How to Publish Your Book

Jane Friedman

THE
GREAT
COURSES

PUBLISHED BY:

THE GREAT COURSES
Corporate Headquarters
4840 Westfields Boulevard, Suite 500
Chantilly, Virginia 20151-2299
Phone: 1-800-832-2412
Fax: 703-378-3819
www.thegreatcourses.com

Jane Friedman
Publishing Industry Expert
and Educator

Ms. Jane Friedman has worked in the book, magazine, and digital publishing industry since the mid-1990s. From 2001 to 2010, she worked at *Writer's Digest*, ultimately becoming publisher and editorial director of the $10 million multimedia brand. Most recently, she led digital media initiatives at *The Virginia Quarterly Review* (*VQR*), an award-winning literary journal published by the University of Virginia. She continues to lecture in publishing at the University of Virginia and is a former full-time professor of e-media at the University of Cincinnati. She holds a B.F.A. in Creative Writing from the University of Evansville and an M.A. in English from Xavier University.

Ms. Friedman specializes in educating authors about the publishing industry to help them make the best long-term decisions for their careers. She has spoken at hundreds of events around the world, including BookExpo America, South by Southwest, the Association of Writers & Writing Programs (AWP), and the International Women's Fiction Festival. She also is known for thought-provoking talks on the future of authorship and has given keynote presentations at national writing conferences, including The Muse & The Marketplace, the University of Wisconsin–Madison Writers' Institute, and PubSmart. In 2013, Ms. Friedman was invited to take part in a three-day collaborative experiment at the Frankfurt Book Fair, sponsored by Arizona State University and Intel Corporation, to write a book on the future of reading, writing, and authorship. She was also an invited participant at 2012 LitFlow, an international publishing think-tank event, hosted in Berlin, Germany.

Ms. Friedman's expertise has been featured by such sources as NPR's *Morning Edition*, Nieman Journalism Lab, and PBS. She also has served on literature grant panels for the National Endowment for the Arts and the Creative Work Fund. She is a regular columnist for *Publishers Weekly*, the leading trade magazine for the publishing industry, and is an adviser to The Alliance of Independent Authors, an international nonprofit professional association for authors. Since 2008, Ms. Friedman has maintained an active blog for writers at JaneFriedman.com, which now enjoys more than 100,000 visits every month and has won multiple awards for its service to the writing community.

Ms. Friedman's feature articles have appeared in *Writer's Digest*, *The Writer's Notebook* (an online publication of AWP), *VQR Online*, *Digital Book World*, *Publishing Perspectives*, *Independent* magazine (published by the Independent Book Publishers Association), *The Huffington Post*, *Writer Unboxed*, and many other print and online venues. Her essays have been published in collections by the University of Chicago Press, Seal Press, Milkweed Editions, and McPherson & Company, as well as Writer's Digest Books, Writer's Market, Writer's Market UK, and The Australian Writer's Marketplace.

Ms. Friedman has published two books for writers: *Beginning Writer's Answer Book* and *Publishing 101: A First-Time Author's Guide to Getting Published, Marketing and Promoting Your Book, and Building a Successful Career.* ∎

Table of Contents

Table of Contents

Table of Contents

Disciaimer

The legal information provided in these lectures is for informational purposes only and not for the purpose of providing legal advice. These lectures may not reflect the most current legal developments in any particular applicable jurisdictions and cannot substitute for the advice of a licensed professional with specialized knowledge who can apply it to the particular circumstances of your situation. Use of and access to these lectures do not create an attorney-client relationship with The Teaching Company or its lecturers, and neither The Teaching Company nor the lecturer is responsible for your use of this educational material or its consequences. You should contact an attorney to obtain advice with respect to any particular legal issue or problem. The opinions and positions provided in these lectures reflect the opinions and positions of the relevant lecturer and do not necessarily reflect the opinions or positions of The Teaching Company or its affiliates. Pursuant to IRS Circular 230, any tax advice provided in these lectures may not be used to avoid tax penalties or to promote, market, or recommend any matter therein.

The Teaching Company expressly DISCLAIMS LIABILITY for any DIRECT, INDIRECT, INCIDENTAL, SPECIAL, OR CONSEQUENTIAL DAMAGES OR LOST PROFITS that result directly or indirectly from the use of these lectures. In states that do not allow some or all of the above limitations of liability, liability shall be limited to the greatest extent allowed by law.

How to Publish Your Book

Scope:

Successfully publishing a book requires a professional approach to the marketplace, with the ability to identify how and where your project fits into the ever-evolving publishing landscape. This course covers the most critical steps to getting a novel or nonfiction book published for a general audience. It also offers an in-depth understanding of how the industry works after you have a book deal, including how to effectively market and promote your work before and after it releases.

In this course, you'll learn to think like an editor or agent, you'll come to understand how a publisher would categorize your work, and you'll discover how to clearly define what type of work you're writing, as well as its commercial potential. Sometimes books are sold on the basis of an idea alone, and sometimes the full manuscript is required. You'll find out what approach is best for your work and what materials to prepare before beginning the submission process. The course will also explain the role of literary agents, including when one is required or preferable and how to tell a good one from a disreputable one.

The number-one tool for getting published, the query letter, is dissected into its five key components, with specific examples of effective queries. The course also analyzes the principles of the novel synopsis, sometimes required in addition to the query, and offers examples of good and bad summarization, plus a key formula to avoid dead-sounding summaries.

For certain types of books, the author must have a platform to the publisher in order get a deal. Because so much confusion surrounds the concept of platform, we'll fully define this term. We'll discuss the various facets of a platform—including online presence, authority and credibility in the market, and ongoing visibility to readers—from a strategic and practical standpoint. You'll also get specific advice on how extensive your platform must be before securing the interest of an agent or publisher.

In addition, the course thoroughly explains the purpose of book proposals, including what questions the proposal must persuasively answer. Although book proposals vary in structure, they have several core elements that require in-depth research; we'll cover these research steps and specific recommended research methods in detail. You'll learn the major proposal sections and elements, as well as the supporting or ancillary materials that can be helpful based on the unique qualities of your proposed book.

We will also look at the challenges of publishing a memoir, including what types of memoirs often fail to gain agent or editor interest and the most common problems in memoirs by new writers.

Before sending a query, proposal, or manuscript, you'll learn how to appropriately format these documents and submit them according to agent and publisher guidelines. We'll define and explain the most common terminology in guidelines for writers. We'll also learn standard communication practices when dealing with agents and editors, as well as if and when to register for copyright in advance of submission. If you're interested in conference pitches with editors or agents, you'll discover how to make the most of such opportunities and analyze examples of weak versus strong pitches.

In the large majority of cases, writers can expect to be rejected multiple times before gaining an acceptance. For this reason, we'll discuss rejection letters and phrases. In cases where no meaningful reason for rejection is offered, you'll learn how to identify potential problems in your manuscript, especially in the opening pages or chapters. Sometimes getting rejected or making little progress can lead to self-doubt, writer's block, and bitterness; we'll also discover how to deal with psychological setbacks in the short term and long term.

In some cases, it can be worthwhile to pay a professional editor to assist in improving a manuscript or proposal. We'll discuss why and when to hire a freelance editorial service, as well as what to expect from the editing process. Alternatively, many informal and formal communities exist to support writers, including writing events and organizations, writing classes and workshops, and writing critique groups. You'll learn about the best resources available and identify which opportunities best fit your goals or skill level.

For writers fortunate enough to be offered a deal, we'll introduce the three categories of book contracts, as well as the most common terms offered by major publishers. You'll learn about the book publishing process from beginning to end, the keys to working successfully with a publisher, and what to expect of the publisher's editorial, sales, marketing, and publicity teams. You'll also get an overview of traditional and digital marketing and publicity efforts, including the mechanics of getting a book onto a national bestseller list.

Because authors share the responsibility for marketing and promoting their books, we'll cover the long-term strategies associated with strong book marketing and platform building, including how to find and engage a readership, build a strong author website, and be active on social media.

If traditional publishing is no longer an option, you'll discover how and when it's possible to successfully self-publish. The course covers different methods of self-publishing, including full-service providers, print-on-demand providers, and e-book retailers/distributors. You'll learn what questions to ask before signing with any self-publishing service and how to find the right professionals to assist you. Because the self-publishing landscape keeps changing, several core sales and marketing strategies have emerged. We'll explore the qualities common to successful self-published authors today, the role of algorithms and metadata in book discoverability, and the challenges self-published authors face in getting attention for their work.

Finally, you will learn how to think beyond the book, especially as the publishing landscape continues to evolve. The use of tablets, phones, and apps has changed how we access many types of information, and young and emerging writers are writing and publishing in new ways and on new platforms. Throughout the course, we'll consider the future of reading, writing, and publishing—and the changing value of the publisher to the writer. ∎

Today's Book Publishing Landscape
Lecture 1

More than 80 percent of people in the United States say they have a book inside them. If you're one of the millions who is writing or thinking about writing a book, the first thing you need to know is that publishing is a business. Publishers and agents look for authors or projects that will make money and provide a good return on investment. In this lecture, we'll first explore this idea of publishing as a business; we'll then take a brief look at the Big Five of publishing and consider the changes affecting the industry today. We'll close by noting some of the challenges authors face—many of which can be overcome with sound knowledge about the industry.

Publishing as a Business

- Although some people like to imagine a long-ago golden era of publishing—a time when selecting and producing the best literature took priority over sales—today's book publishing industry has its roots in Gutenberg-era printers, which were distinctly commercial from the beginning. In the early days of the industry, printers were also publishers and, as such, owned all rights to the work they distributed and sold. Publishers were under no obligation to pay the author—and authors themselves considered it loathsome to write for money.

- One might argue that publishers have remained single-minded in their profit motive since the invention of printing. It's the authors whose business models and attitudes have changed over time. Nevertheless, since the days of Gutenberg, authors have complained about the money-grubbing tendencies of book publishers and booksellers and have had unreasonable expectations about what their publishers can achieve.

- Today, the book publishing industry is once again experiencing monumental shifts, which pose challenging questions for authors.

Despite the many changes in the business, traditional publishing is still an attractive and proven method to reach a broad audience, achieve fame, and become a recognized thought leader. But it's a competitive industry; most estimates put the rejection rate at 99 percent—or higher! As a writer, you should adjust your expectations of the business so that when you are inevitably rejected, you aren't surprised and you know what steps to take next.

- It's also important to realize that there is not a great deal of money to be made in publishing, for either the author or the publisher. As selective as publishers are, they don't market everything they publish, and they have minuscule marketing budgets compared to other consumer products. The lucky few authors who get a publishing deal often realize, after the fact, that their book is just one among thousands of titles released every year, and not many people even know it exists.

Words to the Wise Writer

- Before we discuss the publishing industry, it's worthwhile for you to take an honest look at the reasons you want to become a writer. Don't do it because you've been told by your family and friends that you ought to write a book. You need to write because you're compelled to, because you can't stop yourself from writing, no matter how much anyone tries to discourage you.

- You also need to understand that just as with any other profession, authorship requires years of effort, learning, and practice if it's to become your livelihood. Writing requires commitment.
  - Too many writers rush to submit work before it's ready. They approach publishers or agents with their first book project, sometimes in rough form, and expect to receive feedback and counseling. But that's not how publishing operates.

  - The number-one question to ask yourself before you think about getting published is this: Is this book the best I can make it? Make sure you have put in the work required to produce a publication-ready manuscript.

- The good news in the publishing industry is that you can get agents and editors to consider your work even if they've never heard of you, primarily by following the traditional submission process that we'll discuss in this course.

- Many writers want to know how to increase their odds at getting published, particularly when it comes to capitalizing on current trends in the market. Although we'll discuss trends briefly, your best shot at selling a book to a publisher is to write about what you want to write about and write it as well as you can.

Book Publishing: The Big Picture

- When most people think about book publishing, they envision the *Big Five*—the five New York-based publishers that produce more than two-thirds of all books in the United States. These are Penguin Random House, HarperCollins, Simon & Schuster, the Hachette Book Group, and Macmillan.

- Perhaps the biggest strength of any Big Five publisher is its distribution and reach into the physical retail market. Each of these companies employs a salesforce that focuses on getting retail placement with the biggest possible buy. The challenge for most authors is being able to produce a book that merits this nationwide distribution. Most publishers need to anticipate sales in the tens of thousands of copies to make a project worth their time and investment.

- In part because of consolidation in the industry, the Big Five have been accused of producing homogenous and sometimes even mediocre work. Whether that accusation is fair or not, they are reliably interested in work that demonstrates commercial potential. However, this focus on mass-market, commercial work provides an opening for quality midsize and small publishers to publish in more niche or specialized markets that have been abandoned or neglected by the Big Five.

- Industry estimates put the number of publishing companies in the tens of thousands, but many of those companies don't issue books

The Big Five engage in what's known as *trade publishing*, that is, publishing books that are stocked in an average bookstore for a general audience.

you'd ordinarily find in a bookstore. Further, with the relative ease of digital publishing, small presses have proliferated. To the average author, it can be difficult to tell what kind of sales and marketing muscle a small press has, but probably one of the biggest indicators is how well distributed the publisher is and whether it invests in a print run of books that is used to fulfill orders placed by stores. Many of the new small presses have little trade publishing experience, avoid investing in print runs, and focus on publishing e-books that are primarily distributed and sold on Amazon.

- Of course, Amazon itself represents a critical transformation taking place in today's publishing landscape. It's now possible for an author or a small press to publish books that are on an even footing with the Big Five because they have equal access to distribution on Amazon, the number-one retailer of books. It's estimated that more than 60 percent of books in the United States are now sold through Amazon across all formats—print, digital, and audio.

- Although the number of published titles was increasing through the 1990s and early 2000s, the title count skyrocketed after the e-book became a viable consumer format. From traditional publishers, the number of titles produced in 2013 was a little more than 300,000; in the burgeoning self-publishing market, that number was nearly half a million.

- It's important to note that although more books are being published than ever before, book sales have remained more or less flat, and even this stability has only been possible through e-book sales. According to Nielsen data, the U.S. print book market peaked around 2008 to 2009; print book sales have been on a slow decline ever since.

The Profession of Writing Today

- Until the late 1990s, only one viable option existed for 99 percent of authors seeking publication: to gain acceptance from a traditional publisher. But now that you can publish at the click of a button, the challenge is getting attention in a world of "cognitive surplus." A writer today is competing against thousands more would-be writers than even a couple of decades ago. Thus, respect tends to go to those who earn the attention of readers, not necessarily those who pass muster with the Big Five.

- As a result, publishers have had to focus on PR when they never had to before—and more actively defend their value to authors. There is now a class of successful self-published authors who aggressively speak out against so-called legacy publishers. They portray the Big Five as slow-moving, low-paying, and generally working against authors' interests. But all of this is actually an old story: the ongoing love/hate relationship between author and publisher.

- Something else that has remained consistent is the fact that major publishers can still bank on the ego boost and recognition that most new, unproven authors crave. Even if thousands of authors decided to leave traditional publishing tomorrow, there would be more than enough people to take their place in the system and accept a book deal. Most writers also recognize the need for some type of guidance and expertise from industry professionals.

- What's happening today in the publishing industry is confusing and divisive. For many decades now, authors have felt underserved and unsupported by their publishers; thus, the freedom and power offered by self-publishing is very potent. Authors have separated into camps: those who defend traditional publishing and those who defend self-publishing. In the face of such divergent voices, it's not surprising that most authors struggle to understand their choices.

- Our approach in this course will be more measured. As we'll see, too many authors become paralyzed by change, worried that they'll make the wrong choice and damage their careers. The reality is that there's no single publishing path that's right for everyone. The correct choice depends on your goals and your personality as a writer. And even if you do take a misstep, there's no mistake from which you can't recover.

- We've already noted that the simple act of publishing—the technical aspect—is not difficult in today's market. The challenge for an author is how to make his or her book visible and discoverable in the market, then how to create sustained and meaningful word of mouth about it. Even more important, authors must learn that almost no one can expect to "just write" and have a sustainable career. You'll be far more attractive to a publisher if you're seen as an active marketer and promoter of your book.

- Above all, if you want to realize monetary gain as an author, you must be willing to treat your art as a business. And these two fields don't have to be antithetical. In fact, art and business can each inform the other, and successful writers throughout history have proven themselves savvy at making their art pay. Indeed, committed writers succeed in the industry every single day, especially those who adopt a long-term view and those who know how the industry operates.

Suggested Reading

Eckstut and Sterry, *The Essential Guide to Getting Your Book Published.*

Epstein, *Book Business.*

Striphas, *The Late Age of Print.*

Thompson, *Merchants of Culture.*

Exercises

1. Look at *The New York Times* bestseller list and the Amazon Kindle bestseller list. How much overlap is there between the two? What publishers do you find listed? How many are New York based? How many of the books are self-published?

2. Subscribe to *Shelf Awareness*, a free daily e-newsletter for booksellers. Pay attention to the authors, books, and publishers that get coverage and attention.

Today's Book Publishing Landscape
Lecture 1—Transcript

More than 80 percent of people in the United States say they have a book inside them. If you're one of the millions writing a book, or if you're just thinking about writing one, the first thing you need to know is that publishing is a business, just like any other. Publishers, editors, and agents look for authors or projects that will make money and provide a good return on investment.

While some people like to think there was a golden era of publishing where selecting and producing the best literature took priority—when art was more important than commerce—today's book publishing industry has its roots in Gutenberg-era printers, which were a distinctly commercial trade from the beginning.

In these early days of the industry, the printer served as the publisher as well, and as such, owned all rights to the work it distributed and sold. Publishers then were under no obligation to pay the author—and authors themselves considered it loathsome to write for money.

One might argue that publishers, since the invention of printing, have remained single-minded in their profit motive. It's the authors whose business models and attitudes have changed over time. Early in the history of authorship, you had to be of high birth or have patrons to support your writing. It wasn't until the 18th century, with the rise of literacy, that authorship became closely tied to the commercial success of a book. There is even a specific point in time that historians have pinpointed, called the Magna Carta of the modern author, when in 1755 Samuel Johnson abandoned one of his patrons and committed to living off proceeds from his book sales.

Still, since the days of Gutenberg, authors have been complaining about the money-grubbing tendencies of book publishers and booksellers, who were typically one and the same until the 19th century. The poet Horace warned other writers of the Sosii, the men who published his work and were less than honest in their business dealings. Yet he also acknowledged that without their efforts, his work would have never become so well-known throughout the Roman Empire.

In publishers' defense, historically authors have always had unreasonable expectations about what their publisher can achieve. When authors' complaints reached a critical mass in the late 19th century, publisher G. H. Putnam wrote a landmark guide called *Authors and Publishers* to help improve the PR surrounding publishing companies, as well as outline new operating standards. In 1897, he wrote, "When literary workers complain, it's because they don't understand the business of making and selling books, nor their actual rights and obligations."

Putnam's guide coincided with the rise of literary agents, who by that time were much needed by authors to navigate the growing industry. It was no longer possible for writers to keep up with or learn the complexities of the business.

It seems like the old cliché applies; the more things change, the more they stay the same. The industry is once again experiencing monumental shifts, which pose challenging questions for new and established authors alike. Despite the many changes happening in the business, which we'll discuss throughout this course, traditional publishing is still an attractive and proven method to reach a broad, mass-market audience, achieve fame or celebrity for your work, and become a recognized thought leader.

But it's a very competitive industry. Most estimates put the rejection rate at 99 percent, even 99.9 percent. You need to have the right expectations going into this business so that when you are inevitably rejected, it doesn't come as a surprise and you know what steps to take afterward.

The strange thing about the publishing industry is that while the rejection rate is high, and publishers are quite risk averse, the truth is there's not a whole lot of money to be made in publishing, for either the author or the publisher. If a full-time living is your goal, it's best to do something else—anything else—to earn your money. John Steinbeck famously said, "The profession of book writing makes horse racing seem like a solid, stable business."

As selective as publishers are, they tend to have a let's throw it at the wall and see what sticks approach. They don't market everything that they publish, and they have minuscule marketing budgets compared to other consumer products. The lucky few who get a publishing deal often realize, after the fact, their book is just one among thousands of titles released every year, and not many people even know their book exists.

Before I describe some of the most important facets of the industry you hope to enter, I want to offer a piece of advice to every person who is encouraged by family and friends to write and publish their stories. It's easy to take their encouragement as validation and a sign that you ought to at least try. But you can't listen to these people who tell you to write. You need to write because you think it's good idea. You'll find me reiterating these family-and-friends warnings throughout the course, and that's because it's such a big trap aspiring writers fall into.

I don't want to be dismissive at all about your chances. It's just that too many people approach the publishing industry based on the advice of people who know nothing about it. If someone said you'd make a great doctor, lawyer, teacher, or engineer, do you assume you could undertake those professions based on a passing interest? Let's hope not. Just as with any profession, the profession of authorship requires years of effort if it's to become your livelihood. It rarely happens overnight or based on a passing whim. You need to be committed.

Colette said, "Sit down and put down everything that comes into your head and then you're a writer. But an author is one who can judge his own stuff's worth, without pity, and destroy most of it."

Many writers rush to submit their work before it's ready. And this is another mistake I'll be bringing up often throughout the course. Countless writers approach publishers or literary agents with their first book project, sometimes in rough form, and expect to receive feedback and counseling. But that's not how the publishing industry operates.

The number one question to ask yourself before you think about getting published is, "Is my book really done," or "Have I really thought through this idea? Is it the best I can make it?" Many writers jump the gun or develop anxiety about the publishing process before they've even demonstrated to themselves they can commit to putting in the work required to produce a publication-ready manuscript. They also don't understand how long the publishing process takes; from signed contract to physical book on the shelf will probably take at least one year, if not two.

And that doesn't even count the amount of time it will take to get the contract in the first place; many submissions processes can take a full year or more.

You should also know upfront that when working with a traditional publisher you have to give up a lot of power and control. The publisher gets to decide the cover, the title, the design, the format, the price, and more. You'll have to go through rounds of revisions and change things you don't want to change. But you must approach the process like a professional, and not a high-maintenance artist.

The good news is that the publishing industry doesn't operate based on who you know. You can get agents and editors to consider your work even if they've never heard of you. You can become a successfully published author by following the traditional submissions process that you'll learn about in this course.

However, there is etiquette within the industry that might not follow the standards of etiquette that you're accustomed to. For instance, you'd never call up an agent or editor to ask questions about the publishing process or to pitch your work. In fact, you might not even be contacted with a rejection letter when you do follow all the rules of submitting your work.

While some people think publishing is full of the rudest people they've ever met, the behavior is only a result of them holding onto something that's highly sought after and indeed valuable in the marketplace—the keys to authorship. When thousands upon thousands of people are trying to get your attention every year, it's not possible or realistic to communicate effectively with every person who reaches out to you.

Many writers ask me how to increase their odds at getting published, particularly when it comes to capitalizing on current trends in the market. While we'll discuss trends briefly, the truth is that your best shot at selling a book to a publisher is to write about what you want to write about, and write it as well as you can. It doesn't necessarily matter what's currently selling; the book business is full of unknowns and unexpected. So choose whatever interests you, because the best book you can write is your best book. There's no such thing as the best market for any writer, because so much depends on you.

OK, so let's discuss the big picture of how the industry operates.

When most people think about book publishing, what they're really envisioning are what's known as the Big Five. The Big Five are New York-based publishers that produce more than two-thirds of all books in the United States.

The biggest of these is Penguin Random House, which has more than 200 distinct imprints that it publishes under worldwide. It releases more than 15,000 new titles every year or 25 percent of the world's English language books. It is easily twice the size of the other four players.

The next largest publisher is HarperCollins, with more than 65 imprints. And one of its best-known divisions is Harlequin, which they acquired in 2014. Simon & Schuster publishes about 2,000 titles per year under 35 different imprints.

Hachette Book Group, a subsidiary of the French publisher Hachette Livre, releases about 1,000 books per year.

And finally, there's Macmillan, which is the parent company of well-known imprints such as Farrar, Straus and Giroux, and St. Martin's Press.

The Big Five are all owned by media conglomerates. For example, HarperCollins is owned by News Corporation and Simon & Schuster is owned by CBS. Publishing wasn't always consolidated into the hands of a few media companies, but in the 1980s and 1990s, consolidation began and it hasn't ever really stopped. Eventually, the Big Five are expected to become the Big Four, and perhaps they'll even shrink to the Big Three.

We might ask whether all this consolidation has been good for authors. Unfortunately, it does reduce competition, since imprints within the same house won't bid against each other for books. Therefore the number of publishing options for writers is reduced. However, big publishing companies are better positioned to compete against Amazon, which is considered one of the biggest threats to the business. We'll talk more about them in a minute.

Perhaps the most important strength of any Big Five publisher is its distribution and reach into the physical retail market. This is nearly impossible for a single author to accomplish, but if you publish with a Big Five house, it's a near-guarantee that your book will sit on store shelves across the nation, including Barnes & Noble, independent bookstores, and a range of specialty retail outlets.

Publishers employ a sales force that focuses on getting retail placement with the biggest possible buy. The challenge for most authors who seek publication is being able to bring a project to the table that really merits this nationwide physical retail distribution. Most publishers need to anticipate sales in the thousands of copies to make it worth their time and investment.

In part, due to consolidation, the Big Five have been accused of producing homogenous and sometimes even mediocre work. Whether that accusation is fair or not, they are reliably interested in work that demonstrates commercial potential from the outside. The bright side is that their focus on mass-market, commercial work provides an opening for quality mid-size and small publishers to operate in more niche or specialized markets—those that have been abandoned or even neglected by the Big Five.

While Big Five book titles fill probably 75 percent of every physical bookstore you walk into, and have significant distribution power, smaller and more independent presses can and do compete, particularly when they have strong and recognizable brands. For instance, Graywolf Press is well-known in literary publishing circles for producing some of the highest quality poetry and fiction, and some of their books have hit the *New York Times* bestseller list.

Outside of the Big Five, it's very difficult to make generalizations about publishers. The Big Five encompass what's known as trade publishing. Trade publishing is defined as publishing for a general audience, or publishing books that wouldn't get stocked in your average bookstore. It's often said that publishing is really a dozen different businesses because there can be dramatic differences among publishers. They all have different concerns and trends affecting them.

For instance, New York trade publishing is quite different from K-12 educational publishing, which is quite different from university scholarly publishing. Even within trade publishing itself, there are very different considerations depending the type of book being published. Romance imprints often publish in high volume at low prices since there's significant market demand, while illustrated book publishers produce fewer books at higher prices.

Industry estimates put the number of publishing companies in the tens of thousands, but of course, many of these companies don't issue books you'd ordinarily find in a bookstore. Furthermore, with the relative ease of digital publishing, small presses have proliferated. To the average author or consumer, it can be very hard to tell what kind of sales and marketing muscle a small press has. But probably the biggest indicator is how well distributed the publisher is if they actually invest in a print run of books to fulfill orders placed by retailers.

Many of the new small presses have little trade publishing experience. They avoid investing in print runs, and they focus on publishing e-books that primarily get distributed and sold on Amazon.

Which brings us to one of the most critical transformations of today's publishing landscape that's still playing out. It's possible today for an author or a very small press to publish books that are on an even footing with the Big Five because they have equal access to distribution at Amazon, now the number one retailer of books. It's estimated that more than 60 percent of books in the United States are now sold through Amazon across all formats—print, digital, and audio. If you look strictly at digital sales, Amazon is believed to account for 70–80 percent of all U.S. book sales.

Amazon's power is significant. Appearing on an Amazon bestseller list or being in any way promoted by Amazon can lead to a tremendous sales boost that can't happen in quite the same way through physical distribution or bookstore placement. Amazon is one of the top 10 visited websites in the world, and has about 170 million visitors every month. It's said that one out of every five internet visits involves an Amazon-owned website. Publishers' marketing and sales strength pale in comparison; most of them have very little consumer data, while Amazon has data on millions of book buyers.

So it's hard to overstate Amazon's effect on the book business, at every level, including sales, marketing, and distribution, not to mention its role in the shift to digital book consumption. The launch of the Kindle in 2007 changed the face of book retailing forever, not only changing how books get sold and at what price, but also opening up the field to self-published authors to get their work to market easily and profitably.

While the number of published titles was increasing through the 1990s and aughts, the title count skyrocketed after the e-book became a viable consumer format. From traditional publishers, the number of titles produced in 2001 was around 135,000. By 2013, that number was just over 300,000. Now compare those numbers to what happened in the self-publishing market. Between 2006 and 2011, the number of titles tripled, with nearly a quarter million titles produced in 2011 alone. By 2013, that number had risen to nearly half a million.

What's truly incredible is that these numbers don't even begin to account for all of the self-publishing activity out there. These numbers only count books that have ISBNs, or International Standard Book Numbers, which are used for counting and identifying books. Many self-publishers choose to publish e-books through Amazon and other outlets without an ISBN.

While more books are being published than ever, the bad news is that book sales have more or less remained flat, with some slight gains depending on which sector you look at. This modest growth and stability has only been possible through the addition of e-book sales. According to Nielsen data, the U.S. print book market peaked around 2008–2009, and print book sales have been on a slow decline ever since.

So what does this mean for writers today, especially those seeking publication for the first time?

Until the 1990s, only one viable option existed for 99 percent of authors seeking publication—to gain acceptance from a traditional publisher. While it's popular to say that authors have been self-publishing since the time of Walt Whitman—if not earlier—the chances of gaining credibility and respect without a publisher's stamp of approval were slim to none until books started going digital. So-called vanity publishing has been a frequent and derogatory term for just about any self-publishing effort, a term that's still in use today, but using that term now reveals old-school thinking.

As author Clay Shirky has said, "It is no great or important thing to publish something in the digital era. You can publish at the click of a button." The difficult work lies in getting attention in what he calls a world of cognitive surplus. Cognitive surplus refers to societal phenomenon where people now have free time to pursue all sorts of creative and collaborative activities, including writing.

Ariana Huffington has said, "Self-expression is the new form of entertainment." A writer today is competing against thousands more would-be writers than even a couple decades ago.

More and more, respect tends to go to those who earn the attention of readers, not those who pass muster with the gatekeepers of Big Five publishing.

As a result of this transformation, publishers have had to focus on PR and more actively defend their value to authors, an inconceivable idea just a few years ago. There's a very public and visible class of successful self-published authors who aggressively speak out against so-called legacy publishers. They like to portray the Big Five as slow-moving, low-paying, and generally working against authors' interests.

But all of this is actually a very old story line, only for a new age—the love/hate relationship between author and publisher. It doesn't matter where you look, within the entire history of publishing, you'll always find a mixture of loyalty and vitriol, of partnership and violent disagreement.

But something else has always remained consistent too. Major publishers can still bank on the ego boost and recognition that most new, unproven authors continue to need and crave. Even if thousands of authors decided to leave traditional publishing tomorrow, it's clear there would be more than enough people to take their place in the system and accept a book deal. Most writers also recognize the need for some type of guidance and expertise from industry professionals.

I spent more than a decade working at *Writer's Digest*, where my job was to understand the problems facing writers and provide information and instruction to help them make educated career choices. What's happening today in the publishing industry is confusing to authors as well as hugely divisive. For many decades now, authors have felt underserved and unsupported by their publishers, so the freedom and power offered by self-publishing is very real and potent.

Authors have been separating into camps—those who defend traditional publishing and those who defend self-publishing. These arguments have even sometimes spilled into the public eye, as they did in the summer of 2014, during the very open dispute between Amazon and Big Five publisher Hachette. Authors came down on either side of the debate, some defending the publisher, and others defending Amazon.

When you see such divergent voices and opinions, it's not surprising that authors struggle to understand their choices. My approach is to be measured and provide you with insight and a nuanced understanding of the market. There are tremendous opportunities in the current transformation underway, and I'll help you understand what they are.

Too many authors become paralyzed by the change and are worried they'll make the wrong choice and damage their careers. The reality is that there's no single publishing path that's right for everyone. It depends on your goals as well as your personality as a writer. Even if you do misstep, there's no mistake you can't recover from. Plus it's much better to approach your work as an author in the industry as a long journey, rather than dependent on the success of any single manuscript or project.

I've already mentioned that the simple act of publishing—the technical aspect—is not a difficult thing in today's market. There are more than 32 million books in print. It's estimated that 50,000 new e-books get released for Kindle every month. What overwhelms every author of every stripe is how to get their book visible and discoverable in the market, and then create sustained and meaningful word-of-mouth about it.

With or without a publisher, how does an author build a network to assist in the varied marketing and promotion effort it takes to equal one sale? Given the pace of change, how does an author keep current with the digital and technical advancements that affect how a book gets on the radar of interested readers?

These are among the most significant challenges for a new or unpublished author entering today's market. You should be careful when you encounter publishing advice from authors who are already very well-established in the market, particularly those who got their start before the current digital transformation. Their brands and their readership developed during a different era. Anyone starting a career now has a different set of considerations in play. You can't push the same buttons that were pushed in 2007 and expect the same level of sales or success that were achieved then.

And perhaps most importantly, almost no writer can expect to just write and have a sustainable career. You'll be far more attractive to a publisher if they believe you'll be an active marketer and promoter of your book, and for some genres or categories, they need to see hard evidence you can reach a readership who will buy your book.

It's time to destroy the myth that there was ever an author who didn't have to market, promote, or innovate in order to have a writing career. Erasmus himself organized a network of agents across Europe to actively distribute his works and collect his rewards. Mark Twain sold his work by subscription, which meant that traveling salesmen went door-to-door. At the time, this form of marketing was considered extremely impolite, but Twain was more interested in making a living.

And of course everyone is well aware of Charles Dickens, who released his work in multiple formats, modified his stories based on audience feedback, and masterfully used the serial to garner attention and publicity.

If you're committed to pursuing a full-time career as an author, then you'll be faced with the challenge of staying competitive, current, and discoverable in a shifting digital landscape; of having the right tools to be effective and in touch with your readers; and of developing strong partnerships to help you better market and promote. Assisting with all of these challenges is well within a publisher's ability; only they haven't traditionally put many resources into providing such assistance. They've been focused on their own corporate problems of shifting to a digitally enabled business, and squeezing as many sales as possible out of their mastery of print book sales and distribution.

If you find the right publisher, they'll be an active, long-term partner and resource; they'll help you produce better work; and they'll ensure more sales over the long term. Sometimes the agent fulfills this role alongside or even instead of the publisher.

But the most important thing for you, the new author, to remember is that you're entering a business. If you want to realize monetary gain or reward, you'll have to be willing to treat your art as a business. Art and business don't have to be antithetical to one another. This is the persistent and dangerous myth of the starving artist—that real art doesn't earn money. In fact, art and business can each inform the other, and successful writers throughout history have proven themselves savvy at making their art pay.

While I told you at the very start of this lecture to pursue anything else other than writing to make a living, it's not because good writing is at odds with commercial success; it's that most people aren't willing to make the compromises required or put in the time required to make writing pay. They're looking for what's easy. But writing for publication isn't.

Still, committed writers succeed in the industry every single day, especially those who can adopt a long-term view and recognize that most careers aren't launched with a single fabulous manuscript, but through a series of small successes. You're now taking one of the best steps of all, a step that will distinguish you from thousands of others. You're learning exactly how this industry operates, and by the end of the course, you'll know your best strategy for standing out and getting published.

Defining Your Fiction Genre
Lecture 2

The first step on the path to publication is understanding how a publisher will categorize your work. You should be able to clearly define what type of work you're writing and, even better, have some insight into its commercial viability. This will help set or, perhaps, moderate your expectations of your work's potential and help you better target it in the marketplace. For this reason, over the next two lectures, we'll discuss the genres and categories that represent the majority of books published today. In this lecture, we'll tackle the fiction landscape; then, we'll explore nonfiction.

Commercial versus Literary Fiction

- Fiction publishing can be generally divided into two areas: commercial fiction and everything else. Commercial fiction encompasses well-known genres, such as romance and women's fiction; mystery, crime, and thriller; science fiction and fantasy; and young adult. It also includes what might be generically referred to as mainstream fiction.

- Most people agree that commercial fiction focuses on delivering a great story. There's a clear hero or set of heroes we root for and probably one or more characters who get in the hero's way. The plot has a range of twists and turns, and the story follows a traditional narrative arc.

- This kind of structure has been around for almost as long as humans have told stories, and it's repeated across commercial fiction, with adjustments made to fulfill the requirements or expectations of specific genres. The fact that it uses a formula doesn't mean that such work is boring or derivative but that it builds on proven narrative techniques.

- Work that doesn't fall under the rubric of commercial fiction is often referred to as literary, although there's really no clear definition of this term. It's perhaps safe to say that those who read and write literary fiction tend to have a more pronounced concern with language. They care not just about the story but about how the story is expressed. Literary fiction may also be more likely to challenge the reader than merely to entertain.

- As the term *commercial fiction* indicates, this type of work is positioned to be a moneymaker. In contrast, literary fiction is fairly notorious for selling in low numbers and not making publishers much of a profit. Literary novels, however, may get widespread readership if the book receives major awards, is well reviewed, or both. Most writers don't choose to write either literary or commercial work; rather, they're simply drawn to produce one or the other.

Major creative writing programs almost universally value literary work over commercial.

Varieties of Commercial Fiction

- Romance is by far the bestselling genre of commercial fiction. Its sales exceed $1 billion annually, and it represents between 10 and 15 percent of all fiction read by adults. Romance is read and written predominantly by women. It's often considered one of the easiest ways to break into the business as an author simply because of the volume of titles published and the insatiable demand of the market.
  - Romances are associated with two common conventions: First, a love story must be the focus of the novel, and second, the story must have a happy ending. Outside of those two qualities, romances are diverse, and the genre encompasses dozens of subgenres, such as historical romance, paranormal romance, and romantic suspense.

25

- There are also two formats in the romance genre: series or category romances and single-title romances. Writers usually have the greatest opportunity to break in with series romances; they then "graduate" to writing single titles if they do well.

- Mystery, crime, and thriller fiction represents the second biggest fiction genre—about half the size of the romance market in terms of revenue.

  - A traditional mystery begins with a death or a crime to be solved; the central character is a detective who ultimately solves the mystery. As with romance, you'll find many varieties of mystery, such as cozies, police procedurals, and hardboiled.

  - Thrillers tend to deal with a catastrophe that is about to happen, usually something that will affect many people. The hero of the book must find a way to prevent the catastrophe. In many cases, readers know who the villain is, whereas in a mystery, they try to figure it out along with the detective.

  - Thrillers are more likely to be told from multiple points of view, involve a great deal of action, and offer an emotional thrill. Mysteries tend to be more like puzzles to be solved, focus on mental challenges, and are told only from the detective's or sidekick's perspective. The distinguishing feature of a suspense novel is that the reader knows about facts or clues that the protagonist does not.

  - As far as market trends go, thrillers are more popular now than traditional mysteries. Cozy mysteries and police procedurals are less popular and generate less enthusiasm from publishers.

- The third largest fiction genre is science fiction and fantasy. Science fiction is difficult to define, but essentially, it's speculation about future events and tends to be based in scientific fact. Again, there are a number of subgenres of science fiction, including alternate histories, apocalyptic and post-apocalyptic fiction, dystopias, and time-travel stories. Within the industry, science fiction tends to get lumped together with fantasy as a genre, and there can be some overlap, but fantasy is distinctive for including elements of the supernatural.

- Of course, a novel set during a recognizable period of history gets the additional label of historical fiction. Historicals often operate on a subgenre level of the major genres. For instance, regency romances are romance novels set specifically during the British regency period. Whether you'll have a challenge selling historical work depends on trends in the main genre in which you're working. The most successful mainstream historical novels that don't work within the conventions of another genre are those in which the author documents the life story of a well-known figure.

- If your book doesn't fit into any of the genres discussed so far, then you may have written what's known as *mainstream fiction* or *general fiction*. In simple terms, a mainstream novel is any book that sells well, whether commercial or literary. Other than that qualification, a mainstream novel tends to address contemporary daily realities.

- Inspirational or religious fiction emphasizes Christian morals or life lessons. In terms of market size, inspirational fiction sits between romance and the mystery-thriller genres. It has similar subgenres to those we've discussed, but the stories have religious or inspirational themes. In most cases, religious fiction focuses on the characters' relationship to God.

- A final important genre is young adult (YA). The one unifying feature of this genre is that it features teenage protagonists. This category is fairly new to the industry and has experienced astronomical growth. The most popular YA subgenres are science fiction and fantasy (more often referred to as paranormal in the YA market) and realistic, that is, stories that address social situations with which teens are concerned.

Sales Considerations for Fiction Writers

- Even if your work combines genres, it's important to identify the primary genre. A work that falls outside of every genre is not a selling point for a publisher. To market a product, publishers must be able to identify its audience and point to comparable work that has been successful.

- Another difficulty you might have in selling your book is related to length. The average novel in today's market is 80,000 words, or somewhere between 200 and 300 published pages. The average for science fiction and fantasy can be longer, perhaps 100,000. But once you get up to 120,000 words or longer, you decrease the chances that an agent or editor will be interested in your work.

- The market for collections of short stories is exceptionally small and tends to be literary only. Most mainstream agents and publishers are willing to consider only novel-length work, but many independent and small presses specialize in publishing and promoting short stories. They are often based outside of New York and offer very little money, but there can be prestige and opportunities in having a well-recognized press take on your collection.
  - There is also the potential to publish what's called a *novel-in-stories*, which is a book-length collection of short stories that are interconnected. This sort of approach is uncommon, but it might slightly increase your chances of finding an interested agent or publisher.

  - The market is even less receptive to collections of poetry than it is to short stories. Still, some small, independent presses are devoted to publishing such collections. If you're lucky, you might interest one, but don't expect to earn much money or to see your book in stores.

The Children's Book Market

- The two major areas of interest to writers in the children's book market are picture books and middle-grade books.

- Picture books are meant for younger children, typically pre-readers or beginning readers. They tell a story through both text and pictures. The traditional picture book is 32 pages and has no more than 1,000 words.

- Middle-grade books are for readers aged 9 to 12 who aren't yet ready for YA novels. They might include a few illustrations, but the story is told solely through the text. Middle-grade books are usually 40 to 80 pages long, or about 30,000 words.

- A third category, less often discussed, comprises easy readers. These are targeted at children who are learning to read on their own. Like picture books, they are very short, usually no more than 2,000 words, with plenty of illustrations.

- The age of the target reader is often critical when pitching children's work because such work should address issues that are appropriate for the children's age and use language that fits their reading level. A common mistake made by the beginning writer is to pitch a children's picture book with a great deal of text on every page; such a book is far more appropriate for an older reader.

- These categories are all related to "leisure reading" for children, or reading that happens outside of school requirements. Writers of such books tend to have considerable leeway in how the stories are told and what vocabulary is used. If you intend to write children's books that will be used as school texts, then you need to study the specific requirements and guidelines of educational publishers.

- Some writers think that because children's work is so short, it must be easier to write and publish. The opposite is probably true. Picture books are among the most difficult to get right. The story must be told in very few words and using a limited vocabulary. Further, the writer must know what children are like today—what situations and difficulties they face in current times—and not write only from childhood memories.

Suggested Reading

Brewer, ed., *2016 Poet's Market.*

Randall, ed. *2016 Novel and Short Story Writer's Market.*

Sambuchino, ed., *2016 Children's Writer's and Illustrator's Market.*

Sheer, *The Writer's Advantage.*

Exercises

1. Visit Amazon or Goodreads and search for your genre. In addition to the overall genre, you'll find a listing of all the subgenres or themes within it. Which one seems to best fit your work?

2. Run a Google search for your genre or subgenre plus the word *bestseller*. Which bestselling authors appear in the results? What are the most popular and well-known titles?

Defining Your Fiction Genre
Lecture 2—Transcript

The first step on the path to publication is understanding how a publisher would categorize your work. You should be able to clearly define what type of work you're writing and, even better, have some insight into how commercially viable it is. This will help set or perhaps even moderate your expectations of your work's potential, as well as help you better target it in the marketplace.

That's why over the next two lectures, we're going to spend time discussing the genres and categories that represent the majority of books published today. First, we'll tackle the fiction landscape and then we'll explore nonfiction.

Fiction publishing can be generally divided into two areas: commercial fiction and everything else. Commercial fiction encompasses well-known genres such as romance and women's fiction; mystery, crime, and thriller; science fiction and fantasy; and young adult. It also includes what might be generically referred to as mainstream fiction. Note here that we're primarily talking about novel-length fiction, which comprises nearly all fiction that gets published in book form. We'll grapple with the short story later.

What defines commercial fiction is a matter of great debate, but most people agree it focuses on delivering a great story, usually with a page-turning quality, where it's hard for the reader to put it down. There's a clear hero or set of heroes we're rooting for, and probably a villain or a few characters who get in the hero's way. There will be a range of plot twists and turns, or an element of surprise along the way, and a traditional narrative arc. That means there's building tension that culminates in a thrilling climax, and the story then resolves in a satisfying or definitive ending.

This kind of structure has been around for almost as long as humans have gathered around the campfire to tell stories. So there's this kind of formula you'll see repeated across commercial fiction, with adjustments made to fulfill the requirements or expectations of the genre. That doesn't mean such work is boring or derivative, but that it builds on narrative techniques proven to work time and time again. For example, Joseph Campbell wrote several works arguing for the existence of a monomyth, a term he borrowed from James Joyce's *Finnegan's Wake*. A monomyth is a basic pattern underlying narratives all around the world, which is more commonly referred to as the Hero's Journey. You can find writing instruction books that teach you how to take advantage of the qualities of this monomyth in your own stories.

Work that doesn't fall under the rubric of commercial fiction is often referred to as literary. What literary means depends on who you ask, and if you were to pose the question to a panel of editors or agents, you'd likely hear a chorus of sighs. Nobody likes to define literary, especially in front of an audience of writers. That's because literary writing is sometimes considered more complex, artful, and nuanced than commercial fiction. In other words, smart or deep people write literary work for other smart or deep people, and commercial fiction is for simpletons who probably don't even notice bad writing. That's the stereotype you need to be aware of, and it's a stereotype that commercial writers especially hate having to do battle with in pop culture.

Both literary and commercial fiction can be complex, artful, and nuanced. Neither genre has a claim on those qualities and neither genre has a claim to so-called good writing. However, those who write and read literary fiction do tend to have a more pronounced concern with language. They care deeply about not just the story, but exactly how that story is expressed. The aesthetics of the writing are as important as what happens. On the other end of the spectrum, some commercial writers argue that all that matters is a compelling story—that readers aren't interested in pretty language but in plot and characters they care about.

It's not really possible say that one side is right. It's a matter of personal preference and why you read in the first place. Some people read to be entertained, as an escape; others read to be intellectually challenged. Again, both commercial and literary fiction can accomplish these things—neither has a sole claim over these goals. But as a generalization, commercial fiction tends to focus on entertaining, while literary fiction is more likely to present a challenge. Literary novelists rarely seek to satisfy the reader, but to discomfort them.

If you still struggle with the distinction between the two, ask yourself: Is your book more likely to be assigned in contemporary literature classes, or read while relaxing on the beach? Commercial fiction sometimes has a more ephemeral nature; an author produces it, then moves onto the next book right away, producing usually a book a year. Literary authors, on the other hand, may take 5 or 10 years to write a book, and probably expect their book to be carefully read and analyzed by readers for its many layers of meaning.

As the very name commercial fiction indicates, it's work that's positioned to be a moneymaker. Literary fiction is fairly notorious for selling in low numbers and not making publishers much of a profit. The blockbuster novels tend to help fund the smaller, quieter books that are not destined or positioned to reach a big audience. Some books simply have a blockbuster quality about them, and there are many writing reference books you can read that discuss what these qualities are. Literary novels, on the other hand, usually only get widespread readership if the book receives major awards, is well reviewed, or both. You can get a feel for what the biggest literary names are by looking at the list of National Book Award finalists each year. You'll see names such as Jonathan Franzen, Philip Roth, and Joyce Carol Oates. To understand the biggest commercial novelists, simply look at any week's *New York Times* fiction bestseller list. You're likely to see names such as James Patterson, Nicholas Sparks, Nora Roberts, and Mary Higgins Clark.

Most writers don't choose to write literary or commercial work. Rather they're simply drawn to produce one or the other. However, if you look at major creative writing programs today, you'll find that they almost universally value literary work and aim to produce award-winning literary writers, not commercial novelists. Most commercial authors are not graduates of writing programs. As is well-known, John Grisham was a lawyer before he became a full-time novelist. James Patterson worked in advertising when he produced his first novel.

Now that we've discussed the major divide between commercial fiction and everything else, let's look more specifically about the many varieties of commercial fiction out there.

Romance is by far the bestselling genre. Its sales exceed $1 billion annually, and it represents between 10 and 15 percent of all fiction read by adults. Romance is read predominantly by women and is written predominantly by women. It's often considered one of the easiest ways to break into the business as an author simply because of the volume of titles produced every year, and the insatiable demand of the market.

Romances have two big conventions associated with them: First, the love story must be the focus of the novel. Second, they have happy endings. Outside of those two qualities, romances are diverse and you'll find dozens of subgenres, such as historical romance, paranormal romance, and romantic suspense. When it comes to the inclusion of sex scenes, there's lots of variation here as well. Some romances are considered sweet, where there isn't any sex at all, while others are quite explicit and steamy.

Within romance, you'll also find there are two formats: series or category romances, and single-title romances. If you're familiar with Harlequin romances, then you've probably seen a series romance. The books are numbered in the series and usually released on a monthly basis. Single-title romances are longer and not released as part of a series. Writers usually have the biggest opportunity to break in with series romance; then they graduate to writing single titles if they do well.

Mystery, crime, and thriller fiction represents the second biggest fiction genre; it's about half the size of the romance market in terms of revenue. A traditional mystery begins with a death or a crime to be solved, where the central character is a detective who ultimately solves the mystery.

For example, Agatha Christie and Arthur Conan Doyle are two of the most iconic mystery writers to have ever lived. As with romance, you'll find many different varieties of mystery, such as cozies, police procedurals, and hardboiled.

Thrillers are different from mysteries in that a catastrophe is ABOUT to happen, usually something that will affect many people. The hero of the book has to find a way to prevent that catastrophe from occurring. In many cases, we know who the villain is, whereas in a mystery we're trying to figure it out along with the detective. Thrillers are more likely to be told from multiple points of view, involve lots of action, and offer an emotional thrill thus the name. Mysteries tend to be more like puzzles to be solved, focus on mental challenges, and are told only from the detective's or sidekick's perspective.

Finally, to complicate matters further, some people distinguish between thrillers and suspense fiction. A distinguishing feature of a suspense novel is that the reader knows about facts or clues that the protagonist does not. The reader is left in suspense waiting for something to happen, like a bomb to go off. The protagonist only gradually becomes aware of the danger that they're in.

It's not unusual for a book to have some genre overlap. For example, the bestselling *Da Vinci Code* by Dan Brown combines elements of mystery, suspense, and thriller. But when it comes time to pitch your work, you should choose the one characteristic that is most predominant in your work.

As far as market trends go, thrillers are more popular now than traditional mysteries. Cozy mysteries and police procedurals especially are less popular and generate less enthusiasm from publishers.

The third largest fiction genre is science fiction and fantasy. Science fiction is difficult to define, but essentially, it's speculation about future events, and tends to be based in actual scientific fact. Some of the most well-known authors of science fiction are Philip K. Dick, Ray Bradbury, and Octavia Butler.

You'll sometimes hear science fiction and fantasy referred to as speculative fiction, meaning at the heart of their work is this question of, "What if?" When looking at some of the subgenres of science fiction, you can see the many different manifestations of asking this question: there are alternate histories, apocalyptic and post-apocalyptic fictions, dystopias, and time travel stories. Sometimes these subgenres have very little in common except for the fact they speculate on the future.

A successful science-fiction book, therefore, has a compelling thesis or question at its heart. Margaret Atwood asked in *The Handmaid's Tale*, "What if the ability to reproduce became rare?" In *Fahrenheit 451*, Ray Bradbury asks, "What would happen if books were outlawed?"

Within the industry, science fiction tends to get lumped together with fantasy as a genre, and there can be some overlap. But fantasy is distinctive for including elements of the supernatural, such as magic, supernatural creatures, or shapeshifting. Some of the best-known fantasy series are The Chronicles of Narnia, The Lord of the Rings, and Harry Potter.

What can be challenging for the new fantasy writer is the level of world building that's required in order to have an effective story. Not just anything goes. There needs to be a logic and reason to the supernatural elements or how the magic works. Whatever set of rules gets established needs to be followed from beginning to end.

Probably the most important subgenre related to fantasy is paranormal. In just about every genre, whether romance, mystery, or fantasy, you can find an active paranormal subgenre. Paranormal works are typically set in the so-called real or normal world, but there are supernatural aspects.

If you've written a novel set during a recognizable period of history, it will get the additional label of historical fiction. You often find historicals operating on a subgenre level of the major genres already discussed. For instance, Regency romances are romances set specifically during the British Regency from 1811–1820, and you can also find single-period literary thrillers or historical mysteries. Whether you'll have a challenge selling your work will depend on trends within the main genre you're working in.

The most successful mainstream historical novels that don't work within the conventions of another genre are those where the writer documents the life story of a well-known figure, since it helps ensure a built-in and enthusiastic audience. One excellent example is Hilary Mantel's trilogy about Thomas Cromwell. Historical novels that don't fit in a marquee name can have a more difficult time, but a lot depends on whether the historical period in question is currently in vogue. *Downton Abbey*, for instance, has brought renewed interest to the British post-Edwardian era in popular culture, which in turn affects what editors seek to acquire.

We've now covered the most important and prevalent fiction genres. If your book doesn't fit into any of the genres discussed so far, then you may have written what's known generically as mainstream fiction or general fiction. In simple terms, a mainstream novel is actually any book that just sells really well, whether commercial or literary. Other than that qualification, a mainstream novel tends to address the contemporary and daily realities that apply to everyone. Many book club picks might be considered mainstream fiction because they appeal to a wide audience. Amy Tan, author of *The Joy Luck Club*, is a prime example. Also, sometimes mainstream fiction is simply any kind of genre fiction that breaks out of its conventions or crosses genre boundaries, like you'll find in work by Neil Gaiman or Margaret Atwood.

In our discussion of genre, I did omit a couple of very important fiction categories you need to know about. The first is the inspirational fiction market, which is fiction that emphasizes Christian morals or life lessons. Sometimes this category is called religious fiction, but the term inspirational is more likely to be used when there's not a strong religious message, but the characters' belief in God plays a role in the story. In terms of market size, inspirational fiction sits between romance and the mystery and thriller genres. It has many subgenres more or less identical to those we've just discussed; only the stories have a religious or inspirational theme. For example, the bestselling Left Behind series by Tim LaHaye and Jerry Jenkins is a speculative thriller series that asks the question, "What happens on Earth after the Rapture?" In most cases, religious fiction focuses on the characters' relationship to God.

The other important genre you should know about is the young adult or YA market, sometimes called the juvenile market by industry insiders. One unifying feature of this fiction genre is that it features teenage protagonists. This category is fairly new to the industry and has experienced astronomical growth. In 2004, adult fiction comprised about a third of all books sold in the United States. By 2014, it had dropped to 23 percent, partly as a result of gains in the young adult market. So why did this happen? More adults are reading young adult fiction. If you're an adult who's read Harry Potter, The Hunger Games, or the Twilight series, then you're part of this trend.

The most popular young adult subgenres are science fiction and fantasy, which are more often referred to as paranormal in the YA market. Stephenie Meyer's Twilight—a series about a teenage girl who falls in love with a moody vampire—is the bestselling example here. After the paranormal subgenre, what's known as realistic YA is most prevalent. These are books that address the social situations that teens are most concerned with. John Green, the author of *The Fault in Our Stars*, is well-known for these types of books.

So, if you're writing fiction, do you know your genre yet? Or do you feel like your book includes elements of many genres? Even if you're writing something that combines romance and suspense, or something both thrilling and inspirational, it's important to identify your work's primary genre. What type of reader will your book appeal to the most? If you consider your work to fall outside of every genre—if it's so unique that it can't be labeled—that's not a selling point for a publisher. To market a product, they need to be able to identify its audience and point to comparable work that's been successful.

This is why it's so difficult to sell a book if you pitch it as cross-genre or mixed genre work. It's much better to pick the genre you think fundamentally drives the plot or the characters. Then, once the book is represented by an agent, or sold to a publisher, you can further discuss how to best position the work in the market, given the current trends.

Another difficulty you might have in selling your book is related to length. Most writers go too long. The average novel in today's market is 80,000 words or somewhere between 200 and 300 published pages. The average for science fiction and fantasy can be longer, perhaps 100,000 or a bit more. But once you get up to 120,000 words or longer, you're decreasing the chances that an agent or editor will be interested in your work.

This where writers will rightly point out that many bestselling novels are very long indeed. *The Da Vinci Code* is nearly 200,000 words, or three times the length of a typical novel. As J. K. Rowling passed the midway point of the *Harry Potter* series, the books were exceeding 500 published pages. So what gives?

If you're a first-time novelist, you're an unknown quantity. The longer your book is, the more it will cost to edit, manufacture, and ship. Therefore, the financial risk increases. No editor wants to be responsible for publishing a 500-page commercial failure. Not that they ever want to publish a failure at any length, but the longer the book, the more it will hurt.

There are always exceptions to length rules; just don't count on being one of them. In most cases, a very long manuscript indicates a work where the writer hasn't been disciplined enough in editing it down.

But don't cut back too much. If you have a novel manuscript that's between 20,000 and 40,000 words, you haven't written a novel. You've written a novella. Unfortunately, in the current market, you probably won't be able to find an agent or publisher willing to take a look at your novella, unless it's a more innovative startup, a literary press, or simply an eccentric publisher who likes bucking the trends. You need at least 50,000 words to say you have a novel, and even then, that's quite short by most industry standards and might not be an acceptable length for some publishers.

That said there is growing interest from publishers, especially those in the digital space, to produce what's known as singles. Perhaps you've heard of Amazon's Kindle Singles program, or The Atavist. These are publishing efforts that specialize in shorter works, usually anywhere from 5,000 to 30,000 words. You'll also find publishers more eager to release shorts from authors in between their full-length novels. This allows for continuing visibility for the author and keeps devoted readers engaged and excited for the next work.

Now that we've dealt with the novel length issue, let's discuss what to do should you find yourself with a collection of short stories. The bad news is that the market for such collections is exceptionally small, and when they do sell, they tend to be within the literary market. While there is a market for shorter works in periodicals and online, we're concerned in this course with the sale of book-length work, and trying to collect your shorter works into a salable collection is usually a waste of time. Most agents and publishers are only willing to consider novel-length work. The good news is that there's a wide range of independent and small presses who specialize in publishing and promoting the art of the short story. They will most likely be based outside of New York and offer very little money, but there can be prestige and opportunities in having a well-recognized press take on your collection.

There's also the potential for what's called a novel-in-stories, which is a book-length collection of short stories that are interconnected. This sort of approach is uncommon, but it might slightly increase the chances that someone will be interested.

You should also shelve any expectations you have for collections of poetry you've written. You'll find the market even less receptive to poetry than to short stories. Still, as with short stories, there are small independent presses devoted to publishing such collections. If you're very lucky, you might interest one, but don't expect to earn much money, or to see your book in stores.

Before moving on to the nonfiction landscape, the final area we need to cover is the children's book market outside of the young adult category. There are usually two major areas of interest to writers: children's picture books and middle-grade books.

A picture book is meant for younger children, typically pre-readers or beginning readers. It features pictures on every page and tells the story through both the text and the picture. The traditional picture book is 32 pages and has no more than 1,000 words. Generally, the shorter the better.

Middle-grade books are for young readers ages 9–12 who aren't yet ready for young adult novels. They might include a few illustrations, but the story is told solely through the text. Middle-grade books are usually 40–80 pages in length and have widely varying lengths, but they usually top out at 30,000 words. A well-known middle-grade series is *Encyclopedia Brown*.

There's yet a third category, less often discussed, called easy readers. These are targeted at children who are learning to read on their own. Like picture books, they are very short, usually no more than 2,000 words, with plenty of illustrations. Well-known examples of easy readers include the Amelia Bedelia series and Dr. Seuss books.

The age of the target reader is often critical when pitching children's work, since the work should address issues that would be most appropriate for the child's age, as well as use of language that fits their reading level. A common mistake made by the beginning writer is to pitch a children's picture book with loads of text on every page, where the book would be far more appropriate for an older reader, rather than a beginning reader.

These categories are all related to what we would consider leisure reading for children, or reading that happens outside of school requirements. Writers tend to have considerable leeway in how the stories are told and what vocabulary is used. However, if you intend to write children's books that will be used as school texts, then you need to study the very specific requirements and guidelines that are available from educational publishers.

Some writers think that, since children's work is so short, it must be easier to write and publish, but the opposite is actually true. Especially when it comes to children's picture books, you'll find an extremely competitive market. It seems that every parent, grandparent, teacher, and caretaker has a children's picture book they want to publish. But picture books are among the most difficult to get right. You have very few words, not to mention a limited vocabulary, in which to tell the story. Plus you must know what children are like today—what situations and difficulties they face in current times—and not write only from your childhood memories.

While this lecture discussed what fiction markets are the biggest and easiest to break into, always first consider what you enjoy reading and what you enjoy writing. For instance, we skipped over some genres that represent a very small share of the market, such as westerns and horror, but these genres still have devoted audiences out there. If you're passionate about your subject matter that level of engagement can help you get through the tough patches when you lack confidence or get rejected. Perhaps more importantly, bringing your own passion and talent to a neglected genre or subject matter can produce a revival of interest and create a new trend. After all, when J. K. Rowling wrote the first Harry Potter book, nobody was recommending a middle-grade fantasy series as a way to break in.

Categorizing Your Nonfiction Book
Lecture 3

A ccording to industry estimates, nonfiction makes up the large majority of published work in the United States, perhaps as much as 70 percent. That's not surprising if you've studied the composition of a large bookstore lately. Most of the shelf space is devoted to nonfiction categories. As we discussed in the introductory lecture, it can be difficult to generalize about the publishing industry because it's actually many different industries in one. We could say something similar about each nonfiction category. They each have different market considerations and requirements for success. In this lecture, we'll try to get an overview of this market.

Narrative and Prescriptive Nonfiction

- The biggest divide in the nonfiction market is between *narrative nonfiction* and *prescriptive nonfiction*. Narrative nonfiction tells a true story, often using the techniques of fiction; memoirs fall under this category, as do biographies and autobiographies. Prescriptive nonfiction is driven by information and advice; if you're teaching skills or helping readers improve their lives, then you're in the realm of prescriptive nonfiction.

- Because they are driven by information, prescriptive nonfiction books are most often sold on the basis of an author's platform or visibility in the field. You don't have to be a great writer or artist to produce a bestselling prescriptive nonfiction book; rather, the book must deliver on its promise to readers and be based on your established authority. Readers of such books aren't necessarily interested in being entertained or delighting in what a good writer you are; they want to learn from the wisdom of your experience or unique insights.

- The opposite tends to be true for narrative nonfiction. You need some experience or skill as a writer to produce a memoir, history, or other fact-based work that's meant to entertain through storytelling as much as it informs.

- It's difficult to identify a standard length for nonfiction titles. A narrative nonfiction book might average about 80,000 words, while a coffee table book might not reach 10,000 words. Even within specific prescriptive nonfiction categories, you can find books that range from under 30,000 words to those that are more than 100,000.

  - When you're making a business case for an agent or publisher to take on your nonfiction book, you must include an argument for its length, and you must be prepared to be flexible on this point.

  - Some publishers can't afford to publish a book unless it commands a certain price point in the market, which requires having a minimum number of pages to make the price seem appropriate.

Competitive Categories in Prescriptive Nonfiction

- For large retail bookstores, the most important and often competitive categories in prescriptive nonfiction tend to be religion and business, as well as any titles that fall under diet, health, fitness, or self-improvement. Bestselling books in these categories published by the Big Five tend to be driven by high-profile authors who have name recognition, but smaller presses may be satisfied with significant experience or proven expertise in a field.

- The Big Five publishers often have dedicated imprints or divisions for religious or inspirational titles. Religion is actually one of the few areas that have seen strong growth in recent years, and it remains a robust category in both print and digital.

  - One common question writers have is whether they should pitch their work to a Christian imprint or a more general-interest imprint. The basic rule of thumb—and this applies to fiction, too—is that if you intend to quote scripture or if you're in any way proselytizing, then your book belongs at a Christian publishing house.

  - If this nonfiction category interests you, invest in a copy of *The Christian Writer's Market Guide*, which goes into much more detail than any other resource about the expectations and opportunities in the market.

- Business is another category important enough to merit dedicated imprints or divisions, with more than 11,000 new business books published each year. One expert has identified three main types of business books: (1) self-help business books, such as *The One-Minute Manager*; (2) practical business books, such as those that teach interviewing skills; and (3) Malcolm Gladwell–style books that tell stories supporting a research-based idea.

- For popular categories, such as health, diet, and general advice or self-help, the author usually needs to have credentials or demonstrated success that lends credibility to his or her advice. Successful self-help authors are often TED speakers, multimillionaires, motivational speakers, well-known podcasters, and business founders.

- Not surprisingly, societal trends and current events play a significant role in what types of projects are accepted across a range of nonfiction categories. Most obviously, this directly affects work that falls into the categories of politics and current affairs, but it affects other categories, too. Although it's not usually wise to chase trends, it helps to know when your ideas or projects are in line with, or contrary to, the current zeitgeist line. To find information on current hot topics, read the newspaper or check out Faith Popcorn's *TrendWeek Report*.

Changes in the Nonfiction Market

- A couple of categories in the nonfiction market have experienced significant declines in print sales, affecting what projects publishers will accept. The travel and reference categories have been among the hardest hit. According to Nielsen, travel print book sales have declined 50 percent since 2007, and reference book sales are down by more than a third. The category of crafts, hobbies, and games has also seen a significant decline.

The decline in reference book sales can be attributed to the availability of free information online; even *Encyclopedia Britannica* is no longer being produced as a print edition.

- At the other end of the spectrum, for some categories, such as gift books, coffee table books, and impulse buys, print or physical retail represents the only or best opportunity. Illustrated or four-color books have not made much of a transition to digital sales because of the complexity of formatting across so many different devices. Sales of these books have also suffered because of the overall decrease in foot traffic at physical bookstores.

- You might think that cookbook sales would have declined given all the free recipes and digital recipe organizers now available online, but this category has shown strength in recent years. However, this growth is driven primarily by celebrity chefs and other well-known personalities.

- Some other difficult categories include personal essay collections and humor. To land a book deal for a collection, it's best to focus on small, independent presses; the same is true for themed anthologies with multiple contributors.

Memoirs

- The memoir category is the one that most aspiring nonfiction writers hope to break into, but most new writers working on a memoir as their first project simply haven't developed sufficient skills to tell their story skillfully. In addition, memoir is one of the few categories of storytelling in which good writing doesn't necessarily score you a deal. You must have something new to say that's not like a million other existing stories.

- If you're intent on writing a memoir, one of the most well-known tricks is to pursue a life experiment or stunt. For example, for her memoir *Eat, Pray, Love*, Elizabeth Gilbert went on a trip to three countries to focus on three activities for one month each. Although the stunt memoir isn't a bad idea, it must also have a deeper meaning or insight associated with it.

- To find a fresh angle, you need to figure out why a stranger would care about your story and identify the universal theme. Is it a transformation story, a coming-of-age story, or a cautionary tale? Once you know that, you must be able to sum up the story in one or two sentences, encapsulating the unique perspective of your memoir that hasn't been explored elsewhere.

- Don't expect to sell a memoir that begins in your childhood and ends in the present day. A memoir tells the story of a specific time, a span of months or a few years. Trying to tell your entire life story is a giveaway that you probably don't have a focused or cohesive narrative.

- Trying to fictionalize your life story and pitch it as a "nonfiction novel" isn't a good tactic either. If you're selling your memoir as fiction because the story is salacious or you're afraid of repercussions if people knew it was true, then you're removing a key marketing tactic: Strange or tumultuous events that actually happened make a book more salable. Further, if you have no plans to write fiction in the future, agents and editors will be less interested in you as an author. They'd rather have someone who plans to grow a brand as a novelist.

- It's common for new writers to come up with a book idea that combines elements of narrative or memoir with elements of advice or self-help. For example, you might want to tell the story of advocating for your disabled child, while giving other parents of disabled children information they might need. These hybrid works can be difficult to sell because they don't firmly land in one category or the other. It's probably smart to identify the primary goal of your work and commit to that angle.

Trends in Nonfiction Publishing

- If you're curious about current trends in a particular nonfiction category, visit a bookstore and study how much real estate is devoted to each category. The more limited the shelf space, the greater the chances that only a small number of titles is being acquired in that category.
  - Before Amazon became the dominant retailer, most bookstores stocked many *backlist titles*. *Backlist* refers to titles that aren't new, while *frontlist* refers to titles released within the last 6 or 12 months.

  - The fact that more people now get backlist titles much cheaper in print or digital from Amazon has decreased demand for such books to appear on store shelves. Therefore, the average store tends to focus on the newest titles and the bestselling titles, as well as backlist titles that demonstrate consistent demand.

- Many nonfiction publishers recognize that they have a problem ahead of them, especially those that produce information or advice that can be easily accessed online or via a different medium, such as video. Two publishers, Simon & Schuster and Rodale, have recently announced initiatives related to prescriptive nonfiction offerings. Both intend to offer paid online courses and subscriptions, seminars and workshops, and even mobile applications to boost the profiles of their authors and find new revenue channels.

- As we'll discuss in a later lecture, it's smart to think beyond the book when it comes to nonfiction publishing. Although narrative nonfiction may follow more in the steps of fiction when it comes to the digital transition, prescriptive nonfiction publishers and authors must now consider the many ways information and advice can be delivered, often in more profitable and immediate forms than a book sitting on the shelf.

Suggested Reading

Rabiner and Fortunato, *Thinking like Your Editor*.

Exercises

1. Visit Amazon or Goodreads and search for your nonfiction category or genre. In addition to your category, you'll find a listing of all the subcategories or themes within it. Which one seems to best fit your work?

2. Run a Google search for your genre or category plus the word *bestseller*. Which bestselling authors appear in the results? What are the most popular and well-known titles?

Categorizing Your Nonfiction Book
Lecture 3—Transcript

According to industry estimates, nonfiction makes up the large majority of published work in the United States, perhaps as much as 70 percent. That's not surprising if you've studied the composition of a large bookstore lately. Most of the shelf space is in fact devoted to dozens and dozens of nonfiction categories.

As we discussed in the introductory lecture, the publishing industry can be hard to generalize about since it's actually many different industries in one. You could say something similar about each nonfiction category. They each have different market considerations and requirements for success. The biggest divide when it comes to nonfiction work is between narrative nonfiction and prescriptive nonfiction.

Narrative nonfiction tells a true story, often using the techniques of fiction. That means you'll often find narrative tension, well-crafted scenes, and something like character development. Memoirs fall under this category, as do biographies and autobiographies. If you've seen the movie *Unbroken*, you might know that it was based on a best-selling narrative nonfiction book of the same name by author Laura Hillenbrand. Sometimes narrative nonfiction is called creative nonfiction, though the latter term is most often used within the literary fiction community.

Prescriptive nonfiction is driven by information and advice. If you're teaching lessons, skills, or helping someone improve their life, then you're solidly in the realm of prescriptive nonfiction. Think of prescriptive books as practical books. The reader is trying to achieve something or derive a specific benefit from the book's content.

As such, prescriptive nonfiction books are most often sold on the basis of an author's platform, or their visibility in the field or to the target readership. You don't have to be a great writer or an artist to produce a bestselling prescriptive nonfiction book; rather the book has to deliver on a great promise to readers and be based on your already established authority. The book succeeds based not on the art of your words, but on their benefit and credibility. While good writing is certainly a bonus, and a merely good prescriptive book can become transcendent when written with great artistry, that's not the goal. The reader isn't necessarily interested in being entertained or delighting in what a good writer you are; they want to learn from the wisdom of your experience or unique insights.

The opposite tends to be true for narrative nonfiction. You need some experience or skill as a writer to produce a memoir, history, or other fact-based work that's meant to entertain through storytelling as much as it informs.

While fiction tends to have standard lengths, even across different genres, it's very difficult to talk about a standard length for a nonfiction title. A narrative nonfiction book might average about 80,000 words, just like a novel, while a coffee table book full of illustrations might not even reach 10,000 words. Even within specific prescriptive nonfiction categories, you can find books that are very short, perhaps under 30,000 words, as well as those that extend beyond 100,000. Ultimately, you have to study titles on a category-by-category basis to begin to understand what the standards are.

Also, as you'll find out during the lecture on book proposals, you'll have to make a convincing business case to an agent or publisher for your nonfiction book, which will include an argument for its length. Be prepared to reconsider or be flexible, though. Some publishers can't afford to publish a book unless it commands a certain price point in the market, which requires having a minimum number of pages to make the price feel appropriate. This is why you'll often find nonfiction books that feel padded, or where all the important stuff is contained within a few chapters. It's tough to justify charging $15 or $25 for a book that doesn't exceed 200 pages, and most publishers don't like to price lower than $10 or $15, unless their strategy is to target impulse buyers or go after a very high volume of sales.

We've so far discussed the most critical divide in the nonfiction market, between narrative and prescriptive books. Let's dig a little further into the specific and most important categories of each.

For a large retail bookstore like Barnes & Noble, the most important and often competitive categories in prescriptive nonfiction tend to be business, religion, and then any title that falls under diet, health, fitness, or self-improvement. Bestselling books in these popular categories tend to be driven by high-profile authors who have name recognition. Many have established credits in major publications or regularly appear in the media. You often need a platform to have your project seriously considered by a New York publisher, but smaller presses may be satisfied with significant experience or simply proven expertise in your field. We'll address this platform issue later in another lecture.

The Big Five publishers often have dedicated imprints or divisions for religion or what are sometimes called inspirational titles. For instance, HarperCollins has a global division for Christian publishing. Zondervan and Thomas Nelson, both major Christian publishers, are among HarperCollins's subsidiaries. Religion is one of the few areas that have seen strong growth in recent years, and it remains a robust category in both print and digital formats. Another notable publisher in this area is Hay House, which focuses on New Age, spirituality, and inspirational self-help books.

One common question writers have is whether they should pitch their work to a Christian imprint or to a more general-interest imprint. The basic rule of thumb—and this would actually apply to fiction too—is that if you intend to quote scripture, or if you're in any way proselytizing, then your book belongs at a Christian publishing house. If this nonfiction category interests you, you'll want to invest in a copy of *The Christian Writer's Market Guide*, which goes into much more detail, more so than any other resource about the expectations in this market and the opportunities available.

Business is another category important enough to merit dedicated imprints or divisions, with more than 11,000 new business books published each year. Some of the more notable imprints are Harper Business, Penguin Portfolio, McGraw-Hill Business, Crown Business, and Wiley Business. Jack Covert, co-author of *The 100 Best Business Books of All Time*, observed that there are three different types of business books. First, there's the self-help business book, such as *The One-Minute Manager* or *Who Moved My Cheese?* Then there's the practical business book that teaches you how to write a résumé or interview for a job. Finally there's the Malcolm Gladwell–style book that takes a big research-based idea and tells stories to support that idea.

For popular categories such as health, diet, and general advice or self-help, the author generally needs to have credentials or demonstrated success that lend credibility to their advice. If you look at publishing deal announcements, you'll find authors who are TED speakers, multimillionaires, motivational speakers, well-known podcasters, and business founders. If you think your book should be published because it finally gives voice to the average experience or how a normal person overcomes great adversity, you're headed in the wrong direction. A publisher can't sell an average person's advice for $25, and sometimes they can't even sell an expert's advice for $25.

You'll find—unsurprisingly—that societal trends and current events play a role in what types of projects get accepted across a range of nonfiction categories. Most obviously, this directly affects anything that would fall into the category of politics and current affairs, but it affects other categories too. While I don't advocate chasing the trends, it helps to know when your ideas or projects really go against the current zeitgeist, or when they fall in line. For example, gluten-free living is one of the biggest health trends of recent years, and you'll find it affecting the types of titles produced in the categories of health, diet, fitness, parenting, and cooking. You can even find books in the social issues category that address this particular trend. If you're looking for information on what the hot topics are, you really don't have to go much further than reading the newspaper or looking at the cover lines on the magazine newsstand. But if you really want to get ahead of the curve, try looking at Faith Popcorn's TrendWeek Report.

There are a couple of categories where you need to be aware of significant changes and declines in print sales, which affect how and what projects publishers will accept. The travel and reference categories have been among the hardest hit. According to Nielsen, travel print book sales have declined 50 percent since 2007, and reference book sales are down by more than a third. Obviously this can be attributed directly to the free information available instantly online. When was the last time you considered buying a print dictionary? Even the famed *Oxford English Dictionary* is no longer being produced as a print edition; nor is the *Encyclopedia Britannica*. The category of crafts, hobbies, and games has also seen a significant decline, again due to the growing trend of people going to their digital devices for entertainment, education, and step-by-step instruction.

At the other end of the spectrum, you'll also find categories where print or physical retail represents the only or the best opportunity. This is particularly true of publishers who specialize in gift books, coffee table books, and impulse buys—all the types of books you often find at the bookstore checkout or on display near front of the store.

The publisher Chronicle is well-known for producing beautiful illustrated books across many nonfiction categories that are not only distributed to bookstores, but often get into retail outlets where books are a sideline item—stores such as Anthropologie or Urban Outfitters, or even just independently owned boutiques.

Similarly, illustrated or four-color books have not made much of a transition to digital sales just due to the complexity of formatting across so many different devices. Unfortunately, sales of these books have still suffered because of the overall decreased foot traffic at physical bookstores. Prior to the Kindle, more people were likely to regularly visit the bookstore to buy or browse specific books, then stumble upon something on display they wouldn't have otherwise bought.

You might think that cookbook sales would be negatively affected given all the free recipes and digital recipe organizers now available, but the category has shown strength in recent years. However, don't expect to sell your cookbook project any time soon; the growth is driven primarily by celebrity chefs and other personalities who have significant play on TV, or they otherwise have famous restaurants, or maybe a popular blog. You really need a special platform as an author to get a cookbook deal, especially since cookbooks can be very expensive from an editorial and production standpoint to produce. They're often full-color or illustrated, and may require a photo shoot.

Some other difficult categories include personal essay collections and humor, which is a hard blow particularly for those writers who want to publish a collection of humorous essays, similar to Erma Bombeck or David Sedaris. Unfortunately, I don't recommend trying to sell any kind of book-length work as a humorist or a satirist without having an established track record of publishing in major publications, whether that's in print or online. Almost no publisher will invest in an unheard of humorist or satirist.

Even if not humorous, it's tough to get a collection of personal essays published, although there has been a resurgence of interest lately, with the bestselling success of *Bad Feminist* by Roxane Gay and *The Empathy Exams* by Leslie Jamison. Still, both writers had years of experience behind them before their collections were published. It's best to focus on small and independent presses to land a book deal for a collection, and the same goes if you're hoping to put together a themed anthology with multiple contributors. Just keep in mind, if an agent or an editor happens to read one of your personal essays in a magazine or journal, and they're really excited by it, their first question that they're going to ask will be whether you have a book-length narrative to sell, not an essay collection.

This brings us to the memoir category, perhaps the nonfiction category that most aspiring writers are hoping to break into. Unfortunately, the very new writer working on a memoir as her first project faces a significant challenge in selling her work. She simply hasn't developed sufficient skills to tell her story in a skillful way. Complicating matters, memoir is one of the few categories of storytelling where good writing doesn't necessarily score you a deal. You have to have something new to say; something that's not like a million other stories out there. It can't be about how hard your life has been and how others can survive a hard life too—which, unfortunately sums up the majority of memoirs that are being pitched in today's market. Also, Alzheimer's memoirs or cancer memoirs without a fresh angle are extremely common in the slush pile, and will put you on the road to rejection unless you're able to prove how yours is unique or outstanding in the field.

This raises the question of course, what kind of angle does sell? What constitutes an effective, or fresh approach? First, let's get the obvious out of the way. If you're famous or even a low-level celebrity; if you recently appeared in the national media for either good or bad reasons, that puts you in an excellent position to get a book deal. In most cases, the celebrity doesn't even write the book, a ghostwriter does. Let's assume you don't fall into the celebrity category, which means you shouldn't look at any celebrity's memoir as evidence that a publisher would be interested in yours. For example, Diane Keaton was able to write and publish her mother-daughter memoir because she's Diane Keaton, and her fans want a peek inside her personal life. It doesn't indicate there's a market for your mother-daughter memoir.

One of the most well-known tricks to selling a memoir is to pursue a life experiment or stunt. For example, Elizabeth Gilbert went on a trip to three different countries to focus on three different activities for one month each, and thus we now have her bestselling memoir *Eat, Pray, Love*. While the stunt memoir isn't a bad idea, you can't copy someone else's experiment, it needs to have a deeper meaning or insight associated with it.

To figure out your fresh angle, you need to figure out why a stranger would care about your story and identify the universal theme. For instance, do you have a transformation story? A coming of age? A cautionary tale? Once you know that, you need to be able to sum up the story in one or two sentences, something that really encapsulates the unique perspective of your memoir— something that hasn't been explored before. It can't just be a story about growing up in a small town, or having a difficult childhood; you have to go further. For example: a New York City cop tells the story of how he became a Bronx detective after being a bartender. Or a woman tells the story of becoming a new mother while her parents are being sent to prison. Or a young woman goes on a six-month bucket list adventure with her dying 160-pound English Mastiff.

Notice how these story concepts I just mentioned zero in on a particular period of time in the writer's life. Don't expect to sell a memoir that begins during your childhood and then ends in the present day. That's not actually a memoir. A memoir tells the story of a very specific time, a span of months or a few years. Trying to tell your entire life story is in fact a giveaway that you probably don't have a focused or cohesive narrative.

Writers who are unfamiliar with industry terms will sometimes call their memoir a nonfiction novel, which tends to confuse people inside the industry. Because the biggest genre divide of all is between nonfiction and fiction, any knowledgeable editor will tell you it's impossible to label your book as both at the same time. It's either one or the other. To be fair, some writers use the term nonfiction novel because they're writing a true story that has considerable embellishment added, and they know their story has crossed the line into fiction. An example of this is Karl Ove Knausgaard's *My Struggle*.

For better or worse, Knausgaard's work may inspire more writers than ever to pen novelized versions of their lives. Here I have to be very frank. Most authors who take their life story and fictionalize it aren't going to succeed at selling it—at least not in the United States. If you're selling your memoir as fiction because the story is very salacious, and you're afraid of repercussions if people knew it was true, then you're removing a key marketing tactic— strange or tumultuous events that actually happened make a book more salable. Perhaps more importantly, if you have no plans to write fiction in the future, agents and editors will be less interested in you as an author. They'd rather have someone who plans to grow their brand as a novelist.

Here let's pause to consider the complicated question of ethics when it comes to writing true-to-life stories that rely on memory, or on recreating scenes that we might not have witnessed ourselves. Just about everyone has heard about the publishing scandal from 2006 involving James Frey and his memoir *A Million Little Pieces*. After the book was an Oprah pick, it was revealed that portions of the story were entirely fabricated, resulting in Oprah bringing Frey back on her show for a thorough scolding. The publisher had to pull all copies of the book from stores, and re-release the book with disclaimers from both the publisher and the author.

However, Frey's story is the exception rather than the norm. Both memoirs and narrative nonfiction, to be credible, rely on telling something that's verifiably true. For instance, Rebecca Skloot's *New York Times*–bestselling narrative nonfiction book, *The Immortal Life of Henrietta Lacks*, relies on intimate knowledge of past events and people who've died. Skloot is able to build a believable and ethical story because of extensive research and interviews. While the story is told in scenes and includes dramatic tension, all of the details are based on facts she's able to verify.

Some writers who have a narrative nonfiction idea expect they can research and write it by simply using the tools immediately at hand—which probably means their computer and internet connection, or maybe the local library. This kind of armchair reporting isn't likely to pass muster with a New York publisher. Most successful narrative nonfiction work involves serious legwork, some amount of travel, and plenty of interviews. If you want to build a career in this nonfiction category, staying at home probably won't be an option, and even if it is, you'll have to become skilled at using the phone or online video conferencing to get at information otherwise unavailable.

Creative nonfiction expert, Lee Gutkind, has written at length about the ethics required of narrative nonfiction writers, including memoirists, when constructing stories and scenes. He says it requires even more research than journalism, because a writer can't simply tell what they learn or know. They have to dramatically show it. And when it comes to memoir, while one's perspective and memory are critical to the story, and one's own subjective experience enters into the picture, there's a very good rule of thumb to apply to know if you're crossing a line. Could what you're writing be demonstrated as factually untrue? Is it possible for another person to offer proof that confirms or denies its accuracy?

There are some gray areas, however, such as in the case of composite characters. This is the practice of combining several people into a single character for the sake of a more streamlined or compelling narrative. Whenever you make changes to a story, especially in cases where other people would notice a discrepancy between your story and what actually happened, then that change must be disclosed to your agent, editor, and publisher. They can then assist you in deciding how to handle the situation.

A final word on memoir. It's common for new writers especially to come up with a book idea that combines elements of narrative or memoir with elements of advice or self-help. For example, you might want to tell the story of advocating for your disabled child, while giving other parents of disabled children information they desperately need but would gain only from someone who's been through the same experience. These hybrid narrative/self-help works can be very difficult to sell; they don't firmly land in one category or the other. If the primary goal is to help others and to build a reputation as an expert in the subject matter, I recommend committing to the prescriptive angle. Or, if your motivation is to tell your story or otherwise build your career as a storyteller, then you're better off committing to writing a memoir.

Perhaps the biggest category of nonfiction we have yet to touch on is everything that would fall under the banner of educational publishing. The four largest publishers in the world—in terms of revenue—fall into this sector, including Pearson, Reed Elsevier, Thomson, and Wolters Kluwer. Smaller educational publishers still within the top 20 globally include McGraw-Hill, Cengage, Scholastic, and Springer.

For the most part, these publishers are not what you'd consider trade publishers. If you recall from the first lecture, trade publishers produce books that you find in a typical bookstore and are produced for the average adult reader. These large educational publishers, while they are publishers in name, they have a very different set of concerns and goals than a trade house like HarperCollins. Companies like Pearson are looking at how they can provide a range of services and products that fulfill the needs of not just students, but entire universities.

Furthermore, they have divisions that focus on the needs of specific countries, grades, and even professions. This facet of the publishing business is really its own unique industry—sometimes referred to as the educational services sector. As such, it won't be further considered during this course, since we're really looking at the concerns of trade publishing and writing for a less specialized audience.

If you're curious about current trends in a particular nonfiction category, the best thing you can do is visit the bookstore and study how much real estate each category owns. How many store shelves are dedicated to it? The more limited the shelf space, the more it's guaranteed there's a small number of titles being acquired in that category. In the next lecture, we'll go over this research process in detail, but the key thing to remember is that the big New York publishers have to seriously consider how many copies they can physically place in a store, which means taking into consideration the amount of real estate available in the first place.

Before Amazon became the dominant retailer, bookstores were in the habit of stocking a lot of backlist titles. Backlist refers to titles that aren't new, while front list refers to titles released within the last six or twelve months. The fact that people can now get backlist titles much cheaper in print or digital form from Amazon has decreased demand for such books to appear physically on store shelves. Therefore, your average store tends to focus on the newest titles and the bestselling titles, and those backlist titles that demonstrate consistent demand.

Even more depressing for those who love the browsing experience, the real estate in your average bookstore is becoming more and more devoted to things that aren't actually books. If you've visited a Barnes & Noble recently, have you noticed how much space is devoted to toys, games, and gifts? If you take a look at their earnings reports, you'll probably notice a comment about continued growth in what they call non-book categories, which only further encourages more shelf space to be stolen away from books.

Many nonfiction publishers recognize they have a problem ahead of them, especially those that produce information or advice that can be more easily accessed online, or where a different medium—such as online video— is a more powerful way to reach an audience. Two publishers, Simon & Schuster and Rodale, have recently announced new initiatives related to prescriptive nonfiction offerings. Both intend to offer paid online courses and subscriptions, seminars, workshops, podcasts, even mobile applications to boost the profile of their authors and find new revenue channels for their authors' expertise.

As we'll talk about in more depth in the final lecture of this course, it's smart to think beyond the book when it comes to nonfiction publishing. While narrative nonfiction may follow more in the steps of fiction when it comes to the digital transition, prescriptive nonfiction publishers and authors now have to consider the many different ways information and advice can be delivered, often in more profitable and immediate forms than a book sitting on the shelf.

Researching Writers' Markets

Lecture 4

Once you feel fairly confident about the genre or category of your work, you're ready to begin researching potential markets for it. The research process described in this lecture assumes that you are based in the United States and are seeking publication in the U.S. market. As we'll see, there are three major categories of markets to research: literary agents, book publishers, and competitions. There are also three basic steps in the process: searching major online databases and market guides, conducting online research to dig deeper into each potential market, and categorizing the markets according to fit. This lecture describes the sources you'll use and the research process in detail.

Premium Databases

- *Writer's Market* is the longest continuously published market listings guide. It includes more than 7,500 listings of markets that pay writers, including book publishers, magazines, literary journals, and contests. It's also released in specialized editions by genre, such as *Novel and Short Story Writer's Market* and *Guide to Literary Agents*. The listings are vetted and updated regularly.
  - If you purchase any print edition of *Writer's Market*, you'll receive access to the continually updated online database for free. Alternatively, you can subscribe online for a monthly or annual fee.

  - Each listing in *Writer's Market* includes the following: basic information about the market, often including its mission statement or publishing philosophy; contact information; types of work accepted and, for publishers, the number of titles published each year; types of submission materials to send and timing of submissions; specific tips for authors; and information about pay rates, contracts or author agreements, and typical terms.

- Publishers Marketplace primarily serves people who work inside the industry. It offers a weekday newsletter, called *Publishers Lunch*, with publishing news and analysis; a job board; and a member database. Most writers are interested in the deals database, which has actively reported and archived publishing deals since 2000.

  - For each book deal listed in the database, you'll find the agent who represented the book, the editor and publisher who bought the book, and the author and tentative title, along with a one-sentence hook describing the work. Each deal is categorized and archived by genre or category, and sometimes, if disclosed, the financial size of the deal is reported, though within broad ranges.

  - You can search the deals database for your book's category or genre to see what recent deals have been made and who the representatives were. If the agent or editor listed in a deal report also has a member page on Publishers Marketplace, you can click on the name and find more information, including his or her history of deals.

  - Note that Publishers Marketplace only catalogs deals that are voluntarily reported by agents and editors, and it's far from a complete listing of every publishing deal. However, it can quickly give you insight into who's buying what and what agents are actively selling.

  - When you run your database search, be careful not to search too far into the past. Although it can be instructive to see the history of sales in a category, so much has changed in the past decade or so that only the more recent years will give you a strong indicator of what's marketable right now.

- If you're open to approaching small publishers, then you might add Duotrope to your research list. It's another paid database service and offers about 5,000 regularly updated markets. One of the distinctions of Duotrope is its extensive listing of non-paying markets that publish shorter works, such as poetry, short stories, and essays. Duotrope also collects user-supplied data on how fast or slow markets respond, acceptance rates, and which markets have the most submissions reported.

- Aside from these premium services, a number of other websites also keep track of publishing markets. These include AgentQuery.com, a free database of about 900 literary agents; QueryTracker.net, a database of more than 1,000 agents plus publisher listings; and AAR Online, the website of the Association of Authors' Representatives. You should also check out Manuscript Wish List on Twitter, where agents and editors post the type of projects they're seeking but aren't receiving from writers. Follow #MSWL on Twitter or visit mswishlist.com.

Agency and Publisher Websites

- Once you're armed with an agent or publisher hit list, the next step is to undertake a more in-depth investigation of each market you've found. First, visit the websites of targets on your list. Here, you'll find the most up-to-date information on your prospects, including whether they're open for submissions and current submission guidelines.

- For literary agencies, read the descriptions of all the member agents and determine which one is the best bet for your query. Usually, you should approach only one agent per agency, but check the guidelines to be sure. If the agency lists tips for writers, take note of any advice you'll want to remember when you put together your submissions package. If the agency has an active blog or a news page, look there for comments on the types of queries it is receiving, what has sold recently, and what projects the agency is looking for.

- Publisher websites tend to be far more conservative in their information and advice for potential authors; you may even have to do some digging to find submission guidelines.
  - Make sure to study recent releases on publishers' websites. Usually books are released in two seasons—fall and spring. Looking at an entire season together gives you an excellent

idea of the number of titles the publisher handles and the types of authors and topics it works with.

- ○ Study any formal series or imprints of the publisher that specifically apply to your work. For instance, Sourcebooks, an independent publisher in Chicago, has an imprint specifically devoted to YA books called Sourcebooks Fire. Most imprints have specific guidelines and market considerations that are distinct from those of the overall company.

- When you're researching a small press that may be unfamiliar to you, look for indications that it will be a good business partner. Given the ease of publishing and distributing books in digital format, small publishers now abound. Make sure you ask the following questions when researching small publishers or digital-only presses:
  - ○ Where are the books distributed? In other words, are the publisher's books sold to physical bookstores? The largest publishers sell directly to bookstores, while smaller publishers work with specific distributors, such as Ingram or Perseus, to reach stores. Very small presses may sell their books only through online retailers.

  - ○ Does the publisher invest in a print run or use print-on-demand (POD) only? Asking this question is a backdoor method of determining whether the publisher reaches bookstores. It also indicates the level of investment and commitment a publisher may make to selling and marketing your book. Any publisher limited to POD will probably not have your book distributed to bookstores, unless it also invests in a small print run. Ask the publisher what a typical print run is; most publishers will commit to a minimum of 500 or 1,000 copies of any title they publish.

  - ○ For digital-only publishers, what value do they provide that you need? Most digital-only publishers pay higher royalties but little or no advance. Unfortunately, because so much change is taking place in the digital market, standards haven't been established in this area. You need to study the level of success the publisher's titles seem to have. Ask yourself: Do you want to be part of the family this publisher is building? Do you trust the publisher to be a good editor, marketer, and publicist for your work?

o   What's the editing process like, and will you be assigned an editor? Some small presses publish your work exactly as you submit it, without any copyediting or proofreading. Even if you like the idea of your manuscript remaining pristine, this shows a lack of engagement and care. Virtually no manuscript is ready to publish without considerable editorial work.

o   What marketing and promotion do the publisher's titles receive? What is the baseline marketing plan for every title? Find out the bare minimum activities the publisher commits to; if it does little more than make the title available for sale, you should rethink your choice of publisher.

o   How can you terminate the deal? It's less risky to sign with a small press when there's a definitive way for you to leave if things don't work out. Some new presses are willing to agree to a limited term that's renewable by mutual agreement.

o   Finally, can you speak to recent authors? Find out whether other authors are pleased with the publisher's communication and level of involvement. How much value did the publisher add to the process? Will the author stay with this publisher for his or her next book?

•   Two final steps to take in conducting online research are to check out the social media of publishers in which you're interested and run a Google search on each specific agent or publisher.

Unconventional Research Methods

•   Depending on the type of book you've written and the results of your initial search, you might try a number of other unconventional research methods. For example, one of the oldest recommended methods of finding an agent is to look in the acknowledgments section of a book you've read that's similar to your own. Another tried-and-true method is to ask friends who have been published for a referral to their agents.

For agencies and publishers that are a good fit for your work, find out whether they attend specific conferences or other events; these might give you an opportunity to pitch or meet in person.

- If you're willing to work with a new agent or publisher, then a well-known trick is to keep a close eye on new market announcements. You can find them reported at Publishers Marketplace, on a blog entitled *Guide to Literary Agents*, and on many online writing communities. Also, every October, *Writer's Digest* magazine publishes a special issue highlighting 20 or more agents who are seeking new clients.

- It can also be worthwhile to look at the virtual shelves of Amazon, as well as the actual shelves of your local bookstore or library, to identify more potential publishers. This kind of search is particularly helpful for nonfiction authors, where the variety of specialized presses often outnumbers the guidebooks' ability to capture them all.

- Finally, you may want to think about partnership opportunities outside the traditional publishing industry, such as with corporations, nonprofit organizations, professional societies, and so on. The key here is to look for market affinities between your work and outside organizations or groups. Are you trying to reach the same audience? If you're willing to accept a nontraditional arrangement, you could end up with a published book that ultimately reaches more readers than one from a conventional publisher.

Brewer, ed., *2016 Writer's Market*.

Herman, *Jeff Herman's Guide to Book Publishers, Editors and Literary Agents*.

Exercises

1. Make a list of books that are similar to your own and find them in stores, at the library, or online. Note the publishers and see if editors or agents are mentioned on the acknowledgments page. Research both the publishers and the agents and look for their submission guidelines.

2. If you come up with a list of potential publishers outside of the Big Five, visit your local library and bookstore to see if you can find any of their books on the shelves. Ask the librarian or bookseller if you need help.

Researching Writers' Markets
Lecture 4—Transcript

Once you feel fairly confident about the genre or category of your work, you're ready to begin researching potential markets for it. First, I want you to know this process assumes that you're a U.S.-based author who seeks publication in the U.S. market. Sometimes authors in overseas markets, such as Australia or the UK, believe their home market is too small, and they have a better chance in the U.S. However, it's generally better to start in your home country first, especially if your characters, settings, and themes are tied to your home country. If your book is not culture-specific, however, and you discover an agent overseas who you think is the perfect fit, then there's no harm in pitching as you would an agent or publisher in your home country. Just understand that your book will be sold and targeted to that overseas market first, rather than your own market.

So, you have three major categories of markets to research.

First, literary agents. You'll focus on finding agents if you believe your work has significant commercial potential and is a good fit for a major New York publisher. If your work is more appropriate for a small press, you might still want an agent, but don't limit your search to just agents.

Book publishers are the second major category you'll research. Once you start exploring and uncovering the many different types of publishers that exist, you'll find that some are closed to submissions or open only to agented material. You'll still want to take note of these markets even if you can't submit directly, because you never know when conditions might change.

Third, you might also want to consider researching competitions, especially for literary work. It's not uncommon for short story collections, poetry, or essays to be published by university presses as part of a prize package.

I recommend you take a very methodical approach to this research process. Here's the big picture overview.

To begin, you'll search all the major online databases and market guides. This gives you a very broad hit list that includes every potential market you might approach.

Next, you'll dig deeper into each potential market by doing online research. You want to get your hands on any kind of information that might be available and useful in fully understanding the market.

Then you'll start to categorize the markets according to fit, such as best fit, good fit, and maybe. Sometimes there's not enough information to really know if an agent or publisher would like your material, but keep them on your list for now.

Because you're going to be gathering a lot of information, you'll want to use your favorite note-taking tool or software for this process. I like using Evernote. Other writers use Microsoft Excel. What's important is that you log the information so that you can easily find it later and refer to it during the query writing and proposal process. You might also use this same document to track your submissions process, to keep track of who hasn't responded and who's sent a rejection.

OK, so let's take a close look at the various types of database-style listings available, and what information they offer. Some are free, and some require you to pay a subscription fee. As you might expect, the fee-based services typically offer higher-quality information, and your research process would likely be incomplete without investing in at least one of them.

Writer's Market is the longest continuously published market listings guide. Its first edition was released in 1921 and it's been published annually ever since. It includes more than 7,500 listings of markets that pay writers, including book publishers, magazines, literary journals, and contests. It's also released in more specialized editions by genre, such as *Novel & Short Story Writer's Market*, *Poet's Market*, and *Guide to Literary Agents*. The listings are vetted and updated by full-time editors. They research new markets and regularly contact existing markets for updated information.

If you purchase any print edition of *Writer's Market*, you'll receive access to the continually updated online database for free. Alternatively, you can subscribe online for a monthly or an annual fee.

Each listing includes the following information. First, basic information about the market, often including their mission statement or publishing philosophy; how to contact them; what types of work are accepted and, for publishers, how many titles they publish per year; what submission materials to send and when; specific tips from the editors or agents being listed; and information about how much the market pays, their contract or author agreement, or their typical terms.

Writer's Market can be indispensable if you're undertaking a search for a publisher without an agent. It's also an excellent resource for worthwhile writing competitions. While it's a solid starting point for an agent search, there's another paid resource that you'll want to consult in addition, or instead. So let's cover that one next.

Publishers Marketplace primarily serves people who work inside the industry. It offers a weekday newsletter, called *Publishers Lunch*, with publishing news and analysis. The site includes a job board and a member database, but for our purposes, as writers, what we're most interested in is the Deals Database, which has been actively reporting and archiving publishing deals since 2000.

For each book deal listed in the database, you'll find the following information: the agent who represented the book; the editor and publisher who bought the book; the author and tentative title of the book along with a one-sentence hook describing it.

The deal is categorized and archived by genre or category, and sometimes, if it's disclosed, the financial size of the deal is reported, though within very broad ranges. For instance, a deal where the advance is less than $50,000 is categorized as a nice deal, whereas any with an advance of half a million dollars or more gets labeled as a major deal.

Hopefully the utility of this information is already clear. You can search the deals database based on your own book's category or genre, and see what recent deals have been made and what agents represented them. You can also narrow down your search further by using keywords. Let's say you've written a paranormal romance featuring werewolves. Within your category search, you can type in the keyword werewolves, and see what deals pop up, if any.

Another great benefit of the deals database is that if the agent or editor listed in a deal report also has a member page at Publishers Marketplace, you can click on their name and find out more—as well as see their entire history of deals. It's very uncommon to find specific submission guidelines or other tips for writers on those member pages. Most of this material is available only if you're a member of Publishers Marketplace yourself, although members can elect to have their information available publicly, in front of the subscriber wall.

One important caveat. Publishers Marketplace catalogues deals that are voluntarily reported by agents and editors, and it's far from a complete listing of every single publishing deal. However, it can very quickly give you sharp insight into who's buying what, and what agents are actively selling. When you run your database search, be careful about how far back you go. The publishing industry today is a very different place from the publishing industry of 2001. While it can be instructive to see the history of sales in a category, so much has changed that only the more recent years will really give you an accurate and strong indicator of what's marketable right now.

If you're open to approaching small publishers, then you might add Duotrope to your research list. It's another paid database service and offers about 5,000 regularly updated markets, also vetted by a staff, similar to *Writer's Market*. One of the distinctions of Duotrope is its extensive listing of non-paying markets that publish shorter works, such as poetry, short stories, and essays. For book authors, Duotrope might not be as worthwhile, unless you have a more literary work to sell, or perhaps a collection of poetry or short stories.

A fascinating feature of Duotrope not found elsewhere is its submissions statistics. Duotrope collects user-supplied data to report on how fast or slow markets respond, what their acceptance rates are like, and which markets have the most submissions reported. In other words, you'll have a good idea of which markets are extremely challenging, so you can adjust your expectations accordingly.

Aside from these paid, or what you might call premium, services are a range of other websites that keep track of markets. While some of them may prove redundant if you're using a premium service, they're still worth a look.

One of the most popular is AgentQuery.com, a free database listing of about 900 literary agents. While the site is staffed and it does oversee all the listings, it also allows agents to log in directly and update their profile. AgentQuery offers other perks as well, such as an online community where you can trade query letter critiques with other writers; plus you'll find considerable insights and advice contributed by agents and published authors.

Another good resource is QueryTracker.net, which offers two main features. First, it offers a database of more than 1,000 agents plus publisher listings. Second, you can use the site to help organize and track all of your submissions. As with AgentQuery, the site is staffed and the listings are regularly vetted.

It's also helpful to check out AAR Online, which is the website of the Association of Authors' Representatives. The AAR is a professional organization of about 400 agents, and they list their member directory at their website, which you can search for free. However, the information is pretty bare bones, so its primary use is to confirm whether your agent is an AAR member. If they are, they must follow a canon of ethics in their business practices, and you can read more about those ethical guidelines at their website.

All of these market guides and databases tend to have one thing in common—they can go out of date rather quickly. They also tend to provide you with only the broadest brushstrokes of a particular publisher or agent. It takes further digging to better understand the tastes of a publisher or agent—and don't forget that much of publishing is driven by that subjective thing called taste, not to mention market trends.

To that end, there is one final resource you'll want to browse, and it's called Manuscript Wish List. A phenomenon emerged on Twitter whereby agents and editors tell writers what's on their so-called wish list, or what type of projects they want to sell but aren't receiving from writers. You can stay informed about wish list requests by following the #MSWL hashtag on Twitter, or by visiting mswishlist.com, which automatically tracks what requests have been tweeted.

So, now that you're armed with your agent or publisher hit list, the next step is to undertake a more in-depth investigation of each market you've found. Here's what you should cover.

First, visit their website. You'll almost always find the most up-to-date information at their site, including whether they're open for submissions. Even if you found the submission guidelines elsewhere, always confirm them again on the website, and if you uncover discrepancies, follow the instructions at their site.

For literary agencies, you'll want to read the descriptions of all the member agents and determine which one is the best bet for your query. Usually you should only approach one agent per agency, but again, check the guidelines to be sure, and we'll discuss how to dig further for details about your target agent later.

If the agency lists any tips or advice for writers, obviously you should read them, and take careful notice of anything you'll want to remember when you put together your submissions package. Some agents have an active blog or a news and events page, which can be useful to scan. Particularly within the last 6–12 months, look for any comment on the types of queries they're receiving, what they've recently sold, and what projects they'd like to see more of.

Publisher websites tend to be far more conservative in their information and advice for potential authors. In fact, you often really have to hunt for anything at all mentioning submissions. Check at the very bottom of the site for something that says, About Us or Contact Us if you can't find anything explicitly labeled Submissions. Worst-case scenario, google the publisher's name along with the term submission guidelines, and that will usually turn up something.

While you're at the publisher's site, study their recent releases. Usually books are released in two seasons—a fall list and a spring list. Looking at an entire season together gives you an excellent idea of how many titles the publisher handles, also tells you the types of authors they look for, and what topics they most frequently publish on. In the case of nonfiction, you may end up researching some of these titles in-depth as part of your book proposal and we'll cover that later.

Study any formal series or imprints that specifically apply to your work. For instance, Sourcebooks, an independent publisher in Chicago, has an imprint specifically devoted to young adult books, called Sourcebooks Fire. Harlequin, a romance publisher, has more than a dozen different imprints. Most imprints have guidelines specific to them and market considerations that are distinct from the overall company. It's easy to go down the rabbit hole and get confused at this point. If you find you need a map of how all the pieces fit together, check *Writer's Market*, which every year publishes a very comprehensive listing of all the publishers and all of their imprints.

If you undertake the submissions process unagented, there's an additional component to your research process you shouldn't neglect. Any time you're looking at a small press that's unfamiliar to you, look for signs that it'll be a good business partner and likely to produce a successful book. Due to the extreme ease of publishing and distributing books in digital format, just about anyone can put out a shingle and call themselves a publisher. While working with a newly-minted press might suit your needs, you should know it going in, and adjust your expectations. So, here are some questions to ask when researching small publishers or digital-only presses.

Where are their books distributed? Publishers should clearly state on their site where their books are available or how they can be ordered. Usually the big question for an author is: Are the publishers' books being ordered and shelved in physical bookstores? The largest publishers—the Big Five—sell direct to bookstores, while smaller publishers work with specific distributors to reach stores, such as Ingram or Perseus. Very small presses may only sell their books through major online retailers such as Amazon—which is something authors can do themselves.

Another question to ask is does the publisher invest in a print run or use print-on-demand only? This is kind of a back-door method to figuring out whether the publisher is reaching bookstores. It also indicates what level of investment and commitment is being made to selling and marketing your book. Print-on-demand, also called POD, is a printing technology that allows a publisher to print their books one at a time, as they're ordered. Any publisher limited to print-on-demand will not likely have your book distributed to stores, unless they also invest in a small print run. So, ask the publisher what their typical print run is. Most publishers will commit to a minimum of 500 or 1,000 copies of any title they publish.

Another question for digital-only publishers is what value do they provide that you, the author, need? You'll find many, many varieties of digital-only publishers—everything from special imprints from the Big Five houses to start-up companies. Most digital-only publishers will pay you higher royalties, but no advance—or a very low advance. Unfortunately, because there is so much change still happening in the digital market, you won't find any standards that apply here. It's a bit like the Wild West. So, you'll have to carefully study the titles released, who's authoring them, and what level of success they seem to have. Do you want to be part of the family they're building? Do you trust them to be good editors, marketers, and publicists for your work?

Another question to ask is what is their editing process like, and will you be assigned an editor? Some small presses will take exactly what you give them and publish it, without any copyediting or proofreading. Even if you like the idea of your manuscript remaining pristine, this shows lack of engagement and care. Virtually no manuscript is ready to publish without considerable editorial work.

Another question to ask is, what marketing and promotion do the publisher's titles receive? Ask what their baseline marketing plan is for every title. Do they send out advance review copies? Do they write a press release? Do they submit the book to specific media outlets for coverage? Find out the bare minimum they commit to for every title is really important, and if they do little more than make the title available for sale, you should rethink why you want to publish with them. You can also get a good feel for the sophistication of their overall marketing and promotion by simply studying their online presence and how they present themselves.

Ask the small press how can you terminate the deal? It's less risky to sign with a small press when there's a definitive way for you to leave if things don't work out. Some new presses are willing to agree to a limited term that's renewable by mutual agreement.

Also ask, can you speak to recent authors? This can be the best litmus test of all. Are other authors pleased with the publisher's communication and level of involvement? How much value did the publisher add to the process? Will the author stay with this publisher for their next book?

After you finish studying the website of the agency or publisher, it's time to move onto social media. Twitter is very popular in the publishing community, so you'll likely find a presence there, whoever you research. It's also worthwhile to check for public accounts at Facebook, Pinterest, or Tumblr.

Now, this might sound like you're starting to stalk your targets, and maybe you are a little bit. But here's the thing. Many agents and editors use social media to have conversations with authors, potential authors, and other industry insiders. Studying these communications not only provides insights for the submissions process, but it also helps you figure out the best fit. Is this someone you want to do business with? Do you like their demeanor? What gets them enthusiastic?

You'll also find that some publishing professionals offer specific information and advice for writers through social media, and even invite questions during specific chat windows. These are always good opportunities to ask about that market trend question that's on your mind that maybe only they can answer.

As a final step in your online research process, run a Google search on each of your markets. Put the name of the specific agent or publisher in quotation marks, and see what you get. If you get a lot of results, it can be helpful to add the word interview, submissions, or query. You could also use words connected to your book's genre, category, or theme.

Once you've collected all the insight you can find on your target markets, start to prioritize your list into best fit, good fit, and maybe. Any agent or publisher who is a weak candidate shouldn't be approached—you want to avoid the Hail Mary queries, which will waste your time and theirs. For your best and good candidates, you might further research any conferences or events that these agents or publishers attend. Is there an opportunity to pitch or meet in person? We'll talk more about that process in a later lecture.

If you have any doubts whatsoever about the quality of an agent or publisher on your list, then run a web search on their name, and add the word scam. You're probably not the first person to raise that question, and that search will bring up on message boards where people discuss the legitimacy of publishing markets.

You can also check several sites where industry watchdogs actively post warnings. Writer Beware is the best-known and the most well-respected.

In fact, if you end up having a bad experience with an agent or publisher— especially regarding nonpayment—it's possible to contact Writer Beware with your complaint and ask them to investigate.

You can also check the Absolute Write Water Cooler message boards, or the long-running Preditors & Editors website.

Remember, it's always a red flag when a publisher or agent starts soliciting you out of the blue. If it seems too good to be true, then it is.

OK, while we've concluded the most formal part of the market research process, there are still some other methods to consider, depending on the type of book you have, or if you don't find your results quite satisfying.

One of the oldest recommended methods of finding an agent is to look in the acknowledgments section of a book you've read that's similar to your own.

Just about every author thanks both their agent and their editor. The plus side to this is that you now have an excellent way to open your query letter, which we'll talk about later.

Another tried-and-true method is to ask published author friends—if you have any—for a referral to their agent. Now, the danger here is that your author friend might not believe your book is all that good. If he knowingly sends his agent a dud manuscript, he'll hurt his own reputation and ability to refer other deserving writers. So it can be a delicate situation. Sometimes it's best to ask your author friend if they'd be willing to take a look at your work and offer feedback, which then might lead to a referral. The downside there is that your author friend probably has dozens of other people asking exactly the same thing. So, there aren't any easy answers here, but we'll discuss how to be skillful at networking and community building in a later lecture.

If you're willing to work with a new agent or publisher, then a well-known trick is to keep a close eye on new market announcements. You can find them reported at Publishers Marketplace, which you can access if you're a subscriber; or the Guide to Literary Agents Blog, which posts about new agents; and many online writing communities have dedicated threads focused on such announcements. Also, every year, *Writer's Digest* magazine publishes a special agent issue in October, highlighting 20 or more agents who are actively seeking new clients.

Finally, it can be worthwhile to look at the virtual shelves of Amazon, as well as the actual shelves of your local bookstore or library, to identify potential publishers. This kind of search is particularly helpful for nonfiction authors, where the variety of specialized presses often outnumber the guidebooks' ability to capture them all. And when it comes time to write a nonfiction book proposal, this step will be required anyway.

This market research process I've detailed so far centers on the traditional publishing industry, and stays completely within the confines of its world and its values. But there are other options out there if you're willing to think creatively about how and where your book could be published.

Here's an example. One author I know had traditionally published two books on the global economy and sustainability, which required a really significant travel investment on his part. His publisher offered a very low advance for his third book, and it wasn't enough to cover his costs. However, by his third book, he was a fairly well-known author and brand, with visibility to a valuable target audience of college students. A major adventure travelwear company took notice—a company with which he already had a relationship—and they're now in talks to publish his third book.

Corporations and businesses outside of the publishing industry see books very differently from traditional publishers. For them, what they often see is a content marketing or a branding opportunity, and an author whose good name can rub off on them.

There are similar partnership opportunities with nonprofits, societies, and clubs—just about any organization or company you can imagine. The key is to look for market affinities between you and the group. Are you trying to reach the same audience? Are you working to spread the same message? Can you each add value to what the other one is doing? If you're willing to accept an untraditional arrangement, you could end up with a published book that ultimately reaches more readers than one from a conventional publisher. However, for you the author, this takes a more entrepreneurial approach, and a talent for building mutually beneficial partnerships.

So, we've now finished with the research process. Some writers find all this to be complete drudgery. They want nothing more than to find someone else who can do it all for them. Well, there are, in fact, some services that do exactly that. They'll research the markets, put together your submissions package, send out the queries and proposals in your name, and then report back on the results.

I'll be honest—I'm not a fan of these services. While they may do a good job, I don't think they care about your work and the submissions process as much as you do. If it were me, I'd want to know that sufficient time, attention, and research went into selecting the right agents and editors for my work. Why spend years writing and revising your book only to outsource the very important business decision of identifying its best home?

But there's another reason I recommend you do the work yourself, which is perhaps a little old-fashioned of me: It's good for you. You should do the work that helps you get more familiar with the business side of writing, so you can make better educated decisions over the long-term of your career. Plus, by trying to escape it or pay someone else to worry about it, you're ignoring an important lesson of every writer's life. You have to learn to balance the art and the business.

What to Expect from a Literary Agent
Lecture 5

Of course, the main benefit of having an agent is that it allows you to get your foot in the door of a New York publisher, but there are other advantages, as well. In particular, agents have relationships with editors at many publishing houses, and they're experts in what's selling and how to pitch your work. Further, after your agent has negotiated a deal, he or she will remain closely involved as your book progresses on the path to publication and will run interference with your editor or publisher. An agent may also serve as a career manager, helping you strategize and sell future books, as well as your coach, therapist, cheerleader, and accountant.

Standard and Nonstandard Business Practices

- In the traditional business model, agents make money only when they sell your work. The standard agent commission is 15 percent of everything the author receives, including advances and royalties, and 15 to 20 percent of other possible earnings.

- A small number of agents charge a fee for reading your work, but this isn't routine or a standard practice. Such fees are often indicators of a publishing scam. If you find what appears to be a reputable agent charging a fee, ask whether any critique on the submitted work is offered and whether the fee will be refunded if the agent agrees to represent you and sells your book.

- You might also encounter agents who charge fees associated with submitting your work, such as photocopying or shipping fees. Most agents absorb these expenses as the cost of doing business rather than charging authors, but this practice is not considered unethical.

- You should be skeptical of agents who offer a paid editing service or refer you to an editing service in exchange for representation. Although it's common for agents to suggest revisions of your work before they'll represent you, it's uncommon for them to do this work themselves and charge you for it or to send you to a specific editor for help. In such cases, the agent may be receiving a kickback for referring you.

- Of course, most agreements between agents and authors are formalized in writing. The author-agent contract spells out the timeframe of the representation, the terms of renewal or termination, the agent's commission, and procedures for dispute resolution.

Don't respond to advertisements from agents seeking clients, and be skeptical if an agent contacts you unless you've received recent publicity or attention.

- If you sign with an agent, he or she has the right to be your exclusive agent of record, but your relationship should also give you the freedom to represent yourself or market your own work when desirable. In other words, if you negotiate a deal for your own work, the agent shouldn't earn a commission on it.

- For any and all work that the agent sells, he or she is entitled to earn a commission for as long as that contract remains in effect. In fact, the contract you sign with your publisher will include what's known as the *agency clause*, which is written and provided by the literary agent. This clause binds the agent to the book deal as the agent of record; the agent receives all payments and distributes them to the author until the contract terminates. Even if you terminate the relationship, your agent will continue to receive a 15 percent commission while the publishing agreement remains in effect.

Acquiring an Agent

- When an agent offers you representation, don't feel pressured to agree immediately. If your manuscript is actively under consideration by other agents, you should say so, and ask for a week or two to see if they are interested. You'll also want to ask if the agent requires you to sign a contract, which you'll need time to review. Finally, you'll want a couple of days to go back to your research notes about the agent and formulate a list of questions. If you find yourself in the lucky position of being courted by two or more agents, consider their track records of sales, professionalism, and enthusiasm for your work.

- Note that an agency's size doesn't necessarily correlate with the size of the deal you can expect. Generally, there are several categories of reputable agents: those that consist of only one or two principals, with perhaps a few associates (boutique agencies); midsize and large agencies with many agents and specialized staff members, such as a contracts manager and foreign rights specialist; and mega-agencies that represent other talent besides authors.

- Because it's rare for an agent to represent every single genre, authors who want to pursue multiple genres may need more than one agent. But as a rule, don't shop for more than one agent at a time. Once you've secured your first agent for your first project, he or she will almost always ask what else you're working on. That's your opportunity to discuss your varied areas of interest and your options for representation in another genre.

What to Expect from an Agent

- Finding the right agent doesn't mean that your work will be sent out to publishers immediately. Some agents will help you further refine your manuscript or book proposal, some will ask you for revisions, and others might rework your submissions package to increase its chances of success. Only when the agent is satisfied with the materials and their presentation will he or she start contacting editors.

- Before putting your work out on submission, your agent will probably also discuss the pitch strategy with you, which typically involves a round of submissions to the most desirable editors or, sometimes, an auction.

o Auctions take place when an agent has what he or she thinks is a hot property. The agent might establish a *floor price*—the minimum for which the book will be sold—then make submissions to potential editors, giving a deadline for responses. If one publisher's bid is topped by another, the first publisher is given the opportunity to top the competitor's offer. Obviously, this process hinges on one factor: The book must be one that the industry believes will be a big seller.

o Sometimes before the auction starts, a publisher might try a *preempt*, which is making an offer conditioned on the agent immediately taking the project off the market. If the publisher and author are a good match and the offer is good enough, then a preempt can be a satisfying deal for everyone. Preempts often happen when the editor loves the project and doesn't want to compete with other publishers for it. If the preempt is declined, the agent and author then take their chances with the auction process.

o However the process resolves itself, an agent should never force you to accept a deal or work with a publisher you're uncomfortable with. It's not uncommon for authors to turn down better money with one publisher to go with another house or another editor that offers a better fit.

• Unfortunately, having an agent doesn't guarantee a book deal. If your agent is having a difficult time selling your work, ask for specifics about why. Is the market saturated? Are publishers demanding authors with bigger platforms? Have publishers cut back on the number of titles they're signing?

o Agents should specify what imprints or publishers they've contacted and been rejected by. You can also ask for the rejection letters, although your agent is under no obligation to provide you with specific contact information of editors and publishers.

o Don't assume that your agent isn't "good enough" if your book didn't sell. Ask for an open and frank discussion about any patterns in the rejections you're receiving. Perhaps there's a way to revise your book or its concept to make it more marketable.

- If you feel like your agent is failing you, keep in mind that it may not be easy to find a new one. Just because you've had representation in the past doesn't help you attract it again. And leaving your agency might cause other agents to wonder whether you're a difficult client, especially if they think well of the agency you're leaving.
  - However, if you feel that terminating is your best option, look at your author-agent contract. Some contracts stipulate that you must give the agent at least one year to find a home for the work. Others allow you to terminate the relationship with 30 days' notice.

  - If you part ways with an agent before he or she sells your work, make sure to get a list of all the publishers to which the work was submitted. Unfortunately, if your first agent exhausted every outlet, it's not really possible for another agent to approach those markets a second time. Even if you reconceptualize the book or dramatically revise the manuscript, most editors are unwilling to take a second look at a project they've already considered.

- If the agent path comes to a dead end, another option is to begin the process of submitting your work to smaller presses, niche presses, or digital publishers that the agent didn't pursue because they didn't represent enough of a financial opportunity. If you get an offer from a small press, it's possible to successfully negotiate your own contract if you know what to look for. Alternatively, you can sometimes find an agent to work on an hourly basis to negotiate the contract for you.

Changes in the Agent Model

- In recent years, agents' business models have begun to adapt to self-publishing and digital publishing innovations in the market. Some have started their own digital publishing arms or help their clients self-publish.

- The difficulty here is that traditionally, the only acceptable way for agents to earn money is through sales commissions. The Association of Authors' Representatives (AAR), which is the professional organization for literary agents, prohibits its members from acting as publishers because doing so raises a potential conflict of interest. Therefore, most agents assist with self-publishing only on a commission basis, taking their standard 15 percent on sales.

- Why would an author choose to have an agent assist with self-publishing rather than going solo? Although some authors are well-equipped to be publishing entrepreneurs, others prefer the experience and resources of someone in the industry they trust. In addition, a good agent can help in a strategic manner, providing the same kind of marketing support and insight that a publisher would.

- To be clear, self-publishing through an agent remains an unusual way of working. The overriding goal for most agents, especially for those representing new or unpublished clients, is to sell their authors' work to a traditional publisher. Don't expect to receive an immediate response to your submission with an offer to help you self-publish; that conversation typically takes place only after months of trying the traditional publishing route and by mutual agreement.

Suggested Reading

Sambuchino, ed., *2016 Guide to Literary Agents.*

———. *Get a Literary Agent.*

Exercises

1. Visit the blog entitled "Guide to Literary Agents." Scan recent posts for new agent announcements or Q&As with agents.

2. Visit sites that catalog what agents are currently looking for, such as mswishlist.com, mswlparagraph.wordpress.com, and agentandeditorwishlist.tumblr.com.

What to Expect from a Literary Agent
Lecture 5—Transcript

When looking at the more than 500-year history of book publishing, literary agents are a pretty recent invention. They started appearing in late 19th-century Britain. The publishing landscape was growing in both size and complexity, so writers had greater need of a guide to navigate the market, a person who could protect their interests and negotiate better-paying contracts.

One of the first agents to appear on the scene was a man by the name of A. P. Watt. He was asked by a friend to sell his stories for him, and before long, he was repping major writers of the day, such as Arthur Conan Doyle and Thomas Hardy, among many others.

Publishers weren't initially pleased with this development. William Heinemann was one such publisher. He founded one of the oldest imprints still operating to this day in the U.K. He wrote, "This is the age of the middleman. He is generally a parasite. He always flourishes. I have been forced to give him some little attention lately in my particular business. In it, he calls himself the literary agent."

Soon enough, these so-called parasites became valuable to both the publisher and the author. While agents served as authors' representatives, who could smartly place their clients' work at the best possible publishing house, they also became talent scouts and a trusted filter. Before long, the biggest publishers stopped accepting unagented work, and the gatekeeping responsibility passed to the agents.

Then, as now, agents might be former editors, or they might be lawyers— or neither. There isn't really a formal industry credential for literary agents—anybody can call themselves one. Like editors, they have their own subjective tastes and opinions, and agents tend to specialize in certain types of work.

Whether or not you need an agent depends on several factors. Probably the most important is whether you want your work considered by one of the Big

Five New York publishing houses. They don't often look at authors' material unless it's sent by an agent.

But there are other benefits to having an agent, aside from just getting your foot in the door of a New York house. Today, as was the case 140 years ago, agents know the market better than authors. They have relationships with specific editors at the publishing houses. They're experts in what's selling and how to pitch your work to the right place at the right time. They bring many years of experience, along with a network of contacts—and hopefully a reputation for uncovering talent. Agents are trusted by publishers to bring marketable projects to the table. When an agent represents you, you're getting the benefit of their insider knowledge and contacts.

The advantages of having an agent don't stop there. Once they've negotiated the best deal for you, agents remain closely involved in how your book progresses on the path to publication. They run interference during any disagreements you might have with your editor or publisher. If there's ever a contractual dispute, your agent is the one who will handle it. If there's a problem with payment, your agent is the first to spot it. Most authors appreciate how an agent allows them to focus on the writing work, confident the agent will take care of business and raise red flags if they see something amiss on the path to publication.

The very best agents serve as an author's career manager. They'll be interested not only in your first book, but in how to best strategize and sell your future books. They alternately serve as a coach to help get your work done; a therapist when bad reviews come in, as they always do; a cheerleader to celebrate every win; and a sharp-nosed accountant to ensure you get every dime that's due. A few might even become active in your book's marketing campaign.

Many writers ask, how can I find an agent? The better question is, how can you find the right agent? You want an agent you can trust, who'll be a career-long partner. You need to find an agent who really understands and believes in your work, and is committed to looking out for your long-term interests. It's certainly easy to find the names of agents through online databases and directories, but it's not always easy to find the perfect match.

Be careful, there's an intoxicating excitement of finding an agent interested in your work—especially if you've suffered a string of rejections. Just as you wouldn't go into any business with any person who said, "Hey, let's be partners," you don't want to enter into a business agreement with just any agent. When they sell your book to a publisher, you're entering into a legally binding contract that potentially lasts for the life of that work.

So, let's pause here and go over the standard business practices of a literary agent; what their legal responsibility is, and what commitment you're making when being represented by one.

First, agents are supposed to make money only when they sell your work. Their standard commission is 15 percent of everything that the author receives. That means they'll take 15 percent of your advance, 15 percent of any royalties you earn, and 15 percent of other possible earnings. Later on, when we cover publishing contracts, we'll discuss the many different rights your agent might sell. For now, just remember that the agent gets a cut of everything that comes your way. This of course incentivizes them to find the best opportunities for selling your work and to negotiate better deals.

A small number of agents might charge a fee for reading your work, but this isn't routine or standard practice. Largely you should avoid anyone who charges what basically amounts to a reading fee, because this is how publishing scams typically operate. If you find what appears to be a reputable agent charging a fee, find out if she offers any critique on the submitted work that would offer you some value. Sometimes the fee will be refunded if the agent agrees to represent you and sells your book. Try to determine if the reading fee makes up the agent's primary source of income. Obviously, you want an agent who is most successful at selling, and not reading.

You might also come across agents who charge fees associated with submitting your work, such as photocopying fees or overnight shipping fees. Some agents absorb these expenses as the cost of doing business rather than charging authors—but this practice is considered ethical and some agents still do it.

Another practice to watch for is the agent who offers a paid editing service, or refers you to an editing service in exchange for representation. While it is common for agents to say they'll consider representing your work if you revise it, it's uncommon for them to do this work themselves and charge you for it. It's also questionable when they send you to a specific and approved person to help you. In such cases, the agent may receive a kickback for referring you, which is considered unethical.

Finally, since we're discussing business practices that raise a red flag, do not respond to advertisements from agents seeking clients. If an agent contacts you, your BS meter should go off the charts. Now while it's true that agents seek out clients, it's usually because you've received recent publicity or attention. If the agent makes all kinds of promises to you, or lavishes you with praise, then requests a fee walk the other way.

While agents often work on a handshake agreement with their authors, it's more common these days for an agreement to be formalized in writing. The author-agent contract spells out how long the relationship lasts, how it can be renewed or terminated, the agent's commission, and how disputes get resolved.

Also, while the agent has the right to be your exclusive agent of record, you should have the freedom to represent yourself or market your own work if you want. In other words, if and when you negotiate deals for your own work without the agent's assistance, she shouldn't earn a commission on it.

But for any work the agent sells and negotiates a contract for, she's entitled to earn a commission for as long as that contract remains in effect. In fact, the publishing contract that you sign with your publisher will include what's known as the agency clause. This is a legal clause written by the literary agent and this clause binds the agent to the book deal as the agent of record, who receives all payments and distributes them to the author, until the contract terminates. So, even if you break up with your agent, she's going to continue to receive a 15 percent commission while that publishing agreement remains in effect.

So, as was emphasized earlier, you should sign only with an agent you trust. They oversee and double-check your royalty statements from the publisher, and they're responsible for sending you payments due. If either of you suspect the publisher isn't being accurate or honest in its financial reporting, it's the agent who'll oversee the auditing process.

You might wonder what happens if you think your agent is the one who's being dishonest and needs to be audited. Let's hope you're never in that situation because that's when things get quite ugly. Let's assume everything will go smoothly—which it usually does—and I'll help you understand when an agent might not be as great as they would have you believe.

When an agent offers you representation, you should receive a phone call with the good news. Don't feel pressured to agree to their offer immediately—it's OK to play a little hard to get. If your manuscript is actively under consideration by other agents, you should say so, and ask for at least a week or two to see if those other agents are also interested. You'll also want to ask if the agent requires you to sign a contract with them, which you'll need time to review. Finally, you'll want at least a day or two to go back to your research notes about this agent, formulate a list of questions you might have about how they work, and ask about next steps.

If you find yourself in the very lucky position of being courted by two or more agents, then your phone conversations should give you the first signs of good or bad chemistry. And chemistry may well be the most important factor in deciding which agent you go with. But you should also consider the following factors.

The number one criterion is usually the agent's track record of sales. This can be the best sign of whether you have a so-called good agent. Look at their client list and the publishers they've recently sold to. You should be able to find this information on their website. Are the publishers they sell to the types of publishers you consider appropriate for your work? Ensure your agent has success in repping the type of work you're trying to sell. If she doesn't have the experience or connections you'd expect, then ask her about it—respectfully, of course. Publishing tends to be driven by relationships and by reputation. So, if your agent is trying to break into totally new business territory with your book, you should know that upfront.

Sometimes it's easier to get represented by a new agent who's trying to build a roster of clients, someone who may not have a lot of sales under their belt. Even if an agent's track record's still developing, take a look at her previous experience in publishing. For example, was she formerly an editor at a New York house? Or, what's the experience and reputation of the agency that she's associated with? If she's working at a solid agency with an identifiable track record, or if she has a long history in the publishing world, these are good signs.

The second thing to look for is industry professionalism. This can be tough for an outsider to gauge, but they should be treating you in a way that inspires confidence. They should get back to you in a timely manner, communicate clearly and respectfully. Their business operations shouldn't be cloaked in secrecy, and they should treat you as an equal. If you feel like you're being treated in a shabby way, others might feel the same—and that includes editors at publishing houses.

I should note here, I have observed some unpublished writers who can be quite demanding. Writers sometimes have expectations that are exceptional and outside the norm—at least for the publishing industry. So, be reasonable. You can't call your agent at any hour and have a lengthy discussion, or expect daily contact, or receive near-instant responses to your emails. Remember, most agents work for free until your book's sold and their most immediate responses go to their established clients whose continued book sales pay their bills.

The final thing you're looking for is enthusiasm. Do you get the feeling the agent genuinely believes in you and your work? While agents are certainly interested in a sale, they're also interested in projects that excite them and clients they're proud to represent.

While it's not possible to put a quantitative measure on enthusiasm, think of it this way: Your agent's the person who champions your cause to the publisher throughout the life of your book's publication, and should be there to help resolve conflicts. Does this agent feel like your best champion? You need to feel confident about being in a business relationship with this person. There are few things worse than having anxiety over whether your agent is doing the best job for you.

One thing you shouldn't worry too much about is the size of the agency—this doesn't necessarily correlate with the size of the deal you can expect. Generally, you'll find several categories of reputable agents; those that consist of only one or two principals, with perhaps a few associates—you might call these boutique agencies.

Then you'll find mid-size and large agencies that have many agents on board, and also have specialized staff positions, such as a contracts manager or a foreign rights specialist. Finally, there are mega-agencies that have far greater scope than just literary talent—they deal with all talent. William Morris Endeavor or ICM Partners would be examples of mega-agencies.

Before we tackle what happens when you land an agent, I'd like to advise those writers who might be working in more than one genre. Let's say you're trying to get an agent for your children's book, but you've also got an epic fantasy series, and on top of that, maybe you write screenplays.

It's rare for an agent to represent every single genre, so authors who want to pursue multiple, may in fact need more than one agent. However, don't assume this at the start. And, I don't recommend shopping for more than one agent at a time. Your best strategy is to focus on one project before worrying about the future. Then, once you've secured your first agent for your first project, the agent will always ask, "What else you're working on?" And that's your opportunity to discuss your varied areas of interest. They'll advise you on whether they're suited to represent you across all genres, or if someone else within their agency could represent you. If necessary, they'll release you to find another agent for whatever work they're not able to represent.

OK, so let's say you've managed to find the right agent. That doesn't mean the agent will send your work out to publishers immediately. You'll find that agents' practices vary widely in this regard, but some will help you further refine your manuscript or book proposal. Others will ask you for revisions, and they might rework your submissions package to increase its chances of success. Only when the agent is satisfied with the materials and the sales presentation will they start contacting editors.

You've probably heard that publishers don't spend as much time on editing as they once did, possibly putting more pressure on the agents to fulfill the role of nurturing editor. While it's true that you'll find some agents who are very hands-on editorially, this isn't true of all agents. They aren't supposed to take the place of your editor at the publishing house.

If you want to know if your agent is this hands-on editing type, then look closely at their website, or look for any interviews that they've done, or just ask them directly if they make an offer of representation. There isn't really a right or wrong level of editorial involvement, but agents who are new to the business may be more inclined to put in substantial editorial work. That's because early on, while they're still establishing themselves, they're probably not attracting cream of the crop projects. If you're seeking an agent who is more hands-on, it can be smart to target these so-called hungry agents who are actively seeking clients and may have more time to spend on nurturing your writing talent.

Before the agent puts your work out on submission, they'll probably discuss their pitch strategy with you, which typically involves a round of submissions to the most desirable editors, or sometimes an auction.

Auctions take place when an agent has what she thinks is a really hot property. She might establish a floor price—that's when there's a minimum for which she will sell the book—and then she'll make submissions to potential editors, giving them a deadline for response. If one publisher's bid is topped by another, the first publisher is given the opportunity to beat the competitor's offer. Obviously, this process hinges on one factor. The book must be one that the industry believes will be a big seller. Nothing is more embarrassing for an agent than holding an auction that no one wants to participate in.

Sometimes, before the auction starts, a publisher might do something called a preempt, which is making an offer conditioned on the agent immediately taking the project off the market. If the publisher and the author are a good match for each other, and the offer is good enough, then a preempt deal can be satisfying for everyone. Preempts often happen when the editor loves the project and doesn't want to compete with other publishers for it. If the preempt is declined, the agent and author then take their chances with the auction process.

However, the process resolves itself, an agent would not force you to accept a deal with a publisher you're uncomfortable with. In fact, it's not uncommon for authors to turn down better money with one publisher to go to another house, or another editor, that offers a better fit.

Unfortunately, having an agent does not guarantee a book deal. In fact, these days, it's normal for agents to tell their clients, after several failed rounds of submissions, "Well, I could have sold it five years ago. Today's market is tougher than ever." So, if this is what your agent tells you, hopefully they can offer more specifics about why. Is the market saturated? Are publishers demanding authors with bigger platforms? Have the publishers cut back on the number of titles they're signing?

Agents should specify what imprints or publishers they've contacted and been rejected by. It's your right to know this information, especially after a long period of time has passed. You can also ask for the rejection letters. But your agent is under no obligation to provide you with specific contact information of editors or publishers.

Don't assume that your agent isn't good enough if your book didn't sell. Do however expect an open and frank discussion about any patterns in the rejections you're receiving. Perhaps there's a way to revise your book, or its concept, to make it more marketable. Just don't expect your agent to undertake a revision process with you. Sometimes, it's better for agents to cut their losses if they can't be confident of a sale that's worth their time.

This is a good time to bring up the fact that even if your work merits publication, it might not attract the interest of an agent because they estimate the advance would simply be too low. Many unpublished writers are curious about the kind of advance they might receive, but it's hard to offer a rule of thumb. Advances vary depending on the size of the publisher, the current sales trends in the market, and the excitement surrounding a particular project.

However, to keep your expectations in line, a book advance for an unknown author might not be more than $10,000, maybe $20,000, at a major New York house. Smaller presses commonly offer advances in the low four figures. It's possible for an unknown author to land a six-figure book deal, but in the event this happens to you, remember that the advance is always divided into a few installments, and even $100,000 isn't much to live on. It will be portioned out over two or three years, the agent will take their cut, and you have to pay taxes on what's left. So, don't expect your advance to replace the income from a long-term salary job.

Whatever the scenario, the agent knows that most books don't earn out their advance. That means they won't expect to earn more than several thousand dollars on an average book deal, unless they anticipate the book having a very long sales life. So, when considering whether to take you on, the agent has to go through this mental calculation of hours spent versus potential dollars earned.

If you feel like your agent is failing you, and you want to shop around for another, you might not find it that easy to secure a new agent. Just because you've had representation in the past doesn't help you attract another. In fact, some agents might wonder if you're a difficult client, especially if they think well of the agency that you're leaving.

However, if you feel that terminating is your best option—and it might be— then look at the author-agent contract you signed. What are the rules? Some contracts stipulate you have to give the agent at least one year to find a home for your work. Others allow you to terminate the relationship with 30 days notice.

If you do part ways with the agent before they sell your work, get a list of all the publishers they submitted to. That's the first thing your new agent will want to know. Unfortunately, if your first agent exhausted every possible outlet, it's not really feasible for another agent to approach those markets a second time. So, once a rejection, always a rejection. Even if you re-conceptualize your book, or if you dramatically revise the manuscript, most editors are unwilling to take a second look at a project they've already considered. They would be doing the agent a real favor to reconsider, and most of the time, the answer will still be no.

If the agent path comes to a dead end, another option is to begin the process of submitting the work on your own. You can pitch to smaller presses, niche presses, or digital publishers that the agent didn't pursue because they didn't represent enough of a financial opportunity. If you get an offer from a small press, it is possible to successfully negotiate your own contract if you know what to look for. Or, you can sometimes find an agent who will work on an hourly basis to negotiate that contract for you.

Since we began this discussion of agents, what I've described is all within the bounds of the traditional agent-author relationship. It remains the prevalent model you'll find in the industry. However, as the industry evolves, authors' needs and long-term career growth are no longer defined by selling their next book to a traditional print-driven publisher. Self-publishing and digital publishing projects, which we'll cover later, can play an important role in growing your readership and establishing your career.

As a result, agents' business models have started to adapt in response. They've had to re-envision how they support their authors. Some are starting their own digital publishing arms and helping clients self-publish. The difficulty is that, traditionally, the only acceptable way for agents to earn money is through that 15 percent commission we discussed earlier. The Association of Authors' Representatives, the professional organization for literary agents, explicitly prohibits its members from acting as publishers. That's because it raises a potential conflict of interest when the agent represents the author to traditional publishers while also acting as a publisher herself. Therefore, most agents assist with self-publishing only on a commission basis, taking their standard 15 percent on sales.

Agents who actively assist authors with alternative publishing methods have to be very transparent and careful about their business operations. In an interview, agent Laura Rennert told me, "We have to make sure there's no incentive for us to recommend to our authors that they pursue one avenue or another."

You may wonder how an author benefits from having an agent assist with self-publishing. Why not just go solo? Well, the answer depends on the strengths and assets of the author. Does the author have the existing skills and resources to do it right? How much time does the author have to spend figuring it all out? Some authors are well-equipped to be publishing entrepreneurs, while others prefer the experience and resources of someone in the industry they trust.

Agents I've spoken to about this issue see a long-term benefit in assisting clients with self-publishing and digital publishing, but they point out that it's hard work. The agents who are engaged and invested in their clients' work don't click upload or publish and just walk away. They help in a strategic manner, doing the same work a publisher would, with ongoing marketing support and insight.

Several years ago, when agents first began assisting their clients with self-publishing, some offered a one-size-fits-all model, which usually meant a 15 percent commission on sales, with the author paying freelance costs. Today, some agents have moved to tiers of service, and more customized arrangements, to take into account the unique needs of each author.

To be clear, this remains an unusual way of working. The overriding goal for most agents, especially for new or unpublished clients, is to sell that authors' work to a traditional publisher. Most agents assist with self-publishing efforts only for existing clients. So, don't expect to receive a response to your submission with an offer to help you self-publish; that conversation typically happens only after months of trying the traditional publishing route, and by mutual agreement.

Some authors, when faced with the prospect of finding an agent, feel like they'd rather just self-publish first. Then, if they have some success, they'll consider approaching agents to secure a traditional publishing deal. For most writers, this isn't the right move. Agents are rarely interested in self-published work unless it's hugely successful, and if you're writing a series, they can't sell a second installment to a traditional publisher when the first one has been self-published.

I find that most writers, in self-publishing first, are protecting their egos, or are otherwise impatient to see results, rather than thinking through the best option for their long-term careers. By and large, it's more advantageous to commit to the traditional publishing path until it's clear your work either needs improvement, or it doesn't fit the current model for commercial success.

Writing Your Query Letter
Lecture 6

The query letter is the time-honored tool for writers seeking publication, used by magazine writers and book authors alike. In book publishing, the query functions as a sales letter that attempts to persuade an editor or agent to read your manuscript. A good query has several distinct elements: some customization or personalization of the letter for its specific recipient; a clear definition of the property being offered, including the title, genre or category, and word count; the hook, which is the real meat of the query; biographical information; and the closing. In this lecture, we'll look at each of these elements in detail as they apply to query letters for novel and memoir manuscripts.

Opening the Query Letter

- Personalizing your query can set your letter apart from the hundreds of other queries sitting on an agent's desk. A surprising number of writers do little or even no research when submitting their work, simply blasting their materials to any address they can find. Of course, editors and agents can easily spot blanket submissions, which are often easy rejections, and appreciate those writers who are more thoughtful and considerate.

- There are several ways to personalize your letter meaningfully. If you study the type of books that an agent or editor represents or publishes, you can compare your work to that of an existing client or author. If you've read that an editor has a specific interest in the type of work you write, you can cite that as a reason for your query. Even better, you might mention hearing an agent or editor speak at a conference. The key here is demonstrating knowledge of the marketplace you're trying to enter.

- Here's an example of a strong personalized lead for a query letter: "In a January interview on the *Writer's Digest* blog, you praised *The Thirteenth Tale* and indicated an interest in literary fiction with a genre plot. My paranormal romance *Moonlight Dancer* blends a literary style with the romance tradition." This approach is succinct, knowledgeable, and direct.

- Next in the query, you need to specifically state what you're offering, including your book's title, genre or category, and word count—even though all of these may change at a later date. Including this information signals that you have a fully realized project that's targeted to a particular audience.

- Sometimes, especially if you're writing mainstream or literary fiction or a work that includes elements from multiple genres, it can be useful to draw comparisons between your book and another title or your style and that of another author. Note, however, that such comparisons should be thoughtful. Comparing yourself to a current *New York Times*–bestselling author can come across as arrogant; it's better to demonstrate a nuanced understanding of where your book falls within the literary spectrum.

The Story Hook

- At the core of most query letters is the story hook—probably the most difficult element to get right. Many authors are tempted to cram too much detail into the hook, but this can get tiresome to read; the query becomes loaded down with specifics that don't help sell the story. Instead, you want to boil your story down to just a few compelling elements: the protagonist or main characters and the choices or conflict being faced. Most queries also need to clearly identify the time period and setting, especially if the story is historical.

- Let's look at an example of a mediocre hook we can turn into something much better. This example is adapted from *The Writer's Advantage* by Laurie Scheer. Here's the hook: "Jennifer is a 43-year-old single woman who's had a successful career in advertising and decides at the last minute that her biological clock is ticking; she wants to have a child."
  - This hook isn't interesting or fresh enough to get a manuscript request, but watch what happens if we add another layer:

"Jennifer is a 43-year-old single businesswoman having her first child; at the same time, her 22-year-old niece, Sarah, is also having her first child. Sarah doesn't see the benefit of having a career and wants only to be supported by a rich husband."

- The second hook gives us some conflict; we can see that this might be an interesting story if the two women proceed through the experience together.

• Sometimes your story is compelling, but your query simply fails to capture its unique qualities. Figuring out what's truly special about your story and expressing it in a compelling way is the toughest part of writing the query. To begin a rough draft of your hook, you might try starting with one of the following formulas:
- The first formula answers these questions: What does your character want? Why does the character want it? What keeps him or her from getting it?

- The second formula is to state the character's name with a brief description, describe the conflict faced, and convey the choices to be made.

• A great hook feels natural and easy, as if it was effortless to write, but we all know that conveying a compelling story in just a few words is the test of a great writer. The following is a well-crafted hook describing a novel by Bill Clegg, *Did You Ever Have a Family?*
- "On the eve of her daughter's wedding, a mother is devastated when her home goes up in flames after a gas explosion, killing her ex-husband, her boyfriend, and the young couple to be wed—leaving her the sole survivor."

- As in this example, strong hooks are almost always specific and evocative, which helps set your story apart from others.

• Some hooks are roughly 100 to 200 words, others are a paragraph, and others are a few short paragraphs; much depends on the genre and the nature of the story. In describing the characters, you usually need to mention only the protagonist, the romantic interest or sidekick, and the antagonist. And don't get bogged down in minor plot points that don't affect the protagonist's choices or the story outcome. Finally, don't reveal the ending in your hook.

Dos and Don'ts of Bios

- The next part of the query letter is often a brief biographical note, usually about 50 to 100 words. Here, include your specific publication credits, advanced writing degrees, major professional organizations to which you belong, and possibly, major awards or competitions you've won. You should also highlight any intriguing or unusual research that went into your book. Finally, mention your career or profession, particularly if it lends credibility to your skill in writing a believable story.

- Here's an example of a well-done bio, expressing personality but professionalism, by an unpublished children's writer: "I grew up on a remote farm in South Africa, where I learned to speak Zulu and spent my days exploring bushmen caves and imagining a world filled with mythical African creatures. After my undergraduate studies in South Africa, I went on to complete a master's degree at the University of London and now live in the San Francisco Bay

Red Flags Leading to Rejection

- A query that runs longer than one single-spaced page.

- Direct comments on the quality of your work. Your query should show—not tell—the quality of your writing.

- Explanations of how or why you came to write your book, especially if your motivation is so common as to be a cliché.

- A discussion of trends in the market or your work's target audience. You need to sell the story, not the genre.

Area." The detail offered here directly connects to the work that was being pitched, a story set in South Africa with components of magical realism.

- Be aware that any agent or editor who is interested in your work will Google your name and find your website or blog, whether you mention it in your query or not. If you're particularly proud of your online presence, you might want to reference it in your query. This presence demonstrates that you'll likely be a good marketer and promoter of your work.

- For those authors who have previously self-published their work, including that detail in the query presents a minor dilemma. These days, self-publishing doesn't usually hurt your future chances of traditional publication, but self-publishing credits don't make you more desirable as an author either.

Closing the Query

- In closing your query, you don't have to state that you are querying others simultaneously. However, if the manuscript is under consideration by another agent or editor, state that fact if or when someone else requests it.

- Resist the temptation to editorialize in the closing, proclaiming how much the agent will love the work, how exciting it is, or that it's a sure bestseller.

- Be sure to thank the agent or editor, but don't carry on unnecessarily.

- Never introduce the idea of an in-person meeting. The only possible exception to this rule is if you know you'll hear your recipient speak at an upcoming event. You can mention that you look forward to hearing the speech, but use the event's official channels to set up an appointment.

Final Thoughts on Queries

- The first paragraph of your query should highlight your strongest selling point. If your personalization is weak, you might start by mentioning a referral from another author or referring to a previous meeting you had with the agent or editor. If your hook is particularly compelling, you might also start with that.

- Once your query letter is final, send it out in batches of five or six at a time. Later, you may tweak the letter and send out another wave. If you're targeting the right people and your query is done well, you should receive at least one or two requests for the material after each wave. If you're getting no responses or form responses, reevaluate your query letter to see if you can improve it.

- Submission guidelines may allow for either e-mail or snail-mail queries. E-mail queries can lead to faster response times, but they may also be easier to delete or reject. An e-mail query may have to get to the point even more quickly than a paper-based query. Make sure your e-mail can be read in a glance or two, without scrolling.

- If an agent or editor is receptive to your query, you may be asked to send a few chapters or the full manuscript. A request for an exclusive means the agent or editor wants to be the only one considering the manuscript, and you must promise not to send the work out to anyone else during the exclusivity period. If you receive a manuscript request, ask when you should expect a response, then follow up within a week of that date.

- Finally, if you don't get a response at all from an initial query letter, follow up two to four weeks after the stated response time in the submission guidelines. If no response time is given, wait a couple of months. If you queried via snail mail, include another copy of the query in your follow-up. If you still don't hear back after one follow-up attempt, it's best to assume rejection and move on.

Suggested Reading

Burt-Thomas, *The Writer's Digest Guide to Query Letters.*

Lukeman, *How to Write a Great Query Letter.*

Exercises

1. Write three different versions of your hook—one at 50 words, one at 100 words, and another at 150 words. Test them out on writing group members, colleagues with some distance from your work, or people who are known for offering the truth. See which hooks gets the most favorable response.

2. Once you have a draft of your query letter, ask a friend who doesn't know anything about your book to read it. Without offering any additional explanation or background for the book, ask what questions your friend has after reading the query.

Writing Your Query Letter
Lecture 6—Transcript

As you research agents and publishers and read their submission guidelines, you'll soon discover that almost no one accepts a full manuscript on first contact. Instead, you commonly send a query letter first.

The query letter is the time-honored tool for writers seeking publication. It's used by magazine writers and book authors alike. In book publishing, the query functions as a sales letter that tries to persuade an editor or agent to read your manuscript. At its heart, the query is all about seduction. In fact, it's so much about charming persuasion that you should be able to write the query without having written a single word of the manuscript.

That doesn't mean it's easy. For some writers, the query represents a completely different way of thinking about their book and story. You have to begin seeing your work in terms of a marketable commodity. And to think of your book as a product, you need to have some distance from it. You have to sell the sizzle.

Now, as a reminder even though you could write and send a query without having a completed and polished manuscript, don't. Your work should be the absolute best you can make it before you begin the query process. For novel and memoir manuscripts, only query when you'd be comfortable seeing your book appearing as is between covers on a bookstore shelf. Later on, we'll talk about nonfiction queries and submissions.

I like to think of the query letter as having several distinct elements. First, the query includes some element of personalization. That means you customize the letter for a very specific recipient. Second, you always clearly define the property you have to offer, which means including the title, the genre or category, and the word count. Next there's the hook, which is the real meat of the query—and this is where writers typically have the most trouble selling their story. And then you have the biographical note, and finally the thank you and closing. So let's discuss each of these elements in greater detail.

Personalizing your query can help set your letter apart from the hundreds of others sitting on an agent's desk. A surprising number of writers do little or even no research when submitting their work, and blast their materials to any address they can find. Editors and agents, of course, can easily spot blanket submissions, which are often easy rejections. Speaking as a longtime editor myself, I always appreciated it when writers took time to demonstrate a thoughtful approach. If you consider your query a sales tool, then you're striving to be a good salesperson. And good salespeople develop a rapport with the people they want to sell to, and show that they understand their needs. By personalizing your letter, you can show that you've done your homework and that you're not pushing it out to everyone indiscriminately.

There are several ways to personalize your letter meaningfully. If you closely studied what type of book the agent or editor deals in, you can compare your work to that of an existing client or author. Or if you've read any interviews where they mention a specific interest in what you're writing, you can cite that as the reason for your query. Even better, if you've heard the agent speak or met them at a conference, you can reference that. The key here is demonstrating awareness of the marketplace you're trying to enter. It's not that you want to appear chummy when you're not, but rather informed and deliberate in how you're approaching the publishing process.

That said you're not going to be rejected for not personalizing your query. In some cases, you might find it very hard to personalize the letter in a meaningful way. At the very least, address a specific editor or agent, and try to demonstrate some knowledge of the types of work they deal in, based on your research. This alone will set you apart from the many writers querying, and that's the point. Here's an example of a strong personalized lead for a query:

> In a January interview at the *Writer's Digest* blog, you praised *The Thirteenth Tale* and indicated an interest in literary fiction with a genre plot. My paranormal romance, *Moonlight Dancer*, blends a literary style with the romance tradition.

This is specific, knowledgeable, and direct; and that's really all it takes. Speaking of directness, at some point in the query—and we'll talk about how to structure it later—you need to specifically state what you're offering That means stating your book's title, genre or category, and its word count. Even though the title is known to be tentative, even though the genre could be changed by the publisher later on due to marketing considerations, and even though that word count may change during the editing process, you need to include these details in your query. Such details signal that you have a fully realized project that's targeted to a particular audience. It could also unwittingly signal some problems with your project. So for instance, if your query states that you've written a memoir that's 250,000 words, that fact alone can lead to a rejection, you're selling a project that doesn't fit well within the current market standards.

If you're writing mainstream or literary fiction or a work that includes elements from multiple genres, it can be useful to draw comparisons between your book and another title. You can say that your book is written in the same manner or style as a certain title or author and that it has a similar tone or theme, just be careful of overdoing it. One or two comparisons should be more than enough and the more thoughtful the comparison, the better. Comparing yourself to a current *New York Times* bestselling author can come across as arrogant or too easy; it's better to demonstrate a nuanced understanding of where your book falls on the literary spectrum.

At the core of most query letters is the story hook. This can be difficult to get right and many writers are tempted to cram in too much detail about their story. Too much detail is a huge mistake; it can become tiresome to read and you're loading down the query with specifics that don't help sell the story. Instead, you want to boil down your story to just a few compelling elements—the protagonist or main characters and the conflict being faced—most stories also need to clearly identify the time period and setting, especially anything historical.

When a hook is well-written but boring, it's often because the story lacks anything fresh; it's the same formula without distinction. The protagonist feels one-dimensional, the story angle is something we've seen too many times, and the premise doesn't even raise an eyebrow. The agent or editor is thinking, "Ugh, another one of these?" Let me give you an example of a mediocre hook that we'll turn into something more extraordinary. This example is adapted from *The Writer's Advantage* by Laurie Scheer. "Jennifer is a 43-year-old single woman who's had a successful career in advertising and decides at the last minute that her biological clock's ticking, and she wants to have a child."

If you pitch this, the agent will be waiting to hear the rest of the story. This isn't interesting or fresh enough to generate a manuscript request. But if you can add another layer, watch what happens.

> Jennifer is a 43-year-old single businesswoman having her first child and, at the same time, her 22-year-old niece Sarah is also having her first child. Sarah does not see the benefit of having a career and only wants to be supported by a rich husband.

Now we're getting some conflict—this could be an interesting story if the two women proceed through the experience together. Do you see here how the hook helps an editor or agent gauge if you're a storyteller worth spending time on?

You'll often hear that your story needs to be fresh, and this is exactly what is meant. Of course in the example we just discussed, the problem goes much deeper than the query letter itself; we likely have a story-level issue. Queries, even if they're written well, can fail because they betray what's ultimately a boring story or just a story that doesn't stand out in the current market. Sometimes your story is indeed compelling, but your query fails to capture its unique qualities. Figuring out what's truly special about your story, and then expressing it in a compelling way—that's the toughest part of writing the query. It's common to write dozens of hook variations trying to increase the sizzle. Unfortunately, sometimes great stories in manuscript form just get botched during the query-writing phase, because the writer didn't craft a hook with voice or distinction, or liveliness.

Here's the good news; we can get you started off in the right direction. To begin a rough draft of your hook, I recommend you start with one of the following formulas. The first formula answers a series of three questions: What does your character want? Why does he want it? What keeps him from getting it? The second formula states your character's name with a brief description, describes the conflict she faces, and conveys the choices she has to make.

Whenever I teach a class where we critique students' hooks, just about everyone can point out the weaknesses and explain how to improve them. Now why is that? It's because when you're not the writer, you have distance from the work. When you do come across a great hook it feels so natural and easy, like it was effortless to write. But to convey a compelling story in just a few words is the test of a great writer.

In an earlier lecture, we talked about Publishers Marketplace, an industry news site. If you recall, it offers a deals database, listing books recently sold to publishers. Each deal includes a one-sentence description of the book sold; and these hooks are always well-crafted. Reading the hundreds of hooks at Publishers Marketplace can help you better understand what hooks excite agents and publishers. So let's discuss a couple of very brief but effective hooks.

> On the eve of her daughter's wedding, a mother is devastated when her home goes up in flames after a gas explosion, killing her ex-husband, her boyfriend, and the young couple to be wed—leaving her the sole survivor.

It's quite a hook, isn't it? It describes a novel by Bill Clegg, *Did You Ever Have a Family*. Here's another hook, this time for a memoir: "A single woman in New York decides to date every person who asks her out for an entire year, regardless of the circumstances." This describes a true story by Maria Dahvana Headley, called *The Year of Yes*. Notice in each of these hooks the tight focus on the conflict or unique situation. This is something you'll notice about all strong hooks; they are almost always unfailingly specific and evocative, which helps set the story apart from others that might be similar.

If you're struggling to capture the exact nature and style of your work, remember you can compare yourself to another author or your book to another title, as long as you do it thoughtfully rather than saying, "I'm the next Stephen King." It's also best to compare your work in terms of style, voice, or theme, rather than in terms of sales, success, or quality. You get bonus points if you can compare your work to someone the agent or editor already represents, rather than a title that everyone's talking about from the bestseller lists. For instance, in 2008 agents started rolling their eyes at the number of queries they received that claimed to be the next *Eat, Pray, Love*.

Once you have a draft of your hook, you'll know it can be improved if it runs long. You should be able to write an effective hook in roughly 100-200 words. Some hooks are just one paragraph, or you might have a few short paragraphs; a lot depends on the genre and the nature of the story. You also know you're on the wrong track if your hook has to explain more than three or four characters. Usually you only need to mention the protagonist, your romantic interest or sidekick, and the antagonist. If you're getting sidetracked into minor plot points that don't affect the protagonist's choices or the story outcome, you should probably cut them. Finally, don't reveal the ending in your hook. That actually belongs in the synopsis, which we'll discuss later. You like confidence in your hook, your best strategy is brevity. Brevity gets you in less trouble; the more you try to explain, the more likely you'll squeeze the life right out of your story, so get in and get out.

After you've finished the hook, the next part of the query is often a brief bio note, usually 50 or 100 words. You can consider including any or all of the following information:

First, what publication credits do you have? You have to be specific— you might as well be unpublished if you're not going to name the specific publications or titles. If you have no credits at all, don't say you're unpublished; that point will be made clear by fact of omission. Many querying novelists wonder if it's helpful to list nonfiction credits. It can be; they can show that you have some experience working with editors and an understanding of how the professional industry works. However, scholarly or niche publication credits can be tricky, since they definitely don't convey fiction or narrative writing ability. List them at your discretion, but it's probably not going to be a deal breaker either way.

It always makes sense to mention any advanced writing degrees you have, or major professional writing organizations you belong to. If you've recently attended major writing conferences, that might be appropriate too. Such items signal your seriousness and your intention to develop a career as a writer. However, avoid cataloging every single thing you've ever done in your writing life. Don't talk about starting to write when you were in grade school. Don't talk about how much you enjoy returning to writing in your retirement, even if it's true. Just mention one or two highlights that demonstrate your seriousness and devotion to the craft, if they feel appropriate, and if you're unsure, just skip them.

If your book is the product of some intriguing or unusual research—let's say you spent a year in the Congo, and that informs your characters and plot— mention it. These unique details can catch the attention of an editor or agent. Another relevant thing to mention might be any awards or competitions you've won. If the award isn't widely recognized or known in the publishing community, then the only way to convey the significance of an award is to talk about how many people you beat out. Usually the entry number needs to be in the thousands to be impressive.

The final relevant detail to mention is probably your career or profession. If it lends you credibility to write a better, more believable story, by all means reference it. This is often the case with lawyers who are writing legal thrillers or former detectives writing mysteries. Even if there's not a direct connection, editors and agents are often curious about what background you bring to your writing. Here's an example of a well-done bio, expressing personality but professionalism, by an unpublished children's writer.

> I grew up on a remote farm in South Africa, where I learned to speak Zulu and spent my days exploring bushmen caves and imagining a world filled with mythical African creatures. After my undergraduate studies in South Africa, I went on to complete a master's degree at the University of London and now live in the San Francisco Bay Area.

The detail offered in this bio directly connects to the work that was being pitched; a story set in South Africa, with magical realism components.

Now that we've discussed what you should include, I'll mention a few things that can make you sound like an amateur. Don't talk about how much your mom or your kids love your stories and don't say that all your friends have told you that you should write a book. Among agents and editors, that's considered about the worst reason of all to become an author.

Also, don't talk about how many times you've been rejected or even about your close acceptances, you want to avoid any whiff of desperation or the kind of cloying neediness that would definitely be a turnoff to publishing professionals. While agents and editors are looking for a good story, they're also looking for people who would be enjoyable to work with, rather than an energy drain. Some people call this the airport test—would I want to be stuck in an airport for 10 hours with this person?

Now is probably a good time to give you a heads-up. Just about every agent or editor will do a web search for you if they have any interest in your work. That means they'll likely find your website or blog whether you mention it in your query or not. If you're proud of your online presence and very active, you might want to mention it in your query. This demonstrates you might be a good marketer and promoter of your work. Just remember, it doesn't say anything about your ability to write a great story, and for novelists and memoirists, the art and craft of the story come first.

If you've previously self-published your work, the query presents a minor dilemma. Should you mention your track record as a self-published author? It's really totally up to you. Sooner or later this information is going to come out, so it's all about the best timing. Lots of people have self-published these days, and it doesn't really hurt your chances at traditional publication in the future. If you do mention self-publishing, it's best if you're proud of your efforts and are ready to discuss your success or failure in doing it. If you consider it a mistake or irrelevant to the project at hand, just leave it out and understand it may come up later. And don't make the mistake of thinking your self-publishing credits somehow make you more desirable as an author; that would require incredible sales success.

You don't read much advice about how to close a query letter perhaps because there's not much to it. You say thanks and you sign your name. But you want to make sure you leave a good final impression, so here are a few tips:

You don't have to state that you're simultaneously querying, everyone assumes this already. However, if the manuscript itself is under consideration by another agent or editor, then mention it if or when someone else requests it.

Resist the temptation to editorialize in the closing, or really at any point in the letter. This is where you proclaim how much the agent will love the work or how exciting it is, or how it's going to be a bestseller if only someone would give it a chance. When describing the story, avoid phrases such as, "In this fast-paced thriller," or "in a final twist that will rock your world," or "you'll laugh, and you'll cry."

There's no need to go into great detail about when and how you're available to be contacted. Make sure the letter includes your phone number, email address, and return address. I recommend putting your contact info at the very top of the letter if you're mailing it and if you're emailing it, put it at the very bottom. Don't put your contact info in the query body itself. Thank the agent, but don't carry on unnecessarily or be incredibly subservient or beg.

And finally, never introduce the idea of an in-person meeting. Don't say you'll be visiting their city soon and ask if they'd like to meet for coffee. The only possible exception is if you know you'll hear them speak at an upcoming event, but don't ask for a meeting. Just say you look forward to hearing them speak and then use the conference's official channels to set up an appointment if possible, maybe instead of sending the query. Later we'll discuss how to craft an effective pitch and how to present yourself effectively in person.

Now that we've covered all the query elements, let's go back to the start. I began by emphasizing how you should personalize the letter, but you don't necessarily have to start with that element. The very first paragraph of your query should put your best foot forward. You want to lead with your strongest selling point and if your personalization is weak, then you shouldn't start with that. Some strong ways to start a query include if you've received a referral. A referral is when you've been vouched for or referred by an existing client or author. Or if you met the agent/editor at a conference, and especially if your material was requested, then you would put that information right up front. If you believe that your hook is extra compelling, start with that. Finally, some authors do best to lead with their credentials, prestigious awards, or high praise from a bestselling author. This is especially true for previously published authors, or those who have MFA degrees from well-known programs. If none of these scenarios apply to you, then the default way to begin your query is either with the personalization or with your hook.

Once you have a working draft of your query letter, it's time to check for a few red flags that often lead to a quick rejection. If your query runs longer than one page, single-spaced, you've said way too much; you need to simplify and probably trim back your hook or your bio note. Avoid directly commenting on the quality of your work. Your query should show what a good writer you are, rather than you telling or emphasizing what a good writer you are. On the flip side, don't criticize yourself or the quality of the work; you don't want to come across as self-derogatory.

It can sometimes work against you to explain how or why you came to write your book, especially if your motivation is so common as to be a cliché. For example, many baby boomers have experienced the challenge of acting as a caretaker for their aging parents. If you say this is what inspired your novel on the same theme, agents and editors may immediately draw the conclusion you've written a vaguely veiled memoir or something that lacks spark or freshness in the market, since so many stories with a similar theme get pitched now.

When it comes to pitching a novel, you don't have to talk about trends in the market or its target audience. Your novel's genre already speaks to that, and your publisher will be very familiar with how well that genre sells. So you have to sell the story, and some writers get confused on this point, because it is in fact essential for nonfiction queries to delve into evidence of need in the marketplace. But for fiction, it's the craft that matters at the query stage, and little else.

Once your query is final and the best you can make it, I recommend sending it out in batches of five or six at a time; see what the response is like. Most writers end up tweaking the letter further, then sending out another wave. If you're targeting the right people, and your query is done well, you should receive at least one or two requests for the material after each wave of submissions. If you're getting no response or form responses, reevaluate your query letter and see if you can improve it, or if you've been sending the synopsis or the first five pages along with the query, you may need to consider if any red flags are hidden there. We'll address that in future lectures.

You might wonder if it's better to query via email or snail mail. If the submission guidelines allow for either option, then email queries can lead to faster response times. However, emails can also be easier to delete or reject; they usually have to get to the point even more quickly than a paper-based query. Therefore, it's best to compose your email query outside of your email software, so you can see how long it really is and to edit it carefully. Then when you're ready to send, copy and paste it as plain text without any special formatting.

Make sure it can be read in a glance or two, without scrolling. Don't include your mailing address, special headers or any contact information at the beginning of the email, because that's wasted time and space. Be captivating and essential with your lead sentence and paragraph, because the agent or editor might not reach the end of the message. As far as standard etiquette for terms of address, it's best to open formally, such as Dear Mrs. Smith. If they write back using your first name and sign with their first name, you're welcome to match their formality level in your response.

When you do receive positive responses from your queries, they'll tend to be something like, "Yes, send the first three chapters," or "Yes, send the full manuscript." If someone asks for an exclusive, that means they want to be the only person considering the manuscript, so you have to promise not to send the work out to anyone else during the exclusivity period. I would only grant an exclusive if it's for a very short period, maybe two weeks to consider a full manuscript. When you do receive a manuscript request, specifically ask when you should expect to hear back, then follow up within one week of that date.

Email replies from agents are typically very short. Don't use a positive response as an opportunity to launch into a lengthy reply talking more about yourself and your work; that's better saved for a phone call when the agent makes an offer of representation.

And if you don't hear back at all from an initial query, follow up in about two to four weeks after the stated response time in the submission guidelines. If no response time is given wait a couple months, and if you queried via snail mail, include another copy of the query in your follow up. If you still don't hear back after one follow-up attempt, it's best to assume rejection and move on.

To summarize, the key to every detail in your query is will it be meaningful, charming, or persuasive to the agent or editor? Ideally your query should reveal something of your work's voice or personality, rather than being too stiff. While the query isn't the place to divulge too much personal detail, there's something to be said for expressing something about yourself that provides insight into the kind of author you are—that ineffable you. If you find yourself struggling to perfect your query, the best thing you can do is find a mentor or a published author to read your letter and offer feedback. They usually have that distance required to tell you how to improve your letter and how to make the most effective case for your work.

Writing Your Novel or Memoir Synopsis
Lecture 7

Now that we've tackled the query, we come to what may be the single most despised document you might be asked to prepare: the *synopsis*. A synopsis conveys a book's entire narrative arc and reveals the ending. Unfortunately, there is no standard format or method for writing a synopsis. In this lecture, we'll focus on writing a one-page synopsis that you can use as your default unless specific submission guidelines ask for something longer. Most agents or editors won't be interested in a synopsis that's longer than a few double-spaced pages. In theory, this should make writing the synopsis easier, but as many writers know, boiling down an 80,000-word story into 300 words presents a unique challenge.

Overview of the Synopsis

- For agents and editors, a synopsis helps determine whether or not you can successfully put together a story, especially within the conventions of your chosen genre. A synopsis shows whether your characters' actions and motivations are realistic and make sense.

  o A synopsis can also reveal any problems in your story. For instance, if it turns out that the whole book is a dream or if an act of God resolves the plot, an agent may skip reading the manuscript altogether. A synopsis has an uncanny way of highlighting plot flaws, gaps in character motivation, or a lack of story structure.

  o On the more positive side, a synopsis can reveal the freshness of your story. It also gives you an opportunity to impress an agent or editor with your use of language. Make sure to use active voice rather than passive and the third-person present tense.

- A synopsis must accomplish three things: First, it should tell the story of characters that readers will care about. Generally, the synopsis is written with the protagonist as the focus and shows what's at stake for that character. Second, the synopsis must give a clear idea of the core conflict for the protagonist, what drives the conflict, and how the protagonist succeeds or fails in dealing with it. Third, the synopsis must explain how the conflict is resolved and how the protagonist's situation has changed, both internally and externally.

- Covering these three topics won't leave you much space for detail. You won't be able to mention all the characters or events. You can't summarize each scene or even every chapter, and some aspects of your story will have to be broadly generalized to avoid detailing a series of events or interactions that don't materially affect the story's outcome.

- Don't make the mistake of thinking that the synopsis merely details the plot; if you do, you'll end up with a mechanical account of your story that doesn't offer any depth or texture—a story without emotion. You need to share both the context and the characters' feelings about what's happening in the story. But again, in writing your synopsis, avoid editorializing the narrative.

What Belongs in a Synopsis?
- As you think about what belongs in the synopsis, consider the most important narrative devices that every story uses.
   - First, the story starts with an inciting incident. This incident often puts the protagonist in a situation that increases tension and conflict, forcing him or her to act. Or the protagonist wants something badly but faces an obstacle to acquiring it.

   - Not long after, the story hits the first major turning point, the point at which the character embarks on a journey without any possibility of return to the status quo.

   - Conflict and tension build until the story reaches a climax, which usually happens about three-fourths of the way into the book. The climax is the moment that determines whether or not the protagonist succeeds or fails or when the primary story tension is brought to its crisis point. Portraying this moment effectively is usually critical to a synopsis, as is the inciting incident.

o   As your character deals with the story conflict leading to the climax, he or she will undergo some kind of emotional journey. Your synopsis should clearly indicate what pressures the character is under and his or her approach to dealing with the conflict.

o   Finally, you'll show the falling action and reveal the ending.

- To decide what characters deserve space in the synopsis, you need to look at their role in assisting or generating conflict for the protagonist. We need to see how they enter the story, the quality of their relationship to the protagonist, and how they might change, too.

    o   For example, *Gone with the Wind* has a key romantic interest, Rhett Butler, and his actions or reactions are just as important as those of Scarlett O'Hara. In stories with a scheming villain, we need to know his or her motivations, as well. A good rule of thumb is to limit yourself to mentioning three or four characters by name in the synopsis, but of course, only you can determine the right number, based on the qualities of your story.

    o   Don't let your synopsis get bogged down with the specifics of character names. Use the names of your main characters, but if a waitress enters the story only briefly, call her "the waitress." It's common to type character names in all capitals when they are introduced so that agents or editors can see who the key figures are at a glance.

- The synopsis doesn't necessarily have to tell your story in chronological order; it's more important to make sure that someone unfamiliar with the story can easily understand the sequence of events. The art of the synopsis comes in figuring out how to weave together all the story elements in such a way that everything feels natural. However, you also have to make sure that the synopsis structure matches the structure expected in your genre. A synopsis of a romance should deliver an unfolding love story. A mystery must become more tense and thrilling as it approaches its climax.

What Doesn't Belong in a Synopsis?

- Don't spend any time in the synopsis explicitly explaining or deconstructing the themes your story may address. You don't want to make your book seem like a morality tale.

- Spend only the briefest amount of time on character backstory. A phrase or two is plenty to indicate a character's background, and you should reference it only when it affects how events unfold.

- Avoid including dialogue, and if you do, be sparing. Make sure any dialogue you include is absolutely iconic of the character or represents a linchpin moment in the book.

- Don't ask rhetorical questions or leave questions unanswered. Remember, your goal here isn't to entice a reader.

- Don't split your synopsis into sections or label the plot points. In rare cases, such as a novel with a unique narrative structure, there

A smart strategy for organizing a synopsis is to outline the critical events in your story, which you should be able to jot down without going back to your manuscript.

might be a reason to have subheads in the synopsis, but try to avoid sectioning out the story in any way or listing a cast of characters up front, as if you were writing a play.

- Although your synopsis will reflect your ability to write, it's not the place to get pretty with prose. Leave out any lyrical descriptions or attempts to impress through poetry. In a synopsis, you don't have space to follow the advice "show, don't tell"; you have to tell. For example, it's acceptable to state that your main character is a "hopeless romantic" rather than trying to show it.

- Finally, your synopsis shouldn't be coy or mysterious in any way. The agent needs to know what happens in your book and how it delivers to evaluate whether or not it has money-making potential. Without a clear and accurate synopsis, professionals can't make an informed decision about your project.

Reviewing Your Synopsis

- Once you have a first draft of the synopsis, set it aside for a week or so, then return to it. Do your characters come to life and seem interesting? Does the plot effectively build tension? Does the reader clearly understand what's changed for the protagonist by the end? Does the overall tone or style of the synopsis match that of your novel?

- If you start to get a bad feeling from your synopsis, it may be time to pause the submission process and considering revising your work. Problems with your manuscript won't get resolved by the agent or publisher; instead, you'll get rejected. Because you get only one chance to pitch each work, make sure you resolve any problems that surface during the synopsis-writing stage.

Before-and-After Synopsis Samples

Before: The following synopsis introduces us to too many characters upfront, making it difficult for the reader to keep track of who's who. (Synopsis provided by Daniel Crane.)

> NELL HATLEY, a young law professor in her tenure year at the fictional Coppersmith University near Cincinnati, comes late to a faculty meeting, where she finds a law student, MARY REYNOLDS, opening fire. Nell subdues Mary, but is knocked unconscious. DETECTIVE ALAN SMITH visits Nell in the hospital and reveals that one of her colleagues, LARRY MCINTOSH, was killed and another, HARDEN GHENT, was seriously wounded. In Mary's pocket, the police find a note with McIntosh, Ghent and Nell's names.

After: The revised synopsis provides a little more characterization of Nell and focuses on her story. The reader learns about the inciting incident and keeps the twist of the three names scribbled on a note but holds back information on the other victims in the opening paragraph.

> NELL HATLEY is a young and ambitious law professor in her tenure year at Coppersmith University near Cincinnati, struggling with insecurities about the strength of her scholarship. When she arrives late to a faculty meeting, she finds a law student opening fire. Nell subdues the shooter, but one of her colleagues is killed and another is seriously wounded. In the shooter's pocket, the police find a note with three names scribbled on it—the two victims and Nell's.

Before: In a memoir written by an Indo-American immigrant, the synopsis initially provides too much backstory for what is essentially a straightforward conflict: The protagonist wants something different for herself from what her parents wanted.

> The story opens in the early 1980s, a time in which Indian immigrants were assimilating into American culture in a way

that I call "being brown." I was tolerated in my small town but not accepted. The Asian culture I inherited emphasized hard work and success at all costs, and early tastes of my family's financial success reinforced that the only way to rise above my own alienation was to make money—a lot more than everyone else. However, the path I truly felt called to take, to write, offered absolutely no such promise. There was not one Indian writer on the bookshelves, not an ethnic face on television, and never a non-American name in the newspaper bylines. To aspire to something outside of medicine, engineering or economics seemed equivalent to declaring one's life a failure.

After: The revision conveys the conflict more quickly, personally, and originally.

My physician father hammered his values into me with the conviction that they would lead to wealth and lift me above our alienating immigrant experience. However, I had a deeply spiritual experience at an early age that led me to question my father—and my entire upbringing. Thus began my battle between the pursuit of money and the pursuit of life.

Before: In a complex story involving three storylines, three main characters, and three locations, the synopsis devotes too much space to introducing only one character. (Synopsis provided by Kacie Stetson.)

DAKOTA BROWN, the madam of the notorious black brothel, the Black Orchid, finds an abandoned white baby girl in a gas station restroom. She takes the girl back to the brothel, where her best girl, HERMIONE JONES, takes the child for her own. They name her BRICK for fortitude. For years, they hide her away from the prying gaze of customers. Brick loves Hermione fiercely and descends into abject panic whenever Hermione leaves her side. When Brick is twelve, a john murders Hermione, flinging Brick into the depths of despair. She retreats to the kitchen and teaches herself to cook, a skill for which she shows a mystical talent. When she hits puberty, Dakota enrolls her in the Culinary Academy in the hopes of keeping her away from lustful customers. There, Brick meets HECTOR, a Mexican student who falls in love with her. His advances are met with icy rejection, which only fuel his fire. One night, after months of spurned love, he gets drunk, follows Brick on the way home, and attacks her sexually. Hector gets thrown in jail as Brick plunges into suicidal depression.

After: The revision sums up the character's background quickly to allow space to describe how the story unfolds. Note the use of a dateline to help the reader understand how the story will come together over a period of many years.

Los Angeles, 1963. An orphan girl, BRICK grows up in a notorious brothel, the Black Orchid. At an early age, she teaches herself to cook, a skill for which she shows a mystical talent. A Mexican student, HECTOR, falls in love with her; when his feelings go unrequited, he sexually assaults her. Brick plunges into suicidal depression.

Suggested Reading

Camenson and Cook, *Your Novel Proposal from Creation to Contract.*

Lyon, *The Sell Your Novel Tool Kit.*

Exercises

1. Once you have a draft of your synopsis, highlight every adjective or adverb. Can you eliminate them by choosing a stronger noun or verb?

2. Highlight every character name in your synopsis. Does each character deserve to be specifically mentioned or included? Is he or she critical to how the narrative unfolds? Why?

Writing Your Novel or Memoir Synopsis
Lecture 7—Transcript

Now that we've tackled the query, we come to what may be the single most despised document writers are asked to prepare: the synopsis. Your synopsis conveys your book's entire narrative arc. It shows what happens and who changes, and it has to reveal the ending.

Don't confuse the synopsis with sales copy, or the kind of material that might appear on your back cover, or in an Amazon description. In other words, you're not writing a punchy marketing piece for readers that builds excitement.

Rather, the synopsis is sometimes required because an agent or publisher wants to see, from beginning to end, what happens in your story.

The difficulty is that there's no single standard format or method for writing a synopsis. You'll find different opinions about its appropriate length, which makes it confusing territory for new writers especially.

Here's my biggest recommendation: Keep the synopsis short, or at least start short. We'll focus on how you can write a one-page, single-spaced synopsis and use that as your default, unless the submission guidelines ask for something longer. Most agents or editors won't be interested in a synopsis longer than a few double-spaced pages. In theory, this should make writing the synopsis easier. But as many writers know, boiling down an 80,000-word story into 300 words presents a unique challenge.

Let's back up for a moment. What do agents and editors really get out of this boiled-down version anyway?

The synopsis shows if you can successfully put together a story, especially within the conventions of the genre you're writing in. They're looking to see if the character's actions and motivations are realistic and make sense. A synopsis reveals any big problems in your story, or genre red flags. For instance, if it turns out your whole book is a dream, or if there are acts of god that save the day, an agent may skip reading the manuscript altogether.

A synopsis has an uncanny way of highlighting a book's plot flaws, any serious gaps in character motivation, or just a total lack of story structure. On the more positive side, a synopsis also can reveal how fresh your story is. However, if there's nothing exciting or unique in how your story unfolds—if it's like a million others—your manuscript may not get read.

The good news is that some agents hate synopses and never read them, and those who do understand it's a challenge to write one well. The bad news is they may use this as the first test of your writing ability. Either way, you can impress with lean, clean, and powerful language. From a mechanics point of view, this means using active voice rather than passive, and using third person, present tense.

You'll need to accomplish at least three things with your synopsis, without exception.

First, you need to tell the story of what characters we'll care about, which includes the protagonist. Generally you'll write the synopsis with your protagonist as the focus, and show what's at stake for her.

Second, we need a clear idea of the core conflict for the protagonist, what's driving that conflict, and how the protagonist succeeds or fails in dealing with that conflict.

Finally, we need to understand how that conflict is resolved and how the protagonist's situation, both internally and externally, has changed.

If you cover those three things, that won't leave you much time for detail. You won't be able to mention all the characters or all the events. You'll probably leave out some subplots, and some of the minor plot twists and turns. You can't summarize each scene or even every chapter. And of course many aspects of your story will simply have to be broadly generalized. You want to avoid detailing a series of events or interactions that don't materially affect the story outcome.

Don't make the mistake of thinking the synopsis just details the plot. That will end up reading like a very mechanical account of your story, and won't offer depth or texture—it will read like a story without any emotion at all. Think what it would sound like if you summarized a football game by saying, "Well, the Patriots scored. And then the Giants scored. Then the Patriots scored twice in a row." That's sterile and doesn't give us the meaning behind how the events are unfolding. Instead, you would say something like, "The Patriots scored a touchdown after more than one hour of a no-score game, and then the underdog of the team led the play. The crowd went wild."

What I'm trying to share here is the secret of a good synopsis. You need to share both the context and the characters' feelings and emotions about what's happening. Think of it this way:

You tell about an incident, which advances the story. The character will react or feel something about that incident, and make a decision that further advances the story. As you do this, avoid editorializing the narrative. As you might recall from writing the query, editorializing is when you add phrases such as, "In a thrilling turn of events."

As you think about what belongs in the synopsis, consider the most important narrative devices that every story uses. First, there's an inciting incident that starts the story. This incident often puts the protagonist in a situation that increases tension and conflict, and she's forced to act. Or there's something the protagonist wants very badly, but there's something standing in her way.

Not long after, the story hits the first major turning point, sometimes called the point of no return, where the character embarks on a journey without any possibility of changing her mind. You've probably heard of these plot elements before if you've ever studied structures informed by Joseph Campbell's hero's journey. This can serve as an excellent template for writing a synopsis, especially if your work follows a traditional narrative structure.

Conflict and tension build until we reach the story climax, which usually happens about three-fourths of the way into the book. The climax is the moment that determines whether or not the protagonist succeeds or fails, and when the primary story tension is brought to its crisis point.

Portraying this climactic moment effectively is usually critical to your synopsis, as is the inciting incident. As your character deals with the story conflict leading to the climax, they will have some kind of emotional journey, and your synopsis should clearly indicate what pressures they're under and their approach to dealing with the conflict. Then finally, you'll show the falling action and reveal the ending.

To decide what characters deserve space in the synopsis, you need to look at their role in generating conflict for the protagonist or assisting the protagonist. We need to see how they enter the story, the quality of their relationship to the protagonist, and how that might change as well.

For example, in the case of *Gone with the Wind*, we have a key romantic interest, Rhett Butler, and his actions or reactions are just as important as Scarlett O'Hara's. In stories with a scheming villain, such as Voldemort in Harry Potter, we need to know his motivations as much as we need to know the protagonist's.

A good rule of thumb is to limit yourself to exploring four or five characters in the synopsis, but of course only you can determine the right number, based on the qualities of your story. Whatever you decide, don't let your synopsis get bogged down with the specifics of character names. Stick to the basics. Use the names of your main characters, but if a waitress enters the story only briefly, call her the waitress. Don't say, "Bonnie, the boisterous waitress who calls everyone hon and works seven days a week." That's a huge and unnecessary tangent. When you do mention specific character names, it's common to put the name in caps in the first instance, so it's easy for agents or editors to see at a glance who the key figures are.

Your synopsis doesn't necessarily have to tell your story in chronological order; it's more important to make sure someone unfamiliar with your story can easily follow the story line and understand the sequence of events. The art of the synopsis is in figuring out how to weave together all the story elements in a way that feels natural. There should be transitions between paragraphs that make it clear how the events connect.

However, make sure that the synopsis structure matches the structure expected in your genre. A synopsis of a romance should deliver an unfolding love story. A mystery must become more tense and thrilling as it approaches its climax.

So what doesn't belong in a synopsis? Don't spend any time in the synopsis explicitly explaining or deconstructing the themes the story may address. You don't want to make your book seem like a morality tale or a pedantic read that hits the reader over the head with a lesson.

You also shouldn't spend any time, except in the briefest possible way, on any character backstory. A phrase or two is plenty to indicate a character's background; you should only reference it when it affects how events unfold. This may mean, if you've written a story with flashbacks, you may not include many of those flashbacks in the synopsis. However, if the flashbacks are really about what happens in the book rather than why something happens, then they may belong.

Avoid including dialogue, and if you do, be sparing. Make sure the dialogue you include is absolutely iconic of the character or represents a linchpin moment in the book.

Also avoid asking rhetorical or unanswered questions. Remember, your goal here isn't to entice a reader.

Don't split your synopsis into sections, or label the different plot points. In a few rare instances, there might be a reason to have some subheads in the synopsis due to a unique narrative structure, but try to avoid sectioning out the story in any way, or listing a cast of characters upfront as if you were writing a play.

While the synopsis reflects your ability to write, it's not really the place to get pretty with your prose. So you'll want to leave out any lyrical descriptions or attempts to impress through poetic description. You really can't take the time to show things in your synopsis. You really have to tell, and sometimes this is confusing to writers who've been told for years to show don't tell. The opposite is true in the synopsis. For example, it's okay to just come out and say your main character is a hopeless romantic rather than trying to show it.

Finally, your synopsis shouldn't be coy or mysterious in any way. The agent needs to know what happens in your book and how it delivers. Some writers think a synopsis will kill the enjoyment of reading the manuscript, but this misses the entire point of why the synopsis is being requested. Assume that any agent or editor has seen it all before. Anyone who asks for a synopsis blatantly does not want their curiosity piqued. They want the goods and to evaluate whether those goods have money-making potential. Without a clear and accurate synopsis, some professionals can't make an informed decision about your project.

For memoir writers, there are a few additional and special considerations. As the main character, you should obviously be the focus. The synopsis must convey what makes your story truly extraordinary. The agent or publisher wants to see why your memoir is important to read and will look for signs that your work is about something more universal than just your own life story. As you draft the synopsis, you can try using third person present, as you would with a novel, but first person is more common. Either is acceptable, so try both ways and see which one sounds better.

Sometimes you'll hear about the following strategy for writing a synopsis: Go through your manuscript scene by scene, or chapter by chapter and summarize in a few sentences what happens in each scene or chapter.

This method used to be more popular when agents were actually interested in chapter outlines, which is a pretty rare request these days. Therefore, going through this rather long and tedious process isn't necessary. It gives you a very large amount of material to condense, and it doesn't take into account what scenes are most critical to your protagonist's journey versus what's merely a detail or a subplot.

A smarter strategy is to outline the critical events in your story. You should be able to jot these down without going back to your manuscript. Or, if you used an outline to build your story before you began writing, return to that outline. Another strategy is to use the first paragraph of your synopsis to establish your one or two main characters and the context or the setting of the story. Give the most critical information about character background and motivations, and then segue into the inciting incident.

If you have a very large cast of characters in your book with intertwining story lines—especially if it takes place in different locations—that raises a difficult challenge of how to approach the synopsis. Ultimately, you'll have to decide which characters and story lines deserve treatment in the synopsis, then describe each one from beginning to end. For instance, if you have three key story lines, you might have nine paragraphs, or three paragraphs for each story line representing the three acts of each story. At the start of each paragraph, you'd add a brief dateline with the location, to clarify which storyline we're jumping to.

Now that we've covered how to put a synopsis together, let's look at some examples of synopses, and discuss how they could be improved.

We'll start simply, by looking at how we can describe a plot point with the most efficiency: "At work, Liz searches all over the office for Peter and finally finds him in the supply room, where she tells him she resents the remarks he made about her in the staff meeting."

While there's nothing technically wrong with this sentence, for a synopsis, it's far too wordy. You'll quickly find that a one to two page summary cannot support this level of detail, and you'll need to pare it back. Here's how you'd do it. "At work, Elizabeth confronts Peter about his remarks at the staff meeting."

We don't need to know that she engaged in a long search, or the details of where she found him—unless, of course, these are materially important to the emotional reaction of the characters or how the plot unfolds.

Here's a synopsis with a first paragraph that opens with an inciting incident, but still needs to be improved:

Nell Hatley, a young law professor in her tenure year at the fictional Coppersmith University near Cincinnati, comes late to a faculty meeting, where she finds a law student, Mary Reynolds, opening fire. Nell subdues Mary, but is knocked unconscious. Detective Alan Smith visits Nell in the hospital and reveals that one of her colleagues, Larry McIntosh, was killed and another, Harden Ghent, was seriously wounded. In Mary's pocket, the police find a note with McIntosh, Ghent and Nell's names.

This novel's protagonist is Nell, and while all the characters mentioned in the opening do have a role to play, we don't need to know all their names upfront. It quickly becomes an alphabet soup, and it's hard to keep track of who's who. Here's a rewritten first paragraph for this synopsis:

> Nell Hatley is a young and ambitious law professor in her tenure year at Coppersmith University near Cincinnati, struggling with insecurities about the strength of her scholarship. When she arrives late to a faculty meeting, she finds a law student opening fire. Nell subdues the shooter, but one of her colleagues is killed and another is seriously wounded. In the shooter's pocket, the police find a note with three names scribbled on it—the two victims' and Nell's.

Notice how we're now better focused on Nell's story, which is important for the opening paragraph. We also get a little more characterization of Nell here, in addition to learning about the inciting incident. Finally, we've kept the twist about the three names scribbled on a note. We can learn more about those other victims as the synopsis unfolds.

In the next synopsis example, we're introduced to two minor characters. In this story, the main protagonist, Anna, has inadvertently traveled back in time:

> Anna's closest friends, Sam Dallaire and Zoe Campari, help anchor her to this new reality. Sam, Anna's witty and loyal college roommate, is with her in Australia and provides a voice of sanity amid their boy- and booze-crazy roommates. Zoe, who is in New York studying photography, has been Anna's best friend since a shared love of Kerouac brought them together at 14. She is the only person Anna tells about her time-traveling. Although Zoe begs

Anna for glimpses of the future, Anna is afraid of altering Zoe's path and will not say much.

There's a lot of background information about two minor characters. Neither play a role in the main plot, which concerns a romantic dilemma for Anna. Here's a better way to mention the role of these characters:

> Anna's closest friends, Sam and Zoe, help anchor her. Sam provides a voice of sanity amid their boy- and booze-crazy roommates, and Zoe is the only person Anna tells about her time traveling. Although Zoe begs Anna for glimpses of the future, Anna is afraid of altering Zoe's path and will not say much.

This gives us the texture of the story, and an idea of the pressures Anna must deal with, without getting into the backstory of these relationships, which doesn't affect the story line.

In the next example, a space-opera novel, we have a lot of complex relationships from the outset that need to be streamlined. In the inciting incident, the main character, Zander, is sold into slavery and finds himself serving the most powerful family in the empire, the Bastets. We're then told the following:

> Zander learns that most of the members of the Bastet family are Gifted, having both psychic and magical powers that include, among other things, the ability to tell truth from lie and to read others' thoughts. The matriarch of the Bastet family, the Countess Bastet, is fourth in line for the Imperial throne and rules her family with an iron fist. She is highly Gifted, and even the Empress fears her. Her son, however, is not Gifted, and the Countess uses this flaw to manipulate him and his cousins, Talia and Taryd, by refusing to confirm him as heir. These machinations cause resentment among the cousins, and they hate each other. It is not long before Zander becomes a pawn in the rivalry that consumes them.

This is only one plot line among several others, but it's an important dynamic that creates pressure on the main character of Zander. We need to convey this information, but in a shorter amount of space, and with much less complexity. Here's a more succinct way to handle it:

> Zander learns that most members of the Bastet family have mystical powers that include reading others' thoughts. The matriarch of the family, the Countess, rules her family with an iron fist and—to ensure she retains control over her heirs—she plays the family members against each other. This causes resentment and mistrust, and soon Zander becomes a pawn in their rivalry.

Let's look at an example of a synopsis for a memoir. This story is by an Indo-American immigrant. Her summary begins like this:

> The story opens in the early 1980s, a time in which Indian immigrants were assimilating into American culture in a way that I call 'being brown.' I was tolerated in my small town, but not accepted. The Asian culture I inherited emphasized hard work and success at all costs, and early tastes of my family's financial success reinforced that the only way to rise above my own alienation was to make money—a lot more than everyone else. However, the path I truly felt called to take, to write, offered absolutely no such promise. There was not one Indian writer on the bookshelves, not an ethnic face on television, and never a non-American name in the newspaper bylines. To aspire to something outside medicine, engineering or economics seemed equivalent to declaring one's life a failure.

This is a lot of backstory that boils down to a straightforward conflict: she wants something different for herself from what her parents want. In a revised version, we can convey this more quickly, personally, and also originally:

> My physician father hammered his values into me with the conviction that they would lead to wealth, and lift me above our alienating immigrant experience. However, I had a deeply spiritual experience at an early age that led me to question my father—and

my entire upbringing. Thus began my battle between the pursuit of money and the pursuit of life.

Finally, let's take a look at a more complex story, one that involves three separate story lines with three main characters in three different locations. Those three characters are Blue, Brick, and Jerome. We need to sum up each character's background and situation quickly so that we can spend most of our time on how the timelines unfold. Here's the original introduction for Brick:

> Dakota Brown, the madame of the notorious black brothel, The Black Orchid, finds an abandoned white baby girl in a gas station restroom. She takes the girl back to the brothel, where her best girl, Hermione Jones, takes the child for her own. They name her Brick for fortitude. For years they hide her away from the prying gaze of customers. Brick loves Hermione fiercely, and descends into abject panic whenever Hermione leaves her side. When Brick is 12, a john murders Hermione, flinging Brick into the depths of despair. She retreats to the kitchen and teaches herself to cook, a skill for which she shows a mystical talent. When she hits puberty, Dakota enrolls her in the Culinary Academy in the hopes of keeping her away from lustful customers. There, Brick meets Hector, a Mexican student who falls in love with her. His advances are met with icy rejection, which only fuels his fire. One night, after months of spurned love, he gets drunk, follows Brick on the way home, and attacks her sexually. Hector gets thrown in jail as Brick plunges into suicidal depression.

If each character were introduced with this much detail, we'd reach a full page without even seeing how our main characters end up meeting each other. So we need to minimize this intro to just the essentials:

> Los Angeles, 1963. An orphan girl, Brick, grows up in a notorious brothel, The Black Orchid. At an early age, she teaches herself to cook, a skill for which she shows a mystical talent. A Mexican student, Hector, falls in love with her. When his feelings go

unrequited, he sexually assaults her. Brick plunges into suicidal depression.

We've cut away the backstory of how Brick is found, and we've also removed the characters of the madame and the woman who takes care of her. Neither of these characters play a role in the main narrative arc. What's most important is the mystical talent Brick displays at an early age, and the incident that ultimately results in her meeting the other characters in the book—and that's the attack by Hector. You'll also notice that we've added a dateline, since Brick, Blue, and Jerome live in different places, at different times. This is important to understanding how the story comes together over a period of many years that the novel encompasses.

Once you have a first draft of the synopsis, set it aside for a week if you can, then return to it. How does your protagonist sound? Do they come to life, and feel interesting? Does the plot effectively build tension? Do we clearly understand what's changed for the protagonist by the end? Does the overall tone or style of the synopsis match that of your novel?

If you think you're done, make sure you single-space the synopsis if it's one page. If you're submitting a multi-page synopsis, then double-space it. Put your book title and your name at the top of each page.

Sometimes you'll write your synopsis, and you'll start to get a bad feeling—a feeling that your story has some structural flaws. Maybe you suddenly realize your main character has no backbone, or there's no substantial conflict that needs to be resolved, or the ending falls flat.

When you sense there's a problem with your story, it's time to push pause on the submissions process, and decide if it's time to revise. Problems with your manuscript won't get resolved by the agent or the publisher—instead you'll get rejected. And since you only get one chance to pitch each work, it's critical to make sure you return to your manuscript and resolve any problems that surface at this stage.

The Importance of Author Platform
Lecture 8

During the 1990s, as consolidation swept the publishing industry, agents began to say that they couldn't sell a nonfiction book unless the author had a *platform*. At the time, that meant an author who was in the public eye or had some authority. Today, the concept of platform generally refers to an author's visibility and reach to a target audience. In other words, your platform addresses such questions as: Who is aware of your work, where does it regularly appear, who do you influence, and how many people see it? In this lecture, we'll look at platform requirements for nonfiction and other authors and explore the role that platform plays more broadly in a writer's career.

Platform Requirements for Nonfiction Writers

- With a nonfiction manuscript, it can be difficult to get a deal with a New York publisher unless you have a strong platform. A primary consideration is the context of your visibility and reach. For instance, if you're a marketing executive who has excellent visibility and reach to other marketers, but your book is a self-help guide targeted to housewives, your platform doesn't have the best fit for the book you want to publish. Ideally, you should be visible to the most receptive or appropriate audience for the work you're trying to sell.

- Depending on the category, your authority or credibility in your field is also an important component of your platform. Your authority tends to be critical for books on health, diet, self-help, business, and other categories where readers seek advice from experienced and trusted sources. In other words, avoid differentiating yourself by claiming that your book on a specialized topic is a guide by an outsider—an average person who has dealt with a particular problem. The average person's perspective is almost never a selling point.

- As you take stock of your platform as a nonfiction author, evaluate your strengths in the following areas:
  - Publishing or distributing quality work in media outlets with which you want to be identified and that your target audience reads.

  - Producing a body of work on your own turf that gathers followers, such as a website and blog, e-mail newsletter, podcast, or video series.

  - Being active and visible on social media.

  - Speaking at events that your target audience or community attends.

  - Partnering with peers or influencers to produce creative projects or extend your visibility.

- If you're worried that your platform isn't sufficient to merit a New York publishing deal, then you should spend time building it before you pitch. A great platform won't happen overnight, and for some authors, it can take years of effort.
  - Broadly speaking, publishers won't be impressed unless they see a professional and established website, multiple forms of outreach (blogging, e-mail, or social media), and solid recognition in your community. There should be a perceptible ripple effect whenever you write a new column, post on social media, or are otherwise visibly active. If you speak and nothing happens, your platform probably isn't sufficient.

  - For authors seeking specific numbers that would be impressive to a publisher, consider these: It usually takes a website or blog audience of at least 50,000 visits per month to even spark the interest of an agent. A meaningful e-mail newsletter list should have thousands of names. And your social media reach probably needs to be in the thousands, as well.

o   That said, engagement matters more than numbers. If you can show that the people you reach are responding and sharing your message, that can carry as much weight as a large audience.

- Memoirists and other writers working on narrative nonfiction may be off the hook when it comes to platform. With narratives, the focus tends to be more on the art and craft of storytelling—or the quality of the writing—more than on the platform. Thus, much depends on your credibility as a good writer; an existing track record of newspaper or magazine publication can often be sufficient to get a book deal. To help overcome the platform hurdle, it also helps to have a timely narrative that taps into hot topics.

- Don't despair if your platform is small or nonexistent. You may simply need to reconsider what type of publisher is a good fit for your book. Small presses, especially university presses, have more interest in the quality of your work than your platform.

Blogging for Nonfiction Authors
- Blog-to-book deals have been a trend for some time, but there are several factors to consider before you decide whether that's the right path for you.

- First, blog writing is not the same as book writing. Blog posts should be optimized for online reading. That means being aware of keywords and search engine optimization and understanding how to include meaningful visual and interactive content. Further, blogging isn't a lesser form of writing to be used as a stepping stone to a book deal; it should be treated as an art form in itself.

- Second, long, text-driven narratives don't often lend themselves to the blog format. In addition, personal stories and essays online are a dime a dozen. You typically must put out a high volume of work to break through the noise or have an incredibly unique angle that catches fire.

- Finally, an effective blog is as much about being active within a community as it is about publishing your writing. Good bloggers network and comment on other blogs that share similar topics or themes.

- A genuine interest in blogging is the best reason for any writer to blog. If you don't see the book deal as the end of the road for your blog, then you're in a better position to do it successfully. Blogging should be approached as a long-term platform-building tool rather than a deal maker.

Platform Requirements for Other Writers

- There is significant disagreement about how much time a fiction writer should devote to writing versus platform building. In many cases, novelists are advised to build a platform as if they were nonfiction authors, but that's difficult for writers who don't have any books or credits to their name. For fiction writers, the platform should grow out of the body of their work. Platform building certainly matters for fiction writers, but it's probably not worth spending much time on until you are on the verge of publication.

- That's not to say that platform never plays a role in what fiction gets published.
  - For instance, if you have a M.F.A. in creative writing from Iowa or Columbia, you've already been selected by one of the most competitive degree programs in the United States. Agents and editors are more likely to extend you time and consideration because you've already jumped a difficult hurdle. Getting a credit in a top-tier publication can also ease the path to a book deal.

  - Similarly, if you've been actively writing and contributing to a community site, such as Wattpad, and you've amassed a strong following, a publisher may see a built-in audience for your work.

The Role of Platform in a Writer's Career

- As we said, platform is about your visibility and reach to your target audience or readership. It isn't about self-promotion or hard selling. In addition, platform building is not a one-time event that happens overnight. It is an organic process of gaining visibility, then developing the readership for your work. For all these reasons, building platform is more about putting in consistent effort over the course of a career and making incremental improvements in how you reach readers and extend your network.

People who hold highly recognized positions, have powerful networks or friends, or are associated with influential communities have an easier time building platform than others.

- Because platform building is an organic process, it will grow differently for every author, but in general, platform has six components:

  o Your writing or content that's publicly available, including all of your traditionally published work, self-published work, and online writing.

  o Your social media presence, including the mainstream sites (Twitter, Facebook), as well as online communities and message boards where you're active.

  o Your website; this is usually critical for any ongoing platform activity because it acts as the hub for all your efforts.

  o Your relationships, including the people you know personally, as well as devoted readers.

- Your influence, that is, your ability to get people you don't know to help you out or pay attention to you.

- Your reach—the number of people you can reliably broadcast a message to at any given time.

- In platform building, it's important to remember that you are communicating directly with readers. Be consistent with your voice and style; don't adopt a "marketing voice" that's different from your real voice. Also, focus on what's satisfying and engaging. Publish, post, and share things that fascinate or puzzle you, or ask questions for others to answer.

- The people you reach, either online or off, will be at different stages of commitment to you and your work. For this reason, your communication should be segmented by audience as much as possible. In particular, two types of readers deserve special attention: people who are new to your work and true fans who would buy anything you published. For the first group, offer something for free, such as the first book in a series or a special digital download. For the second, consider providing exclusive communications and experiences, such as early access to new work.

- One final aspect of platform building involves the practice of *literary citizenship*, that is, engaging in activities that support reading, writing, and publishing. This could mean posting about favorite books you've read, interviewing other authors, attending readings, and otherwise making yourself visible as an active writer and reader in the community. These activities demonstrate that you're serious about growing your professional network and potential readership.

Jelen and McCallister, *Build Your Author Platform.*

Katz, *Get Known before the Book Deal.*

Sambuchino, *Create Your Writer Platform.*

Exercises

1. List all the institutions or businesses you have affiliations with that also have something in common with the book you want to write and publish. How many people do these organizations reach, whether through their internal publications, external outreach, or online presence? What opportunities are available for regular contributors, columnists, or guests?

2. Brainstorm a list of people you know—either personally or by reputation—who are influencers or gatekeepers to the audience for your book. What specific steps or actions could you take to develop relationships with some of these people?

The Importance of Author Platform
Lecture 8—Transcript

Platform can be one of the most difficult concepts to explain to authors. Everyone defines it a little differently. But one thing's for sure: Editors and agents are attracted to authors who have this thing called platform.

Legend has it that sometime during the 1990s, as a massive consolidation swept the publishing industry, agents started saying they couldn't sell a nonfiction book unless the author had a platform. At the time, you could have read that as code for, an author who is in the public eye, or an author who can sell books.

In other words, agents became less interested in the average Joe sitting at home who wanted to write a book who had no particular credentials—even if he wrote well or had interesting ideas. Publishers increasingly sought authors who demonstrated some kind of visibility in their community. That is, they wanted people who were regularly in the spotlight, either in the print media or appearing on radio or TV.

Today, the concept of platform has expanded to mean a lot of things, and to cover all types of authors. This has lead to a great deal of confusion as to exactly who needs a platform and when. Sometimes the term is simply used as shorthand for an author's ability to market and promote. Because of that, platform sometimes gets conflated with a social media following. That's not what a platform is.

In the simplest terms possible, I define platform as your visibility and reach to a target audience. Let's break this definition down further.

Visibility is: Who sees your work? Who is aware of your work? Where does your work regularly appear? What communities know about you? Who do you influence? Where do you make waves?

Reach is: How many people see your work? Just how far does it spread? What kind of numbers are we talking about?

We're going to explore platform building in-depth, looking at three different aspects of it.

First, we'll look at platform requirements for nonfiction authors to get a book deal.

Then we'll briefly discuss how platform is considered or required, if at all, for other types of writing.

Finally, we'll look more broadly at the role platform plays throughout a writer's career and beyond the book deal.

When it comes to nonfiction books—with the possible exception of narratives, which we'll cover later—it can be difficult to get a deal with a New York publisher unless you come to the table with a platform—and not just any platform, but the right kind. That's because a publisher cares about the context of your visibility and reach.

For instance, let's say you're a marketing executive who has excellent visibility and reach to other professional marketers. But your book is actually a self-help guide targeted to an audience of housewives. Your platform isn't the best fit for the book you want to publish. Ideally, you should be visible to the most receptive or appropriate audience for the work you're trying to sell.

Depending on the type of book, your authority or credibility in your field is also an important component of your platform. This tends to be critical for books on health, diet, self-help, business, or really any category where readers seek credible advice from experienced and trusted sources.

Avoid being that author who pitches a book on a specialized topic, and tries to set herself apart by saying, "This will be a guide by an outsider, an average person's experience dealing with this problem." The average person's perspective is almost never a selling point.

While I was at *Writer's Digest*, it was very common to receive pitches for articles and books from writers who were unpublished, and these writers would sell themselves as thoughtful failures. That might sound silly, but many different versions of this pitch happen every day. Try to think more like a reader. Would you rather learn from an experienced and successful individual, or from someone without credentials who is muddling through just like you?

As you're taking stock of your platform as a nonfiction author, you'll want to evaluate your strengths in the following areas:

First, are you publishing quality work in media outlets you want to be identified with and that your target audience reads?

Editors will also look to see if you're producing a body of work on your own that's gathering followers, such as a website, and blog, an e-mail newsletter, a podcast, or a video series.

It helps to be active and visible on social media, regardless of whether that's Twitter, Facebook, or some other outlet.

Are you speaking at events that your target audience attends?

And are you partnering with peers or influencers to produce creative projects that extend your visibility?

This certainly isn't an exhaustive list, but it should help you think through what constitutes your platform. With any of these areas, you want to demonstrate how you make an impact. It also helps to give proof of engagement with an audience. This could be quantitative evidence, such as your website traffic or email subscriber numbers. And it could also be qualitative evidence, such as high-profile reviews and testimonials from thought leaders in your field.

If you're worried your platform isn't sufficient enough to merit a New York publishing deal, then you should spend some time building it before you pitch. The drawback of course is that a great platform won't happen overnight. For most authors it takes years of effort—it really amounts to a career built over time.

Often the next question that arises is: How do you know when your platform is big enough? That's a difficult question to answer because there are so many variables.

Generally speaking, however, publishers won't be very impressed unless they see a professional and established website, as well as multiple forms of outreach to the target audience. This outreach could be in person through speaking or teaching, or through online channels. Solid recognition in your community always helps. Author Christina Katz describes it as being able to make waves. That means there should be a perceptible ripple effect that happens whenever you write a new column, post on social media, or are otherwise visibly active. If you speak and nothing happens, your platform probably isn't ready for prime time.

If you're wondering about specific numbers that would be impressive to a publisher, consider this: It usually takes a website or blog audience of 50,000 visits per month, if not twice that, to create even a glimmer in an agent's eye. An email newsletter list should have thousands of names. And your social media would need to be in the thousands as well.

That said, engagement matters more than numbers. If you can show that the people you do reach are responding to your message and helping spread word of mouth, that can carry as much weight as big numbers.

For memoirists and other writers working on narrative nonfiction, you're sometimes off the hook when it comes to platform. With narratives, the focus tends to be on the art and craft of storytelling—or the quality of the writing—more so than your platform. A lot can depend on your credibility as a good writer. For instance, an existing track record of newspaper or magazine publication can sometimes be sufficient to get yourself a book deal.

However, one look at the current bestseller list will often betray publishing's continued interest in a platform: you'll find books by celebrities, pundits, and well-established writers. Their all occupying a fair share of these lists. To overcome the platform hurdle, it helps to be writing a narrative that's timely and taps into current hot topics.

Don't despair if you feel like your platform is nonexistent. You may simply need to reconsider what type of publisher is a good fit for your book. Small presses, and especially university presses, have more interest in the quality of your work than your platform. And it's not uncommon for successful authors to begin their careers with quieter publishers, and then later sign with a New York house once they've built visibility and a strong track record.

Before we look at how platform affects other genres and categories of work, I want to specifically address the practice of blogging for nonfiction authors.

Blog-to-book deals have been a trend ever since I worked as a full-time acquisitions editor. I acquired or oversaw the publication of more than a dozen bloggers-turned-book-authors. So I know that blogs can lead to book deals.

However, you should probably think twice before you decide if this is the right path for you.

First, blog writing is not the same as book writing. Blog posts, to live up to their form, need to be optimized for online reading. That means being aware of keywords and search engine optimization, and understanding how to include visual and interactive content. This is the only way you're likely to get enough traffic that would get a publisher's interest.

Also, it seems strange to have to state it, but blogging, as a form of writing, requires its own unique skill set. Writers who ask, "Can I blog to get a book deal?" probably think of the blog as a lesser form of writing, merely a vehicle to something better. But blogs rarely aspire to become books if they are truly written as blogs. To do it well, you need to treat it as its own artistic forum. If you use your blog as a dumping ground for material that's really meant for print—or for book publication—you're not giving much consideration to the art of the blog.

Second, narrative works don't often do well in blog format. Authors who ask me about the blog-to-book phenomenon are often working on a narrative nonfiction work, such as a memoir. However, long text-driven narratives don't often lend themselves to being chunked up on a blog. And even if you'd like to experiment with that kind of serialization, you'll need to consider how you'll get anyone to pay attention to it.

It's particularly difficult for memoirists to build a platform by blogging. Personal stories and essays online are a dime a dozen—there's enormous competition. You'd have to be putting out a big volume of work to break through the noise, or have an incredibly unique angle that catches fire.

Finally, an effective blog is as much about being active within a community as it is about publishing your writing. An effective blogger networks with other bloggers, and comments on other sites that feature similar topics. It's not possible to blog in a vacuum and expect any kind of attention or traffic.

The best reason for a nonfiction author—or really any author—to blog is that they're genuinely interested in blogging. Building a worthwhile blog that actually has a payoff requires patience and an appetite for online networking and commenting. You won't get recognition overnight, and it takes time to develop a following. Ultimately, it's the buzz you generate and the audience you develop that attracts a publisher to you, not the writing itself—though of course that's important too.

If you don't see the book deal as the end of the road for your blog, then you're in a better position to blog successfully. Approach it as a long-term platform-building tool rather than a book-deal maker.

As final bit of advice, if a blog-to-book deal path is appealing to you, then I highly recommend checking out Chris Guillebeau's "279 Days to Overnight Success." He landed a book deal in about one year based on his blog. However, that wasn't his overriding goal. It was a byproduct. He succeeded because he was laser-focused in his strategy and single-minded in marketing and promoting his blog to all the right people in the blogging community, not the publishing community. In other words, he has the mind and heart of an entrepreneur. Be honest and ask yourself: Does that describe you?

Now that we've covered platform requirements for nonfiction authors, let's consider everyone else, especially novelists.

There is significant disagreement about how much time a fiction writer should devote to writing versus platform building. Some authors say, "Writing is all that matters," while others say, "Audience is all that matters."

I believe novelists have too frequently been advised to build a platform as if they were nonfiction authors. This tends to put the cart before the horse. There's little way to build a platform when you don't have any books or credits to your name. In my philosophy of author platform, it grows out of your body of work. Without an existing body of work, how do you even know who your readers are? We'll talk more about this issue later when we look at platform building for the long-term.

For now, let's just say that platform building does matter for fiction writers, but it's probably not worth spending time on until you find yourself on the verge of book publication. Especially if you're within the first year or two of seriously attempting to write, it's probably premature to focus on building a fiction-writing platform until you have at least some work publicly available.

That's not to say that platform never plays a role in what fiction gets published. For instance, if you have an MFA in creative writing from Iowa or Columbia, you've already been vetted and selected by one of the most competitive degree programs in the United States. Agents and editors are more likely to extend time and consideration because you've already jumped a difficult hurdle. Getting a publication credit in a top-tier publication like The New Yorker can also ease the path to a book deal.

Online followings can also matter. For instance, if you've been actively writing and contributing to a community site such as Wattpad, and you have thousands of readers for your work on that site, that can attract a publisher who sees the proof and profit of a built-in audience. That kind of platform alleviates a publisher's financial risk. This is exactly how *Fifty Shades of Grey* ended up being a blockbuster. Its author started a serialized work of fan fiction online and built up an incredibly huge audience, which led to publisher interest.

So, there are many ways to crack the nut. If you're good at platform building, then consider that a potential path to publication, whether you're a fiction writer, essayist, or poet. But it's not really a requirement for publication in the same way that it is for nonfiction.

Now that we've discussed how your pre-existing platform affects your chances at a book deal, let's talk about its role over the entirety of your career.

And this is a good time to revisit our definition of platform. It's about your visibility and reach to your target audience or readership. Because platform is so often associated with undesirable or time-wasting activities, I'd like to point out what platform isn't about.

It's not about self-promotion or hard selling. It's not about being an extrovert, or annoying everyone you know to buy your book. It's also not about yelling to everyone you can find online or offline, "Look at me!" or "Buy my book!" Platform isn't about who yells the loudest or who markets the best.

Perhaps most importantly, platform is not something that happens overnight, and it's not a one-time event. You aren't going to finish listening to this lecture, follow a three-step formula, and presto, have a platform and be done.

Platform is an organic process of building your visibility to readers. You'll discover and also develop the readership for your work. As I mentioned earlier, your platform grows out of your body of work. This is essential. Platform can't be seen as separate from the work. You don't apply it after the fact. It's the very fabric of how your work gets noticed and shared.

For all these reasons, platform is more about putting in consistent effort over the course of a career. You'll make incremental improvements to how you reach readers and extend your network. It's about attracting other people to you—not begging everyone to pay attention.

Some people have an easier time building platform than others. If you hold a highly recognized position, or have a powerful network; if you have friends in high places, or if you are associated with powerful communities; if you have prestigious degrees or posts, then you do play the field at an advantage.

This is why it's so easy for celebrities to get book deals. They have built-in platform.

Platform building is an organic process, so it grows differently for every single author. It should tie into your unique story or message. It should complement your own strengths and skill set. And ideally it should take into account your target readership—where they're active online or off, and how they behave in response to your work.

That means your platform is as much of a creative exercise as the work you produce. While platform gives you power to market effectively, it's not something you develop by posting "Follow me on Twitter" or "Like me on Facebook" a few times a week.

As I said, I do think new writers should probably back-burner platform building activities. But I don't recommend abandoning them entirely. Even while you're still focused on your writing, it can be helpful to uncover a new mentor, connect with an important influencer, or pursue a new writing retreat opportunity. These things often happen as part and parcel of the platform building process.

To bring the concept of a career-long platform into even clearer focus, I'd like to describe it as having six components:

Number one, and always at number one, is your writing or your content that's publicly available. This includes all of your traditionally published work, self-published work, and all of your online writing.

Two, your social media presence. That means Twitter and Facebook, as well as other social media outlets. Also, don't forget online communities and message boards where you might be active because sometimes these spaces are even more valuable than the well-known social media sites.

Three, your website. This is critical for any ongoing platform activity because it acts as the hub for all of your efforts.

Four, your relationships. This includes the people you know personally, any influencers in your circle, plus devoted members of your readership.

Five, your influence. This is your ability to get people you don't know to help you out, pay attention, and spread the word.

Six, your actual reach. This is the number of people you can reliably broadcast a message to at any particular moment in time.

Notice that social media is only one of the components mentioned. When authors conflate social media with platform building, they tend to suffer burnout, or they begin to question whether it's really a useful practice.

Social media works best when you focus on how to cultivate stronger relationships and connections to existing fans. It also helps when you partner with other authors to extend your visibility to new readers. Sometimes social media can help you create and push out more new work, which is what most writers enjoy doing in the first place.

Here are two examples of writers who used very different approaches to build their audience and platform.

Seth Harwood is a crime novelist who built his readership by producing his work in podcast form. He bought recording equipment, read his work chapter by chapter, and distributed each chapter installment through iTunes and his website. Before long, he had gathered enough of a following that he attracted the attention of a traditional publisher. That publisher released his book in other formats, but he was allowed to continue distribution of the free podcast. He now actively publishes with an imprint of Amazon.

Jeanne Bowerman was an unpublished writer living in rural New York, trying to break into scriptwriting. Because she lacked a network, or any connections at all to the Hollywood industry, she started a weekly Twitter chat where she interviewed experienced screenwriters to help beginners like herself learn from the pros. Fast-forward several years later, and she's now doing paid scriptwriting work and is the editor of *Script Magazine*—and she still runs that weekly Twitter chat.

When new authors ask me if they can just hire someone to build their platform or engage with readers, they're often missing the point. Building a readership, or networking in the community, really only requires one thing: you. You have to be present and authentic. Furthermore, if a third party pretends to be you, you miss the chance to gain insight into your readers. Interacting with readers will always improve your long-term marketing and promotion efforts.

However you decide to directly communicate with readers, it's important that you enjoy the tools or platforms, so you stick with them for the long haul. This is particularly important and too often overlooked. Platform-building activities need time to gain momentum. Just about every author has abandoned an approach too soon, before there was really enough time to see if it would work out.

You also want to be consistent with your voice and style. You don't want to adopt a marketing voice that's different from your real voice.

And you should focus on what's satisfying and engaging for you. If something drains your energy or puts you in a bad mood, that means you haven't found a good fit.

To be an interesting person, you have to be interested in the world, and in other people. You have to be curious. So find ways to publish, post, and share about things that fascinate you or puzzle you. Post questions for other people to answer. Ask people to share something. You may not get it right at first, but playfulness helps, and enthusiasm is infectious.

The people you reach, whether online or off, will all be at different stages of commitment to you and your work. Your communication should respect this and be segmented by audience as much as possible. There are two particular types of readers that deserve special attention and communication.

First, to introduce new people to your work, I recommend the cheese-cube lure. Offer something for free—such as the first book in a series, or a special digital download. Cast a wide net with something broadly appealing. Then, gradually move people into more serious commitments, such as signing up for your email newsletter or buying your book.

For the true fan who would buy anything you ever published, consider special communication and experiences available only to them. You know how your city symphony has a VIP room with cookies and chocolate during intermission, for season subscribers? Think about what your VIP experience looks like, too. For some authors, that means early access and promotional prices for their most loyal fans.

Marketing and promotion ideas usually start by considering what reader relationships and influencer relationships you have in place or can build on. It's easier to start with relationships you have, rather than cold calling strangers when you need help or need to make a sale. This principle is at the very heart of platform building.

The final facet of platform I'd like to cover is something called literary citizenship. This term is used in more literary circles—especially MFA programs—to refer to activities that support the cultural activities of reading, writing, and publishing. These activities could mean posting about favorite books you've read, interviewing others authors, attending readings, and otherwise making yourself visible as an active writer and reader in the community. By doing these things, you can't help but grow your professional network and a potential readership. In some ways, literary citizenship is a more palatable or friendly way of thinking about platform building.

What I've always liked about the literary citizenship movement is that it's simple for people to understand and practice. It aligns well with the values of the literary community. It operates with an abundance mindset, meaning it's not about competition with other authors, but rather collaboration.

It might seem a bit strange that anyone has formalized the process of what could be seen as, well, just being an engaged member of the literary community. Unfortunately, in the literary market, involvement with the readership is often seen as undesirable. Writing for an audience or engaging with them is seen to lessen the art. "I don't write for readers"—you've heard that one before, I'm sure. But it's a very helpful framework for anyone who struggles with this thing called platform. If you find what we've discussed so far to be out of your comfort zone, the literary citizenship approach can feel less like marketing and promotion, and more like a celebration of things you already love.

Kevin Kelly, the founding executive editor of *Wired*, is well-known for a theory called "1,000 True Fans." His theory is that any person who can directly connect with 1,000 people who will buy anything they produce, that can lead to a sustainable living. This idea continues to be debated. Whether you believe it or not, his idea is important on another level: Every person now has the tools to directly reach their audience. This has led to a greater burden for authors, as well as greater expectations from publishers. But it also means a great deal of creative freedom if you do gather a trusting and engaged audience.

I like trying to persuade authors of the value of platform—at least when it can be built organically—because it represents a valuable investment in your lifelong career as an author. You shouldn't rely on a publisher, agent, or consultant to find and keep your audience for you. If you find and nurture your readership on channels that you own, and on your own terms, that's like putting money in the bank.

Researching and Planning Your Book Proposal
Lecture 9

A book proposal is essentially a business plan that persuades a publisher to invest in your book. Instead of writing the entire book, then trying to interest an editor or agent—which is how it works with novels—you write the proposal first. If a publisher is convinced by your argument, it will then pay you to write the book. Many authors find that drafting a rough proposal before writing a book has a number of advantages. Primarily, the proposal requires you to do market research, which offers insight into the content your book should include to be competitive on the shelf. However, book proposals are complex documents; in this lecture, we'll dissect the book proposal in detail.

A Business Plan for Your Book

- As we've said, there are many types of nonfiction, and each category has different market considerations.
  - A sizable platform and expertise is typically required to sell a nonfiction book to a major publisher, especially for such categories as health, self-help, or parenting. For narrative nonfiction and memoir, the quality of the writing generally holds more weight than the business case outlined in a proposal.

  - Because each nonfiction category has its own set of market considerations, not all agents or publishers require you to send a book proposal, and some may want a completed manuscript instead. Read the submission guidelines to learn what your target markets prefer to receive.

- If you're unsure about how much your proposal will matter to a publisher, ask yourself this question: Does your book need to succeed based on its literary merit or its ability to entertain or tell a story? In the second case, the manuscript itself must prove your strength as a writer, and the proposal is likely of less importance. However, if your book is focused on sharing information, you're selling it based on the marketability of your expertise, your platform, and your concept, and your proposal holds incredible weight.

- Proposals vary in length, content, approach, and presentation. Each book requires a unique argument for its existence—or a specific business case—and, thus, requires a unique proposal. However, all book proposals must answer three strategic marketing questions: So what? Who cares? Who are you?

  o The answer to the first question is essentially the reason for your book's existence—the unique selling proposition that sets your book apart from others in the market.

  o The answer to the second question describes your target readership and the size of your audience.

  o The answer to the third question addresses your authority or credentials to write the book and the existence of an appropriate platform that makes you visible to the target audience.

- In preparing a book proposal, keep in mind that editors who work at commercial publishers care about two things: a viable idea with a clear market, paired with a writer who has credibility and marketing savvy. Knowing your audience or market and having direct and specific ways to reach it gives you a much better chance of success. Pitch only the book you know has a firm spot in the marketplace. Don't pitch a book with the expectation that the publisher will bring the audience to you.

Researching the Market

- Before you write your proposal, you need to lay the proper groundwork by researching the market for your work. We can break this research process down into five steps.

- First, identify competing titles. Visit bookstores in your area and study other titles on the shelves where you would expect your book to appear. In addition to recording the titles, authors, and publishers of these books, pay attention to price, length, and format. Read the

© Wavebreakmedia Ltd/Thinkstock.

In researching your book proposal, talk to a librarian to learn which books are popular based on patron demand.

back cover copy: How is the book being positioned? Who does the book seem to target? What promises are made to the reader, or what problems are addressed?

o   Also study the authors' credentials. How are the authors visible in the market? How do they reach readers? Take note of any forewords, introductions, blurbs, or reviews by important people—these might indicate credibility that you'll need, too.

o   Once you've finished studying how the book is positioned and packaged, turn to the copyright page to see how many times it has been reprinted. You can also tell that a book is popular if multiple copies are available for sale.

o   Study the table of contents to get a sense of each book's scope and quality. You don't have to read all the competing titles from beginning to end, but read enough to understand the voice and style of a few authors.

o   Once you've finished the bricks-and-mortar retailer search, go through the same steps with online retailers, especially Amazon.

Make sure you look for e-books, self-published titles, and books published by smaller presses that may not show up in stores.

○ This search should yield a list of 20 or more titles that would be comparable or directly competitive to your book. Finding no comparable titles is not necessarily a good thing. It may mean that your idea is too bizarre to have a market, or maybe the market for your work isn't driven by retail booksellers. Either way, finding no competitive titles—or just a handful of titles—may rule out pitching your book to agents and large commercial publishers unless you have another way to prove there's a market for your work.

• The next step is to research the non-book landscape, particularly digital content and online experts who target the same audience as you do.
   ○ Start by looking for top websites and blogs. Run a general search for keywords and phrases that relate to your book. What will your potential readers find if they turn to Google first? Determine how easy it is to find online information on your topic, whether that information is trustworthy, and whether it's free.

   ○ Video and audio content are additional competitors to books. YouTube is the second most popular search engine in the world after Google, making video an important medium for instructional categories.

   ○ You should also search app storefronts to find relevant mobile and tablet applications, as well as online educational offerings. Basically, you should look at anything that might offer help, education, or resources to your target audience. The goal here is to understand how your audience might fulfill its needs for information from online and multimedia sources, as well as from books, magazines, and events.

• The third step in the research process is to study the authors, experts, and influencers you've discovered. Just as you studied the books and media, dig deeper into the platform and reach of these people to determine how you will set yourself apart. Create a set of notes for each author or influencer you find that includes the following information:

o   Keywords or phrases that seem to be strongly affiliated with the author's brand or presence.

o   Target audience and similarities to your target audience.

o   Published books.

o   Other media outlets used, such as podcasts or video series.

o   Speaking engagements.

o   Social media presence.

- The fourth step is to finely pinpoint your primary target audience. From the beginning, you may have already understood exactly who your book is for. If not, the first three research steps will give you strong indicators about your target audience.

o   It's a red flag if your proposal claims that your book is for "everyone." Maybe it could interest everyone, but there is a specific audience that will be the most likely to buy your book. Who are those people, and how and where can you reach them?

o   The more you know about your primary target market, the better you'll able to build a proposal that speaks to why anyone cares about what you're writing.

- The final step in the process is to analyze how you currently reach your target readers through your platform. The marketing and promotion plan that's included in your proposal is directly informed by your platform. The best marketing campaigns begin with what you have in place today, not what you hope will happen in the future. You need to be honest with yourself about your current position in the market and how you'll collaborate with your publisher on marketing and publicity efforts.

Common Proposal Pitfalls

- The most common pitfall found in book proposals is twofold: no clearly defined market, usually combined with a concept that is too general or broad. Your proposal must show why your idea isn't like a million others. Too many proposed books don't have any compelling element that would set them apart from the competition.
  - Sometimes, a marketable book idea doesn't sell because the proposal concentrates only on the content of the book. Of course, the book's topic is important to the author, but the proposal must show why it's is important to an audience. The proposal is just as much about the book's benefit and appeal to the target market as it is about the content.

  - If you're having a difficult time figuring out what makes your work salable, consider whether it's the first to do something specific—tackle a particular problem, reveal new information, or tell a specific story.

- Another common problem is that too often, writers try to base a book on their own amateur experience of overcoming a problem or investigating a complex issue. This is usually a surefire way to get your proposal rejected, unless you already have a platform or established audience.

- Other reasons your proposal might be rejected include the following: (1) The market is seen as too small for the proposed book (your defined target audience may be too narrow); (2) you don't have sufficient platform to support sales; or (3) the market for books on your topic is dwindling.
  - If you receive the third response, think about whether or not a book is the best medium for your idea. Some editors and agents might recommend that you begin your project as a blog or a website. Too many authors build their book concepts in

a vacuum without any thought to the online conversations already happening.

o   In today's nonfiction market, agents and editors want to see that your book is not the beginning or the end of the road—that it is merely one aspect of your much larger purpose and strategy for developing content and serving a readership, online and off.

o   If the market for books on your topic is dwindling, keep in mind that when executed well, non-book formats can sometimes lead to more opportunity and income than a book itself. Online courses, multimedia companions, and customized experiences tend to command a higher price than books and represent the biggest growth areas for nonfiction authors and experts.

Suggested Reading

Rabiner and Fortunato, *Thinking like Your Editor*.

Exercises

1.   Craft a persuasive 150-word statement that answers the three questions: So what? Who cares? Who are you?

2.   Brainstorm 5 to 10 ways to complete this sentence for your project: "My book will be the first to …." or "This is the only book to …."

Researching and Planning Your Book Proposal
Lecture 9—Transcript

If you want to sell a nonfiction book, the most important document you'll prepare is a book proposal. At its heart, a book proposal explains why your book will sell. Essentially, you create a business plan that persuades a publisher to make an investment. Instead of writing the entire book, then trying to interest an editor or agent—which is how it works with novels— you write the proposal first. If a publisher is convinced by your argument, they'll contract you and pay you to write the book.

Here's the nice thing about book proposals: You can often send them without having to query. And even if the submission guidelines specify you should query first, you could usually get away with sending the proposal on first contact. While few agents or editors will read a fiction manuscript without being queried first, many will flip through a proposal even if they didn't request it.

Some writers find it easier to write the manuscript first, then prepare a proposal. Still, you'll find there are advantages to drafting a rough proposal first. Crafting a proposal requires that you conduct market research. And that research provides you with important insights on what content your book needs to include, or how it needs to be positioned, to be competitive. Even just a little advance legwork can save you a lot of time and energy later. You don't want to spend a year writing and researching your nonfiction book only to find out later there's a competing title that's covered exactly the same territory.

However, book proposals are complex documents. They can take weeks or even months to prepare if you develop and research them properly. An average proposal will probably be between 15 and 30 double-spaced pages, perhaps more. Some proposals can reach 50 or 100 pages.

Before we dive into the qualities of a good proposal, it's important to understand there are many types of nonfiction. Each category has different market considerations. A sizable author platform is typically required to sell a nonfiction book to a major publisher. And if you want to write on topics such as health, self-help, or parenting, you'll need recognized credentials that make you a credible source. Your background should convey authority and instill confidence in the reader.

On the other end of the spectrum, in the case of narrative nonfiction and memoir, the quality of the writing or the manuscript generally holds more weight than whatever business case you express in a proposal. If you have proven journalistic or storytelling skills, that's often the most relevant criteria, while your platform, and marketing savvy might matter less.

Keep in mind that the smaller or more specialized the publisher, the less likely your platform will be a key factor in whether the editor says yes to your book. A university press is more concerned with the quality of your scholarship or ideas than the quality of your platform. As I explain how to build a good proposal, always keep in mind this larger context.

Furthermore—and I admit this part can get confusing—because each nonfiction category has its own special market considerations, a book proposal might not even be required from you. Some agents or publishers will require it. Others may ask for a completed manuscript instead, or they may ask for both. You have to read the submission guidelines to know what each editor or agent prefers to receive, and unfortunately, the requirements just vary a lot. If you're a first-time author pitching a memoir or a narrative nonfiction book, assume you'll probably need both the proposal and a final manuscript. Editors and agents may need assurance that an unknown or first-time author can produce a quality manuscript before they commit.

If you're unsure how much your proposal will matter to a publisher, ask yourself this. Does your book need to succeed based on its literary merit? Does your work need to entertain or tell a story? If so, then the manuscript must prove your strength as a writer, and the proposal is likely secondary. On the flip side, if your book is focused on sharing information or a compelling idea, then you're selling it based on your expertise and your platform, as well as the marketability of your concept. And in that case, your proposal holds the most weight.

Whatever your situation, understand having a finished manuscript doesn't replace sending a formal book proposal if one's required by the agent or editor.

A quick side note here on terminology: You might occasionally hear someone refer to novel proposals, which typically include a query or cover letter, a synopsis or outline, and a partial or complete manuscript. A novel proposal bears little to no relationship to a typical nonfiction book proposal, so don't get confused, because they're not the same thing.

For better or worse, there is no right way to prepare a book proposal, just as there is no right way to write a book. Proposals vary in length, content, approach, and presentation. Each book requires a unique argument for its existence, or a special business case, and thus requires a unique proposal. For example, a coffee-table book on Paris would be pitched differently than a scholarly tome on presidents, or an exposé on a celebrity.

That said, all book proposals do have something in common. They have to answer three strategic marketing questions. While you won't answer these questions in explicitly labeled sections, they'll be running through the mind of every publishing professional who considers your project.

The first question is so what? This is the reason for your book's existence. It's the unique selling proposition that sets your book apart from others in the market. Why is this book needed at this moment in time, and why will readers be compelled to spend $20 or $25 on it? You need to show evidence of need in the marketplace for your work, and this can be tricky to prove. In the research steps I'll outline later, you'll learn several methods to help you find information to make your case.

The second question, which is sometimes inseparable from the first, is who cares? Who is your target readership, or who is the primary audience for your book? What's the size of this audience? What do we know about these readers and their habits as consumers?

Finally, the third question is who are you? You must have sufficient credentials to write the book and an appropriate platform that helps you reach the target audience.

Before I offer more detail about putting together a book proposal, I want to emphasize the following. Editors who work at commercial publishers can be very unforgiving in their analysis of your book idea. They're looking for a viable idea that has a clear position in the market, paired with an author who has visibility to a readership and marketing savvy. You'll position yourself for success if you pitch only the book you know has a firm spot in the marketplace. Knowing your audience well—what problems they have, how they express those problems, and how they behave—this gives you a tremendous advantage when writing the proposal. You need to convince the publisher you have direct and specific experience reaching and understanding your audience. Do not pitch a book expecting that the publisher will bring the audience to you. It's the other way around. You bring your audience and your platform to the publisher.

So, before you write your proposal, you need to lay some groundwork first. You need to research the market and audience for your work. You not only want a well-written proposal, but you want a market-informed proposal. You need clarity about your idea and how that idea is relevant and unique in today's market. Your proposal should also demonstrate a deep knowledge of the community, the network, and the publications surrounding your book's topic. Plus, you'll have a much easier time writing your proposal if you allow plenty of time to conduct this market research in advance. And if you don't already reach your target audience directly, you also need time to prepare a plan for how you'll do that.

I like to break down the research process into five areas or steps.

The first step is to identify competing titles. Visit the bookstores in your area, preferably both an independent bookstore and a chain bookstore. Go to the shelf where you would expect your book to appear. What's there? Study the books closely and take notes. In addition to recording the title, author, and publisher, pay attention to the price, the length, and the format. Read the back cover copy. How is the book being positioned? Who does the book seem to be targeting? What promises are being made to the reader? What problems are being solved?

Also, study the author's credentials. How is the author visible in the market? How do they reach readers? Take note of any particular forewords, introductions, blurbs, or reviews by important people, these might indicate credibility you'll need, too.

Once you've finished studying how the book is positioned and packaged, turn to the copyright page. Look for an edition or printing number. Has the book been reprinted many times? This indicates a strong seller. If you don't see anything, you may instead see a series of numbers counting down. The ending number or lowest number indicates which reprint the book is on. You can also tell how popular a book is, and if it sells quickly when multiple copies are available for sale on the shelf.

Study the table of contents of each book and get a sense of the book's scope and quality. You don't have to read all the competing titles from beginning to end but read enough to understand the author's voice and style.

After you finish researching what's available at bookstores, visit your local library and go through the same exercise. Talking to a librarian can also be helpful to find out what books are popular and what patron demand is like in your book's category.

Depending on that category, you may want to check specialty retailers that carry books in addition to other merchandise. For instance, hobby and craft stores will carry a much deeper selection of books on knitting or home decor than your typical chain store. Cooking stores always have a selection of cookbooks. Try to become more aware of all the places you see books sold, because these are potential marketing and distribution opportunities. It may seem a bit counterintuitive, but books tend to sell better when they're not in a bookstore, where they can get lost among thousands of other titles.

Once you've finished the bricks-and-mortar retailer search, it's time for the online bookstore search. Amazon is the leading online retailer of both print books and e-books, so it's the most important one to tackle.

Go through the same steps that you did for the other stores, only this time you won't be limited to print books. Make sure you look carefully for e-book-only titles, self-published titles, and small press titles that don't often show up in stores, but that may be solid sellers. You can tell a book is popular when it has a very high number of reviews. You can also check its overall sales rank. Just keep in mind that an Amazon sales rank is a very volatile number and changes from day to day.

Often the titles that show up first in your online search will be selling better than all the rest, but perhaps only on that day or week. So dive into the categories and subcategories that Amazon offers. Dig beyond the first page or two of results to see the full scope of what's out there. And closely examine the titles that show up under "People who bought this book also bought."

Once you finish this competing title search, you should have a list of 20 or more titles that would be either comparable or directly competitive to your book. In the next lecture, we'll talk about what you'll do with this list in your proposal.

If you've come up with absolutely nothing that's comparable, that's not necessarily a good thing. It may mean your idea is just too weird or bizarre to have a market, or maybe the market isn't driven by bookstores. Either way, finding no competitive titles, or just a handful, may rule out pitching your book to agents and large publishers. However, there may be another way to prove there's a market for your book, which brings us to the second step in our research process.

You need to take a look at the non-book landscape. It would be a mistake to think that your competition is limited to print book titles. That may have been true 20 years ago, but today, your greatest competition may be a website, an online community, or a video series. You need to conduct a thorough search for digital content and online experts who target the same audience as your book. Here are some of the specific areas you'll want to cover.

First, look for top websites and blogs. Run a general search for keywords and phrases that relate to your book. What will potential readers of your book find if they turn to a search engine first? Determine how easy it is to find online information on your topic, and whether that information is trustworthy. Is the information free, or do you have to pay for it? Is it customized or personalized in some way? How well known are the authors or organizations behind the information?

There are millions of sites and blogs out there, but of course, not all blogs are created equal. Identify major blogs associated with your topic that target your audience. If you're active online and savvy about your subject, you probably already know what the influential sites are, and even better, you may write for them. As you look at sites, take special note of community sites, forums, and message boards because these can be very important to your marketing plan, which we'll cover later.

Video-related content is a more important competitor to books than you might think. YouTube is the number two search engine in the world, second only to Google, making video an important medium for instructional categories, as well as all types of illustrated or image-heavy content.

And don't forget about audio-driven content, such as podcasts distributed through iTunes. For example, you might have heard of Grammar Girl, whose real life name is Mignon Fogarty. Her books were signed and launched after receiving early success with a grammar podcast, which continues to this day. After you check iTunes, look at Audible, too, since audiobooks are one of the biggest growth areas for publishing.

Sometimes mobile and tablet applications can be your competition, so search app storefronts to find anything relevant to your topic. As with any competing product, note the price, the author or content provider, plus the language used and the point of view in the marketing copy.

Finally, don't forget the many different types of online education available, accessible through popular sites like Lynda.com, Udemy.com, and iTunes University.

As you can tell, regardless of medium, I'm encouraging you to study anything that might offer help, education, or resources to your target audience. Your goal here is to understand how your audience might be fulfilling its needs for information from a variety of sources, as well as how that audience is currently being marketed to.

This information may or may not end up informing your competitive analysis, but the upside is that you're developing a comprehensive map of how to market your book when it's published. This will become important as you develop the marketing plan that's included in the book proposal itself.

The third research step is to study the authors, experts, and influencers you found as you completed the first two steps. Just as you studied the books and media, dig deeper into the platform of these people. Ultimately, you have to determine how to set yourself apart. Look for hints about what kind of platform you need to be competitive in the eyes of a publisher. I recommend you create a set of notes for each author you find and consider the following.

What keywords or phrases are strongly affiliated with the author's brand or presence? What audience are they targeting? Is it the same one you're targeting? What are all the books that they've published? What media do they regularly produce? Do they do podcasts or video series? Do they have a blog? Are they regularly speaking at events? Are these events that you should have a presence at, too? What social media presence do they have? And look particularly at their use of Facebook and Twitter, as well as image-driven social media if that's important to your category, like Tumblr, Pinterest, or Instagram.

Ultimately, while these authors or influencers might be competitors, they might also become important collaborators. If they could play a role in your marketing plan, then look for opportunities to build a relationship with them. Your proposal will be all the stronger if you can count them among your network of contacts.

Now that you're deep into the research process, the fourth step is to pinpoint your primary target audience. From the start, you may have understood exactly who your book is for. If not, the first three research steps will give you really strong indicators as to your target audience and what they like. If not, go back and look for clues, look at the marketing language being used, the design aesthetic, how the material is packaged. Successful books and media are geared toward a target audience, even if they have very broad appeal.

Let me share one of the biggest red flags for any nonfiction book proposal; saying that your book is for everyone. Maybe it could interest everyone, but there's a specific audience that will be most likely to buy your book. Who are those people, and how and where can you reach them? Again, the first three steps have probably given you some really good hints and you can also ask the following: What websites and social media outlets seem to be most important or relevant for your target audience? Where does your audience gather online? What else do they read? What do they watch? Who do they listen to in the media?

Knowing the answers to these questions will begin to develop a profile of your target readership, and the more you know about your primary target market, the better you can build a proposal that speaks to why anyone cares about what you're writing. And of course, a deep understanding of your audience leads to a much better book.

The fifth and final research step is to analyze how you reach readers. This is where you really look hard at your existing platform. You should measure how well you currently reach your target readership, through your website or blog, email newsletter, social media, speaking gigs, regular appearances in the media, whatever brings you into contact with readers. This is a good time to refer back to step three of your research and see what the other authors are doing and do you have weaknesses or areas you should improve on?

Your platform directly informs the marketing and promotion plan that's included in your proposal, and the best marketing campaigns begin with what you have in place today, not what you hope will happen, like relying on Oprah to call. You need to be honest with yourself about your current position in the market, and how you'll collaborate with your publisher on marketing and publicity efforts.

If you've been thorough and thoughtful about this five-step research process, it should automatically eliminate the most common weaknesses in book proposals. Let's discuss some of these failings that you need to avoid.

By far the biggest pitfall is twofold. The book has no clearly defined market, and this pitfall goes hand in hand with a concept that is too general or broad.

Your proposal has to show why your idea isn't like a million others, and too many proposed books don't have any compelling element that would make them distinguished in the market. For instance, if you're writing a book on how to live a happier life, there are hundreds if not thousands of books on how to do that. What makes yours unique?

Sometimes a very marketable book idea doesn't sell because the writer concentrates only on the content of the book. You might ask, doesn't the proposal have to focus on the content of the book? This is kind of a classic misunderstanding of the book proposal. Of course, the book's topic or content is important, but the author must show, through the framework of the proposal, why the topic is important to his audience. The proposal is just as much about the book's benefit and appeal to the target market as it is about the content.

This goes back to one of the very initial points we've discussed during this course. Many times, writers aren't looking at their work with a marketer's eye. Try to think about how you'd interest a perfect stranger in your topic. Have you really tapped into current trends and interests when it comes to your project? Are you framing it in an exciting way for an agent or editor? Just because you're fascinated by your subject matter doesn't mean other people will get it. You have to know how to sell it.

If you're having a difficult time figuring out what makes your work salable, consider the following formula. Is your book the first to do or accomplish something specific? Is it the first to tackle a particular problem? Is it the first to reveal new information or a special project? Is it the first to tell the story of something or someone specific?

Another common problem with proposals is that, too often, people want to write a book based on the very personal or amateur experience of overcoming a problem or investigating a complex issue. This is usually a sure-fire method to get your proposal rejected unless you already have a platform or established audience.

Here are a few other reasons an editor or agent might tell you your book idea doesn't work.

First, you may be told the market is too small for the proposed book, and this probably means your defined target audience is so narrow that it doesn't hold enough commercial potential. Maybe you approached too big of a publisher. Big houses may want to sell as many as 10 or 20,000 copies in the first year to justify publication while smaller presses may be fine with just a few thousand copies. Is there a smaller publisher that would be interested because they have a lower threshold of sales to meet?

Second, many authors are told they simply don't have the sufficient platform to support sales. It's not enough to say that you have a blog or a website, or that you're active on social media, you need to have some good numbers, too, and we'll address this in the next lecture.

Another common problem is a dwindling market for books on the topic. A book, even one on a marketable topic, can now sometimes be a less desirable way to deliver information. If your book's information will go out of date quickly, or if it offers more value when it can be accessed on a mobile device through an app, you might find it difficult to sell a print book with that information. And some nonfiction categories, such as reference and travel, have experienced very steep declines in the print market for exactly these reasons.

Still, there are a couple ways you can make a case for a print book.

First, see if you can find evidence that your target audience prefers books. Talk to booksellers and librarians about books in your category. Have they seen shelf space expand or shrink? Are they seeing a move to digital formats or not?

Second, go back to the major competing sites or blogs you found. Some of them may be selling books that offer even more in-depth or valuable information.

Keep in mind that any good editor or agent will probably already know—or at least have preconceived ideas—about market trends in each category. But the more you can reflect your own marketing savvy, the better. Fortunately, if you're writing narrative nonfiction or memoir, you won't have to worry about making the case for a print book. It applies primarily to prescriptive and information-based nonfiction.

Given the significant change happening in the print book industry, authors shouldn't consider a book their first goal or the end goal, but merely one medium, and not always the best medium. Some editors and agents might recommend that you begin your project as a blog or a website, where interactivity and an opportunity for dialogue has more appeal to your audience.

It's true that too many book ideas I see shopped at conferences should really have started out online, or been built as online communities, even if only to test-market the ideas and to learn more about the target audience. The insights that come from being successful with your online content can produce a much more successful print product. Too many authors build their book concepts in a vacuum without any thought to the online conversations that are already happening.

Plus, there's an even greater reason to think about your online strategy. When executed well, online and multimedia offerings can sometimes lead to more opportunity and income than the book itself. Online courses, multimedia companions, and customized experiences tend to command a higher price than your average book and represent the biggest growth areas for nonfiction authors and experts.

So think about what happens when people finish your book. Ideally, readers should have a place where they can continue the conversation with you and other readers and receive updates. The nonfiction authors who tend to be most successful know how to build a community around their ideas and content. Agents and editors will be more excited about your book if they see the potential for a prominent and profitable life beyond the printed page.

Writing an Effective Book Proposal
Lecture 10

O nce you've completed your market research, you're ready to begin writing the book proposal. Even though every proposal is different, they all have several key sections: the overview, target market description, competing titles analysis, author bio and platform, marketing plan, manuscript specification and delivery, table of contents or chapter outline, and sample chapters. We'll discuss each of these, but rather than following the likely order of presentation in the proposal, we'll cover them in the order that you might find them easiest to write.

Competitive Title Analysis

- The competitive title analysis is a good place to start writing your proposal. This section analyzes similar books and explains why yours is different or better.

- To begin, gather all your research and determine which titles are the most important to discuss in your proposal. You should include direct competitors, especially those known as *category killers*. These are well-known titles that are considered the go-to books on their topics. Altogether, this section should include around a dozen titles for most categories.

- For each entry in your competitive title analysis, begin by listing the title, subtitle, author, publisher, year of publication, page count, price, format, ISBN, and specific edition number.

- Next, for each title, briefly summarize the book's key strengths or approach in relation to your own. This is where you differentiate your title from the competition and show why there's a need for your book despite the existence of others. These summaries should run about 100 to 200 words.

- Once you've described all the titles on your list, go back to the beginning and write an introduction to the list that summarizes your book's unique position in the market when compared to the competition. Use such phrases as "This will be the first book to ..." or "This is the only book to ...."

Author Bio

- For the author bio, you might begin with an existing bio, but be sure to tailor it for the book idea you're proposing. Show how your expertise and experience give you the perfect platform from which to address your target audience. If this is a weak area for you, look for other strengths that might give you credibility with readers or help sell books, such as connections to experts or authorities in the field, a solid online following, or previous success in marketing yourself and your work.

- Most author bios are two or three pages, but that length may double when you include details about your platform. A large commercial publishing house will want to know all the numbers related to your online following, including website or blog traffic, e-mail newsletter subscribers, and so on. You should also describe your offline interaction with the target readership, such as speaking engagements; leadership roles in relevant organizations; regular media jobs, such as writing a regular column; relevant recognitions or achievements; and other published works, including sales numbers if they're respectable.
  - To the best of your ability, quantify the impact your online activity has or the extent of your influence. If you blog, consider how many comments you average per post or how many new readers you gain per month. Look at the metrics provided for your social media accounts and see what percentage of your audience sees your posts and clicks on your links.

  - Here's an example of an effective statement you might make about your online activity: "I have 60,000 followers on Twitter, and Twitter is the second-largest source of traffic to my blog, with 2,000 visits per month. More than half the links that I share on Twitter get at least 100 clicks each."

Target Market Description

- The target market description is where you convince potential publishers that an identifiable market of readers exists who will be compelled to buy your book. Although your book may end up having broad appeal, be disciplined in your initial outline of your audience.

- When describing your market, consider the following factors: age, gender, and income level; education level; media and shopping preferences; preferences for gathering spots, either online or offline; and relevant organizations. Also consider whether the economy affects your market; whether your audience is growing, dwindling, or stagnant; and what challenges or problems your readers face.

- Try to include statistics, trend articles, or other research that comments on the problem your book addresses or the audience that you're trying to reach. Government and nonprofit reports, such as those from Pew Research, can be valuable here. You can also try searching Google Trends for indications of your topic's popularity and currency.

- Here's an example of a specific and persuasive statement about an audience: "Consumer surveys indicate that 70 percent of my target audience plans to spend at least $1,000 on hobbies this year, and 60 percent indicated that they buy books about their hobbies." You won't always be able to find that kind of specific information, but don't assume it doesn't exist. Many magazines and websites conduct routine customer research and include extensive data in media kits for advertisers. These can be a rich resource for your market analysis.

- A typical market analysis is two to four pages. Make sure it clearly outlines what's at stake for the target audience—how serious the problem or issue is for them. Agents or editors should know exactly how to find your readers, as well as the approximate size of the readership. They should also know enough about the audience to clearly envision how the book will be successfully positioned and packaged to make a sale.

Marketing Plan

- The marketing plan combines the strength of your platform with knowledge of your target audience. This is where you spell out what you can do to market and promote your own book to readers. Never discuss what you hope to do, only what you can and will do, without publisher assistance, given your current resources. This section generally runs two to six pages.

- A good marketing plan has four facets: First, you want to do everything you can to reach readers directly through channels that you own, such as your blog or e-mail newsletter. Second, you need to effectively tap your personal and professional connections and ask them to help spread word of mouth about your book. Third, you should begin to connect with influencers who reach your target audience. Fourth, you should pursue opportunities that put you in front of your target readership in new ways. In your proposal, you might discuss some of the following marketing activities:
  - Creating a posting strategy tied to the launch of your book for your website or blog.

  - Using existing e-mail newsletter lists to push book sales to people who are already interested in your work.

  - Using social media channels to bring awareness to your book.

  - Ramping up your schedule of speaking engagements to support the book launch.

  - Tapping into special contacts or business relationships you have to get coverage or spread word of mouth for the book.

  - Becoming a regular or guest contributor at a highly trafficked website in advance of your book publication.

  - Persuading early supporters of your book to feature it on their sites, blogs, or podcasts.

- The secret to a strong marketing plan isn't the quantity of ideas you have or even the size of your reach but how well you can put to work the network or advantages you have. You need to show how you can tap into readers and influencers who are already in your network to spread the word about your book. You also need to show that you can take real action that will lead to concrete results and a strong connection to the target readership.

Chapter Outline and Sample Chapters
- At the end of your proposal, you should include a table of contents or a chapter outline for the book, followed by one or two sample chapters.

Book Proposal Elements

- Cover Sheet (including book title, author name, and contact information)
- Proposal Table of Contents
- Overview (1–2 pages)
- Target Market Description (2–4 pages)
- Competing Title Analysis (100–200 words per title for about 12 titles)
- Author Bio and Platform (2–6 pages)
- Marketing Plan (2–6 pages)
- Manuscript Specification and Delivery (1 page)
- Table of Contents and/or Chapter Outline (for an outline, 100 words per chapter)
- Sample Chapters (up to about 25 pages)
- Supporting Materials (include where appropriate; e.g., advance praise may go with the marketing plan; sample clips may fall at the end of the proposal)

- A chapter outline generally works better for narrative or meaty works, especially those that are anticipated to come in at 80,000 words or more. For each chapter, write a brief summary of the idea, information, or story presented, usually 100 words per chapter. If writing a chapter outline seems unnecessary for your book's content, then use a table of contents. The goal here is to show the scope and range of material covered in your book.

- If your book has any special features or sidebars—or any kind of unique presentation of content—make sure to convey that information, as well. Any element that might be used as a selling point to readers should be clearly described and included in your outline.

- Sample chapters must prove that you can deliver on your promise of quality information or storytelling. The best strategy is to include one of the meatiest chapters of the book as your sample. For book proposals pitching a long-form narrative, it's best to include the opening chapters, up to about 25 pages.

Overview, Title, and Other Materials

- Although it comes first in the proposal, the last key element to write is the overview, which is the opening statement and summary of your business case. Typically one to two pages, the overview effectively answers the three questions: So what? Who cares? Who are you? The most compelling and juicy details from your proposal should be in the overview.

- The other detail that you might want to save for last is your book title and subtitle. For nonfiction pitches in particular, it's best to be clear, direct, and benefit-oriented with your titles, rather than vague or overly clever. If you absolutely must get creative with the main title, then make the subtitle explanatory to eliminate any confusion about the book's topic. Most publishers also want to see topic keywords in the title or subtitle to ensure that the book can be easily discovered through online searches.

- Some authors may find it useful to have additional supporting materials in their proposals, and agents and editors are generally accepting of any materials that will help build a good case for your book's publication. One of the more popular inclusions is a foreword, introduction, or some kind of advance praise or testimonial from an influential person or another author. If you've written extensively on the topic in other venues, you may also want to include a few clips of your work.

- For books that require photography or illustrations, include a section that explains how the art will be sourced, obtained, or commissioned. If you intend to create or source the art yourself, include samples in the proposal.

- Finally, if you have ideas for multimedia features—either as marketing and promotional tools or for an enhanced e-book edition or app—create a section in your proposal that addresses those opportunities.

Suggested Reading

Herman, *Write the Perfect Book Proposal.*

Larsen, *How to Write a Book Proposal.*

Lyon, *Nonfiction Book Proposals Anybody Can Write.*

1. Once you have a rough draft of your proposal, set it aside for a few days, then return to it with a fresh set of eyes. As you reread it, look for evidence that there is demand for the book. Does the proposal show why the market needs the book? Often, authors focus too much on the specifics of the content and not enough on why the content will succeed in the market.

2. Many businesses create customer personas, with specific names, to help them understand and make sure they remain focused on their audience. Try creating an ideal reader profile for your book. In about 200 words, describe the reader's daily life and most pressing concerns. Name your reader, and as you write and revise your proposal, keep him or her in mind.

Writing an Effective Book Proposal
Lecture 10—Transcript

Once you've completed your market research, you're ready to begin writing the proposal. Even though every proposal is different, they all have several key sections. We'll discuss each of these sections in depth, but rather than following the likely order of presentation within the proposal document, we'll discuss them in the order you'll probably find them easiest to write. All book proposals should be double-spaced throughout, so keep that in mind when I refer to page lengths.

The competitive title analysis is one of the best places to start. This section analyzes similar books and why yours is different or better. You don't want to skimp or rush here, editors can tell when you haven't done your homework. And whatever you do, don't claim there aren't any competitors to your book. If there are truly no competitors, then editors and agents might conclude there's no market for it.

So gather all of your bookstore and online research, and determine which titles are the most important to discuss in your proposal. You should include direct competitors, especially those known as category killers. These are the well-known titles that dominate the shelf and are considered the go-to books. For example, *What to Expect When You're Expecting* is the category killer in pregnancy books. You might also want to include titles that are more complementary than competitive. They can help better define and pinpoint how your book fits into the overall landscape of titles available.

Overall, your competitive title analysis should include about a dozen titles if the category is popular and far-reaching, such as self-help, business, or health. You might be okay discussing just a few titles if your book is on a very specialized topic or for a very narrow audience.

For each entry in your competitive title analysis, begin by listing the title, subtitle, author, publisher, year of publication, page count, price, format, and the ISBN. If it has a specific edition number, include that, too. You don't need to list things such as Amazon ranking, star rating, or reviews. You also shouldn't worry about knowing the exact sales numbers of the competing titles. There's no way for authors to find out that information, and the agent or editor can look it up for themselves when needed.

So here comes the most important part. You need to briefly summarize each competing book's key strengths or approach in relation to your own. This is where you differentiate your title from the competition. Show why there's a need for your book despite the existence of this other one. This explanation is usually about 100–200 words.

You do have to play a bit of a game here. That's because you don't want to trash the competition, that's bad etiquette. After all, you might end up pitching the agent or editor who worked on a competing book. On the other hand, you can't describe the book neutrally. You need to point out how its approach is different from your own or may have limitations.

If you have trouble figuring out how your title is different, or could be different, then check out the customer reviews for the competing title. You'll often find constructive criticism or insightful comments about how the book could be improved or what territory it fails to cover. For instance, what if you discovered that, for the best-selling titles in your category, recent reviews complain the books aren't keeping up with new information and trends? This would be something to mention in your analysis.

Once you've described all the titles in your list, go back to the beginning, and write an introduction to the list that summarizes your book's unique position in the market when compared to the competition. It's helpful if you can use phrases like, "This will be the first book to…" or "This is the only book to…"

When you're trying to enter a very competitive field of titles, or you have a book that's relevant to two or more categories, you may want to divide your competitive title analysis into subsections, each with its own subhead. For instance, if you're a doctor writing a memoir about your career fighting child abuse, it may be appropriate to discuss memoirs by other doctors, as well as books that address the social issue of child abuse for people working in the field.

After you've finished the competitive title discussion, start on your author bio statement, which is usually two to three pages. It can be helpful to begin with a bio you already use at your website, or perhaps on LinkedIn, the business-oriented social media network. But don't just copy and paste your bio into the proposal and consider the job done. You also have to convince agents and editors you're the perfect author for the book. That means you need to tailor your bio and background for the book idea you're proposing. Show how your expertise and experience give you the perfect platform from which to address your target audience. If this is a weak area for you, look for other strengths that lend you credibility with readers or help sell books, such as connections to experts or authorities in the field, a solid online following, and previous success in marketing yourself and your work.

The worst thing you could do in your author bio is paste in a résumé or CV, and expect someone else to make sense of what's important or relevant to your book. Instead, focus on telling your story in a way that positions you as an ideal author who's headed on an inevitable path to success.

Depending on the nature of your project, you may need to include details about your platform as part of your bio or immediately after. Let's assume you want the best possible deal from a commercial New York house. They're going to want to know all the numbers related to your online following, including website or blog traffic, social media likes or follows, e-mail newsletter subscribers, and so on.

You should also describe your offline interaction with the target readership, at speaking engagements, events, and classes. If you have a strong network in your region or have leadership roles in organizations that are relevant to your book, describe them. Outline any regular media gigs you have, such as being a regular columnist, contributor or guest, and list any accolades, recognition, or achievements that would be relevant to the target audience.

Finally, if you've published other books, you won't be able to get around mentioning your sales history and figures. Even if you don't include these figures, it's the first thing the agent or editor will look up, so it's best to be upfront. Clearly list the figures and offer background on the success or failure of past work.

In terms of online platform, you typically need thousands of engaged followers, and verifiable influence with those followers, to interest a major publisher. And to really stand out from the pack, you need to offer an idea of your growth trajectory. For instance, do you gain 1,000 new blog readers every month? Do you attract 100 new Twitter followers every week?

To the best of your ability, quantify the impact your online activity has, or what your influence is. If you blog, consider how many comments you average per post, or how many people subscribe to your blog via e-mail or RSS feeds. On your social media accounts, look at the metrics provided, see what percentage of your audience is actually engaged, seeing your posts, and clicking on links.

For example, here is an effective statement you might make about your online activity: I have 60,000 followers on Twitter, and Twitter is the number two source of traffic to my blog, with 2,000 visits per month. More than half the links I share on Twitter get at least 100 clicks each.

This shows a highly engaged audience rather than a superficial following. Show that you interact with your readers in a meaningful way, show specifically how and where the market is engaged and growing, and show that you continue to play an active role.

The next section you should write—and this is where we get into more difficult territory—is a description of the book's target market or audience. In as much detail as possible, you should identify who will buy your book. You need to convince a publisher there's an identifiable market of readers who will be compelled to spend money on your information in book form.

As I warned earlier, it can be very tempting to make a broad statement about who your audience is, to make it sound like anyone and everyone is a potential reader. For instance, if you're writing a book about how to be a better leader in the corporate workplace, you might say the audience is anyone who works in a corporate environment. But this isn't very helpful, and it's also rather obvious the book is broadly for that market.

To further refine your audience, focus on who your ideal reader is. Identify not only what demographic they belong to, but take into account their behaviors, motivations, and beliefs. Perhaps that corporate leadership book is primarily for mid-career men at Fortune 500 companies who are looking for a competitive advantage on the executive level. Now we're starting to go somewhere specific and useful.

While your book may end up having broad appeal, be disciplined in your initial outline of who the book will primarily target. After you describe the most likely readers for your book, you can then also describe the potential secondary audiences. But when describing the primary market, consider the following questions. What's their age, gender, and income level? What's their education level? What types of media do they listen to or watch? Where do they shop? Where do they gather online or off? What specific organizations do they belong to? Does the economy affect your market? Is the audience growing, dwindling, or stagnant? What challenges or problems are they faced with?

Your target market analysis will be powerful if you can include statistics, trend articles, or other research that comments on the problem your book addresses. Government and nonprofit reports, such as those from Pew Research, can be very valuable. You can also try searching Google Trends for indication of your topic's popularity over the years, and what news stories broke out on that topic. Just be careful and avoid generic statements. For instance, saying how many search results turn up for certain keywords is meaningless. And you don't need to indicate how many books show up on Amazon in your category. These statistics aren't telling us anything about the audience who will buy your book.

Instead, try to craft statements like, "Consumer surveys indicate that 70 percent of my target audience plans to spend at least $1,000 on their hobby this year, and 60 percent indicated they buy books on that hobby." This is persuasive. You won't always be able to find such specific data, but don't assume it's not out there. Many magazines and websites conduct routine customer research and include extensive data in media kits for advertisers and these can be a rich resource for your market analysis.

A typical market analysis is about two to four pages. You know you're finished when it's clear what's at stake for the target audience, and you've described how your book addresses a problem or issue for that audience. After reading your market analysis, an agent or editor should know exactly how and where to find your readers, as well as the approximate size of the readership. They should also know enough about the audience to clearly envision how the book will be successfully positioned and packaged to make a sale.

You should now be ready to write the marketing plan. A good plan combines the strength of your platform with knowledge of your target audience. This is where you spell out what you specifically can do to market and promote your own book to readers. Never discuss what you hope to do, only what you can and will do, without publisher assistance, given your current resources. A marketing plan will generally run anywhere from two to six pages, sometimes more.

Some authors write their marketing plan in an extremely tentative fashion, talking about the things they are willing to do if asked. This is deadly language, so you should avoid it. Instead, be confident, firm, and direct about everything that's going to happen with or without the publisher's help. Make it concrete and realistic, and attach numbers to everything. A strong marketing plan details how you'll make your audience aware of your book, and builds on what reach you currently have.

I like to think of the marketing plan as having four facets. First, you want to do everything you can to reach readers directly through channels that you own, such as your blog, email newsletter, or social media accounts. These are your existing resources to capitalize on. Second, you need to effectively tap your personal and professional connections and ask them to help spread word of mouth about your book. Third, you should begin to connect with influencers who may not yet be part of your network, but who reach your target audience. Finally, you want to pursue opportunities that put you in front of your target readership in new and hopefully bigger ways. Here are some key areas to consider.

If you have a website or blog that reaches thousands of readers per month, you should have a specific posting strategy tied to the launch of your book. Email newsletters are powerful sales tools. So discuss how you'll use any existing list to push book sales to people already interested in your work. Depending on where you're active in social media, describe how you'll use those channels to bring awareness to your book.

Authors who actively speak or teach should indicate how they might ramp up their schedule of engagements. Will you secure more gigs to support your book launch? Mention any special contacts or business relationships you have that could be tapped to get coverage or spread word of mouth for the book. For example, if you're a former employee of Google, and you're writing a book that would interest the company, would they invite you to speak as part of their Talks at Google program?

If you can become a regular contributor at a highly trafficked website in advance of your book's publication, or if you know you can get guest spots at influential blogs, mention it. Who do you think you can persuade to be an early supporter of the book and featured on their site, blog, podcast, or otherwise recommend it to their audience?

The secret to a strong marketing plan isn't the quantity of ideas you have, or even the size of your reach, but how well and how creatively you can put to work the network and advantages you have. You have to tap into the readers and influencers already in your network and indicate how you'll spread the word throughout that network. You need to show that your ideas are not just pie in the sky, but real action steps that will lead to concrete results and a strong connection to the target readership.

Aside from your own network, it can be helpful to offer a vision of how and where you think the book might receive media coverage. While you might be tempted to go for the obvious big hitters, like the *New York Times Book Review* or *The New Yorker*, think about outlets that your publisher might not already know that reach your book's target audience.

There are some marketing strategies you should avoid discussing in the proposal, even if you know they're frequently used. Anything related to giveaways, discounting or price promotions or advertising is generally not within your control. You can't base your marketing plan around what the publisher would have to pay for, nor should you suggest things that could interfere with normal operations with their business partners. For example, suggesting an Amazon-focused book launch, or giving away the book for free for any period of time, probably won't be an acceptable strategy for most traditional publishers.

You now have the bulk of your business case written. At this stage, if not earlier, I suggest you read a good sample book proposal or two so you can get ideas for how to make your proposal stronger. *How to Write a Book Proposal* by Michael Larsen is a popular guide on book proposals that's been published since the 1980s. It includes several proposal examples, as well as in-depth instruction on every section you need to write.

If you're hitting the average length for most proposals, you probably have at least 10–15 pages focused on the sections I just described. At the end of your proposal, you should include a table of contents or a chapter outline for the book, followed by one or two sample chapters.

A chapter outline generally works better for narrative or meaty works, especially those that are text-heavy and anticipated to come in at 80,000 words or more. For each chapter, you write a brief summary of the idea, information, or story presented, about 100 words per chapter. Sometimes a bulleted list of key points also works well. If writing a chapter outline seems redundant or unnecessary for your book's content, then use a table of contents. And if you want to use both, that's completely acceptable. The most important thing is to show how your book concept will play out from beginning to end, and strongly convey the scope and the range of the material covered.

If you envision your book having any special features or sidebars—any unique presentation of content—make sure that gets conveyed in the chapter outline or in a special section of the proposal. Any book element that might be used as a selling point to readers should be clearly described and included as part of what you think distinguishes your book from the competition.

As for the sample chapters, they have to prove that you can deliver on your promise of quality information or storytelling. If the writing doesn't measure up to the promise made in the proposal, you won't get a deal. Your best strategy is to include one of the meatiest chapters of the book as your sample. Don't slap together a lightweight chapter that might be easy or quick to write but that doesn't showcase your best material.

Memoirists and others who are telling a story are an exception to this. For book proposals pitching a long-form narrative, it's best to include the opening chapters, up to 25 pages or so. Editors need to see that the story starts strong.

Now is probably a good time to pause and directly address the significant challenges facing a memoir proposal. Even though the story you're telling might be a universal one, your proposal is under enormous pressure to demonstrate why your story is unique in the marketplace. And in addition to that, the writing has to be phenomenal. Editors and agents are deluged by stories about addicts, dysfunctional families, aging parents, and cancer survivors. Unless you're a celebrity or have an established audience, your story needs to be unbelievably distinctive in its premise or approach. Just because you've written it doesn't mean the world is hungry to read it. Later in the course, we'll talk more about the story weaknesses that are common to memoir.

Somewhere in the proposal, but typically before the chapter outline, you should include a brief statement that conveys the anticipated length of the book, or the actual length if it's finished. It's also common to state how much time you need to finish the book. Typically, authors are given 6–12 months to write the book after signing. If you need to conduct any special research or have any considerations that affect your ability to complete the project—such as travel costs or the ability to gain access to interview subjects—mention them. This section is usually titled "Manuscript Delivery and Specifications."

The last element of your proposal is the overview, which is the opening statement and summary of your business case. Because it's the hardest to write, I recommend authors save it for last. The overview doesn't need to be more than a couple of pages, but it effectively and holistically answers the three questions: So what? Who cares? And who are you?

The most compelling and juicy details from your proposal should be in that overview, it's kind of like an executive summary. Some agents and editors recommend you envision the overview as your book's back cover copy, which should speak directly to readers trying to decide whether or not to purchase your book, and that's a good way to start.

The other detail that you might want to save for last is your book title and subtitle. For nonfiction pitches, in particular, it's best to be clear, direct, and benefit-oriented with your title, rather than vague or overly clever. If you absolutely must get creative with the main title, then make the subtitle explanatory to eliminate any confusion as to the book's topic.

When crafting a title, assume the editor has seen hundreds of books on your topic. If possible, your book's title should express its benefit or angle to readers right away. Agent Michael Larsen is known for calling this the tell and sell title. The title not only tells readers what the book is about, but it also sells them on it. Usually, you want your book title to be positive and empowering, and to convince book buyers that it will solve their problems or benefit their lives. Also, most publishers want to see your topic keywords somewhere in the title or subtitle, to make sure the book can be easily discovered through an online search. While it's true that the publisher will likely change your title, you should still create something that catches a reader's attention quickly and identifies the book's audience and purpose.

Some authors may find it useful to have additional supporting materials in their proposal. Agents and editors are generally accepting of any materials that build a good case for your book's publication. The more popular elements that can help build a case include a foreword, introduction, or any advance praise from an influential person or another author. Sometimes, if the author lacks sufficient authority on his own, this can really bolster a book's credibility.

Your next question might very well be: How do you gain such advance materials from important people without having a book deal first? The short answer is: You ask very nicely. The longer answer is: Typically, you should only ask people you have some kind of a connection to, or to whom you've been introduced. It is difficult, even impossible, to get endorsements from a completely cold contact. For example, if you wanted to try to get Bill Gates to blurb your book, no amount of calling or emailing his assistants is likely to get you a response unless you know someone close to him. That said, it is possible to get lucky if your book is a really good fit and your timing is perfect.

If you've written extensively on the topic of your book, you may want to include a few published clips in the proposal, especially if any articles had significant media attention or traffic. This can help prove evidence of need for your work in the market. And media-savvy authors may want to link to or reference interviews or clips of them appearing on TV shows or radio, to prove an ability to effectively promote to a national market. The same goes for any author who frequently speaks or teaches; it helps a lot to show what you're like in front of an audience.

For books that require photography or illustrations, you'll need to include a section that explains how the art will be sourced, obtained, or commissioned. You'll also need to discuss any costs or permissions issues that might be involved with obtaining the art. If you intend to create or source the art yourself, include samples in the proposal so the editor can review the quality and appropriateness for book publication.

In the proposal, it's not necessary to discuss what format the publisher should use, such as paperback versus hardcover. That decision remains solely with the publisher, along with pricing. However, if you have ideas for multimedia features—either as marketing and promotional tools, or for an enhanced digital edition or app—create a section in your proposal that addresses those opportunities, and let your publisher lead the discussion on the best format and editions for your work when the time comes.

When you're ready to assemble the proposal, this is what you'll do. First, create a cover sheet for the proposal that includes your book title, name, and contact information and center it all on the page. After that, start a fresh page for the table of contents for your proposal, where you'll list all the proposal sections, and what page number they start on.

The sections are usually put in the following order: Overview, Target Market, Competing Titles, Author Bio and Platform, Marketing Plan, Manuscript Specification and Delivery, Table of Contents, Chapter Outline, and Sample Chapters. But this isn't a strict order. Do what makes the most sense for your project, and additional materials can be added wherever they best fit. Published clips or trend articles typically go at the end, while art and illustration plans are discussed near manuscript specification and delivery.

Before you decide whether your proposal is ready to submit, see if you can find a few people, especially those with business or sales backgrounds, who are willing to take a look and suggest areas to improve. Proposal writing has a lot in common with the art of the pitch, and the best ones demand careful research, a sharp understanding of the audience, and a persuasive framing of the issue if you want to secure the best possible book deal and advance.

Submissions and Publishing Etiquette
Lecture 11

In this lecture, we'll cover the proper etiquette for submitting your work, but first, we also need to address whether you're ready to submit. After you've finished your novel draft, you may be tempted to send it out to agents or editors immediately. But in all likelihood, you'll be rejected. Before you submit a manuscript or book proposal, you must ask yourself: Is this the best I can make it? If you have doubts, take time to correct any weaknesses. Always keep in mind that the publishing industry moves slowly, and it's unlikely that you'll miss an important window of opportunity just by waiting a few weeks to polish your materials before you submit.

Industry Standards for Submissions

- Unless you've found guidelines from an agent or editor that spell out unique formatting requirements, you should submit your materials in accordance with general industry standards.

- For query letters sent through regular mail, use a standard block-letter format, with one-inch margins and single-spaced text. The query letter should look straightforward and professional.

- A book manuscript should be double-spaced throughout. The most common fonts used are Arial, Times New Roman, or Courier in 12-point size. Again, use one-inch margins on all sides.
  - Your manuscript should have a title page that includes the book title, your name, and your contact information, typically centered on the page.

  - Create a header for each page that includes your last name, the title of your novel in all caps, and the page number. Make sure every page is numbered, except for the title page.

  - Each new chapter should start on its own page, about one-third of the way down the page. Center the chapter number and title if there is one. Generally, you should begin the body of the chapter about four to six lines below the chapter number and title.

    ○   Indent for each new paragraph. Don't add spaces between paragraphs or use block paragraphs.

- These same guidelines can be applied to your book proposal, with each new section of the proposal starting on a new page.

- When sending a query via e-mail, be aware that copying and pasting text from your word-processing software into your e-mail often results in strange formatting. For this reason, you should format a special version of your query letter that's only for electronic submissions. Save your query as a simple text file, which will strip it of all formatting. Use all capitals instead of italics for book titles and make sure there are no indents.

    ○   The first line of the e-mail query should be the salutation, and your contact information should go at the bottom. Don't send attachments unless explicitly advised to do so. If you're asked to send attachments, find out what file type is preferred; if in doubt, send documents in PDF format, which can be opened by virtually any type of computer or device.

    ○   The subject line of your e-mail should include the word *Query*, followed by your book title, unless you find other specific guidelines.

- When sending manuscript materials through the mail, print everything one-sided, and keep documents loose or paper-clipped together. Avoid folding materials whenever possible, and don't use binders or protective folders.

Terminology of Submission Guidelines
- Submission guidelines outline the specific submission preferences of publishers and agents. As you'll discover, such guidelines tend to have their own terminology.

- *SASE* is an acronym for "self-addressed, stamped envelope." A SASE is almost always requested for any snail-mail submissions. The agent or publisher will respond to you, often with a one-page rejection letter, using the SASE.

- The term *unsolicited* means that the materials weren't requested from authors. Some markets state in their guidelines that they don't review unsolicited manuscripts, which usually means you need to query first. Other markets may indicate that they don't accept any type of unsolicited material, including queries, which means they are effectively closed. The only way to approach a closed market is to have an agent or to get a referral from an existing author or client.

- Some guidelines may state that *simultaneous submissions* are not accepted. This is a manuscript submitted for consideration to more than one publisher or agent at the same time. Usually the term refers strictly to manuscripts under consideration, not query letters, which are commonly sent out in batches.

- Another term you may come across is *multiple submission*, which refers to sending more than one story idea or manuscript for consideration at a time. Almost no market allows for this, and it should be strictly avoided. Even if you hope to write a series, pitch only the first book in your query, not the entire series. If your first query is rejected, you may query about another project, but you should probably wait a few months before doing so.

- Some guidelines state that previously published work is not accepted. When referring to a book manuscript, this most often means that you shouldn't have self-published the work or otherwise widely distributed it to the public. Posting your work in online critique groups or private communities doesn't count as publication.

Author Rights

- The advice in this section is directed toward writers of prose and poetry. If you are a scriptwriter or playwright, you should refer to the Writers Guild of America for an understanding of your rights.

- It is not possible under current U.S. law to copyright an idea or a title. But note that the likelihood of having your idea stolen is almost zero. You should feel free to share your work with trusted advisers, send it to agents and editors, and talk about it when you're networking at conferences. Unless you are known in the industry for coming up with million-dollar concepts, you probably won't experience idea theft.
  - No matter how valuable you think your idea is, do not tell an editor or agent that you can't disclose the full details without a signed nondisclosure agreement. You will be rejected outright if you withhold information about a project that would help an editor or agent make a decision about whether to do business with you.

  - You must be upfront and clear about every aspect of your project. Don't expect anyone to go out of the way to create a special business agreement with you because you're nervous about idea theft.

- When it comes to protecting written work, you do not have to officially register it with the U.S. Copyright Office for it to be protected under the law. As the law is currently written, as soon as you express your work in tangible form, it is protected. However, you would need to register the work if you found infringement and wished to sue. Also, you

© Devonyu/iStock/Thinkstock.

When you send your work to agents and editors, they know that it's automatically protected under the law and don't need a copyright notice or symbol to remind them of that fact.

don't need to put the copyright symbol anywhere on your work for it to be protected under the law. But if you self-publish your work or otherwise distribute it publicly, then you should officially register it with the U.S. Copyright Office.

- When you submit material to agents or publishers, essentially, you are offering limited-time rights to your work, but you rarely offer all rights. Authors keep copyright to their work, then grant publishers or others permission to exploit those rights on their behalf. Publishers' submission guidelines often indicate what rights they expect to receive as part of a deal. Assuming you haven't granted rights to any other party, then you own full rights and can grant them selectively to anyone you choose.

  o If some portion of your work has been previously published, you must be clear about that upfront. It's generally not a problem, but you must look at the publication contract you signed to be sure.

  o When you publish shorter works, the publication generally takes one-time publication rights that are exclusive for a brief time period, and you continue to have rights to the work afterward.

  o Whatever your situation, to avoid any surprises, make it clear in your query or proposal that portions of the work have been previously published if that's the case.

- Another area where you need to exercise caution is when pitching a work that includes significant material from other published work. For instance, if you want to publish a collection of quotations, you'll quickly run into permission issues. Whenever you quote or excerpt other people's copyrighted work within your own, the most important question to address is: Does the quotation or excerpt fall under fair use?

  o The four criteria for determining fair use take into account the following factors: (1) the purpose and character of the use (e.g., commercial or educational); (2) the nature of the copyrighted work; (3) the amount and substantiality of the portion used in relation to the entire quoted work; and (4) the effect of the use on the potential market for, or value of, the quoted work.

o   Determining whether your use of quoted material is fair falls into one of the grayest areas of copyright law. Many authors decide to ask for permission when quoting more than a certain number of words from a published work. To eliminate all risk, whenever you quote someone else's work within your own, contact the copyright owner of the work—usually through the publisher or agent—and request permission.

o   You do not need permission to quote from works in the public domain, to state unadorned facts, or to mention book titles or authors of other works. You may also not need permission to quote works that are licensed under Creative Commons; this type of license applies to many websites and blogs.

Attracting Positive Attention

- In some cases, authors are approached by agents and editors and are able to sidestep the submission process. The most common method for attracting attention from editors and agents is to get your work published in venues where they scout for talent. For instance, the "Modern Love" column in *The New York Times* is a popular outlet for agents, and its featured writers are commonly approached for book deals.

- A variation on this method is simply to get media coverage in a mainstream publication. The movie *Julie and Julia* began as a blog that attracted attention and was featured in *The New York Times*; its author then landed a book deal.

- Rather than focusing on a book, those with an entrepreneurial spirit can develop a website or blog with content so significant, fresh, and original that it leads to traditional media coverage or an influencer recommendation. Here, you're banking on your ability to develop a story or an experience so powerful that it cultivates a network of connections who will ultimately champion you, almost without being asked.

- Despite these strategies, it's not generally advisable to sit around hoping that someone will notice your brilliance. A proactive writer learns how to pitch his or her work effectively.

Suggested Reading

Jassin and Schechter, *The Copyright Permission and Libel Handbook.*

Sambuchino, *Formatting and Submitting Your Manuscript.*

Exercises

1. Before you submit your materials, read at least one or two popular agent blogs, such as those by Rachelle Gardner or Kristin Nelson. Just about all agents talk about the submissions process, good and bad surprises, and what they wish authors knew before submitting. Reading their frank advice can help improve your materials and make sure you're sending only your best work.

2. Conversely, reading author advice about "what I wish I had known" or "what I've learned" can also help you reassess your situation before submitting. Give it a try; search for writers who discuss lessons learned about publishing. One of my favorites is by author Scott Berkun, "28 (Better) Things No One Tells You about Publishing."

Submissions and Publishing Etiquette
Lecture 11—Transcript

One of the biggest mistakes you can make is to rush to submit your materials to an agent or publisher. So before we cover the proper etiquette of submitting your work, we'll first address whether you're ready to submit because this can be a surprisingly difficult question to answer.

Let's say you've just finished your novel draft. You probably feel elated. It's a major accomplishment to write a book, most people never cross the finish line. So you should feel proud and you're probably eager to get the book out into the world, to make it public, to receive feedback. Maybe your family has already read it and said it's wonderful. So you immediately send it out to a few agents you've found, and then what happens? In all likelihood, you'll be promptly rejected.

Before you submit your work, ask yourself: Is it the best you can make it? Are there any remaining problems you need to address? Don't assume the problems will get fixed later in the process, instead, your work is more likely to be considered unready for publication. You also need to thoroughly research the markets for your work, and be confident you're approaching the right publishers or agents.

As a final step before submitting, carefully review your query letter if you're sending one. Take a look at the first few pages of your manuscript. Are you making the best possible impression? Correct any weaknesses before you start the submissions process. There's almost never a good reason to rush. The publishing industry does not move fast, and it's unlikely you'll miss an important window of opportunity if you wait a few more weeks or even months to submit.

So let's assume you're ready to go. Unless you've found guidelines from an agent or editor that spell out unique formatting requirements—and we'll talk about submission guidelines in a moment—you'll format and submit your material to adhere to general industry standards.

For query letters you send through snail mail use a standard block letter format. Use one-inch margins and single-space all text. Arial or Times are the most common fonts used, in 12-point size. The query letter should look exactly like any other business letter you might send. Don't try to make yours stand out with heavyweight paper, colored fonts, images, or any unusual features. Keep it straightforward and professional.

Your book manuscript should be double-spaced throughout. The most common fonts used are Arial, Times New Roman, or Courier, again, in 12-point size, and use one-inch margins, again, on all sides. If you do this, you'll be 90 percent of the way there. So here's how to handle the rest.

Your manuscript should have a title page that includes the book title, author name, and your contact information, typically centered in the middle of the page. Create a running header for each page that includes your last name, the title of your book in all caps, and the page number. Make sure every page is numbered, except for the title page.

Each new chapter should start on its own page, about one-third of the way down the page. Center the chapter number, as well as the chapter title if there is one. Generally, you should begin the body of the chapter about four to six lines below the chapter number and title. Indent for each new paragraph. Don't add spaces between paragraphs, or use block paragraphs.

These same guidelines can be applied to your book proposal, with each new section of the proposal starting on a new page.

When sending a query letter via email, you need to be especially careful about copying and pasting anything from your word processing software into your email software. There's really no predicting how things will look when that email is opened on the other end, the formatting might become a nightmare. For this reason, you should create a special version of your query letter that's only for sending electronically. Save your query as a simple text file, which will strip out all special formatting. Use caps instead of italics for book titles and make sure there are no indents.

The first line of the email query should be the salutation, and your contact information should go at the very bottom. Don't send an attachment unless explicitly advised to do so, and when you do send an attachment, ask what file type is preferred. If in doubt, send documents in PDF format, which can be opened by virtually any type of computer or device. The subject line of your email should include the word query followed by your book title, or follow any specific guidelines you find.

When sending manuscript materials through the mail, print everything one-sided, and keep documents loose or paper-clipped together. Avoid folding materials whenever possible. Buy an envelope big enough to keep everything flat. It's not necessary to send manuscripts or proposals in binders or protected folders, and in fact, that can be an annoyance when documents need to be photocopied. So keep documents simple, clean, and without window dressing.

These are the rules you should follow in the absence of any other instructions. But both publishers and agents will often have specific guidelines— sometimes called submission guidelines or writers' guidelines—that state their preferences for submissions. Follow these guidelines to the letter, even if they seem eccentric. It's too easy to reject writers who aren't paying attention.

You'll discover that submission guidelines tend to have their own language or terminology. So here are the most common terms you'll find.

SASE is an acronym for self-addressed, stamped envelope. An SASE is almost always requested for any snail mail submissions. The agent or publisher will return their response to you, often a one-page rejection letter, in the SASE.

You've probably heard the term slush pile. This refers to all of the unsolicited material received by those in the publishing industry. Unsolicited means the materials haven't been requested from you. Some markets state in their guidelines that they don't review unsolicited manuscripts, which usually means you need to query first. Other markets may indicate they don't accept any type of unsolicited material, including queries, which means they are effectively a closed market. The only way to approach a closed market is to have an agent, or otherwise get a referral from an existing author or client.

Some guidelines may state that simultaneous submissions are not accepted. A simultaneous submission is a manuscript submitted for consideration to more than one publisher or agent at the same time. Usually simultaneous submission refers strictly to manuscripts under consideration, and not queries, which are commonly sent in batches.

Simultaneous submissions were once frowned upon in the publishing industry. However, they've become a very common practice because agents and editors can take weeks, even months, to respond, and others don't respond at all. So it's rather unreasonable to expect writers to submit their materials exclusively to one market and wait indefinitely before trying another. Also, it's nearly impossible for an editor or agent to know if you have submitted your material simultaneously, and so the consequences are minimal to nonexistent.

But you do want to be professional, transparent, and fair. While it's not necessary in your query to state that you're simultaneously submitting—this is more or less assumed—you should make editors and agents aware when your manuscript is under consideration by multiple parties.

Here's the way this typically plays out. After you get a manuscript request from one professional, if there's a second request, you should let the second person know it's under consideration by another party. If either one asks for an exclusive—meaning they don't want you to send out the manuscript to anyone else while they read it—do not agree unless you put a very defined time period on it. One or two weeks is a reasonable length of time to grant an exclusive, and then when the period of exclusivity has ended, you should ask for an update, and make it clear you'll send the work out to other people who express interest.

Once you have any kind of offer on the table, always go back to the other people who are actively considering the work in manuscript or proposal form. Give them a final chance to express interest, then formally withdraw the work when it's off the market. A brief business letter, stating that you're withdrawing the submission, is all that's needed.

Another term you may come across is multiple submission, which refers to sending more than one story idea or manuscript for consideration at a time. Almost no market allows for this, and it should be strictly avoided. Only pitch one project per query. Even if you're hoping to write a series, pitch the first book, not the entire series. If your first query is rejected, it's okay to query for another if you have another, but the agent or editor will probably feel better about it if you give them a little breathing room. Usually, a few months is a comfortable window of time unless of course they specifically solicit other projects from you.

Some guidelines state that previously published work is not accepted, or that it must be entirely original. When referring to book manuscripts, this most often means that you shouldn't have self-published the work or otherwise widely distributed it to the public. Posting your work in online critique groups or private communities doesn't count as publication. Also, if an excerpt from your work was accepted for publication and appeared in a magazine or a collection, that's rarely a deterrent to an agent or publisher, and it can, in fact, help lead to a book deal.

This issue often leads us to the question of rights, and how to protect your unpublished work before submitting it to publishing professionals. Some writers are particularly concerned about how to prevent their work from being stolen. While I'm not an attorney, years of experience in publishing have shown me that writers can be overly anxious and unnecessarily paranoid, and don't have a clear understanding of the rights to their work that they already own. Plus many warnings you might run across are unnecessary and counterproductive. So my goal here in discussing your rights as an unpublished author is to give you information based on the actual likelihood that something bad will happen to you.

First, a quick side note. The following advice is directed toward writers of prose and poetry. If you are a scriptwriter or a playwright, your situation is slightly different, and you should refer to the Writers Guild of America for an understanding of the landscape.

I'll break down the rights issue in three ways. First, we'll discuss how to protect your ideas, followed by how to protect your unpublished writing, and then your published writing.

It's not possible under current U.S. law to copyright or protect an idea. You also can't copyright a title. So how much precaution should you take to keep your ideas secret? Very little. I guarantee that others have similar ideas and you see it happen all the time in business. Chalk it up to the cultural zeitgeist. While I don't advocate advertising your idea on billboards, or putting flashing lights around it on your website, the chances that an agent, editor, or other stranger will steal your idea, execute your idea better than you, and be able to sell it are next to zero. In other words, it's not worth worrying about.

Share your work with trusted advisers, send it to agents and editors for consideration, and talk about aspects of it when you're networking at conferences. Unless you're known in the industry for coming up with million-dollar salable concepts, it's not likely you'll experience idea theft. In the rare event that idea theft does happen, other people cannot possibly execute or interpret your idea in the same way you can. No one can be you, and that is your best protection of all.

No matter how valuable you think your idea is, don't tell an editor or agent that you can't disclose the full details until they sign a nondisclosure agreement. You will not find any person in publishing who will sign an agreement. They'll also be forced to reject your work if you withhold information that would help them make a decision about whether or not to do business with you. Therefore, be clear and upfront about every aspect of your project. Don't expect anyone to go out of their way and create a special business agreement with you because you're nervous about idea theft.

When it comes to protecting the actual writing itself—such as your unpublished manuscript—you don't have to officially register it with the U.S. Copyright Office for it to be protected under the law. As the law is currently written, as soon as you express your work in tangible form, it is protected. However, you would need to register the work if you ever discovered infringement and wished to sue.

It's also not necessary to put the copyright symbol on your work for it to be protected under U.S. copyright law. There's some amount of confusion about this because it, in fact, used to be a requirement, but it's not a requirement any longer. When you send your work to agents and editors, they know your work is automatically protected under the law and they don't need the copyright notice to remind them. Whether you consider it useful or necessary is up to you, but the copyright notice isn't typically needed unless your work is circulating in an environment where its ownership would be in question.

So, if you prefer to be extra cautious, and you're worried about theft, does it make sense to register your work with the U.S. Copyright Office? Let's review the series of events that have to happen for a lawsuit against infringement to make sense. First, someone must steal your work. Then it would have be developed, packaged, and made desirable for someone to pay for it. The work will have to be discovered in what's a very competitive market. Meanwhile, the person who did the stealing needs to keep a low-enough profile that infringement is not detected, while still making enough money to make the venture worthwhile.

The bigger point here is that most people don't view unpublished writing as an untapped gold mine. It's a lot of hard work to profit from a piece of writing, especially writing from an unknown writer. Therefore, the threat of infringement is very low when you're submitting to already very busy agents and editors. However, if you self-publish your work or begin distributing it publicly, then you should officially register it with the U.S. Copyright Office.

When you begin seeking publication, what you're essentially doing is offering publishers limited-time rights to your work. But here's the important distinction: You are rarely offering them all rights or your copyright. Authors keep copyright to their work, then grant publishers or others permission to exploit those rights on their behalf. In a publishers' submission guidelines, they often indicate at the outset what rights they expect to receive as part of a contract or deal. Assuming you haven't granted rights to any other party, and this is the case with nearly all unpublished work, then you own full rights and can grant them selectively to anyone you choose.

If some portion of your work has been previously published, then you need to be clear about that upfront. This is often the case if you're trying to sell a collection of your essays, columns, or poetry. But novels, memoirs, or other nonfiction books sometimes have portions previously published as well. This is rarely a problem, but you have to look at the publication contract you signed to be sure. When you publish short works, the publication generally takes one-time publication rights that are exclusive for a brief period of time, and you continue to have rights to that work afterward. Whatever your situation, to avoid any surprises, make it clear in your query or proposal that portions of the work are previously published and offer details on where it appeared.

Another area where you need to exercise caution is when pitching a work that includes significant material from someone else's published work. For instance, if you want to publish a collection of other people's writing or a collection of quotations, you quickly run into permissions issues. And this is where we'll need to slow down and explain one of the trickiest areas of copyright law.

Whenever you quote or excerpt other people's copyrighted work within your own, the most important question to address is: Does my use of this work fall under fair use?

There are four criteria for determining fair use, which sounds tidy, but it's not. These criteria are vague and open to interpretation. Ultimately, when disagreement arises over what constitutes fair use, it's up to the courts to make a decision. Let's discuss these criteria.

First, there's the purpose and character of the use. For instance, is your use commercial or educational? If your material will be sold in a book, then your use is commercial, but that doesn't mean you're suddenly in violation of fair use. It does make your case less sympathetic if you're borrowing a lot of someone else's work to prop up your own commercial venture.

Second, what's the nature of the copyrighted work? Facts cannot be copyrighted. For that reason, more creative or imaginative works generally get the strongest protection.

Third, what is the amount and substantiality of the portion used in relation to the entire quoted work? The law does not offer any percentage or word count here that we can go by. That's because if the portion quoted is considered the most valuable part of the work, you may be violating fair use.

Finally, what's the effect of the use on the potential market for, or value of, the quoted work? If your use of the original work damages the likelihood that people will buy the original, you're in violation of fair use. It's important to understand that when we talk about damaging the likelihood people will buy the original work, this isn't referring to negative reviews or criticism, but quoting the work in such a way that the original work would no longer need to be purchased.

For understandable reasons, you may search for a black-and-white rule to apply to figure out whether your use is fair. But determining whether your use is fair falls into one of the grayest areas of copyright law. Still, if you're searching for one or asking around, the biggest rule that you'll find is: Ask explicit permission for everything beyond X. What constitutes X depends on whom you ask. Some people say 300 words. Some say one line. Some say 10 percent of the total word count.

But you must never forget, there is no legal rule stipulating what quantity is okay to use without seeking permission. Major legal battles have been fought over this question, and there is still no black-and-white rule. Any rules you find are based on a general institutional guideline or a person's experience, as well as their overall comfort level with the risk involved in directly quoting or excerpting work. This is why opinions and guidelines vary so much.

The other problem is that once you start asking for permission to reduce your risk that gives publishers or copyright owners the opportunity to ask for money or refuse to give permission, even in cases where the use would actually be considered fair. So you can get taken advantage of if you're overly cautious. It's really a catch-22.

So, bottom line, there are no rules you can apply, only principles. To be 100 percent safe and eliminate all risk, whenever you quote someone else's work within your own, contact the copyright owner of the work—usually through the publisher or the agent—and request permission to use that work.

There are some areas that are black-and-white where you don't need permission. For instance when the work is in the public domain, you don't need to ask permission. Any published or distributed material on which a copyright has expired is considered to be in the public domain, which means it's available for use by any member of the general public without payment to, or permission from, the original author. Whether something falls in the public domain isn't always a simple matter to determine, but any work published before 1923 is definitely in the public domain. Some works published after 1923 are also in the public domain, although the situations and laws surrounding this are very complex.

When you are stating unadorned facts, you don't need permission. If you copy a list of the 50 states in the United States, you are not infringing on anyone's copyright. Those are plain facts.

It's also completely acceptable to mention book titles or authors of other works. You don't need permission to do so because it's kind of like citing a fact. It's also okay to mention things like song titles, movie titles, TV show titles, really any kind of title, in your own work. You can also include the names of places, things, events, and people in your work without asking permission. Again, these are facts.

When a work is licensed under Creative Commons, you may not need permission. You'll know something is licensed under Creative Commons because it's prominently declared on the work itself. For instance, the book *Mediactive* by Dan Gillmor is licensed under Creative Commons, and so are many websites and blogs.

It's very important to remember that when you use copyrighted material in such a way that it cannot be considered fair use, crediting the source doesn't remove the obligation to seek permission. It's expected that you always credit your source regardless of fair use, otherwise, you're plagiarizing.

Finally, because it's so often done by authors of all kinds, be careful when quoting song lyrics or poems in your work, even if they're just used as chapter openers. Because songs and poems are so short, it's dangerous to use even one line without asking for permission, even if you think the use could be considered fair.

While you don't need to seek out permissions prior to submitting your work to agents and publishers, any work you produce that is driven by, or heavily relies on, other people's work could be summarily rejected because of the headache and the expense involved in securing rights.

Before we leave the topic of submissions and publishing etiquette, I want to address one of the more subtle psychological aspects of the process. Writers who are new to the industry, but have very successful careers in their own fields, are often frustrated by the very impersonal nature of submitting their work, and the inability to get any agent or editor to give them the time of day. I get a lot of questions that amount to: How can I avoid the slush pile? Or, how can I get more than 20 or 30 seconds of consideration?

Well, just by virtue of having something to sell that no one has asked for, you can't avoid the slush pile. But it is possible to get approached by an agent or editor and sidestep this entire process.

The most common way is to get your work published somewhere that agents and editors scout for talent. For instance, *Writer's Digest* magazine often includes articles that identify the most popular outlets that agents read. The "Modern Love" column in the *New York Times* is one of these outlets, where it's common for featured writers to then get a book deal. Writer Heather Sellers landed a book deal for a memoir after publishing an essay in *Oprah* magazine about her 100 coffee dates to find true love.

Another variation on this is to get media coverage in a mainstream publication. This can be on a large or small scale, but of course, the bigger the publication covering you, the more likely you'll have agents and editors calling. The blog-turned-book-turned-movie *Julie & Julia* is a classic example of someone being featured in the *New York Times*, and then landing a publishing deal. This is, in fact, the dream for a lot of writers who start blogging or otherwise participate in social media. You're basically banking on your ability to develop a story or an experience so powerful that it attracts media attention, almost without it being solicited. This typically requires either charm or an idea or presence that's very compelling.

The paradoxical thing about being proactively approached by an editor or agent is that they're mostly drawn to people who could not care less about them. Here, it's useful to consider the dating analogy. The most confident person in the room tends to draw the most attention while the ones who beg for attention rarely get it.

I don't think it's really advisable to sit around hoping someone else will notice your brilliance. It doesn't happen that often, and a proactive writer always learns how to pitch herself effectively. Still, there's considerable power in having a community and network of relationships that can come to your aid when you need it, and that could potentially help you bypass the cold query process.

In some groups or communities, there's a strong tradition of giving back to others who are new writers and still getting established. I hear from many writers that their success couldn't have been possible without the tough love or generosity of an important mentor. Also being online and active in social networks opens up more opportunities and chances to meet the right person who can help you.

Not everyone is going to have community-building and networking strengths. But every writer should consider at least one or two ways they can build a support network, become active in a community of like-minded writers, or find a mentor. Getting published is much easier when you know a few people who have the distance, experience, and savvy to tell you how to navigate the industry, and in the next lecture, we'll talk about how you can begin building that network.

Networking: From Writers' Conferences to Courses
Lecture 12

Anyone with an established career knows the role that relationships can play in growth and success. Opportunities often come from the connections you already have in place, rather than from strangers outside your network. Although it's possible to secure an agent or publisher as a relative unknown who isn't involved in the larger writing community, you can shorten your learning curve and enjoy yourself more if you reach out to other writers and professionals during both the writing and the submission process. Even if you don't live in an urban area known for writing and publishing, you can still build valuable connections through online forums, writers' organizations, and conferences. We'll discuss all these networking venues in this lecture.

Conferences and Retreats

- Hundreds if not thousands of writing conferences are held every year in the United States. Some have been run for decades and have a strong tradition of nurturing new writing talent. Although conferences vary widely in their programming and attendance, there are three key reasons to attend one:

  o First, your education and insight into the industry will advance exponentially.

  o Second, a conference can give you clarity about the next steps in your writing career.

  o Third, conferences give you an opportunity to connect with a peer group and find people who can become trusted mentors after the events are over.

- Some conferences are craft-focused, while others are business-focused. Until you have a finished manuscript and are in a position to actively pitch, it's better to attend craft-focused conferences. That

216

way, you can spot potential weaknesses in your work and improve it before you submit.

- Your chances of making close contact with speakers can be greater at a small conference, but large conferences often feature famous authors, agents, and editors as speakers. Determine what's important to you: intimate interactions with a small group or a wide cast of speakers and choices with less personal treatment.

- If you feel confident that your work is ready to submit, then a conference may be the perfect way to sidestep part of the cold-query process. Most conferences offer individual consultations with speakers, editors, or agents, either as part of the registration fee or for an additional fee. Usually, such personal feedback must be scheduled ahead of time, especially if it includes a manuscript critique. When setting up a consultation or appointment, make sure you select the most appropriate agent or editor for your work.

Make sure to attend both formal and informal conference events; even if you don't get to talk to a speaker, you can learn a great deal by just listening to others at lunch.

- Even if you're not pitching, always closely study the background of every speaker, author, agent, and editor who will attend the conference. Having this knowledge may spark questions to ask during panels or social hours.

- During a conference, avoid asking speakers, editors, or agents for favors outright. It's not good etiquette to ask someone to read your manuscript for free or to insist on a referral. It's also not polite to pitch your work outside of the formal appointment times.

- In case you feel at a loss during any conversation at a conference, here are two questions to either spark a good conversation or get one back on track. These questions are inspired by author Michael Ellsberg, who recommends you use them at any gathering to help grow your network.
  - The first question is: What's most exciting for you right now? The second is: What's challenging for you right now?

  - These questions often bring to light information or experiences that help you better understand the life or business of the person you're talking to, while indicating areas where you might be useful.

- Before making a big investment in attending an event, compare the success of the speakers to the success you want to achieve. There should be some commonality there. If possible, ask past attendees about the strengths and weaknesses of the event and whether they felt it was helpful.

- Some people who start out by attending conferences soon discover the value of writer's colonies or retreats. These are places that allow you to write, uninterrupted, for hours each day. Although every colony is slightly different, all provide a private atmosphere meant to encourage writing and the opportunity to interact with other writers, if you desire it. Some colonies have a formal application process that requires writing samples and recommendations, and getting accepted can be a major credit on your bio.

Writers' Organizations

- Many writers find that membership in one of the major writing organizations can be an important component of their professional network. The largest and most active organizations are affiliated with specific genres. They include: the Society of Children's Book Writers and Illustrators (SCBWI), the Romance Writers of America (RWA), the Mystery Writers of America (MWA), and the Science Fiction and Fantasy Writers of America (SFWA).

- In addition to national offices, these organizations have regional chapters that meet regularly. They host annual conferences, offer awards, and produce member magazines and newsletters. If you write in a specific genre, these organizations can be essential to getting focused, in-depth information that isn't known or discussed elsewhere.

- You'll also find a range of state writers' associations with active regional chapters, which are better suited to writers who aren't affiliated with a specific genre. Also look for literary nonprofits that focus on serving writers and the broader reading community. For example, The Loft Literary Center in Minneapolis and GrubStreet in Boston are both successful nonprofit organizations that offer affordable writing classes, bring in speakers, and host community events focused on writing and literature.

- Finally, the Authors Guild is a national professional organization of book and magazine writers. To become a member, you must meet certain publication requirements. The guild is involved in such issues as free speech, copyright, and taxes and represents the interests of writers in Congress and in the courts. Of particular interest to beginning writers, the organization also provides information on standard book and magazine contracts.

Continuing Education in Writing

- Most creative writers will tell you that experience or practice in the art trumps education. However, academic creative writing programs can be valuable because they give you time and space to focus on your writing, and they include regular criticism from professors and peers. Keep in mind, though, that such programs are concerned with the art of writing, not the business.

- Low-residency M.F.A. programs in creative writing are targeted at people who are unable or unwilling to return to school full-time. Instead of attending conventional classes, in these programs, you complete most of your work remotely, in collaboration with professors. Then, you occasionally travel to campus for brief onsite residencies, where you work in-person with professors and other students.

- Because any type of degree program can be expensive, the practical choice for many writers is to invest in local or online writing classes. Look for instructors who have experience helping writers produce publishable work and for courses that offer frequent, detailed critiques of your work, not just lectures or general evaluations.

- The advantage of online classes is flexibility and choice, but probably the most important quality of any class, regardless of environment, is that it pushes you to produce work on a deadline. Sometimes, without that external pressure, it can be difficult to make time to write.

Critique Groups

- A *critique group* is generally made up of three or four writers who provide one another with constructive feedback. Because these groups vary widely in their discipline and focus, you should look for one that shares your values and goals, whether getting published, getting critiqued, or just getting out of the house.

- One danger of critique groups is that when you're working with people at the same level as you, a group discussion may feel like the blind leading the blind. Some members may have particular pet peeves or even bad judgment when it comes to offering feedback. To make sure your group remains constructive and helpful, you might find it useful to adopt the *Lerman method* for offering feedback.

- First, make a specific statement about something you found meaningful or exciting in the work. Beginning with positives is important because writers are often unconscious of what they're doing well.

- Next, allow questions from the writer. This begins a dialogue that supports the writer in solving problems independently.

- The third step is to allow group members to ask questions. This lets the writer know where readers need additional information.

- The final step is a discussion of group members' opinions about what should happen next in the book or how it should be revised.

- If you can't find a good critique group by attending conferences or classes, try seeking out critiques through online forums and communities.

Online Resources

- Of course, there are innumerable online resources available to writers, both from professional sources and from more informal blogs and message boards. Some of these are legitimate and useful, and others have little to no value; the worst are scams. As a general rule, you can trust the recommendations for online resources that come from respected writing publications, such as *Writer's Digest*, *The Writer*, *Poets and Writers*, and *The Chronicle* (published by the Association of Writers and Writing Programs [AWP]).

- As mentioned earlier, Writer Beware is an important online hub for writers who have concerns about any publisher, service, or organization in the writing community. *The Independent Publishing Magazine* by Mick Rooney is a website that regularly reviews and discusses new self-publishing and digital services for writers. It's one of the rare resources that is comprehensive and objective about this sector of the industry.

- For writers actively writing and submitting shorter works or entering contests, Submittable is the industry-wide standard online submissions system. If you're in the literary publishing community, you'll likely end up establishing a Submittable account and using it as a dashboard to check on the status of your submissions. Submittable also runs a site called Submishmash, which attempts to present all the potential creative opportunities available for writers and artists.

- Finally, especially for young fiction writers, Wattpad is becoming one of the most popular community sites for posting writing in serialized form and starting to build a readership. Even major publishers have started partnering with Wattpad to discover and publish new talent found at the site.

Suggested Reading

Levine, *The Writing and Critique Group Survival Guide*.

May, *The Low-Residency MFA Handbook*.

Exercises

1. Visit Shaw Guides and search for writing conferences and workshops in your region.

2. If you write in a specific genre, identify the closest regional chapter of that genre's writing organization and find out when and where its regular meetings are held. If your genre doesn't have a national organization or chapters, see if your city or state has a nonprofit writers' center or organization.

Networking: From Writers' Conferences to Courses
Lecture 12—Transcript

Anyone with an established career knows the role that relationships can play in your growth and success. Future jobs and opportunities often come from the connections you already have in place, rather than from strangers outside your network.

While it's possible to secure an agent or a publisher as a total unknown, without ever getting involved in the larger writing community, I don't recommend it. You can shorten your learning curve and enjoy yourself so much more if you reach out to other writers and professionals during both the writing and the submissions process. Even if you're not living in an urban area known for writing and publishing, such as New York or Los Angeles, you can still build valuable connections through online forums, writers' organizations, and conferences. Let's discuss writing conferences first, since they represent a common first step in meeting people in the publishing community.

There are hundreds, if not thousands, of writing conferences held every year in the United States. Some have been run for decades and have a strong tradition of nurturing new writing talent. The free website Shaw Guides offers an extensive searchable database of upcoming writing conferences. It's possible to limit your conference search by location and by genre, as well as many other factors. This will give you a good idea of the diversity of offerings out there.

While conferences vary widely in their programming and attendance, there are three key reasons to attend one.

First, your education and insight into the industry will advance exponentially. You'll gain an understanding about publishing that's often impossible to get from just reading or hearing about it. Many events put you in direct contact with agents and editors, with opportunities to get immediate feedback on your work.

Second, a conference can offer clarity about your next steps in your writing career. You'll get time away to focus on your work, something that can be hard to achieve if you have a lot of commitments at home.

Finally, you have an opportunity to connect with a peer group, and find people who can be mentors or trusted critique partners long after the conference is over. Some writers—and this includes myself—develop life-long professional relationships with people they meet at conferences.

Now you might be familiar with the reasons to attend conferences, but you might not know how to get the most out of them. Here's how.

Some conferences are craft-focused, while others are business-focused. Until you have a finished manuscript and you're in a position to actively pitch, it's better to attend craft-focused conferences. That way you can spot potential weaknesses in your work and improve it before you submit. You don't want to find out after several months of querying that you broke several cardinal rules in your first pages; or that your protagonist isn't old enough for that YA novel you're writing.

Your chances of an up-close contact with speakers can be better at a small conference, but large conferences can feature famous authors, agents, and editors. Decide what's important to you—intimate interactions with a small group, or a wide cast of speakers with potentially less personal treatment. It can be helpful to know how many people attend an average session or workshop than the total conference attendance number. You'll have a greater chance to ask questions or discuss your work with the instructor if the session sizes are small.

Some large conferences offer intensive workshops by well-known writers or professionals with limited enrollment, which may happen before or after the official event. These opportunities may even be limited to those selected by the instructor, which usually turn out to be the highest-quality experiences.

If you feel confident your work is polished and ready to submit, then a conference is the perfect way to sidestep part of the cold query process. Most conferences offer appointments with speakers, editors, or agents, either as part of the registration fee or for an additional fee. Such personal feedback must usually be scheduled ahead of time, especially if it includes a manuscript critique. If you're paying for an appointment, you should have clarity on what type of materials you should take or shouldn't take to the meeting, so ask the conference organizers if you're unsure. However, don't expect to attend a conference and walk away with a publishing deal. Overnight success stories like that are mostly fantasy.

When setting up an appointment, it's obviously important that you select the most appropriate agent or editor for your work. The responsibility to make the choice is on you. The conferences do not act as matchmakers. So do your research upfront and don't pitch to someone who's not appropriate for your work. In the next lecture, we'll discuss the art of the pitch, and how to make the most of the opportunity.

Even if you're not pitching, always study the background of every speaker, author, agent, and editor who's attending. Be knowledgeable for any chance conversations you have. Being armed with this knowledge up front will spark questions or conversations during panels or social hours. Try not to be that person who asks the obvious question you could've figured out by simply paying attention to the program. Delve deeper. The better questions you ask, the more you'll learn, and the more quality and helpful responses you'll get.

The most important thing to bring with you to a writers' conference is an open and alert mind, ready and willing to listen and learn. Aside from that, take advantage of everything the conference has to offer. Attend all the informal events as well as the structured ones. You may learn as much at lunch as you do at a half-day workshop, because the best shop talk always happens at meal time. Even if you don't get to talk to a speaker, you'll learn a lot just by staying in the circle and listening.

Now that we've covered what you should do, let's cover some things to avoid. Avoid asking outright for favors from speakers, editors, or agents. It's not good etiquette to ask someone to read your manuscript for free, or to insist on a referral if they say no to your work. It's also not polite to pitch your work outside of the formal appointment times. It's better for everyone if agents and editors feel they can freely socialize with writers without feeling pressured. Even if a conversation seems to be going well, don't give any of your materials to agents or editors. Most likely, you'll be putting them in an awkward position where they either have to politely decline or pretend to be interested. The same goes for handing over a copy of your self-published book.

To put it another way, when you enter a conference environment, don't forget everything you know about good social etiquette. Follow the same rules you would follow on any social occasion—don't monopolize the conversation, don't assume familiarity that's not there, and don't speak only about yourself and your work. Whether arising from anxiety, frustration, or simply a sense of urgency, writers can break these rules a little too often at conferences.

If you feel at a loss during any conversation at a conference, then here are two questions to either spark a good conversation or get one back on track. These questions are inspired by author Michael Ellsberg, who recommends you put them to use at all types of events to help grow your network. The first question is What's most exciting for you right now? The second question is What's challenging for you right now?

Why are these questions so useful? They often bring to light information or experiences that help you better understand the other person's life or business, while indicating areas where you might be useful to them. And that's one of the interesting secrets to networking—how can you be helpful to the person that you're talking to?

Now, perhaps it's stating the obvious, but not all conferences are created equal. Some can be disorganized. Others might have speakers with limited experience or expertise. Before you make a big investment in any event, compare the success of the speakers to the success you want to achieve. There should be some commonality there. If possible, speak to past attendees. What were the strengths and weaknesses of the event? How did the event help them?

There are some types of events that you may want to return to. In fact, some writers are devoted attendees of specific conferences and participate every year. This is particularly true of the large annual events held by major professional writing organizations, which we'll discuss next. However, be careful not to let the conferences become the primary facet of your writing life. While conferences present a unique opportunity to connect with professionals and make important creative discoveries, don't make a career out of attending them. If you find yourself attending the same conference every year, pitching the exact same work in the hopes that this time you'll get a different response, you may be clinging to one project instead of making progress.

Which brings us to another type of valuable writing event. Some people who start out by attending conferences soon discover the value of writer's colonies and retreats. These are places that allow you to write, uninterrupted, for hours each day. Though every colony is slightly different, all provide a focused and quiet atmosphere meant to encourage writing. You'll also have the opportunity to interact and discuss your work with other writers, if you desire it. The cost of a stay at a writer's colony varies greatly—some are free, while others offer scholarships or charge a weekly or seasonal rate. Some colonies have a formal application process that requires writing samples and recommendations. Getting accepted into one of them can then become a major credit on your bio.

In addition to attending conferences or retreats, you'll find that membership in one of the major writing organizations can be an important component of your professional network. The largest and most active organizations are affiliated with specific genres. They include: The Society of Children's Book Writers and Illustrators (SCBWI); The Romance Writers of America (RWA); The Mystery Writers of America (MWA); The Science Fiction and Fantasy Writers of America (SFWA).

These organizations have national offices and leadership, but also regional chapters that meet on a regular basis. They host annual conferences, offer awards to recognize achievement in the community, and produce member magazines and newsletters. If you write in a specific genre, these organizations can be essential to getting focused and in-depth information that isn't really known or discussed elsewhere.

You'll also find a range of state writers' associations with active regional chapters. These organizations are better suited to writers who aren't affiliated with a specific genre. Also look for literary nonprofits that focus on serving writers and the broader literary community. For example, The Loft in Minneapolis and Grub Street in Boston are both very successful nonprofit organizations that offer affordable writing classes for members and non-members. They also bring in successful authors to speak, and offer community events focused on reading and literature.

Finally, you may have also heard of the Authors Guild. The Authors Guild is a national professional organization of book and magazine writers. To become a member, you have to meet certain publication requirements. The Guild is involved in such issues as free speech, copyright, and taxes, and they represent the interests of writers both in Congress and in the courts. Of particular interest to beginning writers, the organization also provides information on standard book and magazine contracts.

As you start to explore the networking opportunities in your area—and especially as you uncover the many different classes, workshops, and conferences available—you may wonder how much you should pursue a formal education in writing. While any kind of writing education is valuable, it's far from necessary or mandatory. Most creative writers will tell you that experience or practice trumps education. And much depends on your goals. Academic creative writing programs can be valuable because they give you time and space to focus on your writing. They include regular criticism and feedback from professors and peers, which can be critical for emerging writers to improve and grow.

On the other hand, the habits and rules learned in a university setting may have to be ignored if you want to produce a salable book. Such programs are concerned with the art and the craft, not the business. They're often better suited for writers who intend to teach writing for a living or otherwise continue to work within a university setting.

One significant exception to this is the low-residency MFA program in creative writing. These programs are targeted at people who are unable or unwilling to return to school full-time, and likely have full-time jobs and family commitments. Instead of living on campus and attending conventional classes, in a low-res MFA, you complete most of your work remotely, in collaboration with specific professors who offer feedback. Then, at particular times of year, you travel to campus for brief on-site residencies, when you work in-person with professors and other students.

A drawback to any type of MFA degree, whether full-time or low-residency, is the expense. You can very easily spend $20,000 per year, for a two year program, to earn an MFA. While some programs offer stipends, scholarships, and other types of financial support, be prepared to have a more spartan lifestyle unless you have significant savings to support your education.

But this all assumes you'll be accepted into an MFA program in the first place, and these programs are notorious for accepting a very small percentage of writers who apply. For those who are accepted and can afford it, an MFA degree from one of the top schools, such as Iowa or Columbia, does confer a distinct advantage, both in terms of your network of contacts, as well as when it comes time to pitch. Every agent or editor watches the graduates of the high-ranking programs because they may represent the next generation of top-shelf literary talent. Just remember the point I made earlier, commercial fiction—the type of book most often at the top of the bestseller lists—is not the type of work a typical MFA program accepts or trains you to write. Quite the opposite.

Therefore, the practical choice for most writers is to invest in local or online writing classes. Look for instructors who have experience helping writers produce publishable work. Someone with a sophisticated sense of story or narrative, combined with an understanding of what the industry looks for—that's ideal. While you may be tempted to look for the most well-published instructor, someone who has lots of credits and success, such a person might not necessarily be good in the classroom. You need someone who's expert at providing insightful feedback, and helping you understand your strengths and weaknesses. Look for courses that offer frequent detailed critiques of your work, and not just lectures or general evaluations.

Whether you should look for an in-person class or an online class is really driven by your own personality, skill level, and needs. The advantage of an online class is flexibility and choice—you can take a class from virtually any institution or any author who's offering. You get to work from home and still receive valuable feedback.

But probably the most important quality of any class, regardless of the environment, is that you're pushed to produce work on a deadline. Sometimes, without that external pressure—without knowing someone is waiting to review your work—it can be hard to make time to practice and produce writing on a schedule. Classes provide you the structure and incentive to do that. If you're not sure where to look first for classes, try browsing some of the well-known online education providers, such as Gotham Writers' Workshop, MediaBistro, and *Writer's Digest*.

Hopefully, as a result of participating in conferences and classes, you'll meet other writers who may end up becoming critique partners. A critique partner is someone you trust to review early drafts of your work and offer constructive feedback. Most critique partners work in the same genre and have similar skill levels. Once you reach three or four people who are trading work with one another, you have yourself a critique group.

There are probably more opinions on the value of critique groups than there are writers. That's because a group is only as valuable as the discipline and focus of its members. Some critique groups don't provide much more than an outlet for socializing, and sometimes the socializing can sound more like complaining. The key is to find a group that shares the same values and goals as you, whether it's getting published, getting critiqued, getting support, or just getting out of the house. Avoid those that do nothing other than sit around and gripe.

The other danger of critique groups is that when you're working with people at the same level as you, it may feel like it's the blind leading the blind. Some members may have particular pet peeves or even bad judgment when it comes to offering feedback. To make sure your group remains constructive and helpful, you might find it useful to adopt the following method I learned from another writer. It's called the Lerman Method, named after the choreographer Liz Lerman. It has four steps that should be followed in a strict order. This technique works for any sort of writing or critique process.

The first step is to say what you found meaningful or exciting in the work. It should be a specific statement of where or how the work got to you, and where you entered the world and it became real. For example, I loved that she threw up on him. I split my sides laughing.

Statements of meaning are helpful for writers at any stage of development. They're positive. You're talking about what grabbed you. Beginning with positives has nothing to do with politeness or sugarcoating bad news. Rather, it's important because writers are often unconscious of what they're doing well. Focused on the problems, they discount what comes easy. And that's a mistake, because what a writer does well is what she builds on.

A statement of meaning helps the critique focus on a person's response to the work, rather than their ideas. What you'll find is that people too often love to share their ideas, many of which you should just ignore.

The second step is to allow questions from the writer. This begins a dialogue that supports the writer in solving problems on her own. A writer might ask, did you find this scene or character believable? Or, was this scene confusing? Or, did you find the ending predictable?

Everyone in the group should directly answer the question, and avoid offering ideas or tinkering.

The third step is to allow the critique group members to ask the writer questions. Sometimes what's perfectly obvious to the writer is not obvious to anyone else. Now the writer gets to hear where he's left the reader in the lurch. Your readers might wonder what happened to a character who disappeared, or about the sequence of events. Group members might ask questions that have embedded opinions, if it helps the writer see the process of the reader's confusion. For example, that scene introduced more than five new characters to the story at once. I had a really hard time keeping track of them. Is that your intent?

The final step is a discussion of other people's ideas and opinions about what should happen next in your book or how you should revise. And usually the group has run totally out of time by this point. If not, the writer should suddenly find a reason to excuse herself.

Here are a few other suggestions to ensure that your group is successful.

Set a regular schedule and stick to it. Usually once or twice per month is the best frequency. Then set ground rules and follow them. What will the standard agenda be? How will all the members share work? How will it get distributed and who will distribute it? Does the work shared have to be new? What happens when a member doesn't show or isn't able to contribute?

Some writers would like to start a critique group, but don't know how to go about finding members. If you can't find anyone by attending conferences or classes, you can try seeking out critiques through online forums and communities. Some of the most popular venues are Book Country, Authonomy, and Scribophile. Basically, what happens on these sites are critique exchanges, but of course the quality of critique you receive will vary. You shouldn't worry about theft of your work in any of these communities, mainly because they're private and registration is mandatory. Plus your participation gets tracked and moderators are active.

This brings us to a discussion of the many online resources available to writers, both from professional sources as well as informal blogs and message boards. You could easily spend months, if not years, combing through the advice and networking opportunities available. Some of them are very legitimate and useful, and others have little to no value. The worst are scams. So, how can you tell the difference between a good opportunity and a bad one?

First, you can trust the recommendations of writing publications that have been in the business for decades. These include *Writer's Digest*, *The Writer*, *Poets & Writers*, and *The Chronicle*. Let's discuss each one and how they're different.

Writer's Digest is a for-profit publisher, established in 1920, that offers the most widely circulating how-to magazine for writers. They also publish instruction books and market guides, offer online education, and run annual conferences. And, full disclosure, I used to be the publisher. They regularly feature and discuss new opportunities for writers and point out the most credible and respectable resources in the business. Every year, they round up the 101 Best Websites for Writers, which is a good starting place to learn about valuable online communities and education.

Very similar to *Writer's Digest* is *The Writer*. It's a monthly magazine that was first established in 1887. It offers how-to information related to the craft and the business of writing. You can trust its recommendations and resource lists.

One of the more important nonprofits in the writing community is *Poets & Writers*. It produces a bimonthly magazine focused on the literary publishing community. Its audience is more slanted toward the MFA crowd, whereas *The Writer* and *Writer's Digest* are more focused on writers seeking commercial success. *Poets & Writers* maintains a database of opportunities for writers, especially lists of grants, residencies, and prizes for literary work.

Finally, the Association of Writers & Writing Programs, also known as the AWP, specifically serves the community of nearly 500 writing programs and by extension 50,000 writers in North America. They offer a bimonthly magazine called *The Chronicle* and have an annual conference that attracts more than 12,000 people. You'll find that all types of creative writing students and professors attend this conference, as well as literary magazines and presses, writing events and programs, and all sorts of people in the literary publishing community. If you're an AWP member, you can get special access to their mentorship program, job board, and opportunities for grants and awards.

These four resources represent the highest concentration of opportunities and resources you'll find, but it's still just scratching the surface of what's available. There are a few other important sites you should be aware of.

As we discussed earlier during our research of markets, Writer Beware is an important hub and service for writers who have concerns about any publisher, service, or organization in the writing community. Their site is one of the service arms of the SFWA, the professional organization for science fiction and fantasy writers.

The Independent Publishing Magazine by Mick Rooney is a website that regularly reviews and discusses new self-publishing and digital services for writers. It's one of the very rare resources that is comprehensive and objective about this sector of the industry.

For writers actively writing and submitting shorter works, or entering contests, Submittable is the industry-wide standard online submission system. If you're in the literary publishing community, you'll likely end up establishing a Submittable account and using it as a dashboard to check on the status of your submissions. Submittable also runs a site called Submishmash, which attempts to present all of the potential creative opportunities available for writers and artists.

Finally, especially for young fiction writers, Wattpad is becoming one of the most popular community sites for posting writing in serialized chunks and building a readership. Even major publishers have started partnering with Wattpad to discover and publish new talent found at the site.

Obviously we don't have time to discuss all of the excellent resources and communities out there. But as you explore what's available, and try to determine the worth of the site or blog in front of you, keep this in mind. Depth and nuance don't generate much online traffic. Playing to extremes, unfortunately does.

So, when you read writing advice online—or in any medium—keep this dynamic in mind. The people who talk about the contingencies, and who make allowances for differences—those are the ones to pay close attention to. The black-and-white advice—especially the kind of advice that tries to divide writers into separate groups—take it with a grain of salt.

Pitching Your Book
Lecture 13

As we discussed in the previous lecture, most writing conferences offer opportunities to meet with agents or editors one-on-one and pitch your work. Writers often experience the pitch as a highly intense, emotional, and personal process, but whenever engaging in a business conversation, it's important to have some distance and perspective. Authors who have a business or marketing background, for example, know that getting an idea shot down isn't personal, and they're more likely to be receptive to a conversation about the marketability of a project and alternative routes to success. As we'll see in this lecture, the best approach to a pitch is to try to view it as part of the business of being a writer.

Difficulties of the Pitch

- One of the most common difficulties writers have with pitches is that they may have little experience or practice in pitching. This means that they're nervous before the pitch meeting, and all that anxious energy detracts from the quality of the pitch. Some writers expect their heart and their passion for their work to carry the pitch, but unfortunately, feeling passionate doesn't always translate into a persuasive pitch. You have to know how to position and sell yourself, rather than stress your dedication to your work.

- In addition, some writers place too much importance on the pitch, treating it as the official verdict on whether an idea is worthy of further investment of time. The reality is that there's still a great deal of subjectivity at play in a pitch. Plus, in-person pitches have about the same success rate as a cold query, typically, less than 1 percent.
  - Because you are so focused on hearing a verdict about your work, you might miss out on the biggest benefit of the pitch experience: getting instant feedback on your project. The pitch is your chance to have a meaningful conversation with an industry insider about the market for your work. Such information can dramatically reduce future frustration and

shorten your path to publication.

Sometimes, just five minutes of insightful professional advice received during a pitch meeting can change your perspective, approach, or slant.

o Agents and editors remember those authors who demonstrate flexibility and openness to feedback during the pitch. Publishing professionals look for people they'd enjoy working with and those who are focused on long-term career growth and success. A writer who is too invested in a single project—seeking validation for a book that's the product of a decade of work—can be a red flag. It's a sign of a writer stagnating rather than growing.

Types of Pitches

- There are usually three types of pitches, the first of which is the pitch slam—the equivalent of pitch speed-dating. Here, several dozen agents and editors are available during a concentrated period of time, usually a few hours. Writers line up to speak with a specific agent or editor and get a few minutes to pitch their projects. Pitch slams are typically high-pressure environments, and you need to go in with your pitch memorized. If the agent or editor is interested, you'll be told how to follow up, usually by sending in your materials after the event.

  o You probably shouldn't participate in a pitch slam unless you have submission-ready material—a completed, polished manuscript or book proposal ready to go. It doesn't do you much good to get an invitation to send materials, then follow up 6 or 12 months later when the agent or editor has forgotten you. He or she may still review your materials, but any good impression you made won't work in your favor, and the original invitation might have been based on the timeliness of your idea.

- ○ Also, pitch slams don't offer enough time to have a solid conversation about the marketability of your work or your best path forward. If you're looking for a quick thumbs-up or thumbs-down on your work to assess its immediate marketability, the pitch slam is a good option. If you want professional feedback, you need to consider another type of pitch opportunity.

- A second type of pitch is a scheduled appointment; here, you get 10 to 20 minutes to sit down with an editor or agent and discuss your work. Sometimes, you have to pay extra for these opportunities, or you may get one free appointment with your conference registration fee. Keep in mind that these appointments are valuable only if you're able to select the person you'll meet with, which is almost always the case. Never meet with just any agent or editor; make sure you talk to someone who is actively looking for the type of work you have to offer or has experience editing, selling, or marketing work in your genre or category.

- Perhaps the most meaningful type of appointments are those that include advance review of your materials, such as your query letter and synopsis or even the first 5 to 10 pages of your book. This review gives the agent or editor a baseline understanding of your work before the appointment begins and relieves some of the pressure of explaining your work quickly.

- When you have a pitch appointment, plan to talk less than half the time. Before the meeting, develop a specific list of questions that if answered, would tell you specifically what your next steps are when you leave. Don't attend any appointment expecting to be offered a deal or representation. Go for the learning experience and the opportunity to have a professional consultation. Sometimes it's more valuable to know whether you're headed in the right direction than to succeed immediately with a pitch.

- Pitch appointments result in a high rate of requests for materials because most agents and editors find it easier to agree to look at your materials than to shoot down your dreams. However, most writers get rejected in a businesslike fashion after they submit their materials, just like those who cold query. Even worse, sometimes, there is no rejection at all—just silence. Remember that you have little control over how agents or editors respond after the fact. All you can control is your professionalism during the pitch and how you steer the conversation while you have the agent or editor's ear.

Weak and Strong Pitches: Fiction

- A writer who is nervous about a pitch may read directly from his or her query. This isn't always a bad thing, but you should have a fair amount of confidence in your query before reading it straight through. You won't be helped by a terrible query that includes extraneous detail or editorializing about the quality of your writing. And don't use the pitch as a time to talk about how your friends and family love your work. Just as you did in the query letter, leave out opinions that don't hold weight with a publishing professional.

- Another weak approach to a pitch is to go into mind-numbing detail about the plot and offer no information about the characters. As we've discussed, it's usually best to start with information about the protagonist, although there can be exceptions. For instance, with science fiction or fantasy, it's often necessary to establish a few details about the universe inhabited in the book. Still, be cautious about just relating facts, especially if your listener doesn't understand how they connect to the story.

  o If the agent or editor starts to ask a question about the story, don't interrupt. It's almost always better to find out what your listener is curious about and hear his or her perspective.

  o Not only does this help you understand how agents and editors think about stories, but it may also reveal how well your pitch is working.

- A strong pitch focuses on the main character and the character's problem. When it comes to a fiction, it's much easier to follow a pitch and remain interested when the agent or editor can connect to a character and immediately understand the problem or conflict facing that character. Why will the reader care? What are the stakes? This same approach could be used for a memoir or nonfiction narrative, as well.

- A good technique in pitching is to pause at a question or a moment of tension in your story and wait for the listener to ask for more. Rather, than talking endlessly (which can sometimes happen when you're nervous), remind yourself that you don't have to explain all the details.

- Try to stop just as you've established the key stakes or tension and wait for a reaction from your listener. Let the agent or editor guide the discussion; find out what might catch a reader's attention or what piece is missing. And if the agent or editor asks you to reveal the ending, then you should.

Weak and Strong Pitches: Nonfiction

- In a weak nonfiction pitch, a writer may not elucidate why his or her approach to the topic will be marketable. The agent or editor must have enough information to at least begin to see how a project will be salable. A weak nonfiction pitch may also fail to outline the credentials of the writer.

- Some writers may assume that having an active blog is sufficient to interest an agent or editor in a pitch meeting. However, no matter how well known your blog is, you still need to think through a viable book concept, something that seems competitive with similar titles on the shelves. A strong pitch needs to demonstrate that you have a compelling vision for your book, and especially with nonfiction, you must be able to succinctly and convincingly express tangible benefits to readers.

- In a successful nonfiction pitch, the conversation builds on questions related to the book's market. In particular, the writer must be prepared to address the biggest questions on the agent's mind: Who is the audience for the book? Why are you the best author for it? Why does anyone care what you have to say? Although the pitch meeting might not answer all these questions fully, a good starting answer could lead to a proposal or manuscript request.

The Breakout Feeling

- For all those writers who walk away disappointed from a pitch experience, remember that success is rarely attained in those 5 to 15 minutes. Rather, it comes from all the years of work leading up to that moment, along with the author's appearance of confidence and success—the feeling that he or she is on the verge of breaking out. There's really no way to fake that, and it's what agents and editors are ultimately looking for.

- People who have the breakout "vibe" look and feel prepared and demonstrate a kind of easy confidence that makes them a pleasure to talk to. They ask smart questions and demonstrate curiosity and engagement. Perhaps most important, they appear flexible but resilient when dealing with the business side of publishing. Agents and editors don't fear that something they say will hurt the feelings of these writers because they know they're dealing with professionals.

- When agents and editors meet you and feel as if they'd love to work with you, even if the project you're pitching isn't a good fit, then you're on your way to breaking out.

Suggested Reading

MacGregor, *Step by Step Pitches and Proposals.*

Sheer, *The Writer's Advantage.*

Exercises

1. Write your hook on an index card or a standard-size sticky note. Keep cutting the hook until it fits on one side of the paper. This is about the right length to start your pitch.

2. Practice your pitch until you can recite it on command. Try it out on at least one stranger before pitching an agent or editor.

Pitching Your Book
Lecture 13—Transcript

As we discussed in the previous lecture, most writing conferences offer opportunities to meet with agents or editors one-on-one and pitch your work. I've attended several hundred conferences over the course of my career, and listened to hundreds if not thousands of pitches. While it's important for writers to get out there and interact with professionals and understand how to pitch their work, I also think pitching can be a very difficult process. Here's why.

First, you may have little experience or practice in pitching. This means you may walk into the pitch meeting unbelievably nervous and anxious. All of that anxious energy usually detracts from the quality of the pitch. So many writers who pitch to me fill in the first few minutes with apologies for being nervous. Plus they're not sure what to do, or what to say. Some writers expect their heart and their passion for their book to carry the pitch. Sometimes this works, and sometimes not.

Unfortunately, feeling passionate about your work doesn't always translate into a persuasive pitch. You have to know how to position and sell yourself, rather than stress your dedication to your work. Dedication is often assumed; salability is not.

Second, you may consider the pitch a make-it-or-break-it moment. Some writers place too much importance on that pitch, treating it as if it's the official verdict on whether their idea is worthy of further investment of time. The reality is there's still a lot of subjectivity at play. Plus, in-person pitches have about the same success rate as a cold query, less than one percent typically.

But because you're so focused on this mythic opportunity—and hearing that yes or no verdict—you might miss out on the biggest benefit of the pitch experience—getting instant feedback on your project. This is your chance to have a meaningful conversation with an industry insider about the market for your work. Such information can dramatically reduce future frustration and shorten your path to publication. Sometimes just five minutes of very insightful professional advice can change your perspective, approach, or slant.

Furthermore, if you demonstrate flexibility and openness to feedback during the pitch, the agent or editor will remember that. In today's publishing environment, agents and editors look for people they'd enjoy working with, who are focused on long-term career growth and success. A writer who's too invested in a single project, and seeks validation for a book they've worked on for a decade or more—that can be a red flag. It's a sign of a writer stagnating rather than growing.

Writers often experience the pitch as a highly intense, emotional, and personal process. But whenever engaging in a business conversation—which is what a pitch is—it's important to have some distance and perspective. That's why I find it's usually a pleasure to be pitched by authors who have a business or marketing background. They know that getting an idea shot down isn't personal, and they're more likely to be receptive to a conversation about the marketability of a project and alternative routes to success. To the best of your ability, try to approach the pitch process as part of the business of being a writer.

And to that end, you need to be very diligent in assessing the different varieties of pitch opportunities out there, and pick the one that's right for you given where you're at on the path to publication. There are usually three types of pitches.

One is the pitch slam or speed-dating pitch. This is where several dozen agents and editors are available during a very concentrated period of time, usually a few hours. Writers line up to speak with the agent or editor of choice, and they get a few minutes to pitch their project. As you might imagine, pitch slams are typically high-pressure environments, and you need to go in with your pitch memorized. If the agent or editor is interested, they'll tell you how to follow up, usually by e-mailing or snail mailing your materials after the event.

I don't recommend participating in pitch slams unless you have submission-ready material—a completed, polished manuscript or book proposal ready to go. It doesn't do you much good to get an invitation to send materials then follow up 6 or 12 months later, when the agent or editor may have forgotten all about you. They may still review your materials, but any good impression you made might not work in your favor, and their invitation might have been based on the timeliness of your idea.

Also, pitch slams don't offer enough time to have a solid conversation about the marketability of your work or your best path forward. At many writers' conferences writers have a fuzzy or misdirected goal or path, and no clear idea of how to make progress. If you're looking for a quick thumbs-up or thumbs-down on your work to assess its immediate marketability, the pitch slam is a good option. If you want professional feedback, you need to consider another type of pitch opportunity, such as the scheduled pitch appointment.

A scheduled pitch appointment is where you get a set 10–20 minutes to sit down with an editor or agent and discuss your work. Sometimes you have to pay extra for these opportunities, or you may get one free appointment with your conference registration fee. Regardless of how it's set up, these appointments are only valuable when you're able to select which person you want to meet with, which is almost always the case.

Never sit down to meet with just any agent or editor; make sure they're actively looking for the type of work you have to offer, or have experience editing, selling, or marketing work in your genre or category. This may seem like obvious advice, but every conference is full of writers who assume any agent or editor will do, rather than researching the best person to solicit feedback from.

Perhaps the most meaningful type of appointments are those that include advance review of your materials, such as your query letter and synopsis, or even the first 5–10 pages of your book. This way, the agent or editor has a baseline understanding of your work before the appointment begins. It relieves some of that pressure to pitch your work since it's already on paper.

Now, just because you have 10 minutes or more doesn't mean you've been gifted with time to talk about yourself and your project's background. That would be a critical mistake. No matter how long you have, keep what you say short. As with queries, brevity is your friend. It can take a mere 15 seconds to deliver a convincing storyline. The longer you talk, the less time the agent or editor is talking. And that's why you're meeting with them—to hear their feedback and reaction.

If you can be very disciplined, plan to talk less than half the time. Before the meeting, develop a specific list of questions that, if answered, would tell you specifically what your next steps are when you leave. Don't attend any appointment expecting to be offered a deal or representation. Go for the learning experience and the opportunity to have a professional consultation. Because that's what it is. Sometimes it's more valuable and important to know if you're headed in the right direction, rather than to succeed with a pitch. But I admit this mindset is tough to adopt. Education and course correction are not the dream. The dream is to get an agent or to get published.

Unfortunately, when you approach the pitch with so much of your personal life on the line, agents and editors—as human beings too—don't want to be the one to poke holes in your soul. They'll find it easier to say, "Sure, we'll take a look." And this is the dirty secret of pitch appointments—there's actually a very high rate of agents and editors requesting materials. Many writers compare notes with each other at conferences, to see how many manuscript requests they scored. But this number is ultimately meaningless.

Most writers, just like the ones who cold query, get rejected in business-like fashion upon submitting their materials after the pitch. Even worse, sometimes there's no rejection at all, just silence. Be prepared for this, no matter how well the pitch went. It's just how the business works, and you have little control over how agents or editors respond after the fact. All you can control is your professionalism during the pitch, and how you steer the conversation while you have the agent or editor's ear.

Now that we've covered the basics of pitch appointments and how to approach them, let's get more specific about what you should say during one. We're going to model both weak and strong approaches, depending on whether you're writing a novel or a nonfiction book.

First, let's look at a writer who's pitching a thriller.

Agent: Hello, nice to meet you.

Writer: Hi.

Agent: So, tell me what you've been working on.

Writer: Well, I've never done this before. Is it okay if I just read you my query?

Agent: Sure, go ahead.

Writer: Okay. My novel is titled *The Divinity Dilemma*, Part 1 of the Secret Symbols Series. For so long, we've believed what the church tells us, but there are secrets that they're hiding because they threaten their power. If we knew the real truth, the church would lose its power, money and influence.

Coming in at 188,000 words, *The Divinity Dilemma* is an action-packed thriller and more, with a relatable hero and a pretty companion who provides sexual tension.

Robert Langdon is a handsome Harvard professor who specializes in ancient symbols. He's a serious academic, but he also wears his childhood Mickey Mouse watch everywhere he goes. As a child he accidentally fell down a well and was trapped. As a result, he has claustrophobia, and that gets worked into the story too.

He's also suspected in a murder that he didn't commit. The police wake him up and take him to the Louvre, where the dead body is. The victim is a man Robert knows, who's also curator of the Louvre, and his body is laid out like an old Da Vinci painting—which is unexpected. The police suspect Robert, but he escapes from them with the help of the man's granddaughter.

What follows is a race against the clock across Europe, uncovering secrets and solving puzzles. The writing is compelling and each time there's a puzzle you're on the edge of your seat hoping it'll be solved in time. You also learn a lot about old artists and paintings, and think about them in a different way. They go to England too.

I don't want to give away the ending, but they found out something about Jesus that will blow the reader's mind. My cousin's wife used to be an editor, she read the book and just couldn't believe it.

In this scenario, the writer is reading straight from their query. This isn't always a bad thing, but you should have a fair amount of confidence in your query before reading it straight through. Unfortunately, our writer has written a terrible query, and spends a lot of time during the pitch on details we don't need to know.

First of all, the writer spends too much time upfront discussing the themes and ideas of the story, rather than focusing on the protagonist and the conflict. He also editorializes in his pitch when he talks about it being an action-packed thriller—

Writer: You're on the edge of your seat hoping it'll be solved in time.

—with a relatable hero and that the writing is compelling. This rarely helps. As much as you can, show the qualities of the story through the details you include in the pitch, rather than trying to convince us how the story will make us feel.

You should also avoid sharing details that feel out of place in the short pitch. Even though it can be intriguing in the novel itself to know Langdon's backstory about falling into a well, it's unnecessary here and makes the pitch feel unfocused.

Writer: He's a serious academic but he also wears his childhood Mickey Mouse watch everywhere he goes.

The detail about the Mickey Mouse watch can be an interesting point of characterization, but again in the pitch, it's not grounded or relevant to anything else we're told. So, it's better to leave it out.

Finally, the pitch is also not a great time to talk about how your friends and family love your work. Just like the query letter, leave out opinions that aren't going to hold any weight with a publishing professional.

Agent: Hello, nice to meet you.

Writer: Hi.

Agent: So, tell me what you're working on.

Writer: Did you know that there's an obscure but incredibly well-funded sect of the Catholic Church that adheres to bizarre and sometimes violent practices? And that they're headquartered in an expensive Manhattan high-rise, hidden in plain sight?

Agent: No—

Writer: And that there are ancient pagan symbols—related to worship of nature and the sacred feminine—that still exist in our culture, but for centuries the church has misrepresented those symbols to us as demonic in order to cast them in a negative light; and maintain patriarchy, paternalism, and their position as the only true path to salvation?

Agent: Well—

Writer: And that for almost a thousand years some of history's best-known thinkers—artists, writers, scientists—were members of a secret society, and throughout their work are peppered clues to an earth-shattering and subversive truth?

Agent: If I could—

Writer: Hold on, I haven't gotten to the Fibonacci sequence.

In this pitch, the writer starts by going into mind-numbing detail about the plot and offers no information about the characters. As we've discussed, it's usually best to start with information about the protagonist, although there can be exceptions. For instance, with science fiction or fantasy, it's often necessary to establish a few details about the universe we'll be inhabiting. Still, be cautious about relating a bunch of facts especially if we don't understand how they relate to the story.

If the agent starts to ask a question about the story, avoid interrupting them.

Agent: If I could—

Writer: Hold on, I haven't gotten to the Fibonacci sequence.

It's almost always better to find out what they're curious about and listen to their perspective. This helps you not only understand how agents and editors think about stories, but also tells you how well your pitch is working.

Whether this pitch is better than the previous one depends on your perspective. The writer poses some intriguing questions that might spark the agent's curiosity, but without any knowledge of the protagonist or the conflict, this comes across as a nonfiction pitch rather than a novel pitch.

Agent: Hello, nice to meet you.

Writer: Hi, I was so excited to see you'd be at this conference. Your panel earlier today was excellent. I can't wait to read that new book you mentioned.

Agent: Well, thank you. Yes, that book is fabulous. I'm really excited for my client. So, tell me what you've been working on.

Writer: I've just completed a 190,000-word thriller. It's called *The Da Vinci Code*. The story opens up with academic Robert Langdon who's on business in Paris. He's an expert in the symbols of the ancient world. He's summoned to the scene of a grisly murder in the Louvre. Turns out Langdon is the main suspect, and it's on him to solve the murder and prove his innocence. He races across Europe, one step ahead of the police, uncovering messages hidden in the world's best-known artwork and solving ancient puzzles. Ultimately he uncovers a secret that has been protected by a clandestine society since the days of Christ.

Agent: Wow, okay. So, why is Langdon suspected of this murder?

Writer: At the scene of the murder, the victim has written in his own blood, Find Robert Langdon. The two men knew each other and they were supposed to meet while Langdon was in Paris.

Agent: Okay, and what are these messages? What artwork?

Writer: Well, the most important one is the Last Supper. Langdon finds out that the figure at the right hand of Jesus in Da Vinci's painting is not an apostle, but Mary Magdalene.

Agent: So that's the secret that's being protected?

Writer: No, the secret is that Jesus and Mary Magdalene were married, and that their bloodline can be traced to the present day.

Agent: Okay, you've got me. Send me the first three chapters. I'm a little worried about the length—it's probably about twice as long as I would like—but I'd like to see what you've got.

Writer: Good.

You'll notice in this last version of the hook, we're focused on the main character, and the character's problem. When it comes to pitching fiction, it's much easier to follow a pitch and remain interested when we can connect to a character and immediately understand the problem or conflict facing that character. Why are we going to care? What are the stakes? This same approach would be used for a memoir or a nonfiction narrative as well.

Also notice in this last version how the writer was able to stop at a question, or a moment of tension, and wait for the agent to ask for more. Rather than talk and talk and talk—which sometimes happens because you're nervous—remind yourself that it's okay not to explain all the details. It's more effective to stop just as you've established the key stakes or tension, and wait for a reaction from the agent. Let them guide the discussion; find out what's caught their attention or what piece is missing. And if they ask you to reveal the ending, then you should. Don't worry it's not going to ruin it for them. They can handle it.

Now that we've covered some pitch examples for fiction, let's turn our attention to nonfiction.

Agent: Hello, nice to meet you.

Writer: Hi there.

Agent: So, tell me about your project.

Writer: I know this isn't really an original idea, but I want to write a book about how people can be happier. Like, we can all be so much happier if we were nicer to people and spent more time with our families. We're too focused on things that don't matter and all the while time is passing us by.

Agent: I can see how that's true. But what's your angle on this?

Writer: Well this covers every single possible aspect of how to be happier.

Agent: That's pretty broad. Is it for a specific person, or type of person? Who's your audience?

Writer: It could really help anyone and that's the point.

Agent: Okay, well, what's your background for writing on this topic?

Writer: I was clerking for Justice Sandra Day O'Connor when I finally realized I wanted to be a writer, and didn't want to keep pursuing law. I graduated from Yale Law School.

Agent: So, you left your career in law to become a writer?

Writer: Yes, that's right.

Agent: Maybe consider going back to law.

In this pitch, the writer hasn't been able to elucidate why her approach to the topic is going to be marketable. It feels far too broad as presented, and the agent doesn't have enough information to even begin to see how this will be a salable project. Aside from the topic being too broad, the writer doesn't appear to have any specific credentials in writing self-help. We're not sure why we'd be confident in her ability to pull this off, and she even undercuts herself from the start by saying that she knows her idea isn't original.

Agent: Hello, nice to meet you.

Writer: Hi there.

Agent: So, tell me about your project.

Writer: I've been writing this blog for about a year or so, and it's all about trying to find out what makes us happy. I've been reading all the great thinkers and philosophers on the topic—like Plato and Aristotle—and writing about what I learn about them.

Agent: How many people visit your blog?

Writer: At least a few hundred visits every day. I'm also reading novels and looking at issues of *Psychology Today*. Anything really that relates to happiness, I'm looking at the advice and trying to figure out if the advice works.

Agent: How long have you been blogging?

Writer: A few months now. People really love the blog. They really like to answer the questions that I posed.

Agent: What kinds of people read your blog?

Writer: Everyone really. It applies to everyone. There's so much interest today in happiness, you know, because we're not really paying attention to the things that matter any more. We're just kind of coasting, and not really thinking about how to get more out of life.

Agent: Right, so what's your angle on this?

Writer: I'm interested in all the ways each person can be happy. I'm looking at how we can be happy in marriages, in friendships, at work. How we can have more energy, how we can even be more organized.

Agent: It sounds pretty broad, like it's as much about improving relationships as it is about personal development.

Writer: It is. It's about all of those things. Happiness affects every part of our life. And you can change your outlook by doing very simple things, like singing in the morning, or cleaning your closet, or just reading great philosophers. Just trying to have more fun.

Agent: How is the book organized exactly? What's the structure?

Writer: I'm still working on that, trying to figure it out. I thought I'd start seeing if I could get a book deal first, you know, based on what I've done with my blog, so then I can focus on the book after I get a contract.

Agent: Have you written anywhere elsewhere on this topic, or just on the blog?

Writer: Just my blog, but I've got a great network. I used to practice law, and I know a lot of people from my days at Yale, so I know a lot of people who would buy this book.

In this scenario, the writer is assuming that having an active blog might be sufficient to interest an agent or editor. Unfortunately, no matter how well known your blog is, it would have to be extremely successful to lead to a book deal. You still need to think through a viable book concept, something that feels like it can compete on the shelf against similar titles. You need to demonstrate you have a compelling vision for your book. Especially when it comes to most nonfiction, there needs to be a tangible benefit to readers that can be succinctly and convincingly expressed.

Agent: Hello, nice to meet you.

Writer: Hi there.

Agent: So, tell me about your project.

Writer: I have spent the last year pursuing what I call The Happiness Project. I'm carefully studying the current scientific research on happiness, and then I've been test-driving the wisdom, step by step, to see what happens.

Agent: What do you mean by test driving?

Writer: I adopt very specific resolutions, then measure what happens. For instance, in February, I focused on resolutions to increase happiness in my marriage. In March, I focused on specific steps to improve my friendships to see if it would make me happier.

Agent: Is it working?

Writer: It's surprising what actually works, it's the things you wouldn't expect. Like committing to make the bed each morning. Just having that small bit of order in your life makes a big difference.

Agent: I'm worried the book might be rather broad. Who do you envision as the audience for this book?

Writer: It will mostly appeal to women like myself, people who are raising families and are mid-career.

Agent: So, the self-help reader?

Writer: Yes and no. There's enough tips, advice and wisdom here to make this a solid self-help book, and it should be shelved in self-help. But I'm not trying to preach a method. I'm trying to figure out for people what works from the flood of self-help advice that's out there. What if I could tell you, based on thorough scientific investigation, what small steps to take that really increase happiness?

Agent: So, you think this will really appeal to people who don't typically read self-help?

Writer: Yeah, I think so. There's an audience out there who wonders if any of this self-help stuff really works. This book will answer that question definitively.

Agent: So, what's your background?

Writer: My background is in law. I was clerking for Supreme Court Justice Sandra Day O'Connor when I realized that I actually wanted to be a writer. So far, I've written several biographies that I researched. For this book, I've read and researched very widely. Everything from Schopenhauer to Tolstoy to back issues of *Psychology Today*.

Agent: Have you published anything on this topic yet?

Writer: I've started a blog where I've been interacting with people on the topics and questions in the book. On Facebook, I have a really large following—about 5,000 people—where I pose a Happiness Question of the Day, and I'm getting a lot of comments and collecting more ideas to improve the book.

Agent: So, I guess I should ask the big question—are you happier now?

Writer: I am, yeah. But as I said, it's the small things you don't expect that make you happier.

Agent: I feel like I could benefit from reading your book myself, so I would love to see your proposal.

In this successful version of the pitch, notice how the conversation builds on questions related to the book's market, and that the writer is prepared to address the biggest questions on the agent's mind—namely, who's the audience for the book? Why are you the best author for it? Why does anyone care what you have to say? While the pitch meeting might not answer all of these questions fully, a decent starting answer will lead to a proposal or manuscript request.

For all those writers who walk away disappointed from a pitch experience, remember that success is rarely attained in those specific 5–15 minutes. Rather, it's all the years of work leading up to that moment, and how someone's years of experience give them the appearance of success—that feeling that they're on the verge of breaking out. There's not really any way to fake that, and it's what agents and editors are ultimately looking for.

People who have that breakout feeling look and feel prepared, and demonstrate a kind of easy confidence that makes them a pleasure to talk to. Breakout folks tend to ask smart questions. They demonstrate curiosity and engagement. And perhaps most important, they appear flexible but resilient when dealing with the business side of publishing.

Agents and editors can tell they don't have to fear saying the wrong thing around such a writer, or hurting their feelings. When agents and editors meet you and feel like they'd love to work with you—even if the project you're pitching isn't a good fit—then you're on your way to breaking out.

Avoiding Common Manuscript Pitfalls
Lecture 14

Many agents and editors believe that they can tell within the first page whether or not a manuscript is worth reading further. Most writers, of course, do not like hearing this, but the reality is that impressions about your work are formed quickly, and these impressions are usually more accurate than not. Agents and editors are exposed to hundreds or thousands of manuscripts every year, enabling them to develop intuition about what's worth their time. Most of the time, agents' and editors' rejections are based on identifying red flags or common problems indicating that a work is unacceptable for publication. In this lecture, we'll discuss the two rough categories of red flags: narrative or structural problems and surface-level errors.

Opening Scenes

- To consider whether your first page or scene can be improved, ask yourself this: What is the absolute latest moment in the manuscript that I can begin the story and still not leave out anything critical to the story problem? Writers often take too long to get the inciting incident, the occurrence that sets the story in motion. Often, the best stories sow the seeds of the story problem in some form on the first page.

- For example, consider the opening lines of *The Lovely Bones* by Alice Sebold: "My name was Salmon, like the fish; first name, Susie. I was fourteen when I was murdered on December 6, 1973. In newspaper photos of missing girls from the seventies, most looked like me: white girls with mousy brown hair." In just those three sentences, we get an impressive amount of information, as well as the unique twist that will drive the entire novel: It's narrated by a dead girl.

- Strong openings point immediately to the story tension, without first giving a complete biography of the protagonist or showing the ordinary routine of the characters. It's usually better to allow backstory details to emerge as the story unfolds. Avoid an opening scene that focuses on the mundane details of everyday life, such as getting up and going to work. Instead, share the most distinctive details—the ones that really matter to shaping the story and character from the start.

- Many writers who are new to novel or memoir writing feel compelled to show how the world and the characters they're creating came to be. Novice writers believe that they need to show what everyday life is like in this world so that readers will better understand the change that's coming. Although developing character background, building the setting, and establishing the rules of the world you're creating are important tasks for writing your story, they aren't elements that need to be conveyed immediately in the first chapters.

Action Openings

- Some writers interpret this advice to mean that they must start the story with action. But starting with action isn't necessarily the solution, and it can lead to story openings that are just as boring as those that are loaded down with background detail.

- The important criteria for an action opening are that it provides some context for the action and that readers quickly understand how or why the action is significant to the story. If your opening scene lacks any kind of characterization, the action might not necessarily have any stakes associated with it. We may see people in danger or in pain, but without knowing how that's tied to the overall conflict or story, we don't know why we should care.

- The art of writing lies in knowing what kind of action will provide exactly the right tone and framework for the story. It should be action that engages readers immediately with the main characters. We should begin to form questions about the characters' lives, which builds tension, making us eager to find out what happens next. To test the effectiveness of your opening scene, ask yourself: What questions have been raised about my main character? What will motivate readers to keep turning the pages? What will they want to find out?

- In an effort to create a tension-filled opening, some writers go way overboard in depicting pain or discomfort. For example: "John clenched his throat and tried to stop the flow of blood, but he couldn't. His skin became whiter and whiter, and he broke out into a cold sweat. He felt prickles all up and down his back, and his breathing became intensely labored. He squinted into the sun and wondered if this was finally going to be it."

  o Some writers think this constitutes a tension-filled opening because it shows a precarious situation, but in fact, it shows a misapprehension of the well-known rule "show, don't tell." Not everything can or should be shown or dramatized at length. In fact, especially at the story beginning, it can be better to tell rather than show.

  o Here's how the story about John could be made more effective: "It was during the final hours of his Alaskan wilderness trek that it finally happened. John was attacked from behind. As he tried to stop the flow of blood from his forearm, he rummaged in his pack for the first-aid kit. Then he was attacked again, and that's when he figured this was going to be the end of him."

  o The second version keeps some of the mystery of the first opening, but it avoids strictly focusing on John's physical reaction. Remember that a little description—or "showing"— goes a long way, especially at the start of a story. Dramatizing each event or reaction can slow down a first scene significantly. It's hard to care about any character's pain until we know his or her conflict and motivation. Later on in the book, when we're on the edge of our seats, wondering what will happen to John because we care so much about him—that's the time to slow down, show, and dramatize.

Additional Rules for Openings

- In general, stick to one point-of-view character per scene or per chapter. Opening scenes that give us the thoughts of multiple characters in quick succession can confuse readers about where their loyalty should lie. Try to establish which main character we'll sympathize with in the opening by telling the story from that character's perspective for at least the first chapter or so.

- In an effort to build more uniqueness or tension into the opening, some authors create *false suspense*, raising questions that are either unimportant to the larger story or keep readers in the dark about the basics. Withholding a character's name, age, or identity tends to lead to a lack of reader engagement, rather than creating mystery.

- Prologues are an area of debate. Most writers love them, but editors and agents don't. Inside the industry, they're viewed as a classic form of backstory, with the writing dumping information on the reader before starting the real story. Sometimes, prologues are needed and play an important narrative role; other times, they are more of a crutch for a story that has a weak first chapter. For first-time authors, it's wise to skip the prologue unless it's absolutely necessary. Even then, make it short and have a solid hook.

- Like prologues, dream sequences often fail to present a strong framework for the story. Ask yourself how your dream sequence advances the story, whether it contains relevant conflict or tension, and why it's the best available opening to you. Even if the dream is a key part of the story's tension or overall plot, be careful about including long dream descriptions until readers are further into the narrative and committed to your characters. Similarly, it's best to avoid flashbacks until the reader is a few chapters in and the story conflict is established.

- There's considerable disagreement on the role of dialogue in a story opening—whether it should be used, how it should be used, and how long a dialogue-heavy scene should run before some description is offered. Two good rules to follow here are: (1) Avoid character dialogue in the opening that essentially offers mini-biographies of the characters, and (2) if you start with dialogue, try to be as clear as possible about the context and the identities of the speakers.

- Avoid interior monologue in your opening. Such openings don't give us much of a scene, don't allow us to see the main character interact with others, and don't provide any kind of significant action.

- With a memoir, don't begin by focusing on bitterness or anger. These emotions can't be the sole reason or hook for your story and can lead to quick rejection. The same is true of stories that are focused on pain or victimhood. Writing during the grieving process is a proven method for healing but not for getting published.

- Just as novels do, memoirs must have characters and be told in scenes. Your memoir must have a definitive beginning, middle, and end, not attempt to tell everything about your life. Too many memoirs include extra anecdotes or irrelevant events that don't tie into the narrative arc. Remember: Just because something happened to you doesn't mean that it belongs in your memoir; it must hold interest for others, be necessary to how the story unfolds, and not distract.

© Antonio_Diaz/iStock/Thinkstock.

In evaluating the first pages of your memoir, agents and editors look for a voice or perspective that makes the story compelling and offers vibrancy that will help set it apart from other works on the same topic.

Surface-Level Errors

- Surface-level issues include the mechanics of language, such as grammar, syntax, and punctuation, as well as issues of formatting and style.

- On the subject of grammar, many writers need to learn that perfect grammar has little to do with publishable writing. Certainly, those who have a strong grasp of grammar often have more sensitivity for the nuance of language and, therefore, might be better writers, but facility with grammar has nothing to do with great storytelling. Agents and editors won't praise your error-free prose, but they will praise compelling stories and memorable characters.

- Further, grammar is a surface-level issue that is usually addressed near the end of the writing process and can be corrected or polished by someone else. Most publishers hire freelancer editors to take care of grammar-level and style issues.

- That said, if your work is so riddled with grammatical errors that it distracts from reading, you need to solve that problem before you submit. There's little excuse for repeatedly incorrect punctuation, misspellings, and run-on sentences. Although an occasional error won't be held against you, multiple errors may indicate that you lack the fundamental skills needed for a writing career.

Suggested Reading

Browne and King, *Self-Editing for Fiction Writers*.

Lukeman, *The First Five Pages*.

Exercises

1. If you have a completed manuscript, study your opening chapters. What's the very latest you could start the story and still have everything make sense? In what scene does your main character confront the problem that will persist throughout the book and end up changing the character? Consider how that moment can come sooner.

2. Return to the last few books you've read that match the genre or category in which you write. Analyze the first five pages. What techniques or strategies does the author use to keep you reading?

Avoiding Common Manuscript Pitfalls
Lecture 14—Transcript

If you attend a panel of agents or editors at a writers' conference, and they discuss going through their slush pile, chances are good you'll hear at least one person say they can tell within the first page whether or not a manuscript is worth reading further.

Writers do not like hearing this. Doesn't each story deserve at least one chapter's worth of consideration, if not several chapters, for its best qualities to be recognized? But the reality is that impressions get formed very quickly about your work, even within the first sentence. And while it may seem unfair or unbelievable, first impressions are usually more accurate than not.

Agents get exposed to hundreds if not thousands of manuscripts every year. That level of exposure and immersion in the written word develops their intuition for what's worth their time and what's not. Multiply that over many years, even decades of work in the publishing industry, and you have someone who can spot a story that's salable in the current market.

That's not to say agents and editors don't make mistakes. They do. They overlook great work everyday, and reject books that go on to be bestsellers. There's also a lot of subjectivity that enters into the process. But the large majority of the time, editors' and agents' rejections are based on seeing red flags or common problems that indicate a work is unacceptable for publication.

These red flags can be roughly categorized into two areas: Narrative or structural problems and surface-level errors. We'll explore narrative or structural problems at length because they're by far the most important. And we'll also focus on your story's opening pages or early chapters, because those are most often requested and assessed by agents and publishers. While it may seem like narrative problems are impossible to diagnose on the first page, sometimes the seeds of a story's demise are evident from the story's opening scene.

To consider whether your first page or scene can be improved, ask yourself, what is the absolute latest moment in the manuscript you can begin your story, and still not leave out anything critical to the story problem? Most manuscripts that I read should really start somewhere between page 5 and page 50. New writers especially will commit the cardinal sin of taking too long to get to the inciting incident, or the thing that really sets the story in motion.

The best stories will often seed the story problem, in some form, even if it's just an underlying tension, on page one. As much as possible, your opening scene should hint at or even make explicitly clear what journey we'll be going on.

Consider the opening lines of *The Lovely Bones* by Alice Sebold, which was a bestselling book in the early 2000s. "My name was Salmon, like the fish; first name, Susie. I was 14 when I was murdered on December 6, 1973. In newspaper photos of missing girls from the '70s, most looked like me: white girls with mousy brown hair."

In just those three sentences, we get an impressive amount of information, as well as the unique twist that will drive entire novel. It's narrated by a dead girl.

Here's a famous opening, this time from Franz Kafka's *The Trial*. "Someone must have slandered Josef K., because one morning, without his having done anything bad, he was arrested."

The entire novel is roughly encapsulated by that opening line. Let's look at one more, again a very famous opening. "Where's Papa going with that ax?" said Fern to her mother as they were setting the table for breakfast. That's from *Charlotte's Web* by E. B. White.

Notice how each of these openings immediately points to the story tension, without first giving us a complete biography of the protagonist, or showing us the ordinary routine of the characters. It's usually better to allow backstory details to emerge as the story unfolds. That means you should avoid an opening scene that focuses on the ho-hum details of everyday life.

That includes such scenes as a character hearing the alarm clock, lying in bed deep in thought, getting out of bed, making coffee, and then driving to work. In fact, these kinds of morning routine activities are one of the biggest pet peeves of editors and agents. They're extremely common and appear too often in opening chapters.

So avoid the mundane and focus on only the most distinctive details—the ones that really matter to shaping the story and character from the start.

This is the kind advice that I offer very often, and that agents offer too, but writers find it very hard to accept or implement. This advice basically boils down to you have to learn how to leave stuff out. And I have my own story to help illustrate what I mean.

When I was young, my mom spent many hours each day writing a middle-grade novel. Eager to follow in her footsteps, I conceived of my own novel. I bought a spiral-bound notebook and wrote on the cover, "The Adventures of Superdog." On the first page, I wrote, Chapter 1. And so I began to describe how Superdog came into existence. It felt important to explain the hows and whys of how such a creature came to be. This took at least one page.

Then I started thinking of all the other questions his existence raised. How did he supply himself with food on a consistent basis? How did he come to have shelter and other resources? Where did his magical bone come from? This consumed at least Chapters 2 and 3.

I was obsessed with explaining as logically and clearly as possible the ins and outs of this creature, and getting all the day-to-day questions settled, so that readers would not be confused. Unfortunately, it was dead boring—so boring in fact, I stopped around Chapter 6 or 7. I can't even remember what the story conflict was. I was just too obsessed with the proper setup.

That stuff I was writing was really prep work. I was developing a character background, building the setting, and establishing the rules of the universe I was creating. These were details that I needed to know to write my story, but it wasn't something that needed to be conveyed immediately in the first chapters.

My inclination with Superdog is the inclination most writers have when they're new to novel and memoir writing. Your thought process probably goes something like this: I've got to show how this world came to be. I need to offer an explanation of why this person is how they are now. I need to show what everyday life is like, so that people better understand the big change that's coming.

But you don't, not really. Rather, you need to show the tension the character faces, sooner rather than later, and that means being disciplined about how much stage setting you employ. Otherwise, readers won't stick around to hear about the real story you want to tell. Fill in the backstory as you go, and some of it can help create tension, such as, "Why is Joe so nervous when he's around Mary? When will we learn what happened between them?"

The well-known radio storyteller Ira Glass has said you can create an interesting story out of the most mundane series of events as long as you're able to build tension and anticipation about what happens next. For instance, he suggests what if you simply had your character wake up, and he notices the house is very quiet. And he steps into the hallway, and still, everything is unearthly quiet? And he goes downstairs, and still absolute silence. This is an incredibly boring series of events, but it creates tension because a question is being raised: Why is it so quiet? And so we're waiting to find out.

Here's another way to think about story openings. When you first meet someone new, what do you tell them about yourself? What do they need to know right away? And what will you save for later? You don't have long to convey your life story on a first encounter. A lot has to be summarized and left to the imagination—and it's better that way at the start.

Now, don't mistake everything I've just said and boil it down to the adage, "Start with action." Starting with action isn't necessarily the solution. And worst of all, it can lead to story openings that are just as boring as those loaded down with background detail. A better adage would be "Start with something interesting."

If you do use an action-driven opening, make sure you provide some kind of context for what's happening. Help the reader quickly understand how or why the action is significant to the story. Also, if your opening scene lacks any character development, the action might not have any stakes associated with it. We may see people in danger or in pain, but without knowing how that's tied to the overall conflict or story, we won't know why we should care.

One of the secrets to great writing is knowing what kind of opening action or scene will provide the right tone and framework for the story. Hopefully it will be an opening that engages the reader with your main characters. We should begin to understand who those characters are. Questions should begin to form about these characters' lives, which builds tension. It leads to the reader wanting to know more, to find out what happens next.

To test whether or not your opening page or scene is working hard enough, ask yourself: What questions have been raised about my main character? What will motivate a reader to keep turning the pages? What will they want to find out? Here's an example of a story opening without any significant action.

> A breeze blew in through the open bedroom window. The air was warm and damp. Garbage trucks rumbled by and the newspaper was waiting on the driveway as usual. The smell of coffee wafted up from downstairs. It was time to get ready for work.

Here's how we could improve this opening with some type of significant action.

> His new suit had been carefully laid out the night before, but when Jake put it on, he didn't feel the confidence he was hoping for. Still, he couldn't put it off any longer. He went downstairs to the kitchen, where his wife had already made coffee and was reading the newspaper. She looked at Jake, and said deadpan, "Your office burned down last night."

Here we have a character that we're beginning to know and understand. We have a situation that presents tension for a specific character, and there's an indication of a much larger story problem.

However, in an effort to have a tension-filled opening, I've seen some writers go way overboard in depicting pain or discomfort. Here's an example:

> John clenched his throat and tried to stop the steady flow of his red, sticky blood, but he couldn't. His exposed skin became whiter and whiter, and he broke out into a cold, damp sweat. He felt prickles all up and down his muscled back, and his breathing became intensely labored. His blue eyes squinted into the stinging sun and he wondered if this was finally going to be it.

Imagine that going on for a full page or two, without any further information given to the reader about who John is or why his life is in jeopardy. Some writers think this constitutes a tension-filled opening because it shows a precarious situation.

However, this brings us to the sometimes over-applied rule show don't tell. Not everything can or should be dramatized at length. In fact, especially at the story beginning, it can be better to come right out and tell. Here's an example of how our story about John could be more effective:

> It was during the final hours of his Alaskan wilderness trek that it finally happened. John was attacked from behind. As he tried to stop the flow of blood from his forearm, he rummaged in his pack for the first-aid kit. Then he was attacked again, and that's when he figured this was going to be the end of him.

This keeps some of the mystery of the first opening. We're wondering who or what has attacked John—but it avoids focusing strictly on his physical or bodily reaction. Keep in mind a little description or showing goes a long way, especially at the start of a story. That's because dramatizing each event or reaction can slow down your first scene to an absolute crawl. It's hard to care about any character's pain until we know that character's conflict, motivation, and overall environment. Later on in the book, when we're on the edge of our seat, wondering what will happen to John, because we care so much about him—that's the time to slow down, show, dramatize, and keep us in suspense.

The first version of our John story also suffers from something called overwriting. You can in fact work too hard at painting a picture for readers, and go into an overwrought or flowery description about things that should be plainly stated. Joyce Carol Oates has said, "Storytelling is shaped by two contrary, yet complementary, impulses—one toward brevity, compactness, artful omission; the other toward expansion, amplification, enrichment." When it comes to rushed editors and agents, it's generally safer to favor brevity and artful omission in your opening pages.

There are many other rules you'll hear about opening pages, so let's go over the most common. Keep in mind that many writers successfully break these rules all the time. But the reason the following rules are offered is that they help you craft an opening that readers will care about.

Agents and editors will advise you stick to one point of view character per scene or per chapter. In a nutshell, this means the story should be told from one character at a time. If your opening scene jumps from head to head—meaning we get the thoughts of multiple characters in quick succession—it can confuse a reader as to where their loyalty should lie.

In the early chapters, it can be important to establish which main character we'll sympathize with, and you do this by telling the story from that character's perspective for at least one or two chapters, especially the opening chapter. Published writers may break this rule all the time, but it's difficult for a new author to pull it off successfully. The big red flag is when you have an opening scene with several characters, and no single point of view dominates.

Another rule is that you should avoid opening with ordinary life scenes, where we follow the main character through a routine. As we discussed before, writers like to start with the character waking up to an alarm, or at home in the morning, doing what they normally do, thinking that this is good characterization.

Unfortunately, these types of scenes can add up to a host of everyday life clichés that don't distinguish your story from others in the market. Personally, my least favorite opening, which is fairly common in unpublished work, is the description of the perfect weather outside, with a character waking up in bed, peering out the window, and thinking about the exciting day ahead.

In an effort to build more uniqueness or tension into the opening, you might actually build in what's called false suspense. This is where you raise questions, but these questions are either unimportant to the larger story or keep readers in the dark about the basics. For instance, some writers withhold a character's name, age, or identity for a full chapter, thinking this creates mystery, when it more often leads to a lack of reader engagement.

Prologues are another area of tremendous debate. Most writers love them, while editors and agents don't. The reason they're disliked inside the industry is because they're a classic form of backstory, where the writer dumps a bunch of information into the reader's lap before starting the real story. Sometimes prologues are needed and play an important narrative role, other times they're a crutch for a story that has a weak first chapter. In that case, the better solution is to create a strong first chapter. For the first-time author, a good rule of thumb is to skip the prologue unless it's absolutely necessary. Even then, make it short and give it a solid hook.

Almost as hated as the prologue is the dream sequence. Like the prologue, a dream sequence fails to present a strong framework for the story at hand. Even if you think your dream sequence is different, ask yourself how it advances the story, if it contains relevant conflict or tension, and why it's the best available opening to you. Even if the dream is a key part of the story's tension or overall plot, be careful of going long with your dream description until readers are further into the narrative, and committed to your characters.

Similarly, if you have flashbacks in your manuscript, it's best to hold them until the reader is a few chapters in and the story conflict is established. Some story elements are simply more acceptable or compelling once the important groundwork is laid and you know readers have been hooked.

There's considerable disagreement on the role of dialogue in a story opening—whether it should be used, how it should be used, and how long you can go with a dialogue-heavy scene before offering some kind of description. I think there are two good rules of thumb you can follow.

First, avoid character dialogue in the opening that essentially offers a mini-biography of the characters, to fill readers in on the backstory. This looks amateurish and isn't how people talk to each other.

Second, if you do start with dialogue, try to be as clear as possible about the people speaking and what the context is. Being mysterious about it is a form of false suspense we discussed earlier.

The final rule I'll mention is avoiding interior monologue in your opening. This is where we enter the head of a main character, and follow along with their thoughts for an extended period. The problem is that interior monologue doesn't give us much of a scene, it doesn't allow us to see the character interact with other people, and it completely lacks any kind of significant action. However, this problem is more common with memoirs than it is novels.

In fact, while all of the pitfalls and rules we've gone over apply to all kinds of narratives, whether fiction or nonfiction, I'd like to point out a few special considerations for memoirists. Any memoir that begins by focusing on bitterness or anger will not likely be relatable to readers.

The dilemma, of course, is that many people are motivated to write a memoir for exactly these reasons. But these emotions can't be the sole reason or hook for your story, and if the agent sees nothing but the bitterness or anger on the first page, they'll quickly reject you.

Similarly, if the story seems to be focused on pain or victimhood, and nothing more, you need to revisit your story. Be extra careful with any material you might have written during a grieving process, either at the recommendation of a therapist or as part of a therapy group. Writing through grief and tragedy is a proven method to heal, but it is not a proven method for getting published.

I say this not to be insensitive, but to bring needed attention to the fact that these stories are prevalent, and agents and editors don't find them publishable. If your story opens up with a journal or diary entries, recounting the bad things that have happened to you, that's pretty much an automatic rejection. It's also very telling when a memoir opens with the death of a loved one or a funeral. We start to wonder if we'll get anything more than the writer's own cathartic ride through the grieving process.

Some memoirs don't have any of these problems I've mentioned, but they lack a narrative arc, which an experienced agent or editor can usually detect right away. A memoir needs to be told in scenes, and have characters, just as a novel does. If you're attempting to tell everything about your life, from beginning to end, starting with childhood, where you were born, where you went to school, and you're going to leave no stone unturned, then you're not really writing a memoir.

A memoir needs to have a definitive beginning, middle, and end, and you need to leave out a lot of detail. The difficulty is that it's hard to achieve sufficient distance to see what details are most critical to the memoir. Too many stories include extra anecdotes or irrelevant events that don't tie into the narrative arc, but are fond memories for the writer.

Remember: just because it happened to you doesn't mean it belongs in the story. It has to hold interest for others and be necessary to how the story unfolds.

Finally, when agents or editors evaluate your first pages, they're looking for a voice or perspective that makes the story compelling and offers vibrancy that will help set it apart from other memoirs on the same topic.

Now that we've addressed the higher-level concerns of story in your opening pages, let's discuss the surface-level issues. When I talk about surface-level issues, I'm referring to language mechanics, which includes grammar, syntax, and punctuation. There are also issues of formatting and style.

Most of us learn the rules of grammar in middle school. I remember when I was in eighth grade and we were learning how to diagram sentences and identify parts of speech. I may have been the only student to look forward to those lessons, which were methodical, strict, and exacting. I'm grateful for having a teacher who was able to teach grammar with discipline and comprehensiveness. It provided an important foundation for the rest of my writing career.

However, if I have a frustration with some writers, whether beginning or published, it's how some have an unrelenting obsession and unforgiving attitude toward errors in grammar, spelling, and punctuation. When I worked for *Writer's Digest*, our grammar articles always received the most comments and brought out the fiercest arguments. And whenever or wherever we made a grammatical fumble, in print or online, it was treated as an unforgivable crime.

I have one thing to say about this: Lighten up. Here's why. Perfect grammar has little to do with publishable writing. Certainly, those who have a strong grasp of grammar can be more sensitive to the nuances of language, and therefore might be better writers. But facility with grammar has nothing to do with great storytelling, which is the most important quality for the majority of agents and editors. They're not going to praise your error-free prose; they're going to praise how they couldn't stop turning the pages, or how much they'll remember the characters. Some people also fall in love with the writer's language, but again, that rarely relates to technically correct writing.

So I find it discouraging when writers get anxious about their grammar, or even apologize in advance that their grammar isn't perfect. The much bigger concern is the story, and no amount of captivatingly correct language will add story where there is none.

Furthermore, grammar is a surface-level issue that is usually addressed near the end of the writing process, and can even be corrected or polished by someone else. Most publishers hire freelancers to take care of grammar-level issues, as well as style issues, in the books they publish.

That said, if your work is so riddled with grammatical errors that it distracts from reading, that's a problem you need to solve before submitting your work. There's very little excuse for repeatedly incorrect punctuation, misspellings, and run-on sentences. While an occasional error isn't going to be held against you, it's when the errors happen in every other sentence that it might become clear you might lack the fundamental skills needed for a writing career.

You should also make sure you understand how to properly format dialogue. This is important because it affects the clarity of your scenes and sticks out when incorrect. The most important conventions are these: You should always start a new paragraph when a new person is speaking, and it's most common to use quotation marks to indicate dialogue. You will see some writers breaking these conventions, but I recommend you stick to convention for your first time out.

So we've identified the narrative or structural issues that might lead to rejection, as well as more surface-level concerns that can be a deal breaker. You'll find a range of other reasons cited for rejection, and some will sound ridiculous. I've heard about writers being rejected for using too many adjectives or adverbs, for using passive voice, for bad dialogue attributions, and scores of other reasons.

The most important thing to understand about any feedback you're given is that it's rarely just one thing that leads to a no on your manuscript. It's a whole host of factors that signal to the agent or editor that your writing isn't ready for publication. Most agents and editors will pin the blame on a single element because it's the one that stuck out the most. Unfortunately, this leaves the writer obsessed with this one single infraction, which then leads to overcompensating to correct for it, and that leads to worse writing.

While you should listen to common themes in the feedback you receive, ultimately you have to be true to your own voice and style, and that itself can take years to find and develop. In the end, I hope you're able to successfully break any rules you want to, and always remember that great writers do, all the time.

Hiring a Professional Editor
Lecture 15

There are three primary reasons to hire a professional to review your writing: First, you'll grow as a writer by working with an expert who can point out your strengths and weaknesses and give you feedback on taking your work to the next level. Second, you'll increase your understanding of the publishing industry by experiencing a quality editorial process. And third, you will use the editor's feedback to prepare your work for submission to an agent or publisher. But before you hire anyone to edit your work, you need to understand the different stages of writing and revising, the different types of editing available, and what an editor can and can't do in terms of making your work publishable.

Types of Editing

- *Developmental editing* is most commonly used for nonfiction work, especially by traditional book publishers. Developmental editors (DEs) focus on the structure and content of your book; if they work for a publisher, their job is to ensure that the manuscript adheres to the vision of the work agreed to by all parties to the contract.

  o DEs are often involved while the writing process is still ongoing. They may ask you to justify how the choices you're making as you write will serve the readership. You'll find the DE raising the question of audience again and again: Will the audience understand? Will the audience care? What does the audience need to know at each stage?

  o You should think of DEs as trusted advisors. Their goal is always to produce the best book possible for the reader, and their suggestions are made with an eye toward garnering more sales. They will be concerned with the narrative arc if there needs to be one, the organization of material, and missed opportunities. They'll do their best offer solutions to any inconsistencies or structural problems.

- Of course, authors can be sensitive to feedback that can lead to changing a book's structure or eliminating large sections. As a result, some writers find developmental editing uncomfortable. A thorough development edit will mean letting go of things that may be important to you personally but might not belong in the book from a market-driven perspective.

  - Whether you can overcome your discomfort largely depends on whether you trust your editor and whether you view the editing process as a means of professional development—a way to improve your own abilities and perspective on your work.

- Like developmental editing, *content editing* is focused on structure, style, and overall development, for both fiction and nonfiction. However, content editors almost never work on a manuscript while it's still in progress.

- Both developmental and content editing fall under the category of higher-level editing, a process that inevitably leads to revision and substantive changes in the work. If you're working with an editor at this level, don't expect validation or praise but, rather, an extensive editorial letter and manuscript notations, with detailed advice, to help you successfully revise.

- A thorough developmental or content edit can be quite expensive. An alternative to this type of edit is a more general *manuscript assessment*, where an industry professional reads and assesses the strengths and

Knowing what type of editor to hire requires some level of self-awareness about where your manuscript is in the writing process and what types of suggestions would be beneficial to you.

weaknesses of your manuscript. You won't get page-by-page advice on revision but a broader overview of how to improve the work.

- Sentence- or surface-level types of editing include line editing, copyediting, and proofreading.
  - *Line editing* focuses on sentence structure, word use, and rhythm. Its goal is to create smooth and streamlined prose.

  - *Copyediting* is focused on correcting errors in grammar, syntax, and usage. Some copyeditors also fact-check and point out inconsistencies or lapses in logic.

  - *Proofreading* comes at the end of the editorial process, sometimes after the book is already typeset. At this late stage, an editor looks only for typos, formatting mistakes, and egregious errors.

- Before hiring an editor, it's critical that you understand exactly what level of editing or service will be provided. Don't hire a rules-based editor—someone who will look for sentence-level errors—when what you really need is a big-picture editor to identify strengths and weaknesses in your work.

Hiring an Editor

- One of the best ways to find an editor is to ask other writers for recommendations. You might also check out PublishersMarketplace.com, where you can find freelancers who are knowledgeable about the publishing industry and may even work with traditional publishers and agents. In addition, you can search established associations of editors, such as the Editorial Freelancers Association in the United States and the Society for Freelance Editors and Proofreaders in the United Kingdom.

- Most experienced editors specialize in genres or categories, as well as specific types of editing. You'll get the best results by hiring an editor who has a long track record of editing within your category of work.

- To ensure that there's a good fit and that expectations about the services are clear, an editor may first work on a sample section of your book, for which you may or may not be charged. It's unwise to hire an editor until you feel confident that the two of you are a good match; an editorial review is a big investment, and you want to reduce the possibility of a surprise at the end.

- Avoid any kind of editing situation where you don't know the specific editor you'll be working with, as is often the case with self-publishing or other package services. It's important that you're able to communicate directly with the person editing your work.

- Sometimes, during the submissions process, an agent or publisher may recommend that you retain the services of an editor and resubmit after the revision. You may be sent to a specific service or freelancer who is trusted by the agent or publisher, but always independently vet any recommendations you receive. And remember that it is inappropriate for traditional publishers or agents to charge you for editing services they provide.

- Inexperienced writers too often assume that a friend or colleague who has an English degree or is an English teacher is qualified as a professional editor. Editing isn't about academic credentials or having a good eye for typos. Book editing is a specialized area of expertise, and the average English major has never been exposed to either the book publishing industry or what professional book editors do for a living.

- Seek a professional with a clear record of book-related experience who is willing to share the specifics of his or her writing and publishing credentials. Consider it a good sign when an editor is selective about taking on projects and doesn't have immediate availability. However, you also need to be realistic about who you'll be able to hire. The editors of bestselling books might be perpetually unavailable or out of your price range. They're more likely to turn down manuscripts that they don't think are ready for their level of expertise.

Evaluating Editorial Services

- With the increase in the number of writers self-publishing their work has come an increase in the number of services offering assistance. Before you decide to hire one of these services—or any editor—ask the following questions:

  o Who's behind the service? Do the editors have experience that applies to what you're trying to do? What's the bias, if any, of the people behind the service?

  o What's the business model? Under what terms does the service make money?

  o Is the service transparent? You should expect any freelancer or editorial service to be upfront about the specific services provided.

  o Is the service authoritative? If you don't know what distinguishes a trustworthy and experienced editor or service provider from an inexperienced one, then ask for success stories, testimonials, and recommendations.

  o Are the promises made reasonable or realistic, or does the service seem positioned mostly to make a sale? Ethical services don't overpromise what they're able to provide or lavish praise on you.

- The bottom line is this: Always make sure you need a specific kind of help before you pay for it. Do your research before committing. Get second and third opinions. And have appropriate expectations for how far a professional service can take you.

Beta Readers

- As we've mentioned, the demand for editors has increased with self-publishing, and today, many authors are aware that they need some level of assistance in rewriting and polishing their work. But few authors can afford professional-level, deep editing.

- At the same time, writing processes themselves are evolving. Today, the publishing world is seeing more collaborative work, more serializations, and more publication of works in progress.

- In this changing environment, instead of a formal editing process that aligns with traditional publishing practices, some writers are taking advantage of *beta readers*—smart readers who volunteer to serve as an author's first editors.

- This model is most prevalent in online writing and fan-fiction communities and within the self-publishing community. Authors identify trusted fans or colleagues who are willing to read and offer feedback on unpublished work for free. As authors gain experience and titles under their belt, they may progress from using beta readers to hiring paid editing teams, but they continue to bring in beta readers during certain stages of the editorial process.

- In the world of computer software, beta testers try to identify bugs in software before it is released. In a similar manner, a beta reader helps a writer avoid sending a story out into the world with embarrassing problems. Sometimes, finding a good group of beta readers is as difficult as finding a qualified professional editor, given the amount of time and effort that must be donated. If you're an active member of online writing communities, though, you'll quickly learn how and where to find readers for your own work.

- Beta readers are more closely identified with fiction writing and publishing, although they can be used for any genre. In the nonfiction world, you'll sometimes hear about *crowdsourcing* as a replacement for some level of development and content editing. The crowdsourcing approach makes content available faster, gets real-time feedback from the target audience, and shapes the final product based on collaboration.

- If you decide that beta readers or crowdsourcing might play a role in your writing and revision process, don't forget that the burden will be on you to figure out what advice is actually good and worth acting on and what feedback isn't on target.

- As you go through any editorial process, remember that revision is what separates serious writers from everyone else; professional authors revise their work multiple times, with and without professional advice. If you expect to get anywhere in your writing career, you'll need to find the right process or method for revising. The process of editing is one each writer develops individually through experience and trial and error.

Suggested Reading

Gross, *Editors on Editing*.

Lerner, *The Forest for the Trees*.

Exercises

1. Visit a site where unpublished writers post their work openly for critique from other writers. Popular sites include Book Country, Authonomy, and Kindle Scout. Read a few first chapters and see what captures your attention, then read the comments or critiques. Interestingly, sometimes the best way to improve your writing is to read something that doesn't work at all and identify the reasons behind the errors.

2. If you can't afford a professional editor, explore an online critique community, such as Scribophile, where you can offer feedback on others' work and earn points, then get your own work critiqued by other members.

Hiring a Professional Editor
Lecture 15—Transcript

Writing and publishing advice can feel obvious, or like common sense—have a fresh concept, take out everything that's boring, keep the reader turning pages. But being able to perceive or understand if you've been successful in creating a compelling work requires objectivity than can be hard to achieve on your own.

Have you ever heard of the Rule of 24? It's a rule that many people follow that's very simple: Sleep on everything you write for at least a day. This works for shorter pieces, but 24 hours really isn't enough time when it comes to complex book-length work. We need another kind of rule—perhaps a Rule of 180. Put away your manuscript for one month for every 80,000 words.

One month away starts to create sufficient distance to assess your work without feeling too attached. Even then, it can be difficult to spot the weaknesses in your own work. This raises the question of whether it's worthwhile to hire an industry professional to help you.

There are three primary reasons to hire a professional. The first and maybe most important reason is for the learning experience. You'll grow as a writer by working with an expert who can point out your strengths and weaknesses, and give you specific feedback on how to take your work to the next level. Sometimes, if you have a really great mentor or critique group, you can learn the same things, but the process takes longer, plus there's usually more confusion and doubt along the way. When you pay a professional, you're paying for industry experience and immediately valuable insights that other people might not have.

The second reason to hire a professional is to increase your understanding of the publishing industry by experiencing a quality editorial process. Seeing what good feedback looks like and learning how to apply that feedback is a skill that you'll use again and again. You'll begin to have an intuitive understanding of what kind of attention your work requires, and at what point in the writing process you need feedback. There are different types of professionals who work with you at different stages of the writing and revision process, which we'll cover in detail.

The final reason to hire an editor is to prepare your work for submission to an agent or publisher. For better or worse, this is the key motivation many writers have when they hire an editor. In query letters, I see more and more writers claim their manuscript has been professionally edited, and it's no surprise. People inside the industry are known for emphasizing the importance of submitting a flawless manuscript.

However, when evaluating work that's been edited, I find that it tends to be of lesser quality. Of course, this is quite paradoxical. Shouldn't professionally edited material be much better? Unfortunately, many new writers don't clearly understand what type of editor to use or how an editor is supposed to improve their work. New writers also tend to be more protective of their work and less likely to revise. This results in surface-level changes that don't actually affect one's chances at publication.

When writers ask me if they should hire a professional editor, it's usually out of a vague fear their work isn't good enough, and they believe it can be fixed by a third party. While a good editor can help resolve problems in your work, it often requires just as much work by the writer to revise and improve the manuscript.

Before you hire anyone, you need to first understand the different stages of writing and revising, the different types of editing available, and what an editor can and can't do in terms of making your work publishable. Even the best editor in the world can't turn a mediocre work into a gem. But they can help a very good work become great.

One type of editor you might consider working with is a developmental editor or DE. They're most commonly used for nonfiction work, especially by traditional book publishers. DEs focus on the structure and content of your book. If they work for a publisher, their job is to ensure the manuscript adheres to the vision set out in the book proposal—or basically what everyone agreed to when the book was contracted.

Developmental editors are often involved early and while the writing process is still ongoing. While they don't dictate exactly what the book has to be, as an author you'll be asked to justify the choices you're making, and if they best serve the readership. You'll find the DE raising the question of audience again and again. Will the audience understand? Will the audience care? What does the audience need to know at each stage?

In his essay "Developmental Editing," Paul McCarthy says, "Successful collaboration allows the author to feel sustained and liberated by knowing that she doesn't have to bear the burden of creation, development, and refinement alone." A DE gives you someone else to trust and lean on. Their goal is always to produce the best possible book for the reader, and their suggestions are made with an eye on producing better sales.

They'll be concerned with the narrative arc if there needs to be one, the organization of your material, and missed opportunities. They'll do their best to problem solve and offer solutions for any inconsistencies or structural issues.

However, authors can be sensitive to feedback if it leads to changing the book's overarching structure or eliminating entire chapters. As a result, writers can find this kind of development very uncomfortable, even though it tends to be the most valuable form of editing. A thorough development edit will mean letting go of things that may be important to you personally, but might not belong in the book from a market-driven perspective.

I find that the most resistance tends to come from authors writing personal stories or memoir. It can be hard to see or accept the bigger picture of what a DE recommends. Whether you can overcome your discomfort will largely depend on two things: first, if you trust your editor, then you'll be more likely to listen to their ideas and accept that they may see things more clearly than you can.

Second, writers who see the editing process as a means of professional development—to improve their own abilities and perspective on their work—often tackle revisions with a more accepting and enthusiastic frame of mind.

Similar to developmental editing is content editing. Content editing has more or less the same purpose as developmental editing—it's focused on structure, style, and overall development, for both fiction and nonfiction. However, content editors almost never work on your manuscript while it's still in progress. You'll sometimes hear the term book doctor used quite a bit in connection with this type of work. A book doctor is someone who performs developmental or content editing on your manuscript, almost always after you have a completed draft.

Developmental editing, content editing, and book doctoring fall under the category of higher-level editing. This means the process inevitably leads to revision and significant, substantive changes in your work. It would be nearly impossible for a writer to work with a high-level editor and not end up doing rewrites. While the editor will point out strengths and mark where things are going well, a writer shouldn't expect validation or praise. Instead, you'll receive an extensive editorial letter and manuscript notations, with detailed advice, to produce a successful revision.

A thorough developmental or content edit can be very expensive and sometimes cost prohibitive. An alternative to this type of edit is a more general manuscript assessment, where an industry professional reads and assesses the strengths and weaknesses of your manuscript. You won't get page-by-page advice on revision, but a broader overview of how to improve the work. Fortunately, some higher-level editors also provide assessment services in addition to more intensive editing work.

Earlier I discussed writers who claimed to have their work professionally edited, yet their manuscript quality didn't reflect a professional's involvement. In many such cases, a writer has hired a line editor, copy editor, or proofreader, which are all sentence-level or surface-level types of editing.

Line editing focuses on sentence structure, word use, and rhythm. Its goal is to create smooth and streamlined prose. Copyediting is generally more focused on correcting errors in grammar, syntax, and usage. Some copy editors also fact-check and seek out inconsistencies or lapses in logic. Proofreading comes at the very end of the editorial process, sometimes after the book is already typeset. At this late stage, an editor would only be looking for typos, formatting mistakes, and other egregious errors that shouldn't make it to publication.

The challenge in hiring a professional editor is that the terminology used to describe editing can be very subjective and change from editor to editor, or from service to service. This may seem strange, given that we're talking about an industry that specializes in language, but unfortunately, this is a gray area you'll have to deal with.

Before hiring an editor, it's critical that you're clear on exactly what level of editing or service will be provided. Never hire a line editor or copy editor until you're confident your book doesn't require a higher level of editing first. That would be like painting the walls of your house right before tearing it down. Unfortunately, I've seen writers do a lot of polishing right before a major demolition.

Here's another way to think about the editing process: don't hire a rules-based editor—someone who will look for sentence-level errors—when what you really need is a big-picture editor, who will identify strengths and weaknesses in the work. Some editors can provide all levels of editing, but it would be a mistake to hire an editor to perform all levels of editing in one pass.

Knowing what type of editor to hire requires some level of self-awareness about where in the process you're at, and also what help you would benefit from. Unpublished writers who keep getting rejected may need to hire a developmental or content editor to help get an honest and direct appraisal of how to improve on a big-picture level. Some writers mistake a technically correct manuscript, one that follows all the rules, as the goal of editing. While the polish helps, no polish can make a flawed story shine.

There is no definite number of drafts you should write before you can consider the manuscript finished—but it is possible to overedit. If you find yourself rewriting everything over and over, you might be using editing as a means of avoiding potential rejection. Sometimes it's more important and helpful to get finished pieces into the hands of agents or editors than to spend endless time refining the same manuscript over and over again. Most writers, though, are far more likely to be hurt by too little editing than by too much.

So begins the long journey of learning how to improve your self-editing skills, perhaps among the most important you will ever have. The most common advice you'll receive from anyone is revise, revise, revise. Revision is what separates the serious writers from everyone else. Professional authors revise their work multiple times, with and without professional advice. If you expect to get anywhere in your writing career, you'll need to find the right process or method for revising. The process of editing is one each writer develops on her own, through experience, trial, and error.

Now that you understand what types of editing are available, let's return to the three reasons you might want to invest in a professional. The most important reasons are to learn and grow as a writer, to understand the role of the editor, and to become better at the editing process. Yet your true motivation may be to get closer to a publishing deal. Unfortunately, not even the best editor can guarantee you'll get an agent or publisher if you hire them. You can't buy a magical fix, and there's no editorial formula that will transform your book into a bestseller. If there were, then you can bet the editor would likely be devoting her time and energy elsewhere.

Ask yourself: Will you be comfortable spending $2,000 or $3000 on a high-level edit, maybe even twice that, if your work doesn't succeed in getting published? If the answer is no, then consider one of the crowdsourced editing options I'll be discussing later. If you're comfortable spending that much as an investment in your long-term growth as a writer, an investment that will make your future work better, then that indicates a better and more appropriate mind-set.

If you are in a position to hire an editor, then the next question is: How do you find one? Start by asking other writers. Word of mouth can lead you to someone who is qualified and has happy clients willing to recommend them. If that doesn't lead anywhere, you can check out PublishersMarketplace. com, which you may have already used in the agent research process.

Freelancers who are members of PublishersMarketplace.com are likely more knowledgeable about the industry by virtue of keeping an updated profile at one of the most trafficked sites in book publishing. They might also be actively working with traditional publishers and agents, which is a good sign.

You can also search through established associations of editors, such as the Editorial Freelancers Association in the U.S. and the Society for Editors and Proofreaders in the U.K. These organizations also provide helpful information about what rates to expect, what freelance agreements might look like, and more.

If you run a web search for freelance editors, you'll turn up thousands of choices. So you'll have to learn how to evaluate them based on what information they make available on their website.

First, it's OK to judge them by their website. If you don't get a sense of professionalism and confidence from the site, keep looking. You should be able to find a range of testimonials from happy clients, or if not testimonials, then success stories. If you can't find any, ask. Avoid hiring an editor who can't provide evidence of quality past work.

Most experienced editors specialize in genres or categories, as well as specific types of editing. You'll get the best results by hiring an editor who has a long track record of editing within your category of work. For example, if you're working on a romance, avoid hiring a nonfiction editor, and vice versa.

Also, most experienced editors will work with you on a sample to ensure there's a good fit and that expectations of their service are clear. Sometimes this sample work is done for free, and other times you'll be charged but practices vary, and it's normal either way. I recommend not hiring an editor until you can feel confident the match will work out. It's a big investment, and you want to reduce the possibility of a surprise at the end.

Avoid any kind of editing situation where you don't know the specific editor you'll be working with. This can often be the case with self-publishing services or other package services. It's important that you're able to communicate directly with the person editing your work. You should be able to ask questions and have confidence in the qualifications of the editor. It's not often possible to do this with a middleman obscuring who's really doing the work.

Sometimes during the submissions process, you may hear back from an agent or publisher who recommends you retain the services of an editor, and then tells you to resubmit after you pay for the revision. You may be sent to a very specific service or freelancer they trust. While some agents and publishers do this in good faith, in an effort to be helpful, others receive kickbacks for business they send to freelancers. So be cautious and always independently vet any recommendations you receive. If the publisher or agent recommends their own editing services that they charge you for, this is generally considered a conflict of interest, and it's not appropriate business practice for a traditional publisher or agent.

Inexperienced writers too often assume that their friend or colleague who has an English degree or is an English teacher is qualified as a professional editor. Editing isn't about academic credentials or having a good eye for typos. Book editing is a specialized area of expertise, and your average English major has never been exposed to either the book publishing industry or what professional book editors do for a living.

To save money you may be tempted to hire someone who has less experience. This might be acceptable if you're looking for a rules-based edit or a polish, but ask yourself: Do you really want your book to serve as a practice project for someone else?

I recommend you seek a professional with a clear record of book-related experience who is willing to share the specifics of their writing and publishing credentials. It's also a very good sign when an editor is selective about what projects they take on, and doesn't have immediate availability. Quality editors are in demand, get repeat business, and have their schedules booked well in advance.

However, sometimes it will be necessary to be realistic about who you'll be able to hire. The editors of bestselling books might be perpetually unavailable or out of your price range. They're also more likely to turn down writers or manuscripts they don't think are ready for their level of expertise or involvement. They'll straight up tell you if they don't yet see a strong enough foundation in place to benefit from a high-level edit.

Unfortunately, it's far more common for you to be faced with the opposite situation: There are far more unqualified editors out there offering services and trying to sell you on how they can make your work more publishable. There isn't any formal accreditation process for freelance editors, so anybody can call themselves one, and many set up shop with little experience. Plus the growth of self-publishing has increased the number of people who are putting out their shingle. This means that freelance editors can easily point to published works they've edited, which may not be very high quality.

This raises an important question facing writers. There's a huge increase in the number of writers out there self-publishing their work who need professional assistance. So there's been this increase in the number of services that offer some kind of assistance—ranging from editing to marketing to sales. Who should you trust to help you?

Sadly, I find there's far more unnecessary help offered these days that can waste a writer's time or money. So let's get clear about what writers need on a basic level to produce the most publishable work possible.

First, you should actively read in the category or genre you want to professionally publish in. This helps you understand the basic rules of the genre, what's a fresh idea and what's not, and where you fit into the spectrum of what's out there. Second, you have to do the writing work. Nothing replaces that. Third, you need meaningful feedback, whether that's from a critique group, mentor, or a professional. That's really it, aside from the platform requirements that nonfiction authors have to take into consideration.

Before you decide you're going to pay someone to help you, ask these questions. First: Who's behind the service and do you trust who's behind it? Are there specific names attached? Do they have experience that applies to what you're trying to do? What's the bias, if any, of the people behind the service?

What's their business model? How do they make money? Almost every service has to turn a profit, and there's nothing wrong with that. For valuable or quality help that furthers your career, you should be willing to pay.

Is the service transparent? You should expect any freelancer to be transparent and upfront about what they provide. So take a good look at the service you might want to pay for and look for specifics or examples of what they're providing you.

Is it authoritative? Sometimes this is tough for a new writer to evaluate. If you don't know what distinguishes a trustworthy and experienced service provider from an inexperienced one, then at the very least, look for success stories that match the kind of success you want. Look for a track record and history of achievement in the areas where you need help.

Finally, are the promises reasonable or realistic—or do they seem positioned mostly to make a sale? Ethical services don't overpromise what they can provide, or lavish you with praise. Be suspicious of any freelancer who is overeager to make a sale.

Bottom line, always make sure you need the help before you pay for it. Do your research before committing. Get second and third opinions. And have appropriate expectations for how far a professional service can take you.

The final type of editing and feedback I'd like to address is an area that is quite new and continues to evolve and transform. It's doesn't necessarily fall under the rubric of professional help, but it's sometimes now part of the professional editing process. I'm talking about beta readers.

I've mentioned how the demand for editors has increased, and authors are more acutely aware that they need some level of assistance in rewriting and polishing their work. But very few authors can afford professional-level, deep editing.

At the same time, we're seeing that writing processes are evolving. There's more online and collaborative work, more serializations and more works-in-progress being undertaken. Instead of a very formal editing process that closely aligns with the traditional publishing practice, there's another type of process evolving where smart readers volunteer to serve as an author's first editors—people known as beta readers.

This model is most prevalent today in online writing and fan-fiction communities, and within the self-publishing community. Authors identify trusted fans or colleagues who are willing to read and offer feedback on unpublished work for free. Then sometimes the author will serve as a beta reader in return. As authors gain experience and titles under their belt, they may progress from using beta readers to more formal, paid editing teams—but still continue to bring in beta readers during certain stages of the editorial process.

As you can probably tell, the term beta reader has its origins in computer software. Beta testers try to identify bugs in software and help a developer improve it before an official release. In a similar manner, a beta reader helps a writer avoid sending a story out into the world with embarrassing problems. Sometimes finding a good group of beta readers is as difficult as finding a qualified professional editor, given the amount of time and effort that must be donated.

If you're an active and meaningful member of online writing communities, though, you'll quickly learn how and where to find them for your own work. Beta readers are more closely identified with fiction writing and publishing, although they can be used for any genre.

In the nonfiction world, you'll sometimes hear about crowdsourcing as a replacement for some level of development and content editing. Sourcebooks is one traditional publisher that has experimented with this type of authoring and editing process. Again, people with a background in technology would be very familiar with this type of iterative process and framework. Crowdsourcing makes content available faster, gets real-time feedback from the target audience, and shapes the final product based on collaboration.

Sourcebooks CEO Dominique Raccah has said that the traditional publishing model, with its long schedules and lack of involvement with readers, can be a major weakness and also irritate authors. For nonfiction authors who are experts and highly immersed in their field, a writing process that draws on the wisdom of the community can end up producing a book that is better received, more comprehensive, and more well-researched than one that is produced in isolation from its audience. Some examples of authors who have taken this approach include journalists Dan Gillmor and Chris Anderson.

If you decide that beta readers or crowdsourcing might play a role in your writing and revision process, don't forget the burden will be on you to figure out what advice is actually good and worth acting on, and what feedback isn't on target. This can take a level of discernment and insight that not all new writers have. You can also end up feeling confused by conflicting feedback.

Which brings us full circle to the value of a professional editor. If you've ever heard a published author rave about their longtime editor, then you know what an indispensable role they can play in an author's career-long success. There's a reason that Editor Maxwell Perkins is a legend. He became famous for spotting the talent of F. Scott Fitzgerald, Ernest Hemingway, and Thomas Wolfe. And not only did he spot talent, but he nurtured his authors over many years and books. While he was valued for his ability to see where a story ought to go more clearly than the writer did, he was also cherished for his role as a friend and promoter of his authors' works.

I hope that one day you find your Maxwell Perkins. Despite claims to the contrary, they do still exist, both within publishing houses and as freelancers. Once you find a good match, treat your editor as a prized possession, and valued member of your team. The relationship is one of the most important investments of your career when it comes to fulfilling your potential as an author.

How Writers Handle Rejection
Lecture 16

As we've discussed throughout this course, writers seeking publication must learn to see their writing as a product. When you submit work to an agent or publisher, you're entering into a business transaction, and a large part of the business of publishing involves the rejection of work that doesn't meet a variety of requirements or standards. Of course, that's easy to say. We can all acknowledge rejection as a logical aspect of publishing. At the same time, it's difficult to overcome the emotional sting of being told that the project you've spent years working on isn't worth further consideration. In this lecture, we'll discuss how to let go of rejection or react to it in a constructive manner.

Responding to Rejection Constructively

- Receiving rejections is simply a reality for writers who want to see their work published. But the rejection itself isn't as important as what you decide to do next.

  o First, acknowledge the hurt you feel. Wallow in pain for a set amount of time—perhaps five minutes or five days—then get back to work.

  o Next, avoid parsing vague or form rejection letters. If you get useful feedback, consider it a gift and use it to improve your work. If you violently disagree with any criticism you receive, that might be the rarest gift of all. Put your work aside for a few weeks or months, then revisit it. You may find that the criticism is right on the money.

  o Finally, promise yourself that you won't lose total confidence after rejection. Whatever uncertainty plagues you is natural and part of the process. Sometimes, the best way to deal with it is to continue to read and write what you love.

- Every writer finds coping mechanisms or rituals that help deal with rejection. Some writers keep their work always out on submission, meaning that if one rejection comes back, the work is always under consideration elsewhere. This is smart because it's dangerous to tie all your hopes to one editor, publisher, or agent.

- Once you finish a manuscript, you should also immediately start work on another project. This helps create distance and perspective from the project you just finished—which will inevitably need to be revisited with a more critical eye later.

Common Reasons for Rejection

- The most basic and avoidable reason for rejection is that you submitted your work to someone who is ultimately inappropriate to receive it. This probably means that you didn't properly research agents and editors and adopted a mass submission approach.

- Another common reason for rejection is that something similar was recently published or that you're trying to publish in a category that is saturated. This happens particularly with nonfiction work but can also occur in fiction, when everyone seems to be capitalizing on noticeable trends.

- One of the toughest types of rejections to accept is one that includes a complimentary note but states that the market for the work is too small. If you receive such a letter, you might try approaching a smaller publisher or self-publishing. You might also consider ways in which you can make your book appear more marketable, although this isn't particularly easy. Many talented writers simply don't think like marketers.

- Other standard reasons you might be given in a rejection letter including the following:
  o "Doesn't fit our needs at this time." This is a stock phrase in the publishing world that you shouldn't try to interpret because it could literally mean anything.

- "Doesn't have sufficient market appeal." Again, perhaps the market for your work is too small, or perhaps your work lacks punch.

- "Just couldn't get excited about it." This comment about a fiction work usually reflects a weak story or protagonist.

- "The writing doesn't stand out." Your writing lacks style, sophistication, and voice, or your story is boring, unoriginal, or uninspired.

- "Not fresh enough." For fiction writers, perhaps your plot line is too cliché, your characters are too common, or your story is not unique.

- "You don't have a sufficient platform." This reason is given most often to nonfiction writers who lack adequate credentials, authority, or visibility to the target market.

Personalized Rejections

- Personalized rejections obviously take more time and thought than form letters and are sent only if an agent or editor sees something in your work that might merit consideration in the future. You should consider such communications a sign that you're getting closer to publication.

- Sometimes, a personalized rejection comes with an invitation to submit your next work or resubmit your work if you make changes to it.
  - Never undertake revision to your work unless you believe that the suggestions will improve it. If the feedback opens your eyes to how your work could be genuinely taken to the next level, you should hit the pause button, revise, and resubmit.

  - However, if you have doubts about the feedback, keep submitting and see if you receive any more personalized rejections. If a pattern emerges in the feedback, that's a strong case for revision.

- Whatever happens, there's only one proper response to a personalized rejection, and that's a thank you. Do not try to open up a conversation about the work unless explicitly invited to do so and never argue with a rejection.

  o Getting past the rejection phase and finding a way to build a relationship with a potential agent or publisher often means understanding that person's motivation. Arguing over a rejection or pleading for attention won't accomplish that.

  o If you find an opportunity to talk to agents or editors at a conference, instead of thinking about all the things you want from them

The new rejection in the publishing world is often silence, partly because of the sheer volume of submissions received and partly because editors have grown tired of unprofessional responses to rejection.

or devising clever ways to influence them, demonstrate your curiosity. Ask such questions as: What's the most challenging part of your job? What do you look for in a partnership with an author? What do you wish every author knew before entering into a partnership with you? In response, you'll gain insight that could be useful the next time you submit your work.

Are You Wasting Your Time?

- Let's say that you've gone through the submission process and haven't been able to gain any traction. No agent or publisher has expressed any serious interest, and you don't know whether you can make your work more marketable or you're just wasting your time. Now may be the time to take stock of where you're headed and correct your path if necessary.

- One common time-wasting behavior that leads to fast rejection is submitting manuscripts that aren't your best work. You must give each manuscript everything you've got, with nothing held back, rather than saving your best effort for the future. To be competitive, your book must be better than you ever thought possible. If you think your work has a problem, then it does, and any story with a problem is not ready to be submitted for publication.

- Another time waster is pursuing the wrong path to publication, such as trying to secure a book deal from a major publisher for a niche work. You must be honest with yourself about the commercial potential for your work; not every book deserves distribution to every bookstore in the country.

- Further, some writers—particularly fiction writers—focus on publishing far too early, when they should be focused on writing. Although it's helpful to be active in the publishing community, too many writers develop anxiety about the publishing process before they've demonstrated that they can commit to writing and revising thousands of words—that is, before they put in the work necessary to create a publication-ready manuscript.

Closing in on a Deal

- Three questions often strongly indicate how close a writer is to a traditional publishing deal:
  - How long have you been working on this manuscript, and who has seen it?

  - Is this the first manuscript you've ever completed?

  - How long have you been actively writing?

- Many first manuscript attempts are not publishable, even after revision, yet they are necessary and vital for a writer's growth. A writer who's just finished a first manuscript probably doesn't realize this and will likely take the rejection process hard. At the same time, a writer who has been working on the same manuscript for many years—and has written nothing else—might be tragically stuck. There isn't usually much valuable learning going on when someone tinkers with the same pages over a decade.

- Writers who have been actively writing for many years, have produced multiple full-length manuscripts, have trusted critique partners or mentors, and have attended a few major writing conferences are often well-positioned for publication. They probably know their strengths and weaknesses and have a structured revision process. Such writers often require only luck, and there's an old saying about luck: It's when preparedness meets opportunity.

- Surprisingly, talent may be less relevant in determining how close you are to a traditional publishing contract than two other factors: how much time you put into writing and whether you read enough to understand where you lie on the spectrum of quality.

- Indicators will eventually surface if your work has sufficient quality but isn't suited for commercial publication. You might be told that your work is too quirky, has narrow appeal, or doesn't fit the traditional model. These signs indicate that you may need to think about self-publishing or wait for the publishing winds to change.

- Finally, consider the following timeless factors when your revisiting your writing career and making decisions about your next steps forward:
  - What makes you happy? Happiness is the reason you got into writing in the first place. Even if you put it on the back burner to advance other aspects of your writing career, don't leave it out of the equation for long. Otherwise, your efforts can come off as mechanistic or uninspired, and you'll eventually burn out.

  - What earns you money? Not everyone cares about earning money from writing, and writers who are looking to become rich should probably find another field. But as you gain experience, the choices you make in this regard become more important. The more professional you become, the more you must pay attention to what brings the most return on your investment of time and energy.

- ○ What reaches readers or grows your audience? Sometimes, you'll want to make trade-offs that involve earning less money to grow readership because doing so is an investment in the future. For example, some industry conferences don't pay speakers, but they put you in front of important insiders or influencers in your community.

- • In the end, if you believe that you can't stop writing even if someone tells you that it's a waste of time or won't get you a deal, then you're much closer to publication than another writer who is easily discouraged.

Suggested Reading

Kleinman and Lejarde, *The Science of Rejection Letters.*

Orr, *No More Rejections.*

Exercises

1. Visit LiteraryRejections.com to learn how many times classic works and bestsellers were rejected.

2. Visit RejectionWiki.com to read standard rejection letters from a range of publications.

How Writers Handle Rejection
Lecture 16—Transcript

Rejection can be the number one area of pain, concern, and obsession for writers. After working as an editor for more than 15 years, I still hear second-hand stories about writers who have been wounded by my feedback, many years after the fact. Just about every single time, while I often remember the writer in question, I've completely forgotten what I've said or even what the project was about.

If you talk to other editors and agents, you'll find this is pretty common. So many projects cross our desks and sending rejections is a near-daily occurrence. It's next to impossible to keep mental track of what becomes only one detail of the business.

I tell you this story to help you understand why you shouldn't take rejection personally. As we've discussed throughout this course, when you seek publication, you have to switch mindsets. You have to see your writing as a product. You're entering into a business transaction.

I, too, have had my share of rejection. It gets easier the more you experience it. And especially when you work on the inside of a publishing house or literary agency, and you see how many decisions get made day to day, you realize there is nothing about it that any author ought to take personally or even seriously.

Of course, that's very easy to say. You can acknowledge this aspect of the business as quite rational or logical, but it's quite another thing to overcome the emotional sting when you've spent years of your life on a project that someone spends a few minutes deciding isn't worth further consideration.

When some writers begin receiving rejections, they start to carry around what I call the rejection burden, which tends to color all of their interactions with agents and editors, and even color their future work. You should periodically stop to consider if you've allowed the wound of rejection to transform you or your work into something you never intended.

Here's a parable that I like to share with writers who might be carrying a rejection burden. Two monks come to a muddy river crossing. There they see a young woman dressed in a very fine kimono, obviously not knowing how to cross the river without ruining her clothes. The older monk picks her up and carries her across the muddy river, placing her onto dry ground. The woman does not thank him, but goes on her way. Hours later, the monks find themselves at a lodging temple.

And here the younger monk can no longer restrain himself and his complaints gush forth: "I cannot believe that woman. You kindly carried her on your very own back, and she did not offer thanks." The older monk calmly observes, "I put the woman down some time ago. Why are you still carrying her?"

This isn't to make light of rejection, but to emphasize the importance of being able to let go of it or finding a way to react in a constructive manner. Put another way, the rejection itself isn't as important as what you decide to do next. Here's my suggested method of dealing with it.

First, acknowledge the hurt that you probably feel. Wallow for a set amount of time, whether that's five minutes or five days. When I was a college student, my creative writing professor told us that she would take to bed for a few hours. But when that time runs out, you have to promise yourself that you'll get back to work.

Next, avoid parsing vague or form rejection letters. We'll talk more about this later, but it's mostly a waste of your time and energy. If you get useful feedback, consider it a gift and use it to improve your work. If you violently disagree with any criticism you receive, that might be the rarest gift of all. Put your work aside for a few weeks or months, then revisit it. You might find the criticism right on the money.

It's imperative you not lose total confidence after a rejection, no matter how long the rejection process lasts. Remember that whatever uncertainty plagues you is natural and part of the process. Sometimes the best way to deal with it is to continue to read and write what you love.

Every writer finds coping mechanisms or rituals that work, and the sooner you find your own, the better. Some writers always keep their work out on submission, meaning that if one rejection comes back, the work is always under consideration elsewhere. This is smart because it's dangerous to tie all of your hopes to one specific editor or publisher or agent. Having a lot of irons in the fire can be productive—you always have the possibility of a positive response ahead.

As you become more experienced at sending work out and receiving responses, you'll begin to see that your hit rate—or the number of relative successes you have—will be fairly consistent and also a fairly low percentage of all submissions. The sooner you can learn this about the publishing business, the less rejection will score a lasting hit to your confidence.

I also encourage writers that once they finish a manuscript, the first thing they should immediately do is start work on another project. This helps create distance and perspective from the project you just finished, which will inevitably need to be revisited with a more critical eye later. For genre writers, this process can make a lot of sense if you're working on a series. You can get to work right away on book two as you're trying to sell book one.

While your family and friends should be there to offer moral support during the tough times, be careful when listening to their advice when it comes to next steps on your work. Your family and friends love you and see you in your work. They want you to be happy and to succeed. An editor doesn't know you and is more objective, especially when it comes to marketability. Publishing professionals have distance. You and your closest friends and family may not.

I mention this because at some point, as every writer does, you'll try to determine your next steps based on the rejections you're receiving. Reasons for rejection are incredibly subjective and can boil down to indefinable issues of taste, but let's go over what types of feedback writers most often get.

The most basic and avoidable reason for rejection is that you submitted your work to someone who is ultimately inappropriate for your work. This happens if you didn't properly research agents and editors, or adopted a mass submission approach. Despite all of the resources available to writers, inappropriate submissions still remain the number one reason for rejection, along with submission materials that aren't properly prepared, or that fail to follow the agent or publisher's guidelines.

Another common reason is that something similar was recently published, or you're trying to publish in a category that's saturated. This particularly happens with nonfiction work, but can also happen in fiction when there are noticeable trends that everyone's copying.

Similarly—and this is hard to pinpoint from a form rejection—but your timing may just be bad. Maybe the editor who would've been receptive to your project has left, the publisher has cut back their list, or the market's changed in some way.

One of the toughest types of rejections to accept is when the note is very complimentary. The editor or agent may say they really enjoyed or even loved your work, but the market for it's too small. So what can you do about this? Well, the logical next step would be to approach a smaller publisher, because they have a lower threshold of sales to meet, but if the market is too small for even the small press, then you should probably self-publish.

If that's not what you want, then you have to think through whether it's possible to make your book appear more marketable. This isn't particularly easy, and many talented writers fail to achieve commercial success because they simply don't think like marketers and they have mediocre marketing skills. Conversely, some mediocre writers are quite successful because they know how to position their work so that it entices publishers.

Here are some other phrases you might read in a rejection letter.

"Doesn't fit our needs at this time." This is classic, all-purpose rejection language. It could mean literally anything, so don't try to interpret it. It's a stock phrase that gets used again and again by everyone in the publishing industry.

"Doesn't have sufficient market appeal," means exactly what it says. Perhaps the market for your work is too small, as we just discussed, or maybe your work lacks punch. It's not different enough, unique enough, or special enough for people to take notice.

"Just couldn't get excited about it." If someone makes this comment about your fiction, it usually reflects a weak story or protagonist, or something without a compelling conflict. Your story hasn't emotionally engaged the editor or agent.

"The writing doesn't stand out." This probably means your writing lacks style, sophistication, or voice. It could also mean your story is boring, unoriginal, or uninspired.

"Not fresh enough." For fiction writers, perhaps your plot line is too cliché, your characters are too common, or your story is not unique enough for publication.

"The story is too quiet." This response is common for literary writers who may have a very gently paced book. The characters may be beautifully expressed, but don't do anything of interest. The story probably has too much subtlety and too little action to keep readers turning the pages.

"You don't have a sufficient platform" is a reason given most often to nonfiction writers who lack adequate credentials, authority, or visibility to the target market. We discussed this issue at length in an earlier lecture.

All of these phrases I've just explained might be included in a form rejection. You can usually tell form rejections from the personal ones. A form rejection may not be signed by a specific person, it might not be specifically addressed to you, or it might not say anything specific about your work. It could very well be a photocopied letter that gets sent to hundreds or thousands of writers. Sometimes it clearly states that it's a form rejection.

These stock phrases might also get included in a personalized rejection, which generally hold more weight or deserve more attention than the form rejection. A personalized rejection obviously takes more time and thoughtfulness than the form letter. An agent or editor would only take additional time to write one if they see something in your work that impresses them or might merit their consideration in the future. They might also venture to give you specific insight or guidance on how to improve your work. You can consider such communication a sign that you're getting closer to publication. Agents or editors can tell you're on the verge of producing something great, or might even be accepted by someone else.

Sometimes, a personalized rejection comes with an invitation to submit your next work, or resubmit your work if you make changes to it. It can be difficult to decide what to do next. Should you stop the submissions process to revise? This is something you need to take seriously, but never undertake revision to your work unless you do believe the suggestions will improve it. If the feedback opens your eyes to how your work could genuinely reach the next level, you should hit the pause button, revise, and resubmit.

Accepting feedback and incorporating it into your work will win major points with an agent or editor. This demonstrates serious intent and professionalism. However, if you have doubts about the feedback, keep submitting. See if you receive any more personalized rejections. If a pattern emerges in the feedback, that's a strong case for revision.

Whatever happens, there's only one proper response to a personalized rejection, and that's a thank you. Don't try to open up a conversation about the work unless explicitly invited, and never, ever argue with a rejection. You don't want to make the agent or editor sorry that they tried to help you.

This brings us to a growing phenomenon in the publishing world, which is often surprising to those in other professions. The new rejection is often silence, meaning you'll never receive any response or acknowledgment that your work was even received. So why is this considered acceptable?

Part of it has to do with the sheer volume of submissions that agents and publishers receive, but another reason has to do with some professionals who have grown tired of nonprofessional responses to their rejection letters. It consumes too much time they could more profitably spend on existing clients or projects. They don't like saying no and then having to justify their decision, or saying no multiple times when a writer continues to submit the same work after being rejected once.

I once had a writer contact me and ask how they could respond to an agent who had rejected his work because there was too much passive voice. The writer was frustrated because the agent's diagnosis was in fact wrong—and the agent's misunderstanding of passive voice was clearly leading to unfair rejections.

This is a classic example of an agent who was likely reaching for the most ready reason available to them to reject a work. It may be disheartening to learn that a publishing professional doesn't understand grammar, uses poor grammar herself, or would even reject something on the basis of grammar alone, but ultimately it doesn't matter. Sometimes the reasons you're given are a poor attempt to provide a rational explanation for something that isn't at all rational. The reality is that impressions get formed in seconds, and they're often gut instincts. A reason or explanation is applied only after the fact.

I also meet many writers who emphasize that they just need an agent or publisher to offer serious consideration. You just know your book deserves publication. The only problem is you can't get anyone in the industry to pay attention to you. If only someone would pay attention, you'd have it made. Unfortunately, just about every writer thinks exactly the same thing. Writers have an amazing ability to consider themselves the one exception, but this kind of exceptionalist thinking doesn't get you any closer to publication.

Getting past the rejection phase and finding a way to build a relationship with a potential agent or publisher often means understanding what motivates those agents or publishers in the first place. Arguing over a rejection or pleading for attention won't accomplish that. If you find an opportunity to talk to an agent at a conference, instead of thinking about all the things you want from them or devising clever ways to influence them, be curious instead.

Ask questions like, "What's the most challenging part of your job?" Or, "What do you look for in a partnership with an author?" Or, "What do you wish every author knew before they entered into a partnership with you?" In response, you'll gain insight that could be useful for the next time you submit your work.

When you're not in a position of strategic power—when you want something from someone, but you have nothing proven to offer in return—it benefits you to learn, listen, and find out how you can be a desirable partner.

Most agents and editors do not enjoy being the focus of writer's hopes. If you, as a writer, see yourself as an equal to the people you'd like to work with, you'll be better able to treat communications in a way that doesn't emphasize your need to have something. That in turn removes the emotional tension and power struggle that can enter into your communication. An editor or agent will be more honest and forthright with you if they see you as a professional, and if they can expect an interaction to be productive rather than an energy drain.

More progress than you might think depends on the willingness of agents and editors to help you and advise you, even when they can't represent you or publish you. So bottom line: Be gracious during the rejection process. If you find yourself demonizing people in the publishing industry, taking rejections very personally, feeling as if you're owed something, or complaining whenever you get together with other writers, it's time to hit the refresh button. Return to what made you feel joy and excitement about writing in the first place. Perhaps you've been focusing too much on getting published and you've forgotten to cherish the other aspects.

So let's say you've gone through the submissions process and haven't been able to gain any traction. No agent or publisher has expressed serious interest, and you have very little to go on as far as how to make the work more marketable. It would be helpful to know at this point how close you are to getting your book traditionally published. Wouldn't it be nice if someone could say, "If you just keep at it for three more years, you're certain to make it?"

Even if it's not possible for me to read your work, I can usually say something close to the mark about what your next steps should be. I often see when writers are wasting their time. No matter where you're at from your own publishing path, it's helpful to periodically take stock of where you're headed and revise as necessary.

Let's start by summarizing three common time-wasting behaviors that lead to fast rejection.

First, if you've been submitting manuscripts that aren't your best work, you're doing yourself a disservice. You have to give each manuscript everything you've got, with nothing held back. Too many writers save their best effort for some future work, as if they were going to run out of good material. You can't operate like that. Every single piece of greatness must go into your current project. Be confident that your well is going to be refilled. Make your book better than you ever thought possible—that's what it needs to compete. It can't just be good. Good gets rejected. Your work has to be the best. How do you know when it's ready, when it's your best? If you think the story has a problem, it does—and any story with a problem is not ready.

Second, if you're trying to secure a book deal from a major New York publisher for your very niche or regional work, you're pursuing the wrong path to publication. You have to be honest with yourself about the commercial potential for your work, and not every book deserves distribution to every bookstore in the country.

Finally, some writers focus on publishing far too early, when they should be focused on writing. This mainly applies to fiction writers, since many nonfiction writers do in fact pitch their book before writing it.

If you're a novelist consumed with finding an agent before you've even finished your manuscript, you've got things backwards. While it's helpful for writers to be active in the publishing community by attending conferences or developing relationships with established authors, I see too many writers developing anxiety about the publishing process before they've even demonstrated to themselves that they can commit to writing and revising thousands and thousands of words before they put in the amount of work that creates a publication-ready manuscript.

Whenever I sit down for a consultation with a writer, I ask three questions early on: How long have you been working on this manuscript, and who has seen it? Is this the first manuscript you've ever completed? And how long have you been actively writing?

These questions often strongly indicate how close you are to a traditional deal. Here are a few generalizations I can make. Many first manuscript attempts are not publishable, even after revision, yet they're necessary and vital for a writer's growth. A writer who's just finished her first manuscript probably doesn't realize this, and will likely take the rejection process very hard—and some writers can't move past this rejection.

A writer who's been working on the same manuscript for years and years and has written nothing else might be tragically stuck. There isn't usually much valuable learning going on when someone tinkers with the same pages over a decade.

Writers who've been actively writing for many years, have produced multiple full-length manuscripts, have one or two trusted critique partners or mentors, and have attended a couple major writing conferences are often well positioned for publication. They probably know their strengths and weaknesses and have a structured revision process. Such writers often require only luck, and there's that old saying about luck: it's when preparedness meets opportunity.

Writers who have extensive experience in one medium, then attempt to tackle another—like when journalists tackle a novel—may overestimate their abilities to produce a publishable manuscript on the first try. That doesn't mean their effort won't be good, but it might not be good enough. Fortunately, any writer with professional experience will probably approach the process with more of a business mindset, as well as a good network of contacts to help him understand the next steps.

Notice I have not mentioned talent. I have not mentioned creative writing classes or degrees. I have not mentioned who you know. These factors are usually less relevant in determining how close you are to a traditional publishing contract.

The two factors that are typically most relevant are first, how much time you've put into writing. I agree with Malcolm Gladwell's 10,000-hour rule expressed in his book *Outliers*: The key to success in any field is, to a large extent, a matter of practicing a specific task for a total of around 10,000 hours. The second factor is whether you're reading enough to understand where you lie on the spectrum of quality, and we'll talk more about this in the next lecture.

Indicators will eventually surface if your work has sufficient quality, but isn't suited for commercial publication. You'll hear things like: "Your work is too quirky or eccentric." "It has narrow appeal." "It's experimental." "It doesn't fit the model." Or possibly, "It's too intellectual, too demanding." These are signs that you may need to consider self-publishing or wait for the publishing winds to change.

Pay attention when people enthusiastically respond to something that you didn't expect. I see this happen all the time. A writer's working on a manuscript that no one seems interested in, but has fabulous success on some side project. Or perhaps you really want to push your memoir, but it's a humorous tip series on your blog that everyone loves. Sometimes it's better to pursue what's working and what people express interest in, especially if you take enjoyment in it. Use it as a stepping-stone to other things if necessary.

This brings me to the overall theory of how you should, at various stages of your career, revisit and revise your publication strategy. No matter how the publishing world changes, consider these three timeless factors as you make decisions about your next steps forward.

First: What makes you happy? This is the reason you got into writing in the first place. Even if you put this on the back burner in order to advance other aspects of your writing and publishing career, don't leave this out of the equation for very long. Otherwise, your efforts can come off as mechanistic or uninspired, and you'll eventually burn out.

Two: What earns you money? Not everyone cares about earning money from writing, and I believe that anyone in it for the coin should find some other field. But as you gain experience, the choices you make in this regard become more important. The more professional you become, the more you have to pay attention to what brings the most return on your investment of time and energy. As you succeed, you don't have time to pursue every opportunity. You have to stop doing some things.

For example, a novelist who prefers to dabble in several genres may need to commit to one genre or a particular series where they have the most demonstrable fan base, rather than switching off as the mood suits her. A nonfiction writer who enjoys writing personal essays, which are in notorious oversupply, may have to set that work aside to focus on articles or books that have a higher market value.

Three: What reaches readers or grows your audience? Growing readership is just as valuable as earning money. Sometimes you'll want to make trade-offs that involve earning less money in order to grow readership, because it invests in your future. For example, some industry conferences or events don't pay their speakers, but they put you in front of some of the most important insiders or influencers in your community. Or, more relevant to fiction writers, you may be asked to contribute some of your work to a bundle or anthology, for which you'll be compensated very little or not at all. But if the other contributors have very high stature and established readerships, then you have good reason to believe your work will be exposed to thousands of readers who would've never heard of you before.

It's rare that every piece of writing you do, or every opportunity presented, can involve all three elements at once. Commonly you can get two of the three. Sometimes you'll pursue certain projects with only one of these factors in play. You get to decide based on your priorities at any given point in time.

Earlier, I suggested that it might be nice if someone could tell you whether you're wasting your time trying to get traditionally published. Here's a little piece of hope. If your immediate thought was, "I couldn't stop writing even if someone told me to give up," then you're much closer to publication than someone who's easily discouraged. The battle is far more psychological than you might think, and that's what we'll discuss next.

Overcoming Obstacles to Writing
Lecture 17

Without question, it's difficult to continue writing when you receive no recognition or encouragement, but the longer you let rejection consume you, the longer it will take to reach your goals. Happy writers demonstrate resilience; they understand that failure, loss, and rejection are all part of the game. Rejection is also easier to take when you don't believe the cliché that quality bubbles to the top. In fact, great work is overlooked every day, for innumerable reasons. The best remedy to any setbacks you experience is to genuinely love the writing process, to view rejection as a form of growth, and to take advantage of those opportunities for growth that rejection presents.

Inner Conflicts

- An excellent book by Steven Pressfield, *The War of Art*, is a brief guide to dealing with issues of ego and the persistent battle of self-doubt and arrogance inside every writer. Pressfield discusses the significant role that resistance plays in any creative endeavor and the fact that each of us subconsciously engages in self-destructive behavior that prevents us from doing our best work.

- Similarly, in his series on storytelling, Ira Glass notes that the work you produce early in your career simply isn't good. It's trying to be good, but it isn't because you haven't yet attained the skills to be better. And Glass rightly says that many people never get past that phase. Instead of trying to close the gap between what they know is quality work and the quality they're able to produce, they quit.
  - If you can't perceive this quality gap, then you might not be reading enough. The best way to improve your writing skills—aside from writing more—is to read. As you do, you begin to close the gap between the quality you want to achieve and the quality you can achieve.

  - As Glass says, you've got to produce much that is worthless before you can produce something that's respectable. To

Although you may have the encouragement of family and friends, your motivation to write must come from within.

have an attitude that carries you the distance, you must avoid defensiveness and protectiveness of your work and be patient with the process.

○   You know you're making progress when, looking back, you can understand why your earlier work was rejected, and you believe it deserved rejection. You might even feel embarrassed by your earlier work.

•   Another feeling writers commonly face—and must overcome—is aversion to their own work. Every successful writer has experienced this, but it's not a reason to quit. Good writers are always critical of their own work, and they don't necessarily become less critical even as they improve.

A Writer's Dilemmas

•   At some point in your path, you must honestly answer three questions for yourself. These are dilemmas that come up repeatedly in the business of publishing and can't be addressed by anyone except the individual writer.

- First, are you creating primarily for yourself or primarily for an audience?
  - Producing work for readers means playing by at least some rules of the industry and caring what others think of your work. For long-term success, you'll need to interact with your audience and be available to them.

  - Creating only for yourself means that you find the act worthwhile regardless of who sees your work and that fulfillment comes from the practice itself, not from making your work public or receiving feedback.

  - Of course, you may be creating for both yourself and a readership. But some writers who say they are producing work for an audience aren't willing to make the sacrifices required to do so. You need to identify what you truly want out of your creative endeavors.

- Second, how much of yourself will you share with readers?
  - Having a readership necessitates some kind of persona or brand. If you're confused by this idea, step back and evaluate why you do what you do. What values or passions drive you to produce your work? When you're able to express your reasons for writing, you're on your way to developing an identity or brand for yourself as an author.

  - As humans, we tend to be most strongly attracted to people who are producing work from a deep place, rather than from a superficial drive to make money or become famous. Look at some of the most remarkable author brands, and you'll often find people who exhibit a strong core belief system throughout their work.

  - Some writers claim not to want to be visible, but the act of publishing is to make something public. It means putting yourself out in the world in some form. And given that you must put something of yourself on display, make it something you believe in. Consider the qualities of your work that readers love—that make you and your work human.

- Third, what is your killer medium? The book is often assumed to be the most authoritative and important medium, but that's only because of cultural conditioning. Creative people too often pursue this medium because it has been pushed on them by others. Before you devote a great deal of time and energy to conventional book publishing, make sure that's the appropriate medium for your message and goals.

Talent, Skill, and Determination

- Many writers wonder whether they have talent, but the following questions may be more relevant and meaningful:
  - What makes you remarkable? We each have unique strengths and weaknesses—something remarkable to contribute—and some of us are gifted with the knowledge of what those are. If you don't know, keep asking the question.

  - What's your community? Your environment and the people who surround you are important. Relationships often play a role in your career success. Find someone who can serve as your mentor or guide.

  - What risks are you taking? Playing it safe as a writer will lead to mediocre writing at best. If you're not failing, you're not shooting high enough.

  - How do you deal with change? It's certain that the publishing industry will change, and you'll likely face setbacks on your path to publication. Will you resist change or look for opportunities in it?

- Most writers who haven't succeeded and aren't sure if they can succeed like to hear that determination or persistence is more important than talent, while people who've already achieved some stature tend to argue for the importance of talent. In the end, however, there are a number of reasons that talent may not matter.

o   Neither talent nor skill is always recognized. There are just too many variables that can stand in the way of recognition, such as your background, upbringing, or education. And some people simply have more opportunities or privileges than others.

o   Everyone has some kind of talent, but so what? Your degree of talent is entirely out of your control; thus, to focus on it is fairly useless. If you can't quantify talent and you can't change how much you have, then you're left with doing the work.

o   The people who deserve our admiration are those who work hard to do what they believe in. It takes persistence and bravery to overcome great odds or work harder than others to achieve great things.

- Talent is common and does not set you apart as a writer, but that doesn't mean that just being passionate will make up for not having the skill required to put out a great book. What matters is how your passion translates into good work and smart decisions.
  o   Writers who hope to smooth the path to publication should learn how to be better at seeking advice on next steps and asking good, specific questions.

  o   There are hundreds of instruction books, courses, and videos available on the topics of getting published and self-publishing. Posing questions about these topics to publishing professionals risks disrespecting them.

  o   Instead, for any question you face, go as far as you can on your own through research. Then, when you hit a brick wall, ask a specific question of an expert who can advise you on the next step. That's the way to ask a question that gets results.

Finding Time for Writing
- Writing and revising are nothing if not time-intensive. They take you away from paying work, your family, and other activities that you probably enjoy. When you add in all the additional requirements

that writers have to market and promote themselves, it's difficult to understand how anyone has time for these tasks when publishing pays so little.

- The simple truth is that if you're going to commit to writing and publishing, you must decide what you'll stop doing. This isn't discussed nearly often enough. Everyone has projects and activities that probably fall under the rubric of the writing life but have stopped being fun and enjoyable, or aren't pushing you further, or suck up your time without tangible benefit. Sometimes, you have to stop doing things you enjoy to free up time for something more important to making progress. These are tough decisions to make, but if you don't currently have the time you need, you must stop doing something.

- As you plan your writing schedule, decide what meaningful productivity means for you on a weekly basis—perhaps 250 words a day or a chapter a week. Then, figure out how much time it takes you to meet that level of productivity. If the amount of time scares you, you may have been too ambitious. Scale back to a level where you can be disciplined and consistent. Finally, block out sacred time on your schedule to get the work done.

- It's also smart to introduce some structure into your writing life. You can do this by giving yourself daily or weekly creative writing assignments, scheduling and maintaining time for writing that is always focused on the same task, and constructing both a weekly and a daily goal sheet. Make sure your goal sheet has the following sections:
  ○ Planned accomplishments for the week.

  ○ Other events that may affect your ability to get things done.

  ○ A single task that you promise to complete.

  ○ A "parking lot" where you record things you might forget; this space enables you to free your mind to focus on work.

- Although it's important to have discipline and structure to produce work, you should also maintain self-awareness about whatever processes you set up. Don't get so focused on being as productive as possible that you lose sight of the big picture. When you strive so hard and for so long, the whole reason you started writing in the first place—the real joy and motivation for it—can get completely lost.

Suggested Reading

Lamott, *Bird by Bird*.

Pressfield, *The War of Art*.

Exercises

1. Set a daily or weekly productivity goal for yourself that feels achievable given your day job or other responsibilities. This might be a word-count goal, a page-count goal, or a time-based goal. Firmly commit to this goal for a minimum of three months until you consider readjusting it. Remember that you won't accomplish your goal unless you actually block off time in your schedule for it.

2. Explore the question of what you hope to accomplish through your writing, which is one of the most difficult questions to answer honestly. Try answering this question in 300 words, then cut your response down to 150 words. As a final step, try to reduce it to one sentence. Write this sentence on a sticky note and put it wherever you can see it when you write.

Overcoming Obstacles to Writing
Lecture 17—Transcript

I meet many writers who ask often at a moment of frustration and desperation, "Read my writing and tell me if I should keep trying." I empathize if you're looking for some reason to continue in the face of rejection. It's tough to continue doing something when you receive no recognition or encouragement for it. But the longer you let rejection consume you, the longer it will take to reach your goals. The happy writers I meet have a resilience that you can sense when you talk to them—people who understand that failure, loss, and rejection are all part of the game.

I think rejection can be easier to take when you don't believe the old cliché that quality bubbles to the top. I certainly don't believe it. Great work is overlooked every day for a million reasons. Business concerns outweigh artistic concerns, and some people are just perpetually unlucky.

The best remedy to any setbacks you experience is to genuinely love the writing process, to take advantage of every possible growth opportunity, and to see rejection as a form of growth. And when self-doubt strikes, as it always does, seek feedback from mentors who know you and your work. Avoid seeking validation from strangers, especially strangers in the publishing community. It's not fair to ask them to make that choice for you as to whether you should keep going or not. And in any case, most assurances, while offering a boost to a writer's ego, are ultimately external and momentary.

An excellent book by Steven Pressfield, *The War of Art*, is a brief guide to dealing with issues of ego and the persistent battle of self-doubt, but also arrogance inside every writer. Pressfield discusses the enormous role that resistance plays in any creative endeavor, and how each of us subconsciously engages in self-destructive behavior that prevents us from doing our best work.

Similarly, in his series on storytelling, Ira Glass talks about how when you're early in your career making stuff, what you're making isn't that good. It's trying to be good, but it just isn't because you haven't yet attained the skills to be better. He rightly says that a lot of people never get past that phase. Instead of trying to close the gap between what they know is quality work and the quality that they're able to produce, they just quit.

If you can't perceive the quality gap between what you're producing and what you recognize as good work, you might not be reading enough. The best way to improve your writing skills aside from writing more is to read more. You write and you read, and you begin to close the gap between the quality you want to achieve, and the quality you can achieve. As Glass says, you've got to produce a lot of crap before you can produce something that's of respectable quality. To have an attitude that carries you the distance, you have to avoid defensiveness and protectiveness of your work, and you need patience with yourself and with the process.

You know you're making progress when, looking back, you can understand why your earlier work was rejected and believe it deserved rejection. You might even feel embarrassed by your earlier work. One day, I received a message from a friend and a struggling writer. He announced that he was finally writing again. He commented, "We'll see if I end up hating it, as I have every single thing I've ever written before. I do hope to get over this at some point."

Every successful writer has had to overcome that feeling. It's an important feeling. It's a valid feeling. And if a writer *doesn't* have that feeling at some point, I get worried, and it's exactly because of this Ira Glass crap phase that we all experience.

That's not to say you'll become less critical of your work as you improve. Great writers will always be critical of their own work because they have good taste. It doesn't necessarily get any easier, as just about any successful author will tell you, but that's not a reason to quit.

However, I do want to offer a bit of tough love. I've cautioned in earlier lectures that it's dangerous to rely on family and friends to give you feedback about your work. They can also lead you astray in giving you confidence or motivation. I hear countless writers talk about how their family has encouraged them to write about their lives, or that all their friends love their funny stories. Parents and teachers can also fall into the trap of believing their work has merit because children love what they write.

Basically, you need to ignore your family and friends, who are often dead wrong about what you should or should not do. They're not the ones who will need to dedicate years of their lives or make sacrifices to get published. You need to write because you can't do anything else—because you would suffer if you didn't. If your motivation to write doesn't come from within, then you'll find just about every external validation fleeting.

At some point in your publishing path, you'll have to sit down and honestly answer three questions. These are dilemmas that come up again and again when I talk with writers about the business of publishing, and they are dilemmas that I can't solve for you.

The first question is: Are you creating work primarily for yourself or primarily for an audience? Almost all of my advice in this lecture series is based on the assumption that you want to entertain, inform, or have a readership. Not everyone, though, is concerned with this, nor should they be.

If you're producing work for readers, it means playing by at least some of rules of the industry and caring what others think of your work. For long-term success, you'll need to interact with your audience and be available to them.

If you're creating only for yourself, it means you find the act worthwhile regardless of who sees your work, and that fulfillment comes from the practice itself, not from making your work public or receiving feedback.

Of course, you may be creating for both yourself and a readership, but some writers who say they are producing work for an audience are not willing to make the sacrifices required to do so, which means there's another level to this. Are you creating work for an audience, or creating work for an audience that earns you money? Once money enters the equation, you have to start sacrificing more of what you want and bend to the demands of the market—or else find a generous patron or foundation.

What is it that you truly want out of your creative endeavors? Do you really know?

The second question is: How much of yourself are you going to share—and which part?

Let's assume you do want a readership. This will necessitate some kind of persona. Deciding not to have a persona or removing yourself from visibility—like the infamous Thomas Pynchon—that's also a persona. Some people would use the word brand here, and if you prefer to think of it that way, go ahead. I try to avoid that word because so many writers have a knee-jerk reaction to it. They think that branding diminishes their art or puts them into a box they can't escape.

If you don't like the idea of persona or brand, or if you're just confused by it, then let's step way back and evaluate why you do what you do. What values or passions drive you to produce your work? When you're able to express this why to people, you're on your way to developing an identity or brand for yourself as an author.

As humans, we tend to be most strongly attracted to people who are producing work from a very deep place, rather than from a superficial drive to make money or become famous. Take a look at some of the most remarkable author brands, and you'll find that many exhibit a very strong core belief system through their work. This means that ultimately while you can try imitating someone else's brand or persona, in the long run, you can only be yourself.

I often meet writers who tell me, "I don't want to be visible online. I don't have a brand. I just want people to read my stories." Well, that's not a very workable proposition in the digital age. Just as you figure out how to write a novel, you have to figure out what it means for you to interact with your audience. And, to be honest, I'm not sure I trust writers who say they want to be read but don't want to be visible. The act of publishing is to make something public. It means putting yourself out there in some form. It's unavoidable.

Ask yourself, even if you're shy, what part of yourself can you share and put on display? It's got to be something, so let's make it interesting. Make it something you can believe in and others will believe in it, too. Some of us think famous writers should be aloof, distant, or mysterious, so we imitate aloofness even when it has nothing to do with our personality. Rather than automatically adopting the aloofness of literary celebrity, consider the qualities of your work that readers love, that make you and your work human.

The third question is: What's your killer medium? The book is often assumed to be the most authoritative and important medium, but that's only because we've all been led to believe that through cultural conditioning. Creative people too often pursue mediums that have been pushed on them by other people and because it's the well-worn path. So before you dump a lot of time and energy into conventional book publishing, make sure that's the appropriate medium for your message and goals.

All of this raises the question of how to best focus on your strengths, but people also interpret it as whether they have an aptitude or talent for writing. But this question of talent becomes murky very quickly.

Let me start by telling you a story about my own writing life. I have a BFA in creative writing, and when I was in college, I desperately wanted the professors to tell me if I had talent. I was never brave enough to directly ask the question, but I hoped they might take me by the shoulders, look me in the eye, and say: "Jane, you can't waste this gift, you must write."

Now that I'm a professor, I realize just how irrelevant that question is. I see both talented and untalented students. The ones who impress me are the ones who are motivated and driven to do the work—the ones who push hard despite obstacles. I also clearly see who has a positive attitude and who's unengaged, often without a vision for what they hope to accomplish.

Here are four questions I find more relevant and meaningful than, "Do I have talent?"

First: What makes you remarkable? We each have a unique set of strengths and weaknesses. For some of us, it takes a while before we realize what it is we really want to do and what we have to contribute. But I do believe each of us has something remarkable to contribute, and I hope you're gifted with the knowledge of what that is. If not, keep asking the question.

Second: What's your community? Your environment and the people who surround you are important. Relationships often play a role in your career success. So what I want to know is: Who's your support network? Who's encouraging you? If you don't have anyone who can serve as a guide or a mentor, you need to change that.

Third: What risks are you taking? It's the old cliché—nothing ventured, nothing gained. Playing it safe as a writer will lead to mediocre writing at best. If you're not failing, you're not shooting high enough, which leads me to the next question:

How do you deal with change? The only thing I know for sure is that publishing will change and you'll likely face setbacks in your path to publication. Are you going to tighten up and resist or will you look for the opportunities? If you become frustrated with the publishing industry or how you're being treated by a particular editor or agent, consider these words from Joseph Campbell: "Is the system going to flatten you out and deny you your humanity, or are you going to be able to make use of the system to the attainment of human purposes?"

I tend to side with people who believe determination is more important than talent. To be clear about the definitions, let me explain what I mean when I use the words talent and determination, as well as skill.

I define talent as what you're born with, what doesn't change. When you have talent, it may lead nowhere if you don't have any way to cultivate it or nurture it. The unknowable thing here is quantifying exactly how much talent you've got. It's never been quantifiable, and I'm not even confident it can be separated from other qualities that are important to publishing success.

Skills come with hard work and practice. People can put in the same level of hard work and not attain the same skill level as others. People who have a talent or aptitude for something will gain skills faster and at a more expert level.

Determination helps you overcome challenges, delays, and bad luck. This keeps you in the game when you feel like everything is working against you, and some might call this persistence or grit.

What I've noticed is that most writers who haven't succeeded—and aren't sure if they can succeed—love to hear that determination or persistence is more important than talent. People who've already achieved some level of stature tend to argue for the importance of talent. Successful people have already been selected in some fashion, so they're liable to believe that they have talent that others don't. Maybe they do and maybe they don't. I don't think it really matters for several reasons. Neither talent nor skill is always recognized. This is because there are too many variables that can stand in the way, such as your background, upbringing, or education. Some people have more opportunities or privileges than others.

Also, everyone has some kind of talent, but so what? It's entirely out of our control, so to focus on it is fairly useless. If you can't quantify or really know how much you have—and you can't change how much you have—then you're left with doing the work.

I admire people who push through obstacles to do what they believe in. What's especially inspiring are people who overcome great odds, or who work harder than everyone else to achieve great things. There is usually tremendous sacrifice in that. It takes guts.

So that's why I don't really put much stock in this question of talent. Talent is common and does not set you apart as a writer. However, I don't think this means that just being passionate will make up for not having the skill required to put out a great book. The idea of passion has even become somewhat cheap. We all have a passion these days, but what matters is how that passion translates into good work and smart decisions about that work. Some might say passion is useless without discipline. Others might say passion is useless without acute self-awareness and an ability to make smart decisions about where your efforts will pay off.

Whatever you believe, here's my experience. I've taught hundreds of writers with passion, but I teach few writers with commitment to do the best work possible. The only time when I find passion useful is when it helps you more easily put in the effort or the work required—consistently over time—to become a master in your art.

Writers who hope to further smooth the path to publication should also learn how to be better at seeking advice on next steps and how to ask good, specific questions. This goes back to what I mentioned about making smart decisions about where your efforts pay off. If you're able to ask the right question at the right time, it can be like rocket fuel for your career. The better questions you ask, the better quality responses you'll get, and the more actionable information you'll have.

For example, as a well-known figure in the publishing community, I receive many broad questions along the lines of, "How can I get published?" or "Should I self-publish?" It can make me wonder what kind of response is expected, since hundreds of instruction books, courses, and videos are available on these very topics. Posing such broad questions risks disrespecting the person you're asking unless they're a friend who knows you.

Of course, you're doing an excellent thing right now by taking this course—you're finding out everything you can on your own. For any question you face, go as far as you possibly can through researching it on your own. Then when you hit a real brick wall, confusing issue, or dilemma, ask a very specific question of an expert who can advise you on the next step. That's the way to ask a question that gets results.

One of the reasons I think I'm asked so often, "Tell me if I should keep trying," is because writing and revising are nothing if not time intensive. They take you away from paying work, away from family, and away from other activities you probably enjoy just as much, if not more. Then, when you add in all the additional requirements that writers have to market and promote themselves, you might well ask, "How does anyone have the time to do this when writing and publishing pays so little?"

One question I can count on in every setting—no matter the topic, the gathering, or the audience skill level—is: How do you find the time to do all of this? Sometimes the question is asked in such a way that people seem to think there's a secret they haven't yet discovered. But it's not rocket science, and it's not dependent on having a large inheritance, although that does help.

If you're going to commit to writing and publishing, you have to decide what you'll stop doing—and I'm not talking about cutting out the TV, although maybe you do have hobbies you'll need to set aside. Instead, I'm talking about how you should make a stop doing list.

This isn't discussed nearly often enough. Everyone has projects and activities that probably fall under the rubric of the writing life, but have stopped being fun and enjoyable, or aren't pushing you further, or just suck up your time without tangible benefit. Sometimes you have to stop doing things you enjoy because you have to free up time for something more important to making progress. These are really tough decisions to make, but if you don't currently have the time you need, you have to stop doing something.

As you plan your writing year, consider the following:

Decide what meaningful productivity looks like on a weekly basis. For instance, does it mean writing 250 words every day? Does it mean completing a chapter every week? Decide what works for you. Under no circumstance should you measure productivity based on what someone else does. Then figure out how much time it takes you to meet that level of productivity on a daily or weekly basis. If the amount of time scares you, then you've been too ambitious. Scale back to a level where you can be disciplined and consistent, then block out sacred time on your schedule for you to get this work done.

One of the big lessons I've learned as a writing teacher is that we all need structure. For me personally, it was a hard lesson to learn because many of the things I value cause me to downplay structure. I value things like intrinsic motivation, doing what comes naturally, changing direction upon insight or discovery, and focusing on the journey rather than the outcome.

However, freedom can be our worst enemy. It can lead to procrastination, paralysis, or indecision. And especially for writers who are just starting out, the principles still need to be learned. While we may need room to experiment and explore, we also need meaningful practice and goal posts to measure our progress.

By way of example, the best writing course I ever took in college was an introduction to poetry. The professor was well-known for being a formalist, someone who required the students to write one poem per week using a different and specific form each time. In contrast, most poetry classes focus on free verse since it's the predominant poetic idiom today.

Some of the best work of my college career came out of that class. It's like what Robert Frost said: "I had as soon write free verse as play tennis with the net down." I found the challenge invigorating. It forced me to think harder about my word choices and what I wanted to say. It sharpened my writing skills in a very concentrated way. If you need to introduce some structure into your writing life, here are three ideas.

First, consider daily or weekly creative assignments. You can use writing exercise or prompt books, the kind that force you to go outside your comfort zone. One of my favorite resources for unusual, skill-building exercises is *The 3 A.M. Epiphany* by Brian Kiteley.

Here's an example of a terrific exercise from that book: Describe a happy marriage over at least 10 years. You will have to dispense with focused narrative—summarizing to a large extent, listing details, the reasons you think this is a happy marriage. Is a happy marriage an enviable marriage? Can a couple be too happy, inseparable and insufferable?

Second, have a scheduled writing time always focused on the same task every time. If you don't already have a set time and place for writing that you never deviate from, try this: Pick a 30–60 minute time slot each week that has no chance of being superseded by other responsibilities. Go somewhere that's a treat for you—a coffee shop, a park, wherever you love to go. If it's actually more of a treat to stay home, then stay home as long as you can't be interrupted. Make this your dedicated time to get the same writing task done each week. Never miss it, and always do the same kind of work. I think you'll be surprised and pleased at what happens.

Third, consider both a weekly and daily goal sheet. This is an excellent tool for a writer who is working daily on a long-term project, and who may also have other responsibilities vying for her time. Each week, list what you'd be satisfied with accomplishing, given everything else that's happening in your life. Do not overshoot it. The point is to list what you'd be satisfied with, and it should include the following sections: What do you plan to accomplish in a week? What else is happening that may affect your ability to get things done? What single task are you avoiding that you promise to complete?

And also, a parking lot. This is your free space to list or note whatever you like. I find it's the ideal place to mention stuff I'm worried I'm going to forget. If I keep it the parking lot, I know it's safe, and my mind is free to focus on my work.

After you have your weekly sheet, at the start of each day, use a single, small sticky note to list what tasks from your weekly sheet you have time for. It can be helpful to save your goal sheets so you can go back and evaluate when your most productive times were. Sometimes you'll gain insight into what motivates you to produce more work or your best work.

Even though I'm emphasizing here the importance of having discipline and structure to produce your work consistently over time, the key thing is to maintain self-awareness about whatever process you set up and how you're responding to it.

I'm not actually a stickler for writing or work productivity. In fact, we can get so focused on being as productive as possible that we lose sight of the big picture. When you strive for so hard and for so long, the whole reason you started writing in the first place—the real joy and motivation for it—can get completely lost. It's why in my more humorous moods, I tell people that the best way to get published is to stop caring about getting published. Some

writers put so much pressure on themselves that their most common state is mental exhaustion.

While I have little patience for writers who complain about having a lack of time to write—because we all have to make time for what's important—it's equally important not to carry guilt when you encounter fallow periods, or simply stretches of time where you need to have a bit of empty space. John Cleese once said, "If you're racing around all day, ticking things off a list, and generally just keeping all the balls in the air, you are not going to have any creative ideas."

Look for wisdom that comes only from knowing yourself and what you want. The more you know who you are and what you want, the less you let things upset you. My hope is that every writer I meet will not ask, "Read this and tell me what to do." But instead, "This is my mission, how can I improve and grow?" That kind of attitude puts you on the path to a fulfilling and happy writing career.

The Book Publishing Contract
Lecture 18

To negotiate a book contract in your best interests, you should have some familiarity with the legal language of publishing. If you have an agent, he or she will be knowledgeable about the contract negotiation process, but if you don't, you might find yourself faced with pages written in opaque language. Either way, it's smart to become familiar with the language and standards common to publishing contracts to ensure that you understand what you're agreeing to when you sign on the dotted line. In this lecture, we'll cover three areas of the contract to which you should pay close attention: the grant-of-rights clause, the reversion-of-rights clause, and the subsidiary rights clause.

Grant of Rights and Reversion of Rights

- The *grant-of-rights clause* specifies the rights that you grant or license to a publisher. The act of granting rights does not traditionally mean giving up your copyright; it simply means that you are giving the publisher permission to publish a specific piece of work under certain circumstances, in certain formats, and for a stated amount of time. The *reversion-of-rights clause* spells out when and how your relationship with the publisher ends, meaning when and how all rights revert to you, the author.

- These two clauses generally apply to one of three basic contract models.
  - The most common model is the *life-of-copyright contract*. This term describes a traditional print book publishing contract, which remains in effect potentially for as long as copyright on the work remains in effect.

  - Another model is the *fixed-term contract*. Such contracts have a set time limit—for example, five years—after which all rights revert to the author. Fixed-term contracts are becoming more common and make more sense for works sold primarily in digital form.

- o The third model is the *work-for-hire contract*, under which the author gives up all rights to the work, including copyright. This type of contract is common if you're a ghostwriter or working on an established, branded series for a publisher or book packager.

Life-of-Copyright Contracts
- Despite their name, life-of-copyright contracts are not expected to last until the copyright expires. Rather, the contract typically remains in effect for as long as sales occur.

- Usually, these contracts ask for publishing rights in all formats and mediums, including hardcover, paperback, mass-market paperback, e-books, audiobooks, and more. An agent may try to retain your rights to some formats and mediums and sell them separately.

- Under these traditional contracts, publishers also usually ask for *world English rights* and the rights to sell your book internationally, as well as rights to sell your work in translation. Before granting such rights, you should find out if the publisher has a track record of selling outside North America.

- Most agents limit the publisher's rights grab as much as possible or specify how long the publisher can exploit certain rights. That way, you can get certain rights back within a short timeframe if the publisher has not sold or made use of them.

- For life-of-copyright contracts, negotiating a clear reversion-of-rights clause is critical. Ideally, you want to arrange for a smooth departure after the relationship has ceased to be advantageous or profitable.
    - o An author might want to leave a publisher for a number of reasons, such as the desire to self-publish, lack of marketing or support from the publisher, or the desire to adapt or modify the

work. The desire to terminate may also be connected with how well the book is selling.

- ○ Before e-books, if the publisher wasn't actively printing and distributing the physical book in at least one edition, the author could request a reversion of rights. However, in the age of e-books and print on demand—when any book can be available in perpetuity at nearly zero cost—a publisher can easily keep your book available for sale indefinitely.

- ○ Therefore, it's best to ask for a specific sales threshold that will trigger conditions for you to request reversion of rights. If your book ever sells less than a specific quantity during a 6- or 12-month period or if your royalty payment ever dips below a particular amount, you should be able to request a reversion.

Fixed-Term and Work-for-Hire Contracts

- • For a fixed-term contract, the grant-of-rights clause is much the same as it is for a life-of-copyright contract. However, instead of having an indeterminate end date, the publisher's right to publish the work expires at a specific time.
  - ○ A fixed-term contract can be much simpler than a life-of-copyright contract, but you need to make sure that the contract term doesn't automatically renew. If it does, be diligent about contacting the publisher to terminate the agreement if you want to do so.

  - ○ Fixed-term has been the go-to model for e-book publishers, partly because e-books don't really go out of print. Given how fast the e-book landscape is evolving, few authors are willing to tie up their rights for long, especially if the publisher isn't keeping up with the pace of change.

- • Authors who agree to work for hire relinquish all rights to the work. In comparison to other contracts, there's not much to negotiate here except compensation, which is typically a flat fee and may include royalties.

Subsidiary Rights

- Most boilerplate contracts allow the publisher to sell your work in many ways other than book form. For example, the contract may grant the publisher merchandising rights, dramatic rights, or translation rights. Collectively, these rights are known as *subsidiary rights*, and they can be exercised by the publisher or licensed to others.

- In granting subsidiary rights, consider the following criteria: (1) the publisher's track record of selling or licensing such rights to everyone's mutual benefit, (2) an appropriate split of sales proceeds, (3) the publisher's willingness to seek your approval on certain types of deals, and (4) whether you or your agent is in a better position to exploit subsidiary rights.

- Among the most common subsidiary rights clauses are territorial, translation, multimedia, dramatic, audiobook, and merchandising rights. Publishers also have additional clauses addressing abridgments, anthologies, reprints, book club sales, and so on.

- Ideally, each subsidiary right in the contract should point to a specific sales or licensing activity that the publisher regularly undertakes. You should strike any catch-all clause that says the publisher will pay you a certain percentage for any rights not specified in the contract.

Other Contract Stipulations

- Be sure to check the contract language regarding how much control you have over your book's title and cover, as well as your responsibilities related to delivering the manuscript or content.

- Few authors are granted the privilege of approval over the book title or cover design, but it is reasonable to request and be granted consultation on these issues.

- Most contracts specify that if the writer fails to submit acceptable work or revisions by a deadline, the publisher may either cancel the contract or make revisions on the writer's behalf, sometimes without consultation. If you're worried about the publisher revising your work, try to include language in your contract that requires your approval of revisions or allows you to terminate the contract and take the work elsewhere.

- With book contracts, failure to submit an acceptable manuscript may require you to return any payments made, but sometimes, your agent can negotiate a contract that allows you to keep payments regardless of how, when, or why the contract is terminated. Whether or not a manuscript is considered acceptable is often entirely up to the subjective judgment of the publisher or editor. A good agent will negotiate a narrow definition here, particularly when it comes to revisions. Often, editors are required to write a revision letter, spelling out what changes the author must make to produce an acceptable work.

- The *warranties clause* in a contract requires you to make legal promises about the work. For example, you must guarantee that you haven't granted someone else rights to the work in a way that would interfere with the publisher's rights. You must also promise you've taken reasonable care to ensure that your work is true and accurate and that you haven't plagiarized or violated anyone else's rights by producing the work. If you have any concerns about a potential breach of warranties or liability with your work, consult a lawyer.

Compensation

- When you sign a traditional publishing contract, you receive an *advance against royalties*. As books sell, you earn a percentage of sales for each copy sold (a royalty), which is applied against the advance received. Only once the advance is fully earned do you start receiving royalty payments. Industry insiders estimate that 70 percent of authors do not earn out their advances, but authors do not have to return an advance if the book doesn't earn it.

- The publisher decides what advance to pay you based on a proprietary formula. Its profit-and-loss statement determines whether a book makes financial sense to publish. The decision takes into account a mixture of predictable costs (such as manufacturing) and predicted sales. Sales estimates are determined by looking at an author's past record of sales, recent performance in the book's genre or category, and so on.

- It's not uncommon for Big Five publishers to offer advances that they know won't earn out. One reason for this is that the standard e-book royalty rate of 25 percent is now widely acknowledged to be too low; however, increasing that rate for one author will set off a domino effect, requiring higher e-book royalties for other authors. If an editor really wants to acquire an author or book but can't increase the royalty rates, then a straightforward way to sweeten the deal is to offer a higher advance.

- Royalties will be clearly outlined in the contract based on format. Authors earn a different rate depending on whether the sales are for hardcover, paperback, or e-book. Royalty rates also change depending on the retail sales channel. On average, you can expect

Whenever you're presented with a contract, assume that everything is negotiable; don't be shy about asking to modify boilerplate language.

to earn a royalty of somewhere between 6 and 15 percent on the retail price of your book.

- Most book advances are paid in three installments at certain contractually specified events: contract signing, acceptance of the final manuscript, and publication.

- Read the contract for any indication of publication expenses you must bear, either against your future royalty payments or out of pocket. In traditional book deals, authors almost never cover any costs related to publication. However, it's common for nonfiction authors to bear the cost of indexing. If your book includes art, illustration, or photography, you may also cover some or all of those costs. When costs are charged against future royalty payments, you pay nothing out of pocket, but you won't earn anything from book sales until you both earn out your advance and pay for costs charged against your royalty account.

Suggested Reading

Kirsch, *Kirsch's Guide to the Book Contract*.

Exercises

1. Calculate how much you'd earn over the lifetime of your book if it sold 15,000 copies. Use a royalty rate of 15 percent for a hardcover price and 10 percent for a paperback price. (Base your pricing on how bestsellers are currently priced, assuming the same size and format.)

2. Visit the Publishers Weekly website (publishersweekly.com) and look for the weekly report on announced publishing deals, which sometimes include information about advances and terms.

The Book Publishing Contract
Lecture 18—Transcript

To understand and negotiate a book contract in your best interests, you should have some familiarity with the legal language of publishing. Unfortunately, most writers have limited insight into what publishing contracts look like or what changes are common. Few authors speak openly about their contracts, and virtually no publisher makes their contract available for public scrutiny.

If you have an agent, they'll be responsible and knowledgeable about the contract negotiations process. They'll know how to get the best deal, and you can trust them to make changes that protect your intellectual property and earnings potential.

Of course, not all writers have agents, and you might find yourself faced with a contract full of opaque language. Either way, it's good to become familiar with the language and standards common to publishing contracts so you understand what you're agreeing to when you sign on the dotted line.

There are three areas of the contract to pay close attention to: the grant-of-rights clause, the reversion-of-rights clause, and the subsidiary rights clause.

As I discuss each area, I'm going to temporarily set aside the question of compensation. It varies so much, it's nearly impossible to talk about an average. Only you can decide what money is appropriate for your situation and the work in question. Generally, the more rights a publisher asks for, the more you should get paid. And it's important to remember that regardless of what you are paid initially, the contract can significantly affect what you're paid in the future, as well as your own ability to resell or repurpose your work.

First, let's discuss the grant-of-rights clause and the reversion-of-rights clause. The grant-of-rights is often found at the beginning of the contract and specifies what rights you're granting or licensing to a publisher. The act of granting rights does not traditionally mean giving up your copyright. Granting rights to your work simply means you are granting the publisher permission to publish a specific piece of work under certain circumstances in certain formats for a stated amount of time. The reversion-of-rights clause spells out when and how your relationship with the publisher ends—meaning when and how all rights revert to you, the author.

When it comes to these two clauses, you can generally find three basic methods of working. The most common model is what's known as the life-of-copyright contract. This describes your traditional print book publishing contract, which remains in effect potentially for as long as copyright on the work remains in effect.

Another model is the fixed-term contract. These contracts have a set time limit—for example, five years—after which all rights revert to the author. Fixed-term contracts are becoming more common and make more sense for works sold primarily in digital form.

The third model is the work-for-hire contract. A work-for-hire means you give up all rights to the work, including copyright. There is no reversion-of-rights because you don't hold the rights. This type of contract is common if you're a ghostwriter or working on an established, branded series for a publisher or book packager.

No model is necessarily more favorable than the others. Much depends on the work being contracted, the compensation, and your goals. But life-of-copyright contracts should be expected from any commercial New York publisher, as well as most small presses. So, let's look at each model a little bit more closely.

While it sounds ominous, life-of-copyright contracts aren't actually expected to last until the copyright expires. Rather, the contract typically remains in effect for as long as sales occur. The typical traditional publishing contract will ask for publishing rights in all formats and mediums, including hardcover, paperback, mass-market paperback, e-books, audiobooks, and more. An agent may try to retain your rights to some formats and mediums and sell them separately.

The publisher will also typically ask for world English rights and the rights to sell your book internationally, as well as in translation. Before granting such rights, you should find out if the publisher has a track record of selling outside North America. Now, most agents will limit the publisher's rights grab as much as possible, or they'll specify how long the publisher can exploit certain rights. That way, you can get rights back within a short time frame if the publisher hasn't sold or otherwise made use of them.

One way to limit the publisher's rights is through a reversion-of-rights clause. For life-of-copyright contracts, negotiating a clear reversion-of-rights clause is critical. It can make the difference between a happy ending or a contentious one. Ideally, you want to arrange for a clean and smooth departure after the relationship has ceased to be advantageous or profitable.

But maybe we should first answer the question, why would you want rights to revert at all? After all the trouble it takes to find a publisher, why would you want to leave?

There are many reasons as authors, but the primary motivations are one, you want to publish the book yourself. Two, your publisher is no longer doing a good job of marketing or otherwise supporting the book, so you want to take it elsewhere. And three, you want to do something entirely different with the work that requires you have the rights back—such as adapt it or modify it.

While everyone wants a happy and conflict-free relationship with their publisher, it's best to take the long and probably more realistic view—knowing exactly how you'll make a graceful exit when it's time to move on. If you can't find the reversion-of-rights clause in your contract, look for anything labeled as termination by the author, which refers to the termination of the contract. If nothing happens that would result in a breach of contract, then termination is typically connected with how well the book is selling.

For example—before e-books came along—if the publisher wasn't actively printing and distributing the physical book in at least one edition, the author could request a reversion-of-rights. However, in the age of e-books as well as print on demand—when any book can be made available in perpetuity at nearly zero cost—the publisher can easily keep your book available for sale.

Therefore, it's best to ask for a specific sales threshold that will trigger conditions for you to ask for the rights back. If your book ever sells less than a specific quantity during a six or twelve-month period or if your royalty payment ever dips below a particular amount, you should be able to request a reversion-of-rights.

Just because you request a rights reversion doesn't mean you automatically get the rights back. The contract may leave the door open for the publisher to take action to keep the rights. For instance, it might start selling above the appointed threshold within six months. They may also just drag their feet on a response or find other ways to stall. In such an event, an agent can be of immense value.

For a fixed-term contract, the grant-of-rights clause will look much the same as it does for a life-of-copyright contract. However, instead of an indeterminate end date, the publisher's right to publish the work will expire at a specific time. A fixed-term contract can be much simpler to handle than a life-of-copyright contract, but you need to make sure the contract term doesn't automatically renew. And if it does, be diligent about contacting the publisher to terminate the agreement—assuming you want to do so—and abide by whatever terms are indicated in the contract. A written notice is often required.

Fixed-term has been a go-to model for e-book publishers since e-books don't really go out of print and also because such publishers are newer and have to offer more flexibility to be attractive partners. Given how fast the e-book landscape is evolving, few authors are willing to tie up their rights for very long, especially if their publisher isn't keeping up with the pace of change.

Finally, in the third type of contract—the work-for-hire—authors must relinquish all rights to their work. In comparison to the other contracts, there's not much to negotiate here except the compensation, which is typically a flat fee and may include royalties.

So now that we've covered the grant-of-rights and reversion-of-rights, let's discuss another major area of the book contract: subsidiary rights.

When you're offered a publishing contract, you may be so excited about seeing your work in book form that you don't even give much thought to what other rights are in play. However, most boilerplate contracts allow the publisher to sell many types of rights that go beyond your standard trade hardcover or paperback. For example, the contract may grant the publisher merchandising rights to all aspects of your story, dramatic rights, or translation rights—and much more than that. Collectively, these rights are known as subsidiary rights, and they can be exercised by the publisher or even licensed to others.

When signing a contract, understand what subsidiary rights you are granting and consider the following criteria: One, does the publisher have the means to successfully exploit all of the subsidiary rights it's asking for? Does it have a good track record in selling or licensing such rights to everyone's mutual benefit? Two, authors and publishers split proceeds from subsidiary rights, so does the contract offer an appropriate split? Three, is the publisher willing to consult with you or seek approval on certain types of subsidiary rights deals? Four, are you—or is your agent—in a better position to exploit and profit from the subsidiary rights?

It's not always better to hang on to your subsidiary rights if you or your agent have no means or opportunity to exploit them, when your publisher does. On the other hand, neither do you want to grant a range of subsidiary rights if you're not being paid for your work. Rather than getting into every possible permutation of subsidiary rights clauses, I'll cover the most common—particularly those with the highest potential to affect your earnings.

First, there are rights related to sales territories. If your publisher takes world English rights—which is the right to publish and distribute your book in English around the world—it may have its own publishing subsidiaries in other countries. So it may publish and distribute your book through those subsidiaries, or it may license the rights to a third party. Alternatively, you might be able to negotiate a deal, in which the publisher is granted only North American rights, and you and your agent have the freedom to sell rights to publishers in the U.K., Australia, and so on.

For example, J. K. Rowling's Harry Potter series was published first by Bloomsbury in the U.K., but Rowling and her agent kept her foreign sales rights and auctioned them off to Scholastic in the United States. And Rowling also held on to her e-book rights, which led to the creation of Pottermore.com.

Translation rights are sold separately from territorial rights. Translations are usually created and sold after the English edition is already available. The translation work and cost is the responsibility of the publisher purchasing such rights. Industry insiders predict that publishers may start handling translations of works themselves—with the help of freelance translators—rather than license the rights to other publishers. Also, as e-books become a predominant format, handling translations internally helps reduce the need for foreign publishers to deal with sales and distribution of foreign editions—except for print editions.

Territorial and translation rights deals often happen at international book fairs, such as BookExpo America, the London Book Fair, and Frankfurt Book Fair. Some literary agencies have strong foreign rights departments and will retain these rights whenever possible to maximize your earnings.

Multimedia rights are another area where your agent will try to retain control. Just because a publisher holds e-book rights does not mean you are granting it other electronic or digital rights, such as the right to create an app, a multimedia edition, a website, video games, digital subscriptions, or other electronic content. In my experience, publishers have become more grabby with these rights, given the uncertainty in how the digital landscape will evolve. They may want the latitude to develop your book into an app if the market heads in that direction, but most agents will add in stipulations to prevent abuse.

Dramatic rights encompass TV, movie, and theatrical adaptations of your work, and each of these rights can be negotiated on a separate basis. Authors almost always retain dramatic rights, and literary agencies often have experience in selling options to your work. An option is the right—usually purchased by a production company or director—to adapt your work into a movie or TV show. Options are sold for a specific period of time—such as one or two years—after which the option expires and can once again be sold.

Audiobook rights are another potentially important area of earnings. That's because audiobook sales are on the rise and are sold at a much higher price point than your typical e-book. Whether you can retain audiobook rights depends on the skills and resources of your publisher and the type of project in question.

One sentence or clause will typically lump together all the possibilities related to the merchandising of your work, such as the production of action figures, clothing lines, wine labels, amusement parks—you get the idea. And, authors almost always retain these rights.

Your publisher will likely have additional clauses addressing abridgments, anthologies, condensations, reprints, serialization, book club sales, and much more. Most agents will strike anything too broad reaching or vague in intent. Ideally, each subsidiary right in the contract should point to a specific sales or licensing activity that the publisher regularly undertakes. Beware of any catchall clause that says the publisher will pay you a certain percentage for any rights not specified in the contract. All rights should always be specified.

That said, publishers can't anticipate every single kind of subsidiary rights deal that might happen with your book, and they prefer the flexibility to negotiate deals when the opportunity arises—especially at international rights fairs—without the requirement to consult with the author first. So aim for clarity but be reasonable in your stipulations or demands.

Before we talk about the money part of the deal, you should also check your contract language for how much say or control you have over your book's title and cover. Few authors are granted the privilege of approval over the book title or cover design, but it is reasonable to request and be granted consultation. This means that while the publisher has final say, it'll include you in the decision-making process and presumably take your feedback into account.

Many authors are frustrated by this lack of control, but try to see it from the publisher's perspective. They not only need to get the entire sales and marketing team onboard and enthusiastic about the book's packaging, but they need to pitch it effectively to major accounts, who might ask for their own changes to the cover and title. And, we'll discuss this process at length in the next lecture.

While a publisher knows it's far better to please the author with the packaging if it can, it also knows that an average author has less experience and insight into what sells books. If you do have specific market insight or experience that would lend weight to your opinion on the title or cover, you can try and negotiate for more control; but don't expect to get it.

Most contracts specify that if the writer fails to submit acceptable work or revisions by deadline, the publisher may either cancel the contract or make revisions on the writer's behalf, sometimes without consultation. This first scenario is considered far more reasonable than the second. If you're worried about the publisher revising your work without your consent, try to include language in your contract that requires your approval first or that allows you to terminate and take the work elsewhere.

Failure to submit an acceptable manuscript to the publisher may require you to return any advance payments you received, but sometimes your agent can negotiate the contract so that you keep all payments regardless of how, when, or why the contract is terminated. So you may wonder: What constitutes whether a manuscript's acceptable? Often, that's entirely up to the subjective judgment of the publisher or editor. Therefore, a good agent will negotiate a contract so this term acceptable is more narrowly defined, particularly when it comes to revisions. Often editors are required to write a revision letter spelling out what changes the author must make to produce an acceptable work.

Every author is asked to make legal promises about the work under contract, usually under a clause called warranties. You'll have to guarantee that you haven't granted someone else rights to the work in a way that would interfere with the publisher's rights. You also have to promise that you've taken reasonable care to ensure that your work is true and accurate and that you haven't plagiarized or violated anyone else's rights by producing the work.

Given the warranties you'll be making, publishers will include an indemnification clause that says that if you breach your warranties, you indemnify and hold harmless the publisher from any costs, losses, liabilities, or claims arising out of or in connection to that breach. In plain English, this would include things such as a person, organization, or business suing for defamation, or evidence of plagiarized material. Publishers can charge you for legal costs if they find themselves in hot water as a result of your breach.

Now this can sound pretty scary, and it is serious business if you breach your warranties knowingly or through carelessness. As a result, you or your agent may ask for coverage under the publisher's liability insurance, which insures the publisher in cases of copyright or trademark infringement, libel, and invasion of privacy. Whether you can be insured by the publisher depends greatly on the situation. And some publishers don't even have such insurance to begin with.

Regardless of whether you're insured, always be transparent and upfront with your editor if you have ethical or legal concerns about how the project is unfolding. It's far better to discuss potential conflicts up front, than for the publisher to end up surprised.

Finally, if you're concerned about potential liability with your work, have a frank conversation with your agent or even consult a lawyer. While you may fully trust your editor and have a good relationship with the publisher, it's probably the organization's higher-ups and legal team who will handle any matters of a legal nature.

So now, finally, let's talk about the money. When you sign a traditional publishing contract, you receive an advance against royalties. As books sell, you earn a percentage of sales for each copy sold or a royalty, which is applied against the advance you received. Once the advance is fully earned out, you start to receive royalty payments. Industry insiders estimate 70 percent of authors don't earn out their advance. But authors don't have to return their advance if the book doesn't earn out.

The publisher decides what advance to pay you based on a proprietary formula that you'll never see. Their P&L—or profit-and-loss statement—determines whether a book makes financial sense to publish. It's a mixture of the predictable—such as manufacturing costs—and the unpredictable—namely sales.

When I started working at a midsize publisher in 1998, it was my responsibility as an acquiring editor to put together the P&L for every title I proposed to make sure it would hit the target sales and profit margin before wasting the pub board's time. The pub board was a weekly gathering of key company players in editorial, sales, and marketing who gave the green light to contract authors and titles. Just about every publisher has some version of this pub board meeting.

At this meeting, the sales and marketing team may estimate or otherwise commit to specific sales figures based on retail channel. Bookstores—including Amazon—represent the majority of sales for most Big Five titles. The P&Ls will be done for a specific period—such as the first year of anticipated sales—or it may be done for the expected lifetime of the book. These sales estimates are critical to calculating an advance. So how are those sales estimates determined?

If you've been published before, they'll look at your past sales track record. That's because bookstores and other accounts regularly look at past sales to guide orders in the future. If you're a debut author, they'll use comparable titles to come up with a projection. The publisher also takes into account the recent performance of the book's genre or category across its own list. Then it adds in any potential income from subsidiary rights deals, such as foreign rights sales.

There's a final wild card that comes into play. If your agent takes your book to auction and several editors compete against one another, this will typically drive up the advance far beyond what a P&L would recommend.

So these are the primary factors that drive the sales estimate which affect the size of your advance and also determine your book's final print run numbers. Most publishers avoid keeping excess inventory, since it's like burning cash.

So they'll only print enough books to meet the initial orders or demand, then go back to press when orders clearly outpace available stock.

While it may seem surprising, it's not uncommon for Big Five publishers to offer an advance they know will never earn out. So what's their motivation for doing so? Well, one big reason right now is that the standard e-book royalty rate of 25 percent is widely acknowledged as too low. But publishers do not want to increase that rate. Increasing it for even one author sets off a domino effect, where they have to agree to higher e-book royalties for other authors due to most favored nation clauses in many agent-negotiated contracts. So, if an editor really wants to acquire an author or book, but she can't budge on the royalty rates, then a straightforward way to sweeten the deal is to offer a higher advance.

Speaking of royalties, these will be clearly outlined in the contract based on format. Authors earn a different rate depending on whether the sales are for hardcover, paperback, or e-book. Royalty rates also change depending on the retail sales channel, and they can differ by category or genre of book. On average, you can expect to earn somewhere between a 6 and 15 percent royalty on the retail price of your book. You'll also see royalty escalators—where your royalty increases as the number of sales increases.

A good publisher looks at each title's financial prospects as part of an overall season of titles. If your publisher releases 20 titles every season, they'll likely have a mix of surefire big books and quieter books that involve more risk. If an editor acquires nothing but risky books, she might not keep her job for very long. But one or two low-earning books can be subsidized by better-selling titles. That's why you often hear about the celebrity or blockbuster titles subsidizing the other titles a publisher produces.

All right, let's say you've signed on the dotted line. Most book advances get paid in three installments at certain contractually specified events. The first installment is paid upon contract signing. Another installment is typically paid upon acceptance of the final manuscript. And, the final installment is paid upon the book's publication. Sometimes the advance is paid in four installments, with the final one saved until six to twelve months after the book is released. Now, one might question whether the advance is really an advance in that case, but it happens.

Read the contract carefully for any indication of publication expenses you might bear, either against your future royalty payments or out of pocket. When costs are charged against future royalty payments, you pay nothing out of pocket. But you won't start earning anything from book sales until you both earn out your advance and pay for costs charged against your royalty account.

In traditional print book deals, authors almost never cover any costs related to their book's publication. However, it's common for nonfiction authors to bear the cost of indexing. And, if your book includes art, illustration, or photography, you may cover some or all of the costs. Some digital-only book imprints may charge you for cover design, editing, e-book formatting, even marketing and publicity costs.

When it comes to permissions costs—that is, obtaining permission to quote or excerpt other copyrighted work within your own—authors almost always undertake both the financial and administrative burden of securing permission. That's not to say you're entirely on your own. Your editor will likely assist and advise you with permissions, but remember that the contract puts the responsibility squarely on the author.

Here's some final parting advice on contracts—especially if you're heading into negotiations without an agent—to help ensure you end up with a good deal. First, I recommend you become a member of the Authors Guild, which offers contract review services as well as guides to contract language. Or, if you prefer, you can try finding an agent who's willing to work on an hourly basis to negotiate the contract for you. That can be ideal, but not many agents offer that kind of assistance.

It's best to avoid having an attorney review your contract unless they're well-schooled in publishing business standards or intellectual property law. Sometimes, they'll overreach and have unreasonable expectations, putting you in a very awkward position with your publisher.

But the best parting advice I have to offer is this: Assume everything is negotiable. Don't be shy to ask the publisher what the language means if you don't understand it clearly, and try to modify any boilerplate agreement you're given. The worst that could happen is that the publisher says no. Remember that nearly every publisher's contract is built to protect the publisher's interests, not yours. They are businesses, after all, and you should have just as much interest in getting the best deal you can for yourself.

Working Effectively with Your Publisher
Lecture 19

One day it finally happens: Your contract has been successfully negotiated and signed, and you have a manuscript deadline. For first-time authors, it can be one of the most exhilarating days of their lives, but also terrifying when they realize how much they still don't know. Usually, the time from contract signing to having a book on sale is at least one to two years. During that time, you'll journey through several phases with the publisher, including editorial development, design and production, sales and marketing planning, the book launch, and post-launch PR and publicity. In this lecture, we'll look at several aspects of this process.

Writing and Revision

- At the start of the writing and revision process, you'll be assigned an editor who is responsible for reviewing your work and providing feedback. Because this editor serves as your champion for the book inside the publishing house, developing a strong, collaborative relationship can be one of the most important factors in your success.

- Even if you have a completed manuscript at the time of contract signing, you'll almost always be asked to do revisions. Depending on the publisher and the type of book you're writing, you may be asked to make incremental submissions on the way to the final deadline to ensure that you're making sufficient progress.

- When you submit your work for review, especially if it's a first draft, it may take several months for you to receive any feedback. Ask when you might expect to hear back, and don't check on the response until after that time. If you're concerned about the length of time it's taking, ask your agent for guidance. Sometimes, the contract specifies how much time the publisher has to review and respond, as well as how much time the author has to revise after receiving feedback.

- Writers who are new to the business sometimes consider an editor's requests for revisions to be a personal affront, when in reality, the editor is trying to produce the best possible manuscript for the intended audience. Editors know what works for the market and have the experience and expertise necessary to objectively criticize work. If you don't want to revise your manuscript to the editor's style or suggestions—and you could be right—you can always withdraw the work. In worst-case scenarios, your agent should step in to handle any disagreements that threaten to jeopardize the contract or publication date.

- Respect whatever deadlines you are given. If you think you'll miss a deadline, inform your editor as far in advance as possible and propose a new deadline. The more you communicate about your situation, the more understanding your editor is likely to be. The worst thing you can do is let the deadline pass in complete silence or avoid contact with the editor. Be proactive and professional and work with your editor to ensure that the delay doesn't have an adverse impact on your book.

- Aside from any revisions the publisher requests, you'll also need to read the copyedited manuscript, clarify any vague statements or inconsistencies, and respond to any challenges of fact. The turnaround for such responses is typically two to four weeks. Then, you may have to read *page proofs*—the typeset copy—to check for errors. If you wrote an illustrated book, the publisher may have you review the layout and proofread captions.

- If you're writing nonfiction, you may be responsible for providing an index. Usually, the publisher will hire an indexer at your expense, and the indexing cost appears as a deduction on your royalty statement.

Marketing Planning
- Usually during the late stages of editorial work, the planning process for sales and marketing begins. Your editor is responsible for distributing early versions of your work to the in-house sales and

marketing staff to drum up enthusiasm and support. The editor will also pitch your work during a sales meeting and make suggestions for how the book should be positioned in the market. Decisions will be made regarding your book's format and price at this time.

- Because publishers don't have sufficient money, time, or staff to invest in all the titles they release, it's vital for you to ask questions about the marketing of your work. Most publishers don't have strong direct-to-consumer marketing experience or resources; in other words, they have limited means of directly reaching the target readership. In general, publishers can only hope that a book finds its audience by simply being in stock at stores and discussed in the mainstream media or important review outlets.

- Publishers are known for putting most of their efforts behind A-list authors or books that they're betting will sell big. They will better support a book if it receives an encouraging response or commitment from major retail accounts, such as chain bookstores. Some authors who have been paid a large advance may also be given more support because the publisher has a more significant investment at risk. Unfortunately, all this leaves the majority of authors behind. You should find out early in the process what level of support your book will receive: A-list versus baseline.

- One of the first marketing tasks you'll likely have is the completion of the author questionnaire. This document asks about every facet of your network and platform, including names and contact information for important relationships or professional connections, information about your local and regional media, and more. Be thorough in completing this form. The more the publisher knows about your resources and potential network opportunities, the more it can potentially support your book.

- Out of this questionnaire comes another task for you and the publisher: finding people to blurb your book and, for nonfiction, to potentially write an introduction or foreword. By attaching well-known names to your book, you can add credibility and authority to your work, especially if you're a debut author. The publisher and your agent will help in securing these endorsements, but they will also expect you to reach out to people you know personally.

- If your publisher is serious about your book gaining traction in traditional publishing circles, it will produce an *advance reading copy* (ARC) about four to six months before your book releases. ARCs are sent to trade review outlets, such as *Publishers Weekly*, *Kirkus Reviews*, and *Foreword*. These publications are read by booksellers and librarians to help them make decisions on what to order. The ARCs are also sent to all types of publications and media outlets to help secure additional mainstream reviews and coverage.

- Because the costs of book tours often outweigh the benefits, only A-list authors typically receive book tour support. However, you should plan at least one launch event in your region or wherever you think your book will be most well received. Even a small event will spread word of mouth in your community and put you in touch with booksellers, other authors, and people who can help your book get attention.

The Sales Process

- Roughly four to six months before your book is released, the publisher's sales process will begin. This tends to coincide with the release of the seasonal catalog of titles. Make sure to get a copy of this catalog and study your book's positioning.

- The large traditional publishing houses send out sales teams to call on large accounts, including chain and independent bookstores, wholesalers, distributors, and others. They suggest order quantities to each account based on sales of comparable titles in the market, as well as enthusiasm inside the publishing house.
  - By the time the sales call is made, the marketing department has already outlined the most important initiatives the publisher will invest in to spread the word about the book. Advance praise, a large-scale advertising campaign, and forthcoming

media commitments will all be touted as reasons for buyers to commit to strong sales numbers.

- o   This is why it's important that you as an author communicate what you will do to support your book many months before its release. If your efforts are to have meaning for the initial sales push, the publisher must have them in its plan before the sales call.

- You should be encouraged by signs that your publisher is invested in your book. For example, the publisher may get your book on display at a major retailer or you may be invited to appear with the publisher at an industry event. There's also a chance that you'll be invited to the publisher's offices to talk to the sales and marketing team personally to help build a better relationship, support, and understanding for your work.

- Unfortunately, the majority of authors don't receive special sales treatment, but you can take a number of steps to ensure that your book gets the best possible results.
  - o   First, come up with a marketing plan that you can execute on your own. As we discussed earlier, you should be able to reach your target audience through existing channels, such as your blog, e-mail newsletter, or social media accounts. Tell the publisher what you plan to do along these lines and identify areas where you might need assistance.

  - o   If you have an early start—perhaps two years before the book is due to be released—you can establish a greater online presence and develop relationships with both influencers and your target readership. Make a list of publications where you would like your book to be reviewed and start cultivating relationships with those outlets. Build a database of groups or organizations that would be most interested in your work. As you revise your book, think of products, competitions, or giveaways that might complement the work.

- Around the time the sales calls begin, you'll be introduced to the publicist who will work on your book. He or she will likely schedule a phone call with you to talk about the game plan, what media outlets will be targeted, and how to direct your own requests or needs for assistance.

- Once your book releases, most of the work is done. The marketing and publicity plan will be carried out, but most of the media attention you receive will have been put in place weeks or months earlier. After the release date, the publisher will monitor for reviews and other indicators that the book may take off if invested in a bit more. If nothing happens to help the book gain sales momentum in its first three months or so, the publisher will turn its attention to the next season of books. There's always a new book to market and promote in the hopes of it being the next big winner for the publisher.

Suggested Reading

Lerner, *The Forest for the Trees*.

Rabiner and Fortunato, *Thinking like Your Editor*.

Exercises

1. Ask friends who have published a book through traditional means to describe their experience with the publisher and what they wish they'd known going in or what they'd do differently.

2. Visit a large chain bookstore and closely study books that are on display toward the front of the store or on shelf end caps. (This placement has been paid for by the publisher.) What kinds of books and publishers do you see represented?

Working Effectively with Your Publisher
Lecture 19—Transcript

One day it finally happens: Your contract has been successfully negotiated and signed, and you have a manuscript deadline. For first-time authors, it can be one of the most exhilarating days of their lives. It can also be terrifying when they realize how much they still don't know.

Usually, it takes at least one to two years from contract signing to see your book on sale. You'll journey through several phases with the publisher, including editorial development, design and production, sales, marketing and planning, the book launch, and then post-launch PR and publicity.

The first thing you'll focus on is the writing and revision process. You'll be assigned an editor responsible for reviewing your work and providing feedback. Sometimes this editor is the same one who bought your book. Other times, the acquiring editor will hand you off to an associate for development. Either way, know that your editor serves as your champion for the book inside the publishing house.

That means you want to develop a strong collaborative relationship. Treat it as one of the most important factors in the success of your book because it is. You have may have heard horror stories about authors whose books are orphaned during the publishing process. This is what happens if your editor leaves. And sometimes the book never seems to recover its momentum and receives limited support from sales and marketing.

I hope you don't find yourself in that position, but it mainly just serves to illustrate the critical role of the editor in ensuring your work gets the attention and investment it deserves.

So let's discuss the editorial process. Depending on the publisher and the type of book you're writing, you may be asked to submit partial manuscripts on the way to the final deadline to ensure you're making sufficient progress. Even if you have a completed manuscript at the time of contract signing, you'll almost always be asked to revise.

When you submit your work for review—especially if it's a first draft—it may take several months for you to receive any feedback. Try to be patient. You'll be anxious to hear what the editor thinks, but that editor is also juggling about a dozen other authors and projects—if not more—at various stages of development and production. When you first submit your manuscript, ask when you might expect to hear back and don't check back on a response until after that time.

If you're concerned about the length of time it's taking, ask your agent for guidance. Sometimes the contract specifies how much time the publisher has to review and respond, as well as how much time the author has to revise after receiving feedback.

Writers who are new to the business sometimes consider an editor's requests for revision a personal affront, when in reality the editor is only trying to produce the best possible manuscript for the intended audience. Editors know what works for the market and have the experience and expertise necessary to objectively analyze work.

If you don't want to revise your manuscript based on the editor's suggestions—and you could be right—you can always withdraw the work if it comes to that. But there's a good chance you'll never get your work published if you don't learn to accept constructive criticism from editors.

Authors who have been in the game a long time and have published dozens of books are typically the most open to revision suggestions. Some beginners find this paradoxical, but it isn't once you consider that seasoned authors have attained a level of professionalism and experience that's taught them to respect the editor's eye. Editors are eager to help you achieve your best effort. If there are occasional misunderstandings along the way, don't overlook the editor's essential goodwill toward your work.

In worst-case scenarios, your agent should step in to handle any disagreements that threaten to jeopardize the contract or publication date. Whatever deadlines you're given, respect them. While it's true that publishers try to build in a cushion because authors are notorious for missing their deadlines, don't assume there is one.

If you think, you'll miss a deadline, inform your editor as far in advance as possible, and propose a new deadline. The more you communicate transparently about your situation, the more understanding your editor is likely to be. The worst thing you can do is let the deadline pass by in complete silence or avoid contact with your editor. Be proactive and professional and work with your editor to ensure the delay doesn't have a negative impact on your book.

Sometimes the deadlines are critical for your book to release on the right date and for special marketing and promotion opportunities. You don't want to miss an opportunity that could lead to greater sales because you didn't take your deadline seriously. And of course, your manuscript deadlines are included in your contract too, and publishers may have the right to terminate and ask for the advance back if you fail to deliver your work on time.

Aside from any revisions the publisher requests, you'll also need to read the copyedited manuscript, clarify any vague statements or inconsistencies, and respond to any challenges of fact. You'll probably have about two to four weeks to review the copyedited manuscript and respond. Because it's usually a time-sensitive process, the editor will alert you to the review period in advance so you can block out time on your calendar.

Then you may have a chance to read page proofs—which is the typeset copy—to check for errors. If you wrote an illustrated book, the publisher may have you review the layout and proofread captions to ensure everything matches up properly. If you're writing nonfiction, you may be responsible for providing an index. Usually the publisher will hire an indexer at your expense, and the indexing cost appears as a deduction on your royalty statement.

These are all things you may be asked to do. Each publisher works a little differently, but you should be provided guidelines by your editor that clearly state what's expected of you at each stage of the development and production process.

At some point during the editorial work, the sales and marketing planning process will begin. Your editor will be responsible for distributing early versions of your work to the in-house sales and marketing staff to drum up enthusiasm and support. Your editor will also pitch your work during a season sales meeting and make suggestions for how the book can be best positioned in the market. Important decisions will start to be made regarding your book's format and price. So, let's discuss some of the factors that go into these decisions.

First, there's the question of format. Many years ago, it used to be that most paperbacks were reprints of hardcover books. Today, you can find original fiction and nonfiction issued as paperbacks, and these are called trade paperback originals. Sometimes if these books become bestsellers, they come out in hardcover editions later.

Paperback originals can still be perceived by authors and industry insiders as being of less value or importance, but this stigma has mostly faded as everyone realizes that readers are much more likely to give a new author a shot if the book costs $15 and not $25. Still, publishers and authors often prefer hardcovers because they offer a better profit than paperbacks, even if they do sell fewer copies. And hardcovers also offer authors a higher royalty percentage.

If your publisher releases your book as a hardcover first, the e-book edition will often be released at the same time and then the paperback about 6–12 months after that. The pricing of your book is often driven by the book's format and production quality, the page count, and the conventions of the category or genre your book falls into. Most trade paperbacks—primarily distributed to bookstores—will get priced somewhere between $15 and $20. Trade hardcovers can run anywhere from $20–$35. Mass-market books, which are sold in drugstores and supermarkets, are largely being replaced by e-book sales. They get priced at less than $10.

About 9–12 months before your book releases—or sometimes as soon as your book is signed—the publisher will begin a formal titling process. As we discussed earlier, your contract may give you the opportunity to consult on this process, but the publisher has final say.

About six to nine months before your book releases—after the title's finalized—the cover and interior design process will begin. As with the title, when a publisher accepts a book, it almost always reserves the right to determine the package design.

While you can make suggestions to your editor, never offer to design your book or suggest that your friend or family member be the cover photographer, illustrator, or artist. And don't send mock-ups of how you think the cover should look. Publishers work with their own in-house designers who understand the style and sensibilities of that particular house. You can trust them to make the right decisions for your book—they've probably been in the business longer than you—and they know what sells books. However, if you feel the cover design or title conveys the wrong idea or feel for what you've written, raise your concerns with your editor.

So far, we haven't touched on the sales and marketing process, but the truth is, this process begins from the moment you sign the contract. You'll have the best experience with your publisher if you start asking questions from the very beginning. It's vital you cut through the fog—with the assistance of your agent if needed—on what the publisher will and will not do to market your work. And let's hope your publisher will be honest with you.

The reason you need to do this is because—as you may have heard—not all books are adequately marketed and promoted. First, publishers just don't have sufficient money, time, or staff to invest in all of the titles they release. Second, most publishers don't have strong direct-to-consumer marketing experience or resources. That means they have limited means of directly reaching the target readership to let them know a book of interest is available.

While publishers are well-schooled in reaching bookstores and trade accounts, the marketing opportunities related to those channels are very limited and competitive. The end result is that publishers often rely on hope that a book finds its audience, simply by being in stock at stores and by being talked about in the mainstream media or by important review outlets.

This all results in a mainstream publishing strategy that's akin to throwing a lot of stuff at the wall to see what sticks. Publishers are known for putting most of their efforts behind A-list authors or books that they're betting will sell big. They'll also better support a book if it receives an encouraging response or commitment from important retail accounts, such as a chain bookstore or big-box store.

Perhaps it goes without saying, but this approach leaves the majority of authors behind. You need to find out early in the process if your book will receive the bare minimum of marketing support so you can plan appropriately. Sometimes, if you've been paid a large advance—in the six figures—you can be assured of more support because the publisher has a more significant investment at risk. But don't assume. And as we go, we'll talk through some of the signs of A-list treatment versus baseline treatment.

One of the first marketing tasks you'll likely have is the completion of the author questionnaire. The publisher will send you a document that asks about every facet of your network and platform—including names and contact information for important relationships or professional connections, and information about your local and regional media, and much more. Be thorough in completing this form. The more the publisher knows about your resources and potential network opportunities, the more they can potentially support your book.

One of the well-known rules of marketing is that you should build on existing resources rather than start out cold. Out of this marketing questionnaire will likely come the first task for you and the publisher: finding people to blurb your book and—for nonfiction—to potentially write an introduction or foreword. By attaching well-known names to your book, you can add credibility and authority to your work—especially if you're a debut author.

The publisher—and even your agent—will help you in securing these things. But they'll expect you to reach out to people you know personally, since that's always more effective in getting someone to say yes.

Blurbs are always offered complimentary. You would never pay for them. However, forewords and introductions may involve an honorarium. The size of the honorarium depends on several things: the length of the material required, how well-known or in demand that person is, the complexity of the material to be written, and how big or important your own book is. Rates range from a couple hundred dollars to thousands. If the author is personally interested in your book and you're connected to her, you may pay very little or nothing for a foreword or introduction. And in some cases, the publisher will pay the honorarium or offer to split the cost.

If your publisher is serious about your book gaining traction in traditional publishing circles, they'll produce what's known as an advance reading copy, or ARC, about four to six months before your book releases. ARCs are sent to trade review outlets such as *Publishers Weekly*, *Kirkus Reviews*, and *Foreword*.

These publications are read by booksellers and librarians. They help people in the business make decisions on what to read or order, so they have the most important titles available for patrons and customers. The ARCs are also sent to all types of publications and media outlets to help secure additional mainstream reviews and coverage.

You may be wondering, what about the book tour? For that type of marketing, the costs often outweigh the benefits. Only A-list authors who can be sure of drawing crowds typically receive book tour support. If you're a new author or midlist author, don't expect it. And you should hesitate before planning one on your own. They're time-intensive to plan and execute, and sometimes events are sparsely attended—and that makes the whole effort fairly depressing. Don't embark on a large-scale tour unless you have some confidence of turnout.

However, you do want to plan at least one launch event in your region, or wherever you think you'll get the best turnout. The reasons for this are twofold. First, it's an important and worthy milestone to celebrate, and you'll have friends and family who'll want to support and congratulate you. They'll want an opportunity to brag that they now know a published author. Second, a launch event serves an important marketing function. It helps spread that all-important word of mouth to your community. Even a small book event is likely to put you in touch with booksellers, other authors, and people who can help draw attention to your book.

Roughly, four to six months before your book is released—once your book has a solid cover and title—the publisher's sales process will begin. This tends to coincide with the release of the publisher's seasonal catalog of titles. Get a copy of this catalog by asking your editor. Turn to the page that lists your title. How is it positioned?

If your book has a full-page listing near the beginning, that indicates A-list treatment and support. If it's buried, not so much. What does the catalog say about the publisher's marketing plan for your book? If you've been communicating well with your editor or publisher, nothing you see in the catalog will come as a surprise.

The biggest traditional houses send out their sales team to call on their important accounts, which will include chain and independent bookstores, wholesalers, distributors, and specialty accounts. They'll suggest order quantities to each account based on sales of comparable titles in the market—not to mention the enthusiasm and support coming from inside the publishing house. Remember, it's your editor's job to stoke this support, so hopefully they've done this effectively.

Because a major publisher releases dozens—if not hundreds—of titles per year, not a lot of time can be spent on each title. This may seem a like an exaggeration, but some titles may not be discussed for even a full minute. The A-list titles tend to get the most attention, and the salesperson will emphasize those titles over the others.

By the end of the sales meeting, there's usually a rough indication or informal agreement as to how many copies the account will take, but this isn't a sure thing until the order actually comes through. Sometimes, accounts will ask for changes to a book before they'll place the kind of order the publisher is asking for. For example, it's not uncommon for a buyer at Barnes & Noble to ask for a cover to be changed before they'll commit to a book. In most cases, the publisher tries to please the account if a large sale is at stake.

The account may also push for a better marketing plan or support from the publisher. However, by the time the sales call is made, the marketing department has already outlined the most important initiatives the publisher will invest in. Advance praise will be secured, any large-scale advertising campaign will be committed to, and forthcoming media commitments—such as an excerpt set to run in a major publication—will be touted as a reason to commit to a strong sales number.

That's why it's so important that you, as an author, communicate what you'll be doing to support your book many months before its release. If it's going to carry any kind of meaning for the initial sales push, the publisher needs to have that in its plan before the sales call.

There are a few good signs that your publisher is extra invested in your book. One exciting thing that may happen is that the publisher will secure display space for your book at a major retailer. This requires the publisher to make an investment because every display is paid for, and displays are limited to only the most marketable and sales-worthy titles. It's a significant coup to get display placement, so celebrate it if it happens.

You may also be invited to appear with the publisher at an industry event, such as BookExpo America or an independent bookseller gathering. Such an invitation means you're considered worthy of meeting booksellers, librarians, and other opinion makers who have the power to handsell or place your book in prominent display positions. Finally, there's also a chance you'll be invited to the publisher's offices to talk to the sales and marketing team personally to help build better support and understanding for your work.

But those things don't happen to even the majority of authors. You'll typically have to work at a great distance from your publisher, and you may never meet the sales and marketing team. So here's what you can do at any point after signing the contract to help ensure you get the best possible results.

First, come up with a marketing plan you can execute on your own. This doesn't necessarily take money, but a plan for reaching your target audience through existing channels, such as your blog, an e-mail newsletter, or social media accounts. Tell the publisher what you'll be doing, and identify areas where the publisher could be of greatest assistance to you.

Publishers are much more likely to be helpful if you proactively show them your plan and ask them for what you want. You won't get good results by calling up and demanding to know what they'll be doing to support your book, especially if you haven't demonstrated your own commitment.

If you have a really early start—let's say you sign a contract two years before the book is due to be released—then you're in even a better position. You can begin to establish your online presence and develop relationships with your target readership as well as influencers who recommend books.

For example, make a dream list of online and offline publications where you'd want your book reviewed or mentioned and start cultivating relationships with those sites or people. Identify groups or organizations that would be most interested in your book and start a database of e-mail and snail mail addresses. As you write and revise your work, think of ancillary materials or products that complement the work. Consider competitions or giveaways that would be interesting to someone who enjoys the book.

All of these things can contribute to a strong marketing plan you send to your publisher, which then goes into their own sales pitch to the accounts. You should also inform the publisher if you plan to hire an independent publicist or firm to assist you. Far from being offended, the publisher will see this as a wise investment. But they should know early on so their own team can either collaborate effectively with your publicist or focus on areas that your publicist isn't covering. Look at it as a partnership that will do its best work if the right hand knows what the left hand is doing.

Around the time the sales calls begin—again, about four to six months before your book's release—you'll be introduced to the publicist who'll be working on your book. She'll schedule a phone call with you to talk about the game plan or otherwise send you information on what their process looks like, what media outlets they'll be pitching or targeting, and how to direct your own requests for assistance. This is a good moment to distinguish the role of marketing from that of publicity, since they sometimes get conflated.

Marketing is all about paid placement, such as advertising and sponsorships. With marketing, if you pay for it, it shows up. The attention is guaranteed to be there. Your publisher may or may not have a budget for this, but even if there is one, it's probably very small. Some industry experts say that 85 percent of books get less than $2,000 in dedicated marketing dollars from their publisher. Most bestsellers will get more than $50,000, and it usually reaches into the six figures.

However, marketing alone can't make a book a bestseller because not every book is good enough or appealing enough to the market. And sometimes the timing is simply off. Publicity is the opposite of paid placement. A publicist pitches your book to the media in an effort to get editorial coverage. Usually, a publicist's rate of success is determined by the quality and quantity of her connections. Some publicists concentrate on specialized areas, such as radio or blog tours. But the key thing to remember is that publicity isn't a sure thing. You always hope for it, but you don't always get it.

Publicists at most publishers are stretched to the limit. They might do a great job with the time they have, but they probably won't have time for an in-depth approach, which is why it's often a good idea to hire your own publicist. People need to hear about a book many times and in several ways before they really notice it. Yet most publishers rely heavily on retailer placement above all else. They tend to wait a little too hopefully for that serendipitous word of mouth to occur, usually the kind that comes from book reviewers or other influential figures in the book community.

Very few books have succeeded without any marketing and publicity. Somehow, your book will need to gain visibility to potential readers. You have to think through this problem. Once the book is on the shelf, how does any reader know it's sitting there, or that it exists at all? What marketing has been done?

Most authors on their release date have this horrifying realization. Their book is spine out in a sea of titles, hardly noticeable. But by that time, short of a lucky lightning strike, it's too late to do anything that will lead to a different sales outcome. If the book doesn't sell in sufficient quantities in its first six months on the shelf, it will be returned and not restocked to make way for all the new titles releasing during the next season.

And perhaps most frustrating for you, your publisher will be moving on. Once your book releases, most of their work is already finished. The marketing and publicity plan will be carried out, but most of the media that happens will have been seeded weeks or months earlier. After the release date, the publisher will be monitoring reviews and other indicators that the book may take off if invested in just a bit more.

If nothing happens to help the book gain sales momentum in its first three months or so, the publisher will turn its attention to the next season of books. There's always a new book to market and promote in the hopes of it being the big winner the publisher is looking for.

To avoid disappointment, always start with the assumption that your publisher will do nothing but act as a packager and distributor for your book. And in the next two lectures, we'll discuss some specific marketing strategies you need to know to empower yourself at all stages of the process.

There is some hope on the horizon if your launch is modest or otherwise ends up being a disappointment. Your book could find new life as a paperback release and have a second shot at bestseller lists, as well as editorial coverage. The other piece of good news is that many authors have successfully breathed new life into their old or out-of-print titles by re-releasing them as e-books. There aren't space limitations on digital shelves, and a great new author is always a welcome discovery for a reader, regardless of a book's age.

So no matter how much publisher support you have, or how well your launch goes, take heart in the fact you've created a book that has a lifetime of sales potential ahead of it. And you'll always have new readers who will stumble upon it.

Becoming a Bestselling Author
Lecture 20

A few years ago, a story broke about an author who hired a marketing firm to launch his book onto *The New York Times* bestseller list—and succeeded. But when the firm's less-than-honest methods were uncovered, the results were scandal and embarrassment. What were these methods? In simple terms, all it took was rigging enormous sales of the book during a specific timeframe. The author essentially paid the firm to strategically purchase copies of his book in all the right places. Since that scandal broke, it has become harder to game the system, though authors still look for shortcuts or secrets to bestsellerdom. In this lecture, we'll explore more mainstream ways to achieve that goal.

Overview of Bestseller Lists

- *The New York Times* bestseller list is arguably the most important of such lists because it carries the most prestige and tends to get the most attention and publicity. But it can be the hardest list to hit. It gathers information from many different outlets across the country to determine what titles make the cut, and its sources of information are kept confidential.

- Authors seeking to make *The New York Times* list should note that it is updated weekly; that's why publishers tend to focus activity on selling the book and scheduling events during the launch week.

- Authors always wonder how many book sales it takes to hit the bestseller list. Unfortunately, that question is unanswerable. Each title competes against numerous others for placement on the list during a particular week. Whether you'll make the list depends on who you're up against and how well those titles perform. Still, the number of sales required might be lower than you think. In some categories, you can potentially get on the list with just a couple thousand copies sold.

- Because of the ways in which they're compiled, some people think that bestseller lists are unfair and arbitrary in their focus, but their purpose is to give an accurate reflection of what relatively new titles are being bought and what the general public is currently reading.

Running a Book Marketing Campaign

- It is possible for an author to launch an effective book marketing campaign without a publisher's support or assistance; however, this effort is the equivalent of taking on a full-time job for roughly six months or more, and it usually requires hiring a publicist, PR firm, or marketing consultant to advise and assist you.

- A comprehensive book marketing campaign that results in bestseller status uses a combination of tactics to reach readers. The best approach typically combines online and offline components, and if done right, each amplifies and strengthens the other.

- The first principle in running such a campaign yourself is to concentrate book sales as much as possible within the launch-week window. Your success at achieving this goal largely depends on your online influence. For example, *New York Times*–bestselling author Michael Hyatt literally asked people not to pre-order or buy his book *Platform* until the week of his book launch. But he was able to do this because he had thousands of people reading his blog and receiving his e-mail newsletter, and he offered strong incentives for his readers to wait.

Author Events

- One tactic you can use in your marketing campaign is the author event, which has changed dramatically from the typical reading at a bookstore you may have experienced in the past. Many authors and publicists—as well as bookstores themselves—now plan events in alternative venues, such as bars or clubs. Bookstores and other literary organizations may also sell tickets to author lunches held at restaurants and include a copy of the book with the ticket price.

- Another strategy used by publicists is to partner authors for events and tours because that generally leads to better turnout and a better pitch for media coverage. For instance, one publicist helped several authors organize and promote the Young Authors Give Back Tour, in which four YA authors toured the country and taught writing workshops for teens. That angle got two TV appearances and a feature in the *Chicago Sun-Times*.

- Even if the days of the traditional author tour are over, events still play an important role in visibility and media attention. In fact, media attention is the primary reason authors take the trouble to do events and can sometimes be more important than the number of books sold. Doing an event can be more about making a footprint that leads to greater coverage and new connections, which in turn lead to more opportunities and sales.

- It's important to note that independent bookstores also play a role in turning a book into a bestseller. The American Booksellers Association, a professional organization for independent booksellers, holds regular conventions that are also attended by publishers; some publishers bring along some of their authors who they believe have the potential to break out if supported by the independent bookseller community.
  - The power of *hand-selling*—when bookstore staffs make personal recommendations to their customers—can also play a pivotal role in a new author's success. Such recommendations may be more likely to happen if the booksellers meet the author at an industry convention or otherwise get more personal insight into an upcoming title.

  - For these and other reasons, some authors go out of their way to support independent bookstores as part of a book launch or overall marketing campaign. Some will even adopt an independent bookstore to be their fulfillment center for anyone who wants to find a signed copy. Such relationships help both the bookstore and the book generate more buzz.

- As mentioned earlier, a primary reason to schedule an author event is to help build more media coverage in a particular city or region. Unfortunately, publishing insiders know that the number of media outlets available for such coverage has dramatically shrunk, and the remaining ones are very selective. When you do get a hit in the media, however, it tends to stick with people and make an impact.
  - With persistence, authors can secure publicity or traditional media coverage without their publishers making the call. This effort requires researching media outlets, knowing what they cover, and crafting high-quality pitches that fit the style, tone, and needs of the outlet you're approaching.

  - You must also knock on doors continually with slightly different angles. Even if you hear no, don't stop pitching.

Online Marketing
- One of the greatest challenges for authors is deciding what types of online marketing will work for them strategically based on their starting point, that is, having a large online following versus being an unknown who is unable to score top media attention.

- An e-mail newsletter list is useful for crafting a strategy that you can use in the lead-up to your book's release. If you're like Hyatt and have a strong online presence, you can encourage to people to buy your book via e-mail. If you're a new author and don't have such a list for your first book release, you should start building one through your website and at events.

- Regular blogging isn't necessary to hit a bestseller list, but major blogs and websites can play an important role in spreading word of mouth, which means it can be worthwhile to write guest posts, do interviews, or otherwise try to get featured by bloggers who reach your target audience. It also helps to be an active participant or commenter on blogs that are popular with your readers.

- Often, giveaways can work if done strategically, especially in conjunction with blog interviews and other online appearances.

One popular venue for giveaways is Goodreads, a social media site for books and reading with more than 35 million members. Some authors and publishers offer giveaways of a first book in a series when a new installment is about to launch and enjoy a sales lift across the series after the giveaway concludes.

- If you're struggling to identify online marketing opportunities, examine the activity of authors you admire. What blogs or websites do they appear on? What do they do on social media? What events are they involved in?

- It's also important to be aware of how sales are affected by your online and offline activities. You can do this by tracking your book sales through Amazon Author Central, a free service that allows you to see your Nielsen BookScan numbers—an industry service that tracks individual book sales across most major outlets—and your Amazon sales.

Online promotions, such as the Kindle Daily Deal, have the power to turn a title into a bestseller overnight.

The Future of Book Marketing

- As breaking out becomes increasingly reliant on metadata and algorithms—the computing equations that drive searches and recommendations on Amazon, Goodreads, and other sites—how relevant will traditional book marketing techniques be to an author's success? And given that analyzing algorithms is typically an activity even less accessible to authors than publicity and PR, how will the author-publisher partnership evolve to ensure books get discovered by the right readers?

- Traditionally, one of the greatest values publishers have offered authors is the ability to get their books into stores. This value goes beyond simple distribution; bookstore placement acts as a marketing function, particularly when the book is selected for front-of-store display. The more visible a book is, the better the chances a reader has to stumble on it—and the better the chances of that reader talking about it with others.

- However, if fewer people are browsing bookstore shelves, publishers can't count on the serendipity of the bookstore visitor bumping into a display and taking a chance on a new author. Algorithms and promotions, such as the Kindle Daily Deal, then play an increasingly important role in how readers discover and decide what to read next.

- It's not clear that publishers are well prepared to face this challenge. Although publishers may be unparalleled in their ability to offer print retail distribution and mass-market branding campaigns, they are still catching up with direct-to-consumer marketing.

- Where does this leave the average author? Probably your smartest move is to build a network that you can reach either online or offline. Don't underestimate the difference that your relationships can make. If you make connections, when it's time for your launch or event, you'll see a real and meaningful effect.

Eckstut and Sterry, *The Essential Guide to Getting Your Book Published.*

Exercises

1. Compare three bestseller lists, those of *The New York Times*, *USA Today*, and Amazon. What titles appear on all three lists, and what publishers are represented? What titles appear only on one list?

2. Study the main *New York Times* bestseller list every week for a month. How much does its composition change from week to week? What publishers are represented?

Becoming a Bestselling Author
Lecture 20—Transcript

A few years ago, a story broke about an author who hired a marketing firm to launch his book onto the *New York Times* bestseller list—and succeeded. But when the firm's less than honest methods were uncovered, it resulted in scandal and embarrassment. What were these methods? In simple terms, all it took was rigging enormous sales of the book during a specific timeframe. The author, more or less, paid the firm to strategically purchase copies of his book in all the right places. Since that particular scandal broke, it's getting harder to game the system in this way, though authors still look for shortcuts or secrets to bestsellerdom. Once you hit one of the major bestseller lists that creates its own marketing momentum and additional sales.

For the purposes of this particular lecture, arguably the *New York Times* bestseller list is most important, since it carries the most prestige and tends to get the most attention and publicity. But it can be the hardest list to hit. It gathers information from many different outlets across the country, to determine what titles make the cut. It remains confidential which particular retail outlets the *New York Times* surveys, but it takes into account both physical bookstore sales and online retail sales, such as Amazon. If you visit the *New York Times* website where they make the bestseller lists available, you can read their own statement about their methodology, which is rather intricate and offers some important qualifiers regarding when and if it takes into account e-book sales.

Here's the most important thing to remember for any publisher or author who seeks to call themselves a *New York Times* bestseller—the list gets updated weekly, so usually your efforts will be engineered to give a book its best chance to make the list on a very particular week. That's why publishers tend to focus activity on selling the book and scheduling events on the specific launch day and week of the book. The other quirk of getting on bestseller lists is that pre-orders that happen in the months prior to release, typically get counted when the book finally goes on sale. That also increases the likelihood that the launch week, or the first week of sale, is the most likely time for authors to hit the list.

The big question that authors always ask is, "How many book sales it takes to hit the bestseller list?" Unfortunately, the question is unanswerable. Your title will be competing against a lot of others for placement on the list during a particular week. Some books will sell in amazing numbers, others won't. So it depends on who else you're up against and how well those titles perform. Still, the number of required sales might be lower than you think. In some categories, you can potentially get on the last spot of the bestseller list with only a couple thousand copies sold. It just depends on the week.

So, being a *New York Times* bestseller doesn't actually tell you much about how many copies any book has sold. Compare this situation to the music industry, where if a record goes platinum, you know it sold a million copies. There are no such official designations in book publishing, and sales figures are almost never released. Furthermore, bestseller lists typically exclude titles that are known as perennial sellers. For instance, the Bible is the bestselling book year after year in the United States, but you won't find it on any bestseller list. The same is true of books that are typically found on classroom reading lists, as well as test prep guides, and self-published books. You might say bestseller lists are biased toward a certain type of book, and that's partly true. Some people think the list is unfair and seemingly arbitrary in its methodology and focus. But it is trying to give an accurate reflection of what relatively new titles are being bought, and what the general public is now reading.

Before we discuss how books get launched onto bestseller lists, perhaps it's worth raising the question of whether or not it's worth the trouble—since it does take a significant amount of time, money, and energy. If your book hits a major bestseller list, it does create a tremendous ripple effect—more people hear about the book, more sales get triggered, more requests flow into your publisher or agent for rights, translations, and subrights, and you're likely to get more invites to do media or to speak. Not to mention you're in an excellent position to sign your next book deal. It's possible, if not desirable, for an author to launch that kind of effective book-marketing campaign without a publisher's support or assistance. Mainly, it requires time and energy because it will be the equivalent of taking on a full-time job for roughly six months or more. It will likely require hiring a publicist, PR firm, or marketing consultant to advise and assist you.

A comprehensive book-marketing campaign that results in bestseller status, uses a combination of tactics to reach readers. It would be unusual to focus solely on social media, or solely on events, to generate word of mouth. The best approach typically combines online and offline components, and if done right, each amplifies and strengthens the other.

The first principle most authors should adhere to, is concentrating the book sales as much as possible within the launch week window, for reasons explained earlier. Many of the strategies discussed will have the best payoff when this timing is kept in mind. You'll need to conduct an aggressive sales campaign that encourages everyone to buy the book during a very specific week, even on a specific day. Whether you can run such a campaign depends on where and how you might've already established yourself online as an author. For example, *New York Times* bestselling author Michael Hyatt, literally asked people not to pre-order or buy his book *Platform* until a specific week, the week of his book launch. But he was able to do this because he had thousands of people reading his blog and receiving his e-mail newsletter, so when he gave his specific instructions, he had a large audience listening.

You may wonder why Hyatt didn't also run a pre-order campaign, which is a common strategy. There is some amount of risk entailed with pre-order strategies, because most pre-orders will happen through Amazon. Then Amazon will release the books when they have them to ship, which can mess up your precision timing if that happens to be before the pub date. The other important detail was that Hyatt created a significant incentive for people to take action only when he wanted them to. If readers e-mailed Hyatt a dated receipt of their book sale, regardless of where or how they purchased it, he sent them several bonuses, such as access to his audio-video curriculum and previous digital books. He began teasing this offer weeks before the pub date, encouraging people to wait. And it worked; he sold more than 11,000 books during his first week on sale, and hit the *New York Times* list. Of course, not everyone launches a book with the resources that Hyatt has. Aside from being a well-known blogger who reaches hundreds of thousands of people every month, he's also the former CEO of Thomas Nelson, a major publisher. So, he had some connections not all of us have. But it does show you the power of making a focused and concentrated effort on getting your sales to hit within a specific timeframe.

Now that we've discussed that overarching goal you should keep in mind, let's look at specific tactics that all authors can use to reach it, starting with the author event. Publishers typically schedule authors for bookstore events the first week or the first month the book goes on sale. If publishers are focused on hitting a bestseller list, they'll schedule authors at stores that they believe are the so-called reporting stores that are used by the *New York Times* to determine the bestseller list. However, the multi-city book tour is mainly a thing of the past, even if *New York Times* bestselling authors still go on tour for their new releases. Plus, bookstores aren't always the best place for events these days. Much of the general public is inclined to go somewhere only if it feels like a party or a special event, rather than visiting the bookstore and listening to an author read their work. Therefore, many authors and publicists—as well as the bookstores themselves—now plan events in alternative venues, such as bars or clubs. Bookstores and other literary organizations sell tickets to author lunches held at restaurants, and the ticket price includes a copy of the book. Such events feel more social, and they avoid the lower perceived value and less compelling nature of the reading-signing format.

Another strategy used by publicists is to partner authors for events and tours, since that generally leads to better turnout and a better pitch for media coverage, which is an important component we'll discuss later. As an example, one publicist helped several authors organize and promote the Young Authors Give Back Tour, in which four young adult authors, who had all published before the age of 25, toured the country and taught writing workshops for teens. That angle got two TV appearances and a feature in the *Chicago Sun-Times*. Even if the days of the traditional author tour are over, events still play an important role in visibility and media attention. As one publicist told me, media is the primary reason you take the trouble to do events, and that can sometimes be more important than the number of books sold. Doing an event can be more about making a footprint that leads to greater coverage and new connections, which in turn lead to more opportunities and more sales.

Before we leave the topic of events entirely, it's important to recognize the related role that independent bookstores can play in turning a book into a bestseller. Some say they're the key to success on the *New York Times* bestseller list—meaning that if your book only sells in chain stores or on Amazon, it may not have as good of a chance to hit the list. The American Booksellers Association, which is a professional organization for independent booksellers, holds regular conventions for booksellers that publishers also attend. Some publishers bring along their authors if they have potential to breakout if supported by the indie bookseller community.

The power of hand-selling can play a pivotal role in a new author's success. This is where the bookstore staffs make personal recommendations to their customers, and get behind a book in a focused way. They might put books on prominent display because they believe the book deserves a big readership. This is much more likely to happen if the bookstores meet the author at an industry convention, learn about the book from the publishers' staff, or otherwise get an up-close-and-personal look at an upcoming title. It's a more personal approach to bookselling than what often happens with chain retail accounts. For many reasons, some authors go out of their way to support their independent bookstore as part of their book launch or overall marketing campaign. Some will even adopt an indie bookstore to be their fulfillment center for anyone who wants a signed copy. When authors do that, it gives the bookstore something to offer that their competitors can't. And that means the bookstore is likely to put it on their Facebook page, or tweet about it, or help the book generate more buzz.

As was mentioned earlier, a primary reason to schedule an author event is to help build more media coverage in a particular city or region. Unfortunately, publishing insiders know that the number of media outlets available to pitch for coverage, has dramatically shrunk. The field is very competitive, and it makes all media outlets very selective, across radio, TV, and print. However, when you do get a hit in the media, it tends to stick with people and sell books. One publicist told me if you're driving in your car, and you hear NPR's Terry Gross have a conversation with an author, that interview is going to resonate with you much more than if you saw the interview online.

With persistence, authors can secure publicity or traditional media coverage even without their publisher making the call. However, it typically takes months of effort, of continually knocking on the door in a slightly different way, for the same thing. Even if you hear no, you don't stop pitching. You don't get deterred by resistance. However, you need a series of very high-quality pitches that fit the style, tone, and needs of the outlet. You'll have to take the time to research media outlets, know what they cover, and write a persuasive e-mail that shows how you and your fit into the editorial mission of the outlet. And, of course, don't forget to take into account the importance of timing, because you want to make sure that your biggest publicity hits come during the same week as your events, all of which you want to hit during your book's launch week. And you have to factor in the lead times required for each media outlet, so that you're pitching far enough in advance.

As you can probably tell, an effective and quality pitch process is time-consuming, and this is where you have to evaluate where your time and effort are best spent. Mass-scale media pitches usually require a freelance publicist to assist you. It's possible for authors to manage the process on their own, if they have an extra eight hours in the day. Even if you do, it's also a publicist's job to stay on top of current events and news stories, and see how to draw connections in a book pitch—and many authors don't have the skill set for that.

There is an author who, like Michael Hyatt, reached the *New York Times* bestseller list without specifically pursuing offline advertising, mainstream media, or publicity. And he didn't just hit it for one week—he hit the list and stayed there for months. The author is Tim Ferriss, author of *The 4-Hour Workweek*. His book was simultaneously number one on the *New York Times* list and the *Wall Street Journal* list. And he was a first-time author. How did he do it? According to his own claims, he started by ruling out book signings or author events. He instead focused on creating word of mouth through all the best blogs. As a well-known blogger himself, this wasn't particularly difficult for him to accomplish. Because he was able to build a great deal of strategic buzz through well-known bloggers and online interviews, that led to offline media pursuing him for interviews and quotes. When the calls came, Ferriss was prepared. He had already invested in media training and he had a reel of himself that he used to establish himself as a viable guest to TV producers. If you dig a little deeper into Ferriss's success story, though, you'll end up realizing that from the beginning, he was focused on developing blog traffic and buzz for his book long before his launch, mostly through offline activities. He focused a lot of his time on attending and speaking at events where bloggers were the attendees, helping ensure that later on, they'd remember him, feature him, and link to him. Furthermore, for someone who claimed to rule out book signings or author events, Ferriss in fact held a very well-attended pre-launch party, based on his in-person connections. He partnered with three friends to host a birthday party for themselves in San Francisco that also doubled as his book launch. More than 250 people attended, many of them top bloggers in his industry. He gave away his book, signed copies, offered lots of free booze, and buzz from the party alone led to media coverage.

As you can see, Ferriss is in fact a classic example of how online and offline build on each other to create success. Yet, it's still the surest way to start a debate in a room full of writers. Ask them about the value of online marketing and social media. On one side of the debate, you have those who argue that reader engagement through social media contributes to long-term career success and visibility, including getting onto the bestseller lists. On the other side, you have people who have participated in some form of online promotion, and who found it a waste of time or a major distraction, without a meaningful impact on sales.

Most publicists will tell you that when it comes to online marketing, so much depends on what your starting point is. Some people are interested in online marketing because that's the primary method they have available to them for building recognition. Some new authors or books will not score top media, so they instead focus on getting something easy, and work up. Therefore, one of the biggest challenges for authors is deciding what types of online marketing will work for them strategically, based on their starting point.

If you're like Hyatt, and have an e-mail newsletter list you can use to encourage people to buy your book, you need to put together a specific strategy for using it in the lead up to your book's release. It's easy for people to miss something that gets posted on social media, but just about everyone reads their e-mail, even if it just takes a long time. New authors may not have such a list ready for their first book release, but a recurring theme emerging from successful authors—both traditionally published and self-published—is that you should start building one through your own website, and at events, in preparation for future releases. We'll talk more about this in the next lecture.

Regular blogging isn't necessary to hit a bestseller list, but as you can tell, major blogs and websites can play an important role in spreading word of mouth, which means it can be worthwhile to write guest posts, do interviews, or otherwise try to get featured by relevant bloggers who reach your target audience. It also helps to be an active participant or commenter on blogs where your readers hang out. Just keep in mind that it's a small number of websites that actually have influence and traffic. If you do any marketing on a small blog or website, make sure its audience is a good fit for your book, so you don't invest too much time for too little return. Plus, there has to be an element to the interaction that will encourage people to actually buy the book.

While an online interview or event, may be a great way to interact with a lot of people or get visibility, if there's no specific link to buy the book, no call to action, or a discount incentive, it's easy to end up wasting your time. Often giveaways can work if done strategically, especially in conjunction with blog interviews and other online appearances. One popular venue for giveaways is Goodreads, a social media site for books and reading, with more than 35 million members. Some authors and publishers offer giveaways of a first book in a series, when a new installment is about to launch, and enjoy a sales lift across the series after the giveaway concludes.

If you're struggling to figure out what to do for your marketing strategy, take a look at books or authors you admire. What does their activity look like? What blogs or websites did they appear on? What do they do on social media? What events are they involved in? Can you emulate those things? Still, it can be difficult to decide which opportunities might be worthwhile, since they can be as much about creating word of mouth, as selling books. A happy accident can always happen even if the sales aren't there. For instance, maybe very few people attend one of your bookstore events, but you develop a really great rapport with the bookstore owner. Then she later recommends you for a magazine feature on emerging authors. You never know what might happen. Whatever you do, measure things when it's possible. Be aware of how sales are affected, on a day-to-day basis, by your online and offline activities. You can do this by tracking your book sales through Amazon Author Central. You can sign up for this free service way in advance of your book's on-sale date. It will allow you to see your Nielsen BookScan numbers, an industry service that tracks individual book sales across most major outlets. By checking the data and asking your publisher for any additional insight they might have on their end, you'll have an excellent indication of how you're doing.

We've now covered what might be considered fairly traditional ways to reach the bestseller list and make your book a success. But there's more to book sales than just marketing, publicity, and word of mouth. Increasingly, retailers such as Amazon are able to create a bestseller by simply featuring it prominently as a deal on their website, or e-mailing customers about it. And the book doesn't necessarily have to be a new release anymore to become a bestseller. As an example, thriller novelist Jamie Freveletti, saw one of her novels, *Dead Asleep*, selected as the Kindle Daily Deal. It wasn't a new release, but Freveletti's novel became the number one bestseller at Amazon, and remained in the top ten for several days. Freveletti says this success came as a complete surprise; her publisher had no involvement in securing the promotion. She speculates that Amazon's algorithms were tripped—that there was something about the sales behavior of her work that indicated to Amazon it could break out big if given special promotion on the site.

Online promotions like the Kindle Daily Deal, have the power to turn a title into a bestseller overnight. Until recent years, when sales lightning struck, it would do so in the form of a favorable *New York Times* book review or a call from Oprah. But the increasingly dominant role of Amazon—and the ability of readers to discover a book through online retailers and Internet search—is changing what it means to successfully market a book. It also calls into question the value of traditional bestseller lists like the *New York Times*, which rarely reflect what books are moving in big numbers digitally or predominantly through Amazon. Some say the truest of all bestseller lists is in fact the *USA Today* list, which tracks all formats of a single title and rolls up the sales into one number. The *New York Times* doesn't do anything even close to this, and in fact maintains separate lists based on format.

As breaking out your book becomes increasingly reliant on metadata and algorithms—those ever-changing computations that drive searches and recommendations on Amazon, Goodreads, Google, Apple, and other sites—how relevant will traditional book-marketing techniques be to an author's success? And given that analyzing algorithms is typically an activity even less accessible to authors than publicity and PR, how will the author-publisher partnership evolve to ensure books get discovered by the right readers?

Traditionally, one of the biggest values publishers have offered authors is the ability to get their books into stores. It's a value that goes beyond simple distribution. Bookstore placement acts as a marketing function, particularly when the book is selected for front-of-store display, or has cover-out placement, rather than spine-out placement. The more visible a book is, the better the chances of a reader stumbling upon it—and the better the chances of that reader talking about it with other readers.

In fact, Ferriss himself attributed good distribution to his book's staying power on the *New York Times* bestseller list. The more books that appeared on shelves, the more books that sold. If more chains feature a book, or give it prominent placement, sales are nearly guaranteed to increase. However, if fewer people are browsing bookstore shelves, publishers can't count on the serendipity of the bookstore visitor bumping into a front-of-store display and taking a chance on a new author. Algorithms and promotions like the Kindle Daily Deal then play an increasingly important role in how readers discover and decide what to read next.

It's not clear if publishers are well-prepared to face this challenge. While publishers may be unparalleled in their ability to offer print retail distribution and mass-market branding campaigns, they're still catching up with direct-to-consumer marketing. Next door to publishing, in New York City's advertising and marketing agencies, you'll find best practices in digital and consumer marketing that aren't necessarily known by the major houses.

Even publishers who eventually learn best practices, however, can be ultimately be stymied by changes in the marketplace. Toolsets change quickly, and most publishers are focused on marketing the upcoming season of titles. That means they have little time for experimentation or looking ahead at what might work next.

Where does this leave the average author? Probably the best thing you can focus on is the same thing that Hyatt and Ferriss focused on. If you build a network you can reach either online or offline, and they trust you, they'll come out when your book releases. Don't underestimate the difference that your relationships can make. If you make connections, when it's time for your launch or event, you'll see a real and meaningful effect.

While you might not be able to keep up with every nuance of what's changing in digital marketing or book publishing, and you won't be able to control what your publisher does to support your book, you'll always benefit from building your own platform and overall brand. And that's what we'll talk about next.

Career Marketing Strategies for Writers
Lecture 21

O ne of the most common disappointments experienced by authors during the traditional publishing process is lack of or perceived lack of marketing and promotion support. In fact, publishers tend to do more to market and promote books than authors realize, but authors should not depend on anyone else to build their brands or expand their direct connections with readers. Your publisher is focused on the short term—its immediate return on investment. You must take care of the long-term career building, which includes taking ownership of your brand and your vision for it and building direct connections with readers. Both of these tasks are like contributing to a retirement account, a long-term investment that pays off over time.

Author Websites

- An essential task for any author today is to establish a website that serves as a hub and information clearinghouse for everything he or she publishes. A website serves as your primary calling card in the digital age. Whatever type of marketing strategy you pursue, it will be more effective with a website in place.

- There's some truth to the belief that a bad website or an out-of-date website can be more damaging than no site at all, but most authors are quite capable of constructing and maintaining sites after being educated properly. Further, no site has to be perfect at launch. Authors can start small and build their skills and presence over time. It may even be worthwhile for an unpublished writer to start a website.
  - Starting a site when you're unpublished helps you get over the learning curve of set-up and maintenance well before you need the site. Building a simple site today should enable you to have a robust and effective one in the future, when it's most important.

  - Also, having a site helps slowly extend brand awareness, especially if you're active on social media or elsewhere online. This tends to be particularly important for nonfiction authors who are building their authority and reach in order to persuade a publisher to offer a contract.

- ○ Finally, having a site opens up opportunities. You never know who might be looking to contact you or might simply be intrigued by stumbling across your site.

- If you're an unpublished author, your site needs only one or two pages. Include a short bio, mention any credits or media appearances, link to your social media accounts, and briefly describe the type of writing work you do. Don't belabor your unpublished status.

  - ○ Your professional bio should run about 100 to 200 words. You may also include a professional head shot if you have one or another good photo.

  - ○ You might include a tagline or description in your site header that clearly describes your brand or the kind of work you do. For example, novelist CJ Lyons uses the tagline "Thrillers with Heart."

  - ○ Next, you should have a page dedicated to your published or forthcoming books. You might have a separate page for each book or product, or you might combine them. Regardless, don't skimp on the details, and always include links to where your books can be purchased in both print and digital form.

  - ○ Always let readers know where else you're active online. This is important because some visitors may never return to your site. One visit may be your only chance for potential readers and others to find and connect with you on social media—at the moment they're interested.

  - ○ You should also mention notable media coverage, good reviews, testimonials, or a significant following you have on another platform. Such positive attention constitutes *social proof*; that is, it sends out strong signals that other people have found your writing worthwhile.

- Even established authors are susceptible to a number of common mistakes in constructing websites.
  - For example, some sites have unclear or confusing navigation that makes it hard for new visitors to find what they're looking for. Most statistics show that a website has roughly seven seconds to get its point across; thus, your homepage needs to offer clear paths to the most popular information, such as your most recent publication or current project.

  - Sites that take a long time to load, require special plug-ins, or don't work on all devices frustrate visitors and cause them to leave quickly. Today, most websites receive 30 to 50 percent of their traffic from mobile devices, which makes a mobile-friendly site a near requirement.

  - Finally, don't make it difficult for people to get in touch with you. Offer a contact form, give a specific e-mail address, or provide contact information for your agent, publicist, or publisher.

- Facebook is not an adequate replacement for an author website for a number of reasons. First, although it may be hard to imagine, Facebook may eventually fall out of favor; it's also true that not everyone is on Facebook. Perhaps most important, you can never control what Facebook or any other social media platform does with its design and functionality, its user interface, and your followers. Your insights into your readership are limited to what Facebook itself measures and decides to pass on to you.

Author Blogs

- Unfortunately, many authors receive bad advice about blogging and end up blogging poorly because they believe that a blog is nothing more than a way to increase book sales. In fact, blogging is a great marketing tool, but few people know how to do it well.

- Meaningful blogging requires patience and persistence, as well as a willingness to learn what makes for compelling online-driven or online-only writing. This type of writing is not the same as writing for formal publication or in other genres or mediums—or even for websites other than your own.

- If you have to ask, "What do I blog about?" then you probably shouldn't be blogging. If the writing is too forced or contrived, your blog may be doomed from the start, or you may not stick with it. But if you approach blogging because it seems as if it would be fun, then it can be incredibly important to your engagement with readers and overall audience growth.

- Once you have a site or blog established, mostly, you need to be patient. Traffic will grow organically as you produce or publish more work. Be sure to link to new blog posts on each social media network where you're active. With the link, offer an intriguing question, lead-in, excerpt, or explanation of why the post might be interesting to people on that specific social network.

Google Analytics is a free service that tracks traffic to your website; it shows how people find your site and what pages are most popular.

E-Mail Newsletters

- Your website should also have an e-mail newsletter sign-up to enable you to communicate directly with your audience. But before you start a newsletter, decide on the frequency with which you will publish and stick to it. Your efforts will be more successful if you're consistent with your timing. Also, keep your e-mails short and structured, and make sure that people understand what they'll get if they subscribe.

- In the content of your e-mail newsletter, try to provide value or otherwise focus on other people or quality content. For example, her monthly newsletter, author CJ Lyons features a Q&A with another novelist. This offers something appealing to her readers, who are thriller fans; helps out another novelist; and gives Lyons a valuable means of serving her community.

- Aside from a sign-up form on your own website, the only tool you need to start a newsletter is a service that automates the subscription process, stores the subscriber addresses, and archives newsletter issues. Never add a name to your e-mail list unless you are given permission to do so and never sell your readers' information.

Social Media

- Social media is extremely useful for building relationships in the writing community, actively marketing a book, and nurturing reader relationships. Of course, the key benefit that everyone's after with social media is a visible effect on sales. But you'll be successful at marketing through these platforms only if you have built trust and forged relationships on each network.

- Social media is excellent at building awareness of who you are and what you stand for. Over time, you become more visible and identifiable because you show up consistently and have focused messages. It's usually only after this recognition and trust develops that you can run a successful social media campaign that focuses on the sale of a particular book. If you don't have these relationships or trust in place, ask your friends and influencers who do to help spread the word about you.

- Social media typically works best for long-term awareness efforts, relationship building, audience development, and general networking. It is not terribly effective for the hard sell. All the information about why people might like your book—along with the sales pitch—should be on your website.

Other Communications

- When your book is set to launch, brainstorm a list of all the meaningful relationships you have, and divide the list into three groups: (1) people who would probably like to be alerted to your new work, perhaps old classmates or coworkers; (2) people who have significant reach or influence with your target readership; and (3) your existing and devoted fans.

- For the first group, friends and acquaintances, write a brief announcement and include a link to your website for all the book details. For the second group, write a brief, personalized note about your book promotion efforts and offer one to three concrete ways in which your recipient could help, such as tweeting about your book on a specific day. For the third group, your fans, write a general note asking for support in any way they feel comfortable.

- You should also brainstorm a list of all the gatekeepers to your readers with whom you do not yet have a relationship, including specific individuals and websites or blogs. For example, if you write romance, popular romance review blogs are such gatekeepers. Do those blogs accept guest posts? Can you contribute to the community in some way? If you want to grow your readership, you'll have to look beyond your existing network.

- Many times, when an author's marketing efforts fail, it's because the author tried to go it alone. When you see a successful author, what you see may be only the visible aspects of his or her presence or platform. What you can't see are all the relationships and conversations that go on behind the scenes that contribute to a more amplified reach.

Suggested Reading

Grahl, *Your First 1,000 Copies.*

Hyatt, *Platform.*

1. Select a few published titles that are similar to your own and visit the authors' websites, as well as the Amazon pages for their books. Look for any and all media attention and publicity received for their work or business relationships that are in play. Study what these authors do on social media to interact with readers and promote their work.

2. Visit the websites of authors whose work you admire. What opportunities do readers have to interact with each author or receive information? What, if anything, does the author offer to readers that's totally free?

Career Marketing Strategies for Writers
Lecture 21—Transcript

While everyone's situation is unique, authors tend to experience the same disappointments during the traditional publishing process. The most common disappointment—and the one that can have the most damaging effect on the author-publisher relationship—is lack of marketing and promotion support.

Sometimes this is more perceived than real. Publishers do a pretty poor job of letting authors know about all the things they do to market and promote books, especially within industry channels, that the author might not see visible evidence of.

Whatever your experience, it's essential that you not depend on your publisher or your agent to build your author brand, or be responsible for growing your direct connection with readers. Publishers will be focused on the short-term, or their immediate return on investment. You have to take care of the long-term career building.

While you may delegate tasks or hire help, the author should take ownership of their brand and build a vision for it. It also largely falls on your shoulders to undertake marketing activities that don't have immediate payoff, but are important for future success and sales. Building direct contact with readers is building up your own 401k, a long-term investment that pays off over time.

The first and most important step in this journey is establishing your author website—a website that serves as a hub and information clearinghouse for everything you publish. Yet it's not unusual for authors to be told by their publishers that an author website isn't necessary or effective. Publishers may say you're better off creating and maintaining a Facebook page instead. We'll talk about Facebook later, but for now, all you need to know is that publishers are dead wrong in this advice.

A website is the number one calling card for a successful digital-age author. Whatever type of marketing strategy you pursue, it's more effective with a website in place. That's not to say that every author should put the same amount of time and energy into it—every author's career is different—but given how much book discovery is moving online, there's no reason any published author should say no to a website.

One of the problems, however—and here's the reason many publishers don't encourage authors to build one—is that few people are educated on best practices or design for author websites, or what websites are good at, or how they integrate into a larger online presence. There's a learning curve here that few publishers want to be involved in, so it becomes easier to say "Don't bother because you won't do it right."

There's some truth to the belief that a bad author website or an out-of-date website, can be more damaging than no author website at all. However, I think it's a mistake and a disservice to authors, to make them believe a website is some sophisticated piece of technology they can't handle or maintain. I've seen many writers, some as young as 15 years old and others beyond 60, who successfully start and maintain their sites after being encouraged and educated properly.

This is part of being a capable author in the digital age, and it's essential if you want to grow your career over the next 5, 10, or 20 years. The good news is that you don't have to launch and perfect everything at once. You can start small, and build your skills and presence over time. It may even be worthwhile to start a website while you're unpublished, for several reasons.

To begin with, it helps you get over the learning curve. While it's easy nowadays to get a full-fledged site up and running in 24 hours, you'll likely need to learn some new systems and become accustomed to new tools. I think it's a mistake to start the website building process, only on the day you need a site. Instead, educate yourself in advance. Try building a simple site today, so you can have a robust and effective site when it's most important to you.

Also, having a site helps slowly build your brand, especially if you're active on social media or elsewhere online. This tends to be particularly critical for nonfiction authors who are building their authority and reach to readership, to persuade a publisher to offer a contract. It's never too early to start making positive impressions. This leads to another reason to get a site up sooner rather than later.

It opens up opportunities. You never know who might find your site. You never know who's listening, you never know who's searching. When I finally started my own website that wasn't connected to my employer, many more opportunities opened up, because it was then clear how people could contact me, what I could offer, and who I was already offering it to.

Of all these reasons to start a website early, the biggest benefit is usually to get comfortable with the tools before you really need your site to pay off. So, what do you say on your site if you're still unpublished?

You can keep it simple. You only need one or two pages. Include a brief bio, mention any publishing credits or media appearances, and link to your social media accounts. Don't belabor your unpublished status. You deserve to have a site even if you're unpublished; it helps indicate your seriousness about your craft and career. But you don't need to explain at length your journey to get published or your attempts to find an agent. Briefly describe the type of writing work you do, and leave it at that.

Every published author's website should include the following elements. First, you should have a bio or about page. I recommend a brief bio of about 100 to 200 words, and a professional headshot if you have one. You can expand in many different ways, but a short bio up front is very helpful and essential, for those looking for the quick facts.

It can also be helpful to have a tagline or description in your website header—something that appears on every page—that clearly describes your brand or the kind of work you do. For example, novelist CJ Lyons, uses the tagline "Thrillers with Heart."

Next, you should have a page dedicated to whatever books are forthcoming or already published. You might have a separate page for each book or product, or you might combine everything together. Regardless, don't skimp on the details, and always include links to where your books can be purchased in both print and digital form. Also let readers know where else you're active online, so they can follow you there, too. This is important because some visitors may never return to your site. This is your chance, at the moment someone is interested, for them to find and connect with you on social media. You should also offer an e-mail newsletter signup, which we'll discuss in more detail later.

If you have notable media coverage, good reviews, positive testimonials, or a significant following on a specific platform, let it be known. This is called social proof; we're all very susceptible to strong signals that other people have found something worthwhile. Now that we've covered what you should do, let's discuss some of the most common mistakes that get made, even by very established authors.

Some sites have unclear or confusing navigation that makes it hard for a new visitor to find what they're looking for. This decreases your site's effectiveness because people who end up at your site will not likely read more than a couple pages of it. In fact, most statistics show that a website has roughly seven seconds to get its point across. So it needs to be clear on the homepage, what's important. Offer clear paths to the most popular information. Don't build your site for yourself—build it for readers.

For example, if you're actively writing and publishing books, people who end up at your site, are likely seeking further information about your latest work. That's why the latest book cover or project should often be on the homepage and marked as such. Readers may also be seeking an overview of all the work you have to offer, so make it easy for them to find a page that offers the full list. If you have a series, have the series title in your main menu.

If your site takes a long time to load, requires special plug-ins, or doesn't work on all devices, you're going to lose a chunk of your visitors who get frustrated and leave. Today, most websites receive at least 30–50% of their traffic from mobile devices, which makes having a mobile-friendly site a near requirement.

Finally, don't make it a mystery as to how people can get in touch with you. Offer a contact form or give specific directions for how to reach you. If you prefer, offer contact information for your agent, publicist, or publisher.

At this point in my discussion of author websites, particularly at writers' conferences, I'm often asked: Why not just use Facebook? Isn't that where everyone is spending their time already? Why would people even visit my site? Why bother with all the effort especially if a bad website could be more damaging than no website at all?

It may be hard to envision, but Facebook may eventually fall out of favor. By choosing Facebook instead of an author website, you're favoring the short-term over the long-term. You're investing your time and energy in a platform that may lose effectiveness, or disappear in several years. It may benefit your current campaign or initiative, but you can never be sure it's going to benefit your second or third book. In the meantime, your author website will remain unfinished, and people who don't use Facebook, will become incredibly difficult to identify and reach. Even though it may seem like it, the entire world is not on Facebook.

Perhaps most important, you can't control what Facebook or any other social media platform does—with its design and functionality, or with its user interface, and with your followers. You're limited in what you control, and your insights into your readership are limited to what Facebook itself measures and decides to pass on to you. While it's true that a site with more than a billion users has attractive qualities to anyone trying to reach readers, just realize you don't call all the shots.

I hope that I've convinced you that a website is a critical part of your long-term career toolbox. At this stage, the next big question is, "Should I blog?" When I observe writers on the path to publication, the chain of events often goes something like this: The book nears its publication date, and the author knows she needs to market and promote, the author receives advice that blogging is a good way to market her book, she then wonders "What should I blog about?"

If you're unpublished, you might also hear advice that blogging will help you land a book deal, which we covered earlier. Sadly, many authors blog poorly because of so much bad advice surrounding how blogging is a way to accomplish some goal associated with book sales. While it is, in fact, a great marketing tool, few people know how to do it well.

Speaking for myself, I started blogging because it seemed like a fun creative outlet—a practice that would build discipline and better engagement with my community. After seven years of active blogging, it became the core of my overall online marketing strategy. So I'm not down on blogging, but I was willing to put in years of effort, and I also improved as I went along. My best blog posts didn't start appearing until I was several years in.

You can be a quicker study than I was and be a lot more strategic. I recommend reading author Chris Guillebeau's free guide, "279 Days to Overnight Success," to understand how to blog meaningfully. Unfortunately, many authors pursue blogging without any understanding of the medium, and also as little more than a means to an end.

Meaningful blogging requires patience and persistence, as well as a willingness to learn what makes for good, compelling online writing. It's not the same as writing for formal publication or in other genres. If you have to ask, "What do I blog about," maybe you shouldn't be blogging? If the action is too forced or contrived, your blog may be doomed from the start, or you may not stick with it.

On the other hand, I encourage you to experiment. If it kind of does sound like fun, then, as I said, it can be incredibly important to your engagement with readers and overall audience growth, especially if you're writing nonfiction.

Once you have a site or blog established, mostly you need to be patient. Traffic will grow organically as you produce or publish more work. Most authors don't need to worry too much about driving traffic in isolation from that. But there are ways to make the whole engine more robust and hardworking, so I'll share some ways to ensure you're following best practices.

If you do blog, always link to new blog posts on each social media network where you're active. But don't just post a link, offer an intriguing question or personalized comment on why the post might be interesting to people who follow you. While it might be possible to automate postings across your social networks whenever a new post goes live, it's far more effective to give each post a personal touch based on what you know appeals to a particular group.

Always include your website address on all offline materials. Whether it's business cards, books, bookmarks, or postcards—any kind of print collateral—don't forget to put your website address on it. It's best to install Google Analytics on your website from the moment it goes live. Google Analytics is a free service that tracks traffic to your site and what people do with your site. By looking at your analytics, you can uncover whether or not your social media accounts are having any impact on sending people to your site. You'll also learn how people find your site overall. This kind of information is invaluable when making difficult choices about where to spend your marketing time. The data also helps you improve your site, because you'll see how people behave when they visit, what pages are most popular, and what path people take from the beginning to the end of their visit.

Last but not least, you should have an email newsletter signup on your website. It allows you to communicate reliably and directly with your audience from one book to the next. You want the power of direct engagement with your readers, without the danger of websites folding, platforms changing, or publishers merging.

Because most people are overwhelmed with unwanted email, it may seem counterintuitive to categorize the e-mail newsletter as one of the more effective forms of digital communication. However, e-mail has proven to be a more long-term and stable tool than social media, which is constantly shifting. E-mails can't be missed like a social media post that disappears in readers' feeds as more posts follow it. You truly own your e-mail list, unlike Facebook or Twitter accounts.

And if you use people's e-mail addresses with respect, those addresses can become resources that grow more valuable over time. Getting started with an e-mail newsletter is simple and also free, but let's review a few principles before getting to the technical aspects. Decide on your frequency and stick with it. Your efforts will be doubly successful if you're consistent with your timing. For published authors, monthly is a common frequency. If you choose a low frequency, such as quarterly or even annual, you run the risk of people forgetting they signed up, which then leads to unsubscribes.

Keep your e-mails short, sweet, and structured. Hardly anyone will complain that your e-mails are too short; the more frequently you send, the shorter your e-mails should probably be. It can also help to deliver the same structure every time. Be specific and honest about what people are signing up for. You should create a newsletter sign-up form that tells people what they'll get if they subscribe. This leads us to the question of what you actually put in this newsletter.

The only limit is your imagination. While the business intent is to keep in touch with readers and let them know about your new book releases, you should also be a welcome presence in the inbox. This means trying to provide value, or otherwise focus on other people or quality content. Ask yourself: What do you love sharing with other people? What are you already curating or collecting? What do people ask you about all the time? Or what do you have special insight or expertise on?

For example, in each monthly newsletter, bestselling thriller novelist CJ Lyons, offers a Q&A with another novelist. This accomplishes several things: It offers something appealing to her readers, who are thriller fans, it helps out another novelist, who gets increased visibility to an audience of 20,000 plus subscribers, and it gives CJ Lyons a means to serve her community in a valuable way.

To start getting subscribers, you of course need a sign-up form on your website. As fans of your work visit your site, they'll see this sign-up form pretty unmistakably. Make sure it's available in your header, footer, sidebar, or somewhere that it consistently shows up regardless of where people enter your site.

Aside from your own website, the only tool you need is a formal e-mail newsletter service that automates the subscription process, stores the e-mail addresses, and archives the newsletter issues. Some of the most popular services are MailChimp, TinyLetter, and Campaign Monitor. MailChimp is often a good choice because it's free to use until you reach 2,000 subscribers.

One of the most important rules of running an e-mail newsletter is that while it is possible to manually add names to your list, you should never add someone unless she gives you permission to do so. The number one reason e-mail newsletters get a bad reputation is because people break this rule all the time. Just because you connect with someone on LinkedIn or through a conference, doesn't mean you automatically have permission to add that person to your e-mail newsletter list.

Also, pay readers the utmost respect by never selling their information or sending strong, impersonal sales and marketing messages, also known as blasts. Most people will sign up for your newsletter because they want to hear from you personally. Maintain subscriber trust by keeping the messages as intimate as possible, and in your voice.

OK, we've now covered what I consider the building blocks for any marketing strategy you pursue: An author website, and an e-mail newsletter signup. No matter what kind of author you are, get these in place first. We've so far avoided any discussion of social media, even though most new authors, upon securing a book contract, are advised they need to establish a Twitter account, a Facebook page, or any number of social media profiles. Why? To sell their book, of course.

This presents an immediate dilemma: If you're not already active on these channels, of your own interest and volition, you now have the mindset of using these tools to sell. More importantly, you may have no idea what that means beyond telling people to buy your book, like your page or follow you. The other problem is that social media, while not going away, is constantly in flux. Its use is also highly dependent on the type of work you write and publish—not to mention your own personality and comfort level.

To help you out of this dilemma, I want to first focus on the principles behind social media use, as well as all online marketing, since the landscape changes so rapidly. I'm going to focus on the three most common benefits of using social media. One, building relationships in the writing community, two, actively selling a book and encouraging word of mouth, three nurturing reader relationships.

Building relationships is the kind of activity that's largely unquantifiable, but it's also where nearly every single person starts out, at least if you're not a celebrity. As you learn to use any social media tool, there's a warming up period as you come to understand the community, its language, and its etiquette. Most people begin by reaching out to the real-life people they already know on the network, then branch out and connect with people they haven't met in person before.

So what's the purpose of this? Well, why do any of us attend social functions? To have a good time, to network with others, and to be informed about the community. The key benefit that everyone's after, of course, is a visible effect on sales. But you'll only be successful at marketing on social media, if you've been building trust and forging relationships on each network. Nobody likes a stranger barging into the room and loudly announcing a sale. It's considered rude.

But let's be honest, many people have been told to get on social media in preparation for a book launch, and have no interest in using it beyond a marketing and sales effort. That people feel this obligation or burden is one of the greatest failures of the publishing community, but let's set that aside and instead discuss how to do it without rubbing everyone the wrong way.

Social media is excellent at building awareness in the community, of who you are and what you stand for. Over time, you become more visible and identifiable, because you show up consistently and have focused messages. It's usually only after this recognition and trust develops, that you can run a successful social media marketing campaign that focuses on a sale.

If you don't have relationships or trust in place on social media to help you be successful, here's a work-around. Get your friends and influencers who already have relationships and trust in place, to help spread the word for you.

Bottom line, don't lean on social media for the hard sell. Social media typically works best for long-term awareness efforts, relationship building, audience development, and general networking. It is not terribly effective for repeatedly telling people, "Buy my book." All of the information about why people might like to buy your book—along with the hard-hitting sales pitch—should be on your website.

Now we come to the third benefit of using social media. Once you're an established author, it's going to be an important means of nurturing reader relationships. It helps you stay engaged with your audience, and grow it for the long term. I believe this is actually where the most difficult challenge lies, or where the real pinch comes into play. This is when authors have to balance writing time, with time spent interacting with their audience.

There's a lot of value to be gained from nurturing that connection, and it can even inform what you write next. Yet every author has to form a strategy they're personally comfortable with and can sustain with reasonable comfort. It's hard to prescribe a formula because this comes down to your personality and also where you're at in your career. Your priorities will change, and your social media use will fluctuate. That's natural and expected.

When does social media use reach its limits of utility? That's kind of like asking how much time it takes for two people to maintain a good and productive relationship. The answer is different for everyone. If social media is starting to drag on your time and resources to do other things more important to you such as writing it's time to reassess.

While I don't recommend analyzing time spent on your social media, it's helpful to check in with yourself on how the activity is making you feel. Energetic or drained? Positive or anxious? Empowered or jealous? Whenever you experience more negative emotions than positive, it's time to step back from whatever networks are causing these emotions, and decide if you should find another place to focus your marketing efforts.

Some writers are advised to get on social media before publication, in order to grow their audience, and this does make sense for nonfiction authors who need to build visibility and authority in their field. But for fiction authors, it can make little sense. How can you build readership around work that hasn't yet been made public? You can build relationships, and be part of a community, but you're not necessarily cultivating a readership. A potential readership, maybe.

But there's a big difference here that's not acknowledged frequently enough, and also leads to a lot of frustration and claims that social media doesn't work. As an unpublished writer, are the people you're engaging with online the sort who will love to read what you write, when it's published? Let's assume yes. To turn those potential readers into actual readers, requires showing up consistently within your community over a long period of time, being consistent in your communication to that community, and then of course delivering work that aligns with all of your previous activity and messaging.

When the book arrives, it should feel like the exclamation point at the end of a sentence, emphasizing what people sensed was already there. And if the work you produce is quality, you not only have a reader, you have a fan who will spread word of mouth to others.

In whatever way you decide to use social media, there's another step you should be taking, whenever you have a book launch, that will make all of your marketing that much more effective.

Brainstorm a list of all the meaningful relationships you have—people you can count on to read your e-mails. You shouldn't have strangers or acquaintances on any of these lists. Divide your list into three groups. One, people who would like to be alerted to your new work, such as coworkers and friends. Two, people who have reach or influence with your target readership, like a blogger or a published author. Three, your existing fans who may be willing to spread the word about your work to their friends and connections.

For the first group of friends, after the book goes on sale, write a brief email describing it, then include a link to your website or Amazon, for all the details. Don't send a batch email to the entire group, but rather send each individual a form letter and personalize them if you have time.

For the second group of influencers, write a brief, personalized note to each person about your book promotion efforts, and offer one to three concrete ways they could help you. Maybe they could tweet about the book on a specific day, excerpt the book on their website, or interview you on their blog. Base your suggestions on things you've actually seen them do.

For the third group, the one with your fans, write a brief note asking for support in any way they feel comfortable, and provide specific examples of what that support looks like. You can even give them specific messaging that they can copy and paste into a Twitter post or similar. If you have a few really avid fans, you might consider a more personalized note to them.

So few authors do any of this. Taking the time to write personalized e-mails will dramatically increase support from your network. You shouldn't try to market and promote your book on your own; it takes a village, as they say. I also recommend you brainstorm a list of all the influencers who reach your readership, but who you don't yet know. For example, if you write romance, then popular romance review blogs would act as an influencer and gatekeeper to your readership. Do those blogs accept guest posts? Can you contribute to their community in some way? If you want to grow your readership, you'll have to think beyond your existing network.

Many times, when an author's marketing efforts fail, it's because they tried to go it alone. When you see a successful author, what you see are just the visible aspects of their presence or platform. What you can't see, are all of the relationships and conversations that go on behind the scenes that contribute to a more amplified reach.

When you're an early career author, you may not have many relationships to draw on initially. You may also feel that your website is lacking, your social media following is meager, and your email list is miniscule. But with each new book or piece of writing you publish, you'll gain visibility and new fans that will help you during the next launch. New authors have to be patient and play the long game. Have faith that the time you spend on marketing activities, even if it doesn't produce sales today, will produce sales tomorrow.

The Self-Publishing Path: When and How
Lecture 22

As we've discussed, authors today have more power and control than ever in deciding how and when to publish. Technology has enabled us all to be active creators, publishers, and distributors, without needing the permission or approval of the so-called gatekeepers. This message of empowerment is so strong that authors are beginning to ask why publishers are needed in the first place. What value do they add to the process? In fact, the value added by a publisher depends on your own personality and strengths as an author. In this lecture, we'll begin by discussing the value of publishers; then, we'll talk about specific scenarios in which you may not need that value.

The Value of Traditional Publishers

- One of the primary benefits of working with a publisher is that doing so will help you produce the best possible product that fits well into the marketplace. Publishers have decades of experience in packaging books that sell. They understand how to build off your strengths, while minimizing the appearance of your weaknesses.

- In addition, it's useful to have someone to tell you when something isn't working. Most people don't have the gift of being so distant from their work that they can see where it's succeeding or failing. To develop to your maximum potential, you need someone to create a little discomfort.

- The bottom line is this: If you want to compete in an increasingly crowded marketplace, you need the most professional quality possible. Although it's true that publishers can put out low-quality work, they're far more consistent in the quality they achieve than what you find across the majority of authors who self-publish.

- Not every author has the time—or wants to spend time—learning about and administering the self-publishing process and finding assistance they can trust. For some writers, having a publisher frees them to focus on other aspects of the writing, marketing, and promotion process.

Goals of Self-Publishing

- Self-publishing most frequently enters the conversation when writers have experienced a "near miss" with a publisher or the traditional submission process has failed to produce an acceptance. In other words, self-publishing is often seen as a last resort, rather than the first and best option.

- Before you commit to self-publishing, identify your primary goal for doing so. This goal will affect what service you choose, how much money you spend, what format you use, and how satisfied you are at the end of the process. Three common goals are to experience the satisfaction of seeing your work in print, to strengthen expertise and visibility for nonfiction authors, and to prove the gatekeepers wrong.
  - If your primary goal is to see your work in print form, then the key question is: How much help or service do you need or want to make that happen? It is possible to write a check, hand over a Word document, and get a printed book in your hands very quickly. Many full-service publishing providers offer a range of packages to choose from, with the average cost somewhere between $1,000 and $2,000. Just don't expect any sales to come from this effort.

  - A common goal for nonfiction authors is to maintain visibility in a specific field or profession. Self-publishing can be especially helpful to those who speak often, have a ready audience, and are existing authorities in their field. Such authors should avoid full-service providers because they collect royalties on every book sold. Instead, these authors should contract out all services or hire a professional to manage the process. This ensures that the author controls all property, rights, and profits after the book is finished.

- Many who self-publish harbor a secret goal of proving the gatekeepers wrong. These authors hope that once their work is in print, those who rejected them earlier will see their success and now want to sign them.

Deciding to Self-Publish

- Despite all the success stories, few authors make a living from their self-published work or go on to traditional book deals. If you envision yourself as a thriving independent author, you need to also see yourself as a long-term entrepreneur. You'll need marketing experience—or a willingness to acquire some—and the time to be active online, because most of your sales will be through online retailers.

- It's generally ill-advised to self-publish if you don't have a strong idea of who your readers are, if you don't have any online presence, or if you're hoping to get lucky. Many self-published authors hope to go on to a traditional deal, but if they couldn't interest a larger publisher in a book before it was self-published, they're unlikely to find a buyer afterward, unless they rack up significant sales on their own.

- It's also true that there is still a stigma attached to self-publishing. Most traditional media outlets will not review or consider self-published books for editorial coverage. It may also be difficult to find a marketing or publicity person to work with you. With a self-published book, you must build credibility on your own, and in the process, you will battle against a number of preconceived notions about the quality of your work.

- That said, there is an active community of self-published, independent authors who are ready to share their strategies and tactics to help newcomers. If you're diligent in following best practices, approach the process with an entrepreneurial spirit, and feel committed to producing books on your own for years to come, you may become a success story.

- The self-publishing industry was revolutionized in the late 1990s by the advent of print-on-demand (POD) technology, which allows books to be published one at a time. Nearly every self-publishing service uses this technology to create, sell, and fulfill orders for print editions. This eliminates the need for inventory and warehousing, not to mention the risky investment in a print run that might not sell. It also explains why self-published books are almost never stocked in bookstores; copies are printed only when they've already been purchased.

- The self-publishing approach that's been around the longest is the formal full-service publishing provider, better known by the derogatory term *vanity press*. Such services will publish your book in whatever formats you want, but they take a significant cut of your profits.

- If you want a full-service approach with better earnings potential, you can look for companies that help you produce your book strictly on a work-for-hire basis, meaning that they earn no royalties off your sales. However, these services tend to be far more expensive than the other type of provider because they're more personalized and focused on quality.

- If you're comfortable with very little to no service, you can use the major services that distribute POD specifically for self-published authors, such as Amazon's CreateSpace and IngramSpark. With these services, which are virtually free, you can often see your book for sale at major online retailers in as little as 48 hours.

- This entire process becomes simpler if you plan to self-publish and distribute your book only in e-book format. E-book services typically fall into two categories.
  - First, there are retailer-specific distribution and sales services that are 100 percent free to use, such as Amazon's Kindle Direct Publishing. As an author, you work directly through a self-service interface to make your work available for sale almost

instantly. It's as simple as opening an account, uploading your book files, and pushing the "Publish" button.

- Also available are e-book distribution services, such as Smashwords. They offer a centralized site to upload your work, which they then push out to all the major online e-book retailers. Some e-book distributors charge an upfront fee, while others take a percentage of your sales.

- Understand that these services are not publishers. They are distributors and retailers. They take no responsibility for the quality of your work, but neither do they take any rights to your work. You use these services on an at-will basis. If you decide you've made a mistake in publishing your e-book, you can remove it from availability as quickly as you uploaded it.

- When using an e-book retailer or service, keep the following pointers in mind:
  - First, check to see if the retailer or service is exclusive or nonexclusive. Most work on a nonexclusive basis, which means that you can sell your e-book at many different retailers at once.

  - Second, you should always be in control of the price. Although some retailers may have reasonable pricing restrictions, such as not allowing you to price below $0.99, the standard practice is to give the author complete control over pricing. However, most e-book retailers mandate that you not offer more favorable pricing elsewhere.

  - Third, you should always understand how much money you'll earn on each book sale. For example, Amazon Kindle offers you 70 percent of your book's list price as long as you price between $2.99 and $9.99. If you price outside that range, you'll earn 35 percent.

  - Fourth, make sure you understand how much freedom you have to make changes to your e-book after it goes on sale. Retailers

Because the cover of your book is often your number-one sales tool, especially for online sales, make sure you hire a professional designer to create it.

generally allow you to upload revised files as often as you like, but distributors may require you to pay a fee to make changes.

○ Finally, check what formats are required from you. Most retailers allow you to upload a Word document, which is then automatically converted into whatever format is needed. Most services offer guidelines and preview programs to ensure that your e-book looks good before it goes live.

Professionalism in Self-Publishing

- Two mistakes commonly made by self-publishing authors are not hiring a professional editor to review your work line by line and not hiring a professional designer to create your book cover.

- Further, if you want to tackle self-publishing in the most professional way possible, you should establish a small press. Give this press a name, even if you'll be publishing only your own work. You will use this press name when you self-publish through online retailers, on the copyright page of your books, and anywhere else the name of the publisher is seen or requested.

- As part of this process, you should buy your press its own set of ISBNs, which are the industry-standard identification numbers for books. If you want your book to have any chance of being stocked or distributed in a retail environment, this number is required.

- You might also look into two final self-publishing models: self-publishing with an agent's assistance or partnering with a publisher. Both approaches may give you the benefit of assistance from industry insiders, but they also involve some costs. Make sure you carefully research such arrangements and understand their terms before you reach an agreement with either an agent or a publishing partner.

Suggested Reading

Kawasaki, *APE: Author, Publisher, Entrepreneur.*

Levine, *The Fine Print of Self-Publishing.*

Exercises

1. Visit Smashwords, an online retailer of many thousands of self-published e-books. Look at the bestselling titles in your category or genre (filtered by most units sold), then search for those same books at other retailers. How well distributed are these books? How many formats are they available in? Where can they be ordered? Where do these books seem to have the most reviews or the highest ranking? Do they have ISBNs, and how are they priced? Also study the authors' websites. How do they appear to be marketing and promoting their work? How many titles have they published? How active are they on social media?

2. Brainstorm several keywords that readers might use to search Amazon if they wanted to find a book like yours, then search Amazon using those keywords and see what titles turn up. How many are self-published versus traditionally published? (You can often identify self-published titles on Amazon because the publisher is listed as CreateSpace or Amazon Digital Services, although this is not always the case.)

The Self-Publishing Path: When and How
Lecture 22—Transcript

There's incredible emphasis these days on how authors have more power and control than ever in deciding how and when to publish. Technology has enabled us all to be creators, publishers, and distributors, without needing the permission or approval of the so-called gatekeepers.

This message of empowerment is so strong that authors are beginning to ask why publishers are needed in the first place. What value do they add to the process? The truth is, the value they add depends on your own personality and strengths as an author, and there are definitely some types of authors who have nothing to gain from working with a publisher.

First, I'll discuss a few ways that publishers generally add value. Then we'll talk about specific scenarios where you may not need their value.

To begin with, publishers push you to achieve the best quality for the target market. Working with professionals who are experts in their field will help you produce the best possible product for the marketplace. Publishers have decades of experience in packaging books that sell. They also understand how to build off your strengths and make them the focus, while minimizing the appearance of your weaknesses.

Plus, it's useful to have someone to push you, to tell you where things are not working. Most people don't have that gift of being so distant from their work that they can see where it's succeeding or failing. To develop your maximum potential, you need someone to create a little discomfort.

What it boils down to is this: If you want to compete in an increasingly crowded marketplace, you need the most professional quality possible. And while it's true that publishers do put out low-quality work, they're far more consistent in the quality they achieve than what you find across the majority of authors who self-publish. There are subtle cues in every product and service we purchase, small signs that indicate quality. People may not be able to name them or point them out, but they feel them, and self-published work can lack these important cues.

If you self-publish without ever having experienced the traditional publishing process, you may lack insider knowledge into what professional quality looks like. Traditionally published authors who self-publish later in their career don't have this problem as much. They know the process and they know the huge improvements that can be made by a professional. But people who haven't experienced that professional touch may not yet have a good measuring stick. There are ways to overcome this if you hire the right freelance professionals to help you. However, not every author has the time—or wants to spend the time—learning about and administrating the self-publishing process or finding assistance they can trust. Some writers just don't have the interest or the patience. They prefer having a publisher so they can focus on other aspects of the writing, marketing, and promotion process.

You don't need a publisher, but writers can greatly benefit from partnerships or professional assistance at different points in their careers. Part of a successful author career is understanding what assistance you should seek and when, based on the goals you're trying to achieve.

Self-publishing most frequently enters the conversation when writers have experienced a near miss with a publisher or the traditional submissions process has failed to produce an acceptance. Meaning that self-publishing is still often used a last resort, rather than the first and best option.

I know how difficult it is to secure an agent or publisher, but it doesn't become any easier to reach your goals after you've self-published, unless you're sitting on top of the Amazon bestseller list week after week.

So before you commit to self-publishing, ask yourself: What's your primary goal in doing so, because that affects everything. It affects what advice I give you, it affects what service you choose, it affects how much money you spend, it affects the format, it affects how satisfied you are at the end of the process.

While I can't possibly cover every goal a writer might have in self-publishing, I'll cover the three most common.

One common goal is the satisfaction of seeing your work in print form. This goal assumes that even if you don't sell any copies of your book or see it distributed in bookstores, you'll be satisfied with just having your work published.

If this is truly your goal, then the key question becomes: How much help or service do you need or want in making this happen? It is possible to write a check, hand over a Word document, and get a printed book in your hands very quickly. Many full-service publishing providers offer a range of packages to choose from, with the average cost somewhere between $1000 and $3000. Just don't expect any book sales to come from it.

So imagine your finished book in your hands. You're giving it to friends, family, and colleagues, you never sell more than a handful of copies, and you never see it on store shelves. No agent or editor ever hears about it. Do you feel satisfied with that outcome?

A common goal for nonfiction authors is to build their expertise and visibility in a specific field or profession. Self-publishing has always been a popular option for professional growth and development. It can be especially helpful to those who speak often, have a ready audience, and are existing authorities in their field.

Often such authors—who are really businesspeople rather than writers—know more about their market than a mainstream publisher. And their topic may be too specialized to be seriously considered for trade publication.

In this case, usually one of the most important considerations is how to maximize your profit. You should avoid the kind of full-service providers I mentioned earlier, since they might collect a royalty on every book you sell. Instead, you should contract out all the services yourself or hire a professional to manage the process for you. This ensures you control all intellectual property rights and profits after the book is finished.

So imagine in this scenario your book being available in your place of business, through your business partners, or through major online retailers like Amazon. Imagine selling it at your speaking engagements and having the book referenced by colleagues as a good resource. It's probably not visible outside your own professional circle, and it's not marketed to a general audience or distributed nationally at bookstores. Do you feel satisfied with that outcome?

Another goal I'd like to mention is the one that's secretly held by many who self-publish. It's the goal of proving all the gatekeepers wrong. You're going to publish your book anyway and be so successful that those people who rejected you are incredibly sorry they didn't see the light. You can go about conquering the world in this way, but before you head down this path, you need to be honest with yourself and understand the limitations you'll face.

Back in the olden days of self-publishing, before there were e-books, the message to authors was much simpler: Don't self-publish a book unless you intend to definitively say no to traditional publishing for that project. There was a stigma, and in some ways, it helped authors avoid a mistake or a bad investment.

Today, with the overselling of self-publishing, too many authors either decide they won't even try to traditionally publish, even if they have a viable commercial project. Or they assume it's best to self-publish first and get an agent or publisher later, which is patently false. Some authors end up self-publishing for the instant gratification or to avoid what's increasingly seen as a long, exhausting, and rather dumb process of finding an agent or securing book contract.

Yet, take note: These days, the number one inquiry I receive is how a self-published author can transition to traditional publishing. Usually it's because the author is disappointed with their sales or exposure. Other times, that was their plan all along. These authors ask me, in many different ways, "How can I get my self-published book the exposure it deserves?"

I support entrepreneurial authorship and authors taking responsibility for their own career success. But I would like to see more authors intelligently and strategically use self-publishing as part of well thought-out career goals, rather than as a stepping-stone to traditional publishing. It's not any easier to interest an agent or publisher when you're self-published, and since new authors are more likely to put out a low-quality effort, chances are even lower their book will get picked up.

Before you self-publish, consider whether any of the following conditions describe you. If so, then you're on a better path than most self-publishing authors I encounter.

First, does your work present challenges for the traditional or commercial market? If you don't know how commercial your work is or if a traditional publisher would be interested in it, you need to find out. Are you about to enter a very competitive field, a very niche market, or a growing category with lots of opportunity? Know the challenges ahead of time and while you're at it, study the marketing strategies and platform of successfully independent or traditionally published authors you find. If you can't be bothered to do this market research, then you're less likely to be a successful self-published author.

Second, can you commit to entrepreneurial authorship for several years? If you feel self-publishing is your next best step rather than, say, writing a new work, then commit to that plan for several years and preferably over several titles. You need to build a core audience as you release each new work. If you switch genres every time, you'll likely find yourself spinning your wheels because you have to find your audience again with each new book.

Look at the most successful indie authors, and you'll find many are writing a series and have lots of books on the market. Having more books means you have a lot more room to develop marketing strategies and find your audience. If you have only one book and you're wondering why it's not going anywhere in its first three months on sale—well, you're expecting too much too soon.

And third, are you patient enough to wait for agents and editors to approach you? Novelist Hugh Howey is a successful independent author who has an agent, but continues to self-publish. Because of that, he's often asked by writers how they can effectively approach agents and editors, and he always advises: Wait for them to come to you. That's how you know when you've reached the level of success necessary to interest the traditional market.

And if you've done your job right, that's exactly what will happen. Only by that time, you may enjoy your success and your profits so much you don't want to share them with an agent and publisher, so it can be quite a catch-22.

While I don't like to discourage authors from experimenting with self-publishing, it doesn't help when it's approached as a stopgap measure or a short-term strategy. Have your eyes wide open about the likelihood it's going to work for you, your category of work, and your ability to be your own best promoter.

And sadly, while people still talk about a new and level playing field for self-published authors, the truth is there is still a stigma that will plant a variety of obstacles in your way. It may not be fair, but it's the reality. Most traditional media outlets won't review or consider self-published books for editorial coverage. They already have far too many titles to consider from traditional houses alone, and this is a simple method for them to cut down on the number of requests that they receive.

Also, it'll be difficult to find a marketing or publicity person to work with you, because they probably know even better than you the barriers to media coverage. With a self-published work, you're starting out with an unwanted handicap. You're having to build credibility on your own. Since anyone can self-publish these days—and anyone does—you're doing battle against a lot of preconceived notions about the quality of your work.

That said, there is an active community of self-published, independent authors who are ready to help newcomers, and share strategies and tactics of what worked for them. If you're diligent in following best practices, approach the entire process with an entrepreneurial spirit and feel committed to producing books on your own for years to come you might find yourself one of the success stories that people write about. And despite the myths that still get passed around, self-publishing doesn't kill your chances at a traditional deal later.

Now that we've covered if, when, and why you might self-publish, let's cover the question of how. There are several types of services you need to know about, and before I dive into them, I want to explain the fundamental operating principles of these services.

While it can be fairly straightforward and inexpensive to get a print book in your hands, virtually no self-publishing service can get your book physically stocked in bookstores. They may claim to distribute your book to such stores or make your book available, but this is very different from actually selling your book in bookstores. Bookstores almost never stock titles from any self-publishing service, although they can special order them for customers when asked.

The other thing to understand is that the entire self-publishing industry was revolutionized in the late 1990s by the advent of print-on-demand technology, which allows books to be printed and published one at a time. Nearly every self-publishing service uses this technology to create, sell, and fulfill orders for the print edition of your book, and this eliminates the need for inventory and warehousing, not to mention the risky investment in a print run that might not sell. Once you understand this important facet of most self-publishing services, it begins to make more sense why your book is not stocked anywhere. Copies are only printed when they're already paid for.

Finally, distributing a print or digital book to major retailers, or making it available to order through wholesalers, is something that anyone can do. You can do it, your neighbor can do it, and your publisher can do it. So that's not what you're paying a service to do. Rather, you're paying them to create the product itself so that it's ready to be distributed and sold. How much effort they put into creating that product depends entirely on what you pay them. And even if you pay them a lot, the service you get may be fairly basic.

So let's look at some of the major types of services you could use, starting with the print-focused services.

The approach that's been around the longest is the formal full-service publishing provider, better known by the derogatory term, vanity press. If you're able to pay the asking price, then they'll publish your book in whatever formats you want. You'll have to sign something that looks very similar to a publishing contract to get started. Unless you pay the service a lot of money for the best possible package, you'll likely receive a template design, limited editing, and limited attention. The stereotypical vanity press makes their money on upselling you services you probably don't need, but that doesn't stop them from taking a significant cut of your profits when sales do occur. As a result, these companies tend to be viewed very negatively by professional independent authors.

If you're still looking for a full-service approach, but with better earnings potential, you can hire a company that helps you produce the best possible book strictly on a work-for-hire basis. That means they earn no royalties off your sales. However, these services tend to be far more expensive than the other type of provider because they're more personalized, and aren't going to attempt to upsell you to make their profit.

If you're comfortable with very little to no assistance, you can go straight to the major services that distribute print-on-demand books to all major retailers, specifically for the market of self-published authors. The two biggest players in the industry are Amazon's CreateSpace and IngramSpark.

While CreateSpace does offer some à la carte services if you need them, such as cover design, interior design, and copyediting, you can use them for free and see your book available for sale in major online retailers in as little as 48 hours. The only catch is that you need to have printer-ready PDF files for your book, and getting to that point can pose a significant challenge for an inexperienced author.

All of the above assumes that you're interested in producing and selling a print copy of your book. The entire process becomes even simpler if you plan to only distribute in e-book format. While it's ideal to offer both print and e-book formats, most self-published authors sell far more digital copies than print. E-book publishing also presents a lower barrier to entry and lower costs for most authors.

For e-book publishing, there's an entirely different set of principles and services you need to know about, and the services typically fall into two categories.

First, there are retailer-specific distribution and sales services that are 100 percent free to use. Amazon's Kindle Direct Publishing is the most well-known and prominent, but you'll find almost identical services from competing retailers such as Barnes & Noble, Apple, and Google. As an author, you can work directly through a self-service interface to make your e-book available for sale almost instantly. It's as simple as opening an account, uploading your book files, and pushing the publish button.

Then you'll also find e-book distribution services. These services offer one centralized place to upload your work, and then they push it out to all the major online e-book retailers. These systems are also easy to use and endeavor to make it effortless to publish your work—no special expertise or knowledge required. E-book distributors operate on a variety of business models. Some charge you an upfront fee, while others take a percentage of your sales. Smashwords is one of the most well-known of e-book distributors and has been around the longest, but there are several others, and some provide you with additional free and paid services if you need them.

Because e-book publishing is an area that's ever shifting, with new services coming out onto the market all the time, it's useful to understand the underlying principles that are at play, so that you can evaluate new offerings or packages as the landscape evolves.

First, understand these services are not publishers. They're distributors and retailers. That means they take no responsibility for the quality of your work, but neither do they take any rights to your work. Authors use these services on an at-will basis and have to accept the terms of service, meaning you won't be negotiating the terms of sale with Amazon for instance. If you decide you've made a mistake in publishing your e-book, you can remove it from availability as quickly as you uploaded it. You are acting as the publisher and making all the choices associated with the publication of your e-book—no one else is.

Second, always check to see if the retailer or service is exclusive or nonexclusive. For the most part, all retailers and services work on a nonexclusive basis. That means you can sell your e-book at many different retailers at once, and this is generally to your advantage. You don't want to limit where your e-book may be sold, just as no publisher limits where their e-books are sold. However, Amazon does offer special perks to authors who agree to sell exclusively with them, and this program is called Kindle Select. Whether it's worthwhile to limit your distribution to Amazon in exchange for those perks is a matter of great debate in the author community.

If you do agree to some kind of exclusive arrangement that limits where your e-book can be sold, make sure there's a specific term that you're agreeing to. For instance, Amazon only asks for 90 days of exclusivity in exchange for those perks, and given how fast the market conditions can change for e-books, it's wise not to tie up your rights for too long.

Third, you should always be in control of the price. While some retailers may have reasonable pricing restrictions, such as not allowing you to price below 99 cents, the standard practice is to give the author complete control over pricing. There is one caveat to this: Most e-book retailers, especially Amazon, mandate that you not offer more favorable pricing anywhere else.

Fourth, you should always be able to find clear information about how much money you'll earn on each book sale. For example, Amazon Kindle offers you 70 percent of your book's list price as long as you price between $2.99 and $9.99. If you price outside that range, you'll earn 35 percent. Always read the fine print for any retailer or distributor you're doing business with. You'll be surprised at what you find. In the case of Amazon, you'll be charged a very small fee on each book sale related to digital delivery charges, but only if you're earning a 70 percent royalty, not 35 percent.

Fifth, make sure you understand how much freedom you have to make changes to your e-book after it goes on sale. If you're working directly with retailers such as Amazon, you can upload new and revised files as often as you like. It's a self-service system, and they don't care. However, if you're using an e-book distributor, you might have to pay fees to make changes.

Finally, check what e-book formats are required from you. Most retailers make it as easy as possible for you to get started and allow you to upload a Word document, which is then automatically converted into whatever e-book format is needed. However, for this conversion process to go well, you'll need to unformat your Word document to avoid bad results. Most services offer extensive guidelines, preview programs, and other ways of ensuring things look okay before your e-book goes live.

You could also hire a firm to produce professional e-book files for you, which is recommended if your book has special formatting concerns, such as a large number of images, charts, graphs—any feature that might not convert smoothly into e-book form.

Before you hit the publish button on either a print book or an e-book, you should be aware of the two biggest mistakes that authors make. One is not hiring a professional editor to review the work line by line. Traditional publishers use an in-house editor, copy editor, and a proofreader for each book they publish. While you may not need three different people looking at your work, at the very least, you need a good copy editor or proofreader to catch errors.

The other big mistake is not hiring a professional designer for the cover. Your book won't be taken seriously if it doesn't look appropriate for your genre. Too many authors design their own covers, or use artwork provided by family and friends. The cover of your book is often your number one sales tool, especially when it's sold primarily online, and you want to make a positive impact and avoid an amateurish cover. If you decide that self-publishing is in fact the best choice for you and you want to tackle it in the most professional way possible, here's what I suggest in addition to hiring a professional editor and designer.

Consider establishing a small press. It can either be part of an existing company you own and named as such, or you can start one fresh. The most important thing is that you give this press a name or identity, even if you'll only be publishing your own work. You'll use this press name when you self-publish through online retailers, on the copyright page of your book, and anywhere else where the name of the publisher is seen or requested.

While your press doesn't need to be registered as an official LLC or corporation, having a formal name goes a long way toward indicating your seriousness of intent. And down the road, if you're very successful, you can of course establish it more fully and professionally, and even consider publishing other people's work aside from your own.

As part of this process, I recommend buying your press its own set of ISBNs, which are the official industry standard identification numbers for books. If you want your book to have any chance of being stocked or distributed in a retail environment, this number is required. When you buy your ISBNs, you should buy them from Bowker in the United States. This is the originating company for ISBNs, and Bowker offers you the best pricing. At Bowker's site, you'll indicate the name and location of the press, along with details about each title you publish. Whenever someone in the publishing industry looks up your ISBN, they'll see your book's official record, including the name of the publisher, when it was published, and other kinds of metadata.

Now, to clarify: While it's perfectly okay to self-publish your work without an ISBN—and many successful authors do—I recommend that anyone pursuing publishing as a long-term entrepreneurial business start thinking professionally from the start, and an ISBN indicates professionalism.

We've so far covered the self-publishing options that the vast majority of authors use. However, there are additional models and services that might work better for you.

For one thing, there is a growing number of literary agents who assist authors with self-publishing, typically in exchange for 15 percent of profits—the same amount they take for traditionally published titles. Some authors bridle at the thought of agents taking a commission on self-published work, but the real question is would you benefit from having someone inside the industry assist you? Arguably, once again, it depends on the personality of the author, her existing skills, and resources, and how much time she can spend on the self-publishing process. Some authors are well-equipped to be entrepreneurs, while others prefer the experience and resources of someone in the industry they trust.

Before self-publishing with an agent's assistance, you should ask the agent a few questions about the business arrangement, since agents work in very different ways. First, you'll want to know who covers the costs associated with self-publishing. In most cases, you'll have to cover the cost, but sometimes the agent will cover expenses and then deduct them from your earnings.

Also, find out how long you must commit to giving the agent 15 percent of sales on your work. It shouldn't be indefinitely, which leads us to the final question of how or when your agreement with the agent can be terminated. Some agents may ask you to commit for at least a year or more to ensure they have a chance to recoup their investment of time and resources. You'll also find that if you become very successful as a self-published author, you can find an agent to represent you and help with the administrative aspects of distributing and selling your work, especially overseas and for translation.

Aside from agents, there is a growing number of publishers of all sizes experimenting with partnership and hybrid approaches to publishing. This typically means you won't receive an advance and you'll likely end up paying something out of pocket, but you'll have the support and assistance of a highly qualified publishing team. Usually these partnership models have some kind of vetting process, and they may offer distribution you wouldn't be able to get on your own. Just be careful about partnering up with anyone, and carefully research the services that seem to be selling you a little too hard. Some of the newest publishers may offer little more than digital distribution and administration that you could accomplish on your own, while others offer invaluable market experience and connections.

Despite the self-publishing bestseller stories you'll hear about, always remember that the success rate for indie authors isn't that different from traditional publishing. Few authors make a living from their self-published work or sell more than a hundred copies. If you envision yourself as a thriving independent author, you also need to see yourself as a long-term entrepreneur, and not all authors are up for that. It requires marketing savvy or a willingness to acquire some, plus an ability to be exceptionally active online, since most of your sales will be through online retailers. If that describes you, then consider the digital publishing world your oyster, because it's never been easier to access the same tools and distribution paths that the New York houses use—and to forge your own path to publishing success.

Principles of Self-Publishing Success
Lecture 23

In an earlier lecture, we discussed the ways in which books are launched onto bestseller lists. We also noted that the time-honored ways to generate word of mouth for books, such as bookstore signings and media coverage, don't work as well as they used to. The digitization of reading and publishing has changed the rules about what generates word of mouth. Another unintended consequence of the rise of the digital marketplace is that the book launch itself may be outdated. Many independent authors have noted that launch sales can be disappointing compared to what happens once a book gains traction around online reviews and reputation. In this lecture, we'll discuss how these changes translate into tactics for self-publishing success.

Optimizing Books for Online Sales

- One of the main issues in optimizing books to be seen and discovered online is metadata comprehensiveness and strategy. In general, *metadata* refers to everything that is not the content itself but how that content is described and classified.

  - For example, the original form of metadata in publishing was the book jacket. Now, it's the information and keywords on a book's product page on a retailer's website. Selecting what information to include there requires the same care and attention as the cover.

  - Metadata includes such information as cover image, author bio, excerpts, reviews, region codes, prizes or awards, target audience, table of contents headings, and more. One industry study showed that when a book's metadata is improved, online sales can lift by as much as 28 percent.

- It's impossible to know exactly what goes into the secret sauce of any retailer's algorithm or how those algorithms will change over time, but most digital marketing is focused on helping algorithms "see" books better. In online retail environments, this basically means that keywords drive the discoverability and visibility of your book. Keywords relevant to your book's theme or topic must be included in the metadata, as well as in excerpts and reviews.

- The first step in identifying appropriate keywords is to choose the right category for your book, particularly on Amazon. For example, on Amazon, you might choose: Women's Fiction > Single Women. Because every category or genre is surrounded by certain expectations—for example, a romance should have a happy ending—the category you choose should be a good fit to avoid disappointing readers. If you're unsure about the categories, check those for several books that are similar to yours.

- The second step is to identify the best keywords to describe your work. A *keyword* is a word or phrase associated with the characters, themes, or ideas in your book. The tricky part is to identify keywords that your readers will actually use to search online. Before you publish your work, brainstorm a list of words and phrases that might be associated with it. Also ask editors, family members, and others who've read the manuscript to suggest keywords.

- Next, test your keywords by searching for them on Google and Amazon. This step works as a kind of verification of the language people use when searching. Pay special attention to the auto-complete feature of Amazon and Google, which will attempt to "guess" what you're searching for. These guesses can provide helpful clues about how people conduct searches in your category. Also, when using Google, check the bottom of the results page to find similar terms that people have used to search for your topic.

- In almost all cases, specificity is good, and vague or generalized terms are bad. For example, "family relationships" could pertain to many different types of stories, but "father-daughter relationships" is much more specific and better for a search.

- Once you settle on keywords that make the most sense, you'll use these when you upload and publish your book to Amazon and other retailers or distributors. You should also use the keywords in the book description that customers read. The goal here is to have keywords that match for the title (for nonfiction), for the description, and behind the scenes in the keywords metadata box.

Your Amazon page may be the first and only one a reader looks at when deciding whether to purchase your book; make sure you provide a full description of the book and complete your author profile.

Pricing and Giveaways

- Independent novelists tend to charge very little for their work online, usually between $0.99 and $2.99. Many believe that these low prices encourage readers to take a chance on unknown fiction writers. In contrast, nonfiction authors should price according to the competition and what the market will bear. Sometimes, prices in nonfiction categories are just as high for digital editions as print editions.

- When you begin the process of selling your book online, you'll be asked whether you want to enroll in Amazon's KDP Select program, which requires you to sell exclusively through Amazon for 90 days. If your readers buy a significant number of your books from other retailers, you probably aren't interested in this program, but if you have no readers yet, then building an audience on Amazon before branching out to other venues might be a good idea.
  - If you commit to the KDP Select program, Amazon will give you 5 giveaway days out of the 90 days you're enrolled. Giveaways are well-known to boost sales and visibility of your book even after they end, and it's impossible to offer giveaways on Amazon unless you're enrolled in this program.

  - The KDP Select program also allows your book to become available as part of the Kindle Owners' Lending Library, as well as Kindle Unlimited, the Amazon e-book subscription service.

You get paid each time someone borrows your book through these services, and the pay can be roughly equivalent to a sale.

- On the subject of giveaways, some people believe that they create misleading expectations among readers (that all your books will be free) or cultivate the wrong type of reader (one who wants only a cheap read). Of course, like any promotion, giveaways can result in both good and bad leads. Strategic authors learn over time how and where to use the giveaway incentive to increase the number of high-quality leads they receive.

  o The giveaway can be a powerful tool because it's a way to get attention when there is not yet any demand for your work. Especially if you have no publisher backing you, then it's important to provide social proof to potential readers or give them an indication of the merit of your work before they invest in it.

  o With giveaways, independent authors may run into trouble if they have only one or two books to sell and nothing else to offer readers or if they don't establish any means to contact readers in the future, whether via e-mail newsletter or social media. The other catch is that the quality of your work must match the expectations of your audience. If it doesn't, no amount of giveaways will help you.

  o Whether you use KDP Select or not, giveaways can be an effective part of a larger marketing strategy. But before you use them, make sure you understand your reader funnel and the demand curve for your work.

Garnering Reviews

- In addition to leading to visibility and new readers, giveaways can also result in more reviews for your work, and getting a good number of reviews early on can tip the scales in your favor. Although no one knows what the Amazon algorithm favors, most authors see that once they have around 60 to 70 reviews, the visibility of their books on Amazon is improved. It's also well-known that readers make buying decisions based on the content of reviews.

- One method of encouraging reviews is to enroll in the KDP Select program. Another option is to do a giveaway on Goodreads, a social media site for books and reading with more than 35 million members. Goodreads is favored by both traditional publishers and self-publishers for getting the word out and generating pre-publication buzz. The drawback is that Goodreads gives away physical books only, which requires a small investment from the author and won't work at all for authors who are publishing only in e-book format.

- A more e-book–friendly solution is to use an e-mail marketing service that targets readers looking for cheap or free reads, such as BookBub. Any author can submit work to BookBub to be considered for inclusion in e-mail promotions to readers, as long as the book can be downloaded from a major retailer and is offered for free or at a major discount. If your book is accepted for promotion, you'll be charged a fee based on a variety of criteria. This type of promotion can lead to a wave of new reviews on Amazon or Goodreads.

- Finally, the old-fashioned way of getting book reviews is to go door-to-door and ask for them. Several major online directories, including the Book Blogger Directory and The IndieView, list book reviewers and book bloggers that you can pitch for review coverage. You can also try contacting reviewers in Amazon's Vine program, which is a group of people hand-selected by Amazon as among the best reviewers on the site.

Releasing New Work

- Both publishers and successful authors know that writing and releasing a new work is one of the best and most reliable marketing tools for boosting sales of previous and future books. This phenomenon can be so pronounced that successful authors have counseled beginners to all but stop marketing efforts and, instead, focus on producing new work.

- This is probably the most boring advice possible, but the truth is seldom glamorous. Few authors want to hear that the way to build their career is to work hard for a long time. Although you may want to find readers for the book you already have instead of writing a new one, the painful reality is that if you're a self-publishing author who only ever writes one book, your chances of succeeding with it in a meaningful way are very low.

- Authors who are advanced in their self-publishing strategies tend to develop long-term series, with each release building on the characters and tension in the previous books and creating an irresistible hook for readers. We can see an interesting parallel in the binge-watching that's now common with TV series available on demand. Authors tap into the same kind of addictive potential by building out a story arc over a number of books.

- Having more books out there also aids in generating more word of mouth. You'll have more readers telling their friends that they absolutely must read your books. But the first step is to write books that are worth sharing. Reading is a significant investment of time, and accepting a book recommendation is, therefore, an act of trust. Most people will suggest only those books that give readers an excellent experience, not just an interesting story.

Suggested Reading

Gaughran, *Let's Get Visible*.

Penn, *How to Market a Book*.

Truant and Platt, *Write. Publish. Repeat.*

1. Look at the Amazon Kindle bestseller list; you'll notice it's divided into free titles versus paid titles. Look at some of the free titles and try to find some in your category or genre. Download and sample at least one of them. Is there another book by this author for readers to buy next? Does the author ask you to sign up to receive another free book? What strategies does the author use to make the most of the giveaway, if any?

2. Sign up for the free BookBub e-mail newsletter in your category or genre and study the discounting and giveaway strategies being used.

Principles of Self-Publishing Success
Lecture 23—Transcript

Earlier, we discussed how books get launched onto bestseller lists. While these methods can also be applied to self-published titles, the playbook has to shift for two reasons.

First, it's extremely unlikely your book will be nationally distributed to bookstores. That means most of your marketing efforts will be online-based, to drive people to buy your book through online retail channels. Second, if you're a first-time author, you may have limited resources and relationships, so your efforts may be slanted toward free marketing and promotion activities that you can tackle from home.

Fortunately for the independent author, the time-honored ways to generate word of mouth that are available to traditional publishers—such as bookstore signings, traditional media coverage, and critical reviews—those things don't work as well as they used to. The digitization of reading and publishing has fundamentally changed the rules on what generates word of mouth.

Another unintended consequence of the rise of the digital marketplace is that the practice of the book launch itself may be outdated. The idea of the book launch originates with traditional publishing, where the first few months of sales can make or break a book in terms of placement in stores. There's only so much shelf space available, and if your book doesn't sell, it has to clear the way for something else. But in the digital age where online shelf space is unlimited, your book doesn't have to hit immediately.

Successful self-publishing author Joanna Penn has said that launch sales can be generally disappointing compared to what happens once the Amazon algorithms kick in, once a book gains traction around reviews and reputation. Likewise, bestselling indie author Hugh Howey has said many times he doesn't have a timeframe for a book to do well. He says, "It's a real slow burn."

This is a very different model than what traditional publishing is accustomed to. Plus publishers are beginning to realize that effective digital marketing especially works best across a range of titles or on an author brand basis, rather than on a title-by-title basis.

We'll discuss how these changes translate into strategies and tactics for self-publishing success. We'll start with the very important issues of metadata, algorithms, and optimizing your book to sell through online retailers.

When experts talk about optimizing books to be seen and discovered online, metadata is a big part of what they're talking about. Metadata can be a confusing term since its meaning varies by industry and context, but generally, it means everything that's not the content itself, but how we describe and classify that content.

For example, the original form of metadata in publishing was the book jacket. Now, it's the information and keywords on a book's product page on a retailer's website, and it requires the same care and attention as the cover. Metadata includes such information as cover image, author bio, excerpts, reviews, region codes, prizes or awards, target audience, table of contents, and a lot more. One industry study showed that when a book's metadata is improved, online sales can lift by as much as 28 percent.

Since it's impossible to know exactly what goes into the secret sauce of any retailer's algorithm or how those algorithms will change over time, most digital marketing isn't about gaming the system or knowing the algorithm, but rather helping algorithms see the books better. In online retail environments, this basically means that keywords drive discoverability and visibility of your book. Keywords relevant to your book's theme or topic need to be included in the metadata, as well as in excerpts and reviews.

So let's describe the basic process of identifying the keywords that matter to your book, to help ensure your book is found when a relevant search happens.

The first step is to choose the right category for your book, particularly on Amazon. Amazon's considered the most important online retailer because it sells more books than anyone else, plus it sells the highest volume of self-published work. You can choose two categories for your work on Amazon out of hundreds available. An example of a category would be Women's Fiction—Single Women.

Every category or genre has certain expectations surrounding it—for example, romances should have a happy ending—so the category you choose should be a good fit to avoid disappointing readers. If you struggle with this, choose several authors whose books are similar to yours, and check what categories they're in, and that will help you to find the appropriate category.

The second step is to use the best keywords to describe your work. A keyword should be a word or phrase associated with the characters, themes, or ideas in your book. But here's the tricky part: You want to use keywords based on the words that people actually use to search online. Often the language you would use is not the language that your reader might use.

Also, a keyword doesn't have to be just one word. For example, if you were writing a novel set in 18th-century England that phrase—18th-century England—would become a keyword associated with your work.

So before you publish, brainstorm a list of words and phrases that might be associated with it. You could ask editors, friends, and family who've read the manuscript to suggest keywords as well, or how they would go about searching for a book like the one you've written.

Next, test out your keywords by searching Google and Amazon for them. This works as a kind of verification of the kind of language that people use when searching. Pay special attention to the auto-complete feature of Amazon and Google. They'll attempt to guess at what you're searching for, and this can provide really helpful clues as to how people conduct searches in your category. Also, when using Google, check at the very bottom of the search results page for similar terms that people have used to search for the topic. In almost all cases, more specificity is good and more vague or general terms are bad. For example, family relationships as a keyword could pertain to many different types of stories, but father-daughter relationships is a much more specific keyword and better for a search.

Once you settle on the keywords that make the most sense, you'll use these when you upload and publish your book to Amazon and other retailers and distributors. Amazon allows you to specify up to seven keywords. You should also use the keywords in your book description that customers read. However, make sure any marketing copy is reader-friendly and not just a list of data points. Your goal is to have the keywords match across the title if you're writing nonfiction, description, and also behind the scenes in your keywords metadata box.

As a side note on Amazon: Because they represent such a high percentage of book sales in the United States—especially for self-publishing authors— keep in mind your Amazon page may be the first and only page a reader looks at when deciding whether to purchase your book. So you should spend a considerable amount of time making sure that you've completed your book's description page fully, and then do the same for your Amazon author profile. Leave nothing blank.

The next major strategy for self-publishing authors centers on pricing and giveaways. If you check Amazon's e-book bestseller lists, you'll see that independent novelists charge very little for their work, usually between 99 cents and $2.99. Some argue this devalues the work, while others say that it's appropriate for an e-book from an unknown author. Whatever your perspective, just understand that if you're an unknown novelist, your competition will probably be priced at $2.99 or less to encourage readers to take a chance. Typically, the more well-known or trusted you are, the more you can charge.

There's another layer of complication to all this. Amazon is well-known for paying 70 percent of the list price to authors who price their e-books between $2.99 and $9.99. The percentage plummets to 35 percent for anyone who prices outside this range, so this is why you find novelists periodically switching their price between 99 cents and $2.99. Authors maximize volume and visibility at the low-price point and attempt to get on bestseller lists, then switch to $2.99 to maximize profits.

You'll notice I keep mentioning this as a strategy for novelists. That's because nonfiction authors should price according to the competition and what the market can bear. Sometimes prices are just as high for digital editions as print in nonfiction categories.

There's yet a third layer of complexity and it's called Amazon KDP Select. This program is so important to Amazon that it's the first thing they'll ask when you begin the process of self-publishing your book: Do you want to enroll in KDP Select?

KDP Select requires that you sell exclusively through Amazon for 90 days. If your readers buy a significant number of your books from other retailers, then you probably don't want to anger them by only selling your book through Amazon. But if you have no readers yet, then building an audience on Amazon before branching out to other venues might be a good idea.

So why would you grant Amazon exclusivity like that? For two reasons. First, if you commit, they'll give you 5 giveaway days out of the 90 you're enrolled. Giveaways are well-known to boost sales and visibility of your book after the giveaway ends, and it's impossible to offer a giveaway on Amazon unless you're enrolled in Select. Second, if you commit, your book will become available as part of the Kindle Owners' Lending Library, as well as Kindle Unlimited, the Amazon e-book subscription service. You get paid each time someone borrows your book through these services, with the payment based on how many pages actually get read.

Established authors who have several published titles sometimes rotate content through KDP Select because they can get a significant number of paid lends and new readers from the program. Newer authors with limited readership sometimes have nothing to lose by granting Amazon exclusivity while they use Select to build their audience, hopefully land on Kindle bestseller lists, and also increase their number of customer reviews.

However, some indie authors say that giveaways don't work as well as they used to. There's a lot of competition and it's tougher to gain visibility through Amazon. Plus the algorithms favor books that are bought rather than given away. But if your free days land you at the top of Amazon's free bestseller list, that exposure might be worth it in terms of increased sales for the days following a free promotion, not to mention the number of readers who now have your book. This could lead to more reviews and increased sales of your books. Still, if you only have one book, this is a difficult strategy. You might see increased sales of that one book after a giveaway, but now there's nowhere for readers to go next—there's nothing else for them to buy.

This brings up the larger question of whether or not you should give away your books at all and if so, when. Some people think giveaways create bad expectations among readers, and even possibly cultivate the wrong type of reader, the one who only wants a cheap read. However, there's a larger and more important strategic question that authors need to ask in relation to giveaways, and that's a question about what kind of reader funnel you're creating.

Giveaways are popular for good reason. They're a classic, frictionless way to make people aware of your work. Just about every industry has some way of using free to their advantage, particularly game, software, and app developers. If you can get a sufficient number of people in the door and they like your stuff, you can sell them other things once you have some kind of trust or relationship in place.

If you've seen the famous Alec Baldwin speech in *Glengarry Glen Ross*, it's the same idea being expressed: A-I-D-A. First, get people's attention, whether through an ad, a freebie, or media coverage. That creates interest. And if all goes well, you have a decision and action to make a purchase.

I don't find it useful to discuss giveaways in the abstract because unless we can tie them to a particular strategy for a particular author at a particular time, it's impossible to evaluate them. If the giveaway leads to paying fans down the road, it's smart. If the giveaway leads to no further action, it should be reconsidered. Don't assume that your giveaway will lead to unrealistic expectations from readers that all of your books will be free. When we get a free cheese cube at the grocery store, we don't expect to carry away the whole wheel of cheese without paying. When we consider ourselves fans of an author, we might expect promotional pricing for buying early and, of course, fair pricing in general, but not free stuff forever.

If there is a serious problem with giveaways in the indie author community, it might be that giveaways can attract low-quality readers, but they also attract high-quality readers, too. And this is how business works. Some leads will be good, other leads will be bad. Strategic authors learn over time how and where to use the giveaway incentive to increase the high-quality leads and reduce the low-quality leads.

So, the giveaway is one of the more powerful tools in your arsenal because it's a way to get attention when you may not have anything else going for you. There's no demand for your work yet, and especially if you have no publisher backing you, then it's important to provide social proof to potential readers or have some way of indicating merit before they'll invest time or money. Even established authors do giveaways, often by making the very first title in their series available for free, to introduce readers to their work. That acts as a gateway drug to the rest of the books available.

Where indie authors run into trouble is when they only have one or two books to sell, and they have nothing else to offer readers. Even worse, they don't establish any means to contact the reader in the future, whether via e-mail newsletter or social media, so there's no funnel or path for readers to follow. It becomes a dead-end road. The potential fan finishes the book and then you lose them, and maybe they'll find your next book, if and when it comes, or maybe not. The other catch is that your work has to have quality that matches the expectations of your audience. If it doesn't, no amount of giveaways will help you. When the cheese tastes bad, people stop taking the samples.

So the bottom line is that, whether you use KDP Select or not, giveaways themselves can be an effective part of a larger marketing strategy. Just don't use them without considering your funnel, as well as your demand curve. If you have fans who value your work, they aren't seeking everything for free—and in fact, once you have a fan base, they'll be looking for experiences that are much better than a free book.

As you become more experienced as a self-publisher, it won't take you long to realize that in addition to giveaways leading to visibility and new readers, it also results in more reviews for your work. And getting a good number of reviews, early on, can tip the scales in your favor. While no one knows what the Amazon algorithm favors, most authors see that once they have around 60 to 70 reviews, their book's visibility on Amazon is much improved.

Search considerations aside, though, it's well-known that on Amazon, as well as other sites like Goodreads, readers will look at the reviews and make buying decisions based on the content of those reviews. For self-published authors in particular, the reviews become critical in assuring readers of quality. The big question, of course, is how to encourage and receive the number of reviews that will help you sell your work.

The KDP Select option, which offers you five free giveaway days, is the most frequently cited strategy for new authors, but of course we've discussed the drawbacks of that program, and you might not want to use it. Another method is to do a giveaway on Goodreads, a social media site for books and reading with more than 35 million members. One of the most important elements of the site is the Goodreads star rating, which is based on reader reviews. Goodreads is favored by traditional publishers and self-publishers alike for getting the word out and generating pre-publication buzz. The drawback here is that Goodreads only does giveaways of physical copies, which requires a small investment, and won't work at all for authors who are publishing in e-book format only.

I'd like to make a quick aside about Goodreads because it's an important social network of avid readers, with people actively looking for the next book to read. But it's developed a notorious reputation with some authors due to a few isolated acts of author-reader animosity. This is because authors have used the site inappropriately to market and promote their work, and they've also asked readers to remove critical reviews, so then readers have found ways to retaliate against those authors in ways that have been rather ugly.

So here's what I recommend: At the very least, sign up for a Goodreads author account and make sure that your profile is connected to any books you've published. But beyond that, don't try to game the Goodreads system or try any kind of hard sell. Accept friend requests and build connections if you like using the site, and take advantage of Goodreads tools for advertising or use their giveaway system. But never respond to or argue with negative reviews. That's only going to make readers angry.

So back to the question of giveaways. There's a more e-book-friendly solution if you have a bit of money to spend. You can now find a range of e-mail marketing services that target readers looking for cheap or free reads. One of the biggest services out there is BookBub. They reach millions of readers directly via e-mail. Their lists are highly segmented into specific categories and genres. Any author can submit their work to be considered for promotion in their e-mails to readers, as long as the book can be downloaded from a major retailer and as long as you're offering the book for free or at a major discount. If your book's accepted for promotion, then you'll be charged a fee based on a variety of criteria. Most authors find this e-mail-based promotion highly effective, since it's going to a list of people actively looking for new e-books to read or purchase. It can also lead to a wave of new reviews as readers finish the book and leave their thoughts at Amazon or Goodreads.

Finally, there's the old-fashioned way of getting book reviews, which is by going door-to-door and asking for them. There are several major directories online that list book reviewers and book bloggers. Two of the bigger directories are the Book Blogger Directory and The IndieView. You can also try contacting reviewers in Amazon's Vine Program, which is a group of people hand-selected by Amazon as among the best reviewers on their site.

It's generally not worth your time to send your book to traditional or mass media outlets for review. Very few will accept a self-published book for coverage. If you want to try it, though, I recommend approaching them well in advance of your release date, up to three to six months prior to publishing. Assuming you have the money to spend, you can make a digital advance reading copy available through a service such as NetGalley. This is the same service that traditional publishers use to distribute books to reviewers and other professionals. Of course, you can also send print copies, but this gets very expensive very fast, and only make that investment if you have considerable confidence in the quality of the book you're sending and if you think you have a reasonable chance of getting someone's attention.

And now's a good time to mention whether or not hiring a publicist or marketing assistant is a good idea. I've heard a lot of nightmare stories from authors who were working with a book publicist or marketer and didn't get what they wanted out of the relationship or the investment, and I think that sometimes this happens because of misaligned expectations, or even a misunderstanding of what working with a publicist can achieve. A publicist can be very helpful in securing mainstream media coverage. If that's the only reason you have to hire one, then you probably shouldn't. The odds are stacked against self-published titles getting any attention.

But marketers and publicists can offer tremendous value aside from media coverage. They can assist with activities you could do yourself, but they can often do them better, more efficiently or more knowledgeably. They can save you time to focus on other high-value activities, and they can help you avoid marketing tactics or campaigns that they know are problematic, or point you toward new and useful tools they've discovered. If you have money to hire marketing and publicity help, make a list of the specific outcomes you're looking for the publicist to achieve. Share this with each publicist you might hire and ask them for a proposal, along with their fees. Before hiring a publicist, research other campaigns they've worked on. Have they achieved the kind of results you're looking for? And talk to their past clients if at all possible.

So we've now covered three of the major marketing strategies for authors: Optimizing your book's metadata, being strategic with pricing and giveaways, and gaining critical mass on reader reviews.

Earlier, I mentioned that publishers are beginning to realize that effective digital marketing works best across a range of titles, or on an author brand basis rather than a title-by-title basis. This holds true for self-publishing authors. In fact, just about everyone has now discovered that writing and releasing a new work is one of the best and most reliable marketing tools for boosting sales of previous books and future work. This phenomenon can be so pronounced that successful authors have counseled beginners to all but stop marketing efforts and just focus on producing a new work.

It amounts to the most boring advice possible, but the truth is seldom glamorous. Few authors want to hear that the way to build their author career is to work hard for a very long time. While you may want to find readers for the book you already have instead of writing a new one, the painful reality is that if you're a self-publishing author who only ever writes one book, your chances of succeeding with it are very low. Your footprint is simply too small, and you're going to get lost in the noise. After enough books and time, you're more likely to reach a critical mass, when your ideal readers will find it hard to miss you. This leads to the so-called overnight success some writers see after spending thousands of nights writing.

Authors who are very advanced in their self-publishing strategy tend to develop long-term series, so that each release builds on the characters and tension in the previous books, creating an irresistible hook for readers. You can see an interesting parallel in the binge-watching that's now common with TV series available on demand. Authors are tapping into the same kind of addictive potential by building out a story arc over 3, 5, 10 or more books. To see this model at work, you can study successful indie authors such as Bella Andre, CJ Lyons, and Hugh Howey.

Having more books out there also aids in generating more word of mouth. You'll have more readers telling their friends that they absolutely must read your books, but the first step is to write books that are worth sharing. Reading takes a significant investment of time, and accepting a book recommendation is therefore an act of trust. Most people only suggest books that give readers an excellent experience, not just an interesting story.

You'll notice that throughout this discussion, we haven't touched at all on social media marketing such as Facebook or Twitter. If you're a new author without an established reader base, then social media might not get you very far unless you've been actively using those channels prior to your book release. They can be very useful for letting your first circle of fans know about your work early in your career, but as far as finding strangers and telling them about your book? You'll find it has very limited hard sales potential.

Some indie authors, especially those in the romance community, harness social media in a very different way from the average author. They employ street teams, or groups of super fans who advocate for their work by writing reviews and spreading the word on social media. In exchange, authors offer their street team early access to new work, special promotions, and merchandise.

As you gain experience as a self-published author, you'll notice that the indie community tends to be more experimental, innovative, and collaborative in figuring out how to make their books visible to new readers. Commercial fiction authors in particular are known for banding together and releasing bundles at low prices, then marketing to their audiences cooperatively. The collective effort and value then rockets their work onto bestseller lists, gaining them a fresh audience they didn't have before.

Perhaps most intriguing of all, authors who have succeeded on their own as self-publishers have been able to make greater demands on publishers when it comes to digital marketing. When speaking at a publishing industry conference in 2013, bestselling author Sylvia Day said she expects a comprehensive marketing plan that covers everything she's not doing herself. To pass muster with Day, she says publishers need to broaden her audience, not just sell to her existing audience. She says when it comes to digital marketing, no traditional publisher can compete with what she accomplishes on her own.

So, even though a self-publishing author may begin at a disadvantage by not having bookstore distribution, any author who directly reaches her audience does have a chance at outperforming a traditional publisher when it comes to online sales. Authors who track and analyze their efforts and make adjustments to maximize their impact, have more direct access, control, and insight into their readership, keywords and all. That's something publishers sometimes can't deliver, whether they want to or not.

But by far the best advantage a self-publishing author may have is time. Time is always on your side if you're happy to keep producing new work. To repeat Hugh Howey's advice, "It's a real slow burn." Treat your marketing strategy as a marathon, not a sprint. Focus on reaching new readers, one reader at a time.

Beyond the Book: Sharing Ideas in the Digital Age
Lecture 24

For hundreds of years, the book has been the primary vehicle for sharing knowledge and authority, and to some extent, it still is. But for sharing ideas, telling stories, or wielding influence, authoring a book is only one tool or method available to us today—and not always the best one. We now have the best speakers and thinkers lecturing through YouTube and online courses, in-depth reporting delivered through multimedia websites and blogs, and on-demand, professionally produced podcasts. For this reason, it's important to consider the story or message you wish to share, rather than focusing on the container; there are many ways besides a book to write, publish, and share ideas in the digital age.

The Book in the 21ˢᵗ Century

- It's not true that the book is dead, but the ways in which the book has traditionally been sold and distributed are on the way out. By the end of 2012, nearly half of U.S. book sales—including both print and digital books—were made through online retailers, particularly Amazon. Large chain bookstore sales used to dominate the market, but their share is now less than one-fifth of all book sales in the United States.

- In discussing the future of publishing, it's important to separate the future of the book itself from the future of writing, reading, and literacy.
  - Many people value long-form reading and the experience of deep immersion in a book. But the number of heavy readers who avidly consume books has always been a minority of the total population. Most studies show that we read as much as we ever did, but what, where, and how we read are changing.

  - Pew Research shows steadily increasing adoption of mobile and tablet devices in the United States, and mobile-driven media consumption is far higher in other parts of the world.

Regardless of what you are writing or publishing, to be successful for the long term, a mobile strategy must be part of the equation.

- Despite these fundamental changes, another myth we need dispel is that publishers are going away. It's simply not true that there is no longer any value in traditional publishing. But that doesn't mean that there won't be further consolidation among publishing houses and a continued evolution of the business model.

The Future of Nonfiction

- For the foreseeable future, we will experience a revolution in how we find, use, and share information. On the most practical level, authors who understand when and how a book is needed or valuable for their audience will have a leg up on the competition.

- In particular, for nonfiction authors, the book simply cannot be the end of what you offer. Agents and editors want to see that a book is just one aspect of your much larger purpose and strategy for serving an audience.

- Publishers who specialize in reference already understand that some books are too expensive to produce for how fast they go out of date and how easily the same information can be found for free online. Thus, some nonfiction publishers have stopped talking about books and now focus on *content strategy*, recognizing the need to deliver information in adaptable forms through different channels, formats, and environments.

- Going even further, the CEO of one large educational publisher has said that his company's job is not to deliver information or content but to develop services. By that, he means servicing universities, students, and professionals with online courses, assessment, workflow tools, communities, and of course, digital books.

The Future of Fiction

- Publishing futurists tend to draw a line between the future of novels and other forms of narratives and the future of non-narrative books. If you're working in a non-narrative format, you tend to compete against multimedia offerings that didn't exist even a few years ago. If you're working in narrative-driven publishing, such as fiction, then you tend to focus more on the ways in which the digital age is changing how those stories are discovered and consumed by readers.

- Significant questions have arisen regarding how readers interact with digital books and whether the reading and writing process will become more social. For example, Bob Stein, founder of the Institute for the Future of the Book, argues that as we move from the printed page to the screen—to networked environments—the social aspect of reading and writing moves to the foreground. Once this shift takes place, the lines begin to blur between reader and writer. Stein suggests that authors will take on added roles as moderators of communities in nonfiction and designers of complex worlds for readers to explore.

- A related topic here is the idea of *transmedia*—a term from the entertainment world. It focuses on the story world first and the methods of distribution second. *Star Wars* might be considered transmedia—something that spans film, TV, books, video games, merchandise, and more—but of course, it didn't start out that way. The most progressive people in media are looking at how stories can be established and evolve without putting any one medium first but, instead, growing or adapting the story in different ways across many channels.
  - For example, recently, a group of writers collaborated to produce a serialized story that was released over a period of six months through an iPhone app. Readers could contribute to the story during that period and use their phones to unlock new chapters.

  - We may slowly be moving into an era that embodies an entirely new concept of what an author is and does. Rather than being solitary creators, authors may become moderators or collaborators who synthesize and express many people's ideas.

- One area where we find a strong social component and collaboration in writing and reading is in the fan fiction community, where readers create new stories based on well-known characters and story worlds. Fan fiction enthusiasts and other writers congregate in online communities, such as Wattpad, where they often post stories in serialized form.
  - One of the reasons that Wattpad is attractive to young writers is that it offers a chance to directly reach and grow a readership, even if it means giving away the writing for free. Wattpad is able to ping a devoted readership whenever a new story or installment is posted.

  - Unlike traditional publishing or even self-publishing, in which authors have limited insight into their readers and no means to interact with them, Wattpad offers a platform for ongoing conversation. And Wattpad's larger vision is just that: to foster a stronger connection between the reader and writer.

The Future of the Author

- Although serials and fan fiction are sometimes dismissed by industry insiders as low-quality work that won't affect traditional publishing, others have begun to speculate that these markets might be in a position to do exactly that. These sites deliver a social reading experience that's already much better than the traditional e-book experience. They feature stories in smaller and more addictive chunks and offer better integration into pop culture. And the authors are responsive to their readers.

- More than a few people see such developments as a threat. The extent of the danger, however, depends on the goal of the writer. If the goal is sales and long-term readership growth, there might not be any harm at all. But if interacting with readers impedes the writer from pursuing his or her primary purpose, then the call to engagement may be detrimental. This, in fact, has been the conclusion of many "literary" authors, or those who see their purpose as producing something that goes beyond entertainment.

- Some serious writers argue that distance is the writer's friend and that mystery plays a significant role in our love of books. Writers who engage more with readers are overexposing themselves and demystifying their work for everyone who follows them. What will become of the authors who hold this philosophy?

- It seems that our culture's concept of authorship is destined to change. As thought leaders in publishing have pointed out, the concept of the author as an original genius is a fairly recent one that came into being with the printing press and copyright. The digital era likely entails a new type of authorship, one that is built on resampling, remixing, and collaborating. Authors may evolve to be leaders, moderators, and synthesizers of information, rather than dictators in control of it.

- Another facet of this is the idea that we now live in a time of universal authorship, in which anyone and everyone can write for public consumption. Although

Writing today and in the future will encompass many possible models—beyond the book—for creating stories and sharing information.

that might not mean writing a book for publication, it includes commenting, blogging, posting updates on social media, and being active in online communities.

- ○ This has resulted, predictably, in a deluge of free and cheap information and entertainment options. Of course, the quality varies tremendously, but still, people have more good things to read, watch, or otherwise consume than they could possibly need. Thus, the challenge becomes how to be more visible, valuable, or attention-grabbing than the next person.

○ For this reason, authors who are more engaged and responsive may have more options, freedom, and success in the future. There's enough choice and community out there that most of us have only the time and money to devote to things we can feel a part of, or believe in, or simply can't get anywhere else.

• Authors will become known and be supported through many paths. Those with business savvy will be successful on their own. Others will have productive partnerships with publishers, editors, agents, or managers. Some authors will be known for making a living through their stories alone, while others will capitalize on value-added or digital media endeavors. And another segment will continue writing without the expectation that their art should sustain a living.

○ A new generation of authors is coming—a generation of those who enjoy the act of creating things across mediums and aren't tied to the book form. They will use visuals, be proficient with code, and enjoy crafting a range of experiences.

○ You don't have to wait for someone to validate you before trying something new. You can reach your readers directly and experiment with how to deliver your story. The world of publishing now has so many new tools, services, and distribution methods, with low or no start-up costs, that your only limit is your imagination.

Suggested Reading

Bhaskar, *The Content Machine.*

McGuire and O'Leary, eds., *Book: A Futurist's Manifesto.*

Nash, "The Business of Literature."

1. Watch the first 10 minutes of Simon Sinek's well-known TED talk "Start with Why." If your book is the "what," then what is the "why" behind it? In what other ways might your "why" be expressed, aside from a book?

2. Jot down the names of several authors whose books you read without fail. Then, research whether their work takes any other shape or form. How else do their messages manifest themselves in the world? For example, nonfiction author Alain de Botton founded The School of Life to bring philosophy into the daily lives of people. Novelist Hugh Howey allows fan fiction writers the freedom to publish stories derived from his work without fear of copyright infringement.

Beyond the Book: Sharing Ideas in the Digital Age
Lecture 24—Transcript

As much as my own career has revolved around the reading, writing, and publishing of books, the book can, in fact, have limitations. Stating this is close to sacrilege in some circles, and not just for those who work in publishing. For hundreds of years now, the book has been the primary vehicle to share knowledge and authority, and to some extent, it still is.

But there's another history of the book that isn't often acknowledged, and that's its history as a business. The book was one of the very first products that was mass marketed and sold, and today, with hundreds of thousands of books published every year, books are dramatically overproduced in the hopes of achieving profit or launching a career. Very few reach the level of shaping culture or influencing ideas.

If your goal is to share ideas, tell stories, or wield influence, authoring a book is only one tool or method available today, and not always the best. We now have speakers and thinkers lecturing through YouTube and online courses. We have in-depth reporting delivered through multimedia websites and blogs. And there's a renaissance of on-demand, professionally produced podcasts—and that's only a few of the mediums that weren't available to most of us even 20 years ago.

It's possible to thrill at a beautifully written passage that fundamentally shifts how we see ourselves and the world, and at the same time acknowledge that the physical form of the book, as well as the e-book, doesn't always fit or easily fit into the multifaceted digital network we're immersed in on a daily basis.

This is why I try to help writers think beyond the book. Consider the story or message that you wish to share rather than focusing on the container. There's been so much aspirational focus on writing and publishing a book without consideration of the many other ways we can write, publish, and share ideas in the digital age.

And when it comes to nonfiction, as we've discussed early in this series, the book shouldn't be the be-all, end-all of what you offer. Agents and editors want to see that your book is merely one aspect of a larger strategy for serving an audience.

This is the headline message I want you to remember, but I'm going to dive deeper into some of the most talked-about trends and dynamics shaping the publishing industry of the future, and why I believe in that headline message.

The first myth we need to put to rest is that the book is dead. That's not what we're talking about. However, that doesn't mean print publishing won't fundamentally change over the coming decades. Futurists often argue that the print book will become something like a souvenir or collectors' item. There will probably always be an audience for print—just enough people to ensure that paper books are an enthusiast product, similar to vinyl for music lovers.

However, the way the book has traditionally been sold and distributed will fade. By the end of 2012, nearly half of U.S. book sales and that includes both print and digital books, happened through online retail. As most people know, online retail is dominated by Amazon. Large chain bookstore sales used to dominate the market. Their share is now less than one-fifth of all book sales in the US.

While many people talk about whether the percentage of e-book sales is growing or not, it's actually more important to keep tabs on where the majority of sales are happening, regardless of format. This directly affects how books are discovered, and puts more power into the hands of tech and media giants such as Amazon, Google, Apple, and Facebook.

Pew Research shows steadily increasing adoption of mobile and tablet devices in the US, and this is one area where the US is actually behind. In other countries, whether it's third world countries where mobile devices are essential to daily life, or Asia, where fast and cheap wireless connectivity can be more ubiquitous, mobile-driven media consumption is higher. This only amplifies the control that tech and media companies have over how books get discovered.

Consider that you and most people you know probably own at least one device made by Amazon, Google, or Apple. These companies have volumes of consumer data and insight into book consumption and readership, far more than the publishers themselves. These consumer tech companies are able to observe, analyze, and reach very distinct audience segments that are invisible to many publishers. Their algorithms, silently at work behind millions of online transactions, are becoming more and more powerful at identifying what each of us wants to see next.

Large publishers continue to struggle with these developments and with the increasingly fragmented audience for media, and this is the primary reason why they come under so much criticism from people outside the industry. But the other myth we need dispel is that publishers are going away. While many self-published authors might have you believe there's no longer any value in traditional publishing, it's simply not true. That doesn't mean there won't be further consolidation among publishing houses, and a continued evolution of the business model. Generalist publishers in particular will have a tough road ahead, not least because it's becoming harder to market to a general audience in the digital age.

Some futurists argue that publishers must push themselves to become leaders of the community of readers and writers who have matching interests. They say publishers should add value and credibility to communities of authors and readers—through the act of publishing, of course, but also through other forms of leadership and support that go beyond print publishing and extend into events, services, grants, fellowships, reading groups, and much more.

This idea of building community is a hot topic in publishing circles, mainly because it's seen as a way to develop connections with readers in a way that doesn't depend on large tech companies. But it requires intimate knowledge of and respect for communities of readers, combined with creativity and imagination in serving them. Publishers that survive—whether they focus on traditional print or digital media—will likely need to become indispensable to the communities they serve.

While at one time a publisher might have been indispensable by delivering quality ideas and stories, a publisher who does that today—and nothing more—can be seen as merely adding to the burden we all now face. There are too many wonderful things to read, and too few signposts as to what's worth our time. Thus, the publisher needs to be a beacon, to offer a strong signal amidst all the noise, and organize ideas, content, and stories within an identifiable and useful context.

I've dispelled two myths so far: That the book is dead and that publishers will go away. It's also important to separate the future of the print book, or even the book itself, from the future of writing, reading, and literacy. Most studies show that we read as much as we ever did—but what, where and how we're reading is changing. While some people place tremendous value on long-form reading and the deep immersion in a book, the reality is that avid book readers have always been in the minority of the total population.

For a long time to come—for at least as long as the printing press revolutionized all aspects of society—we'll experience a revolution in how we find, use, and share information and stories. On the most practical level, authors who understand when and how a book is needed or valuable for their audience will have a leg up on the competition.

There's now incredible pressure on traditional publishers who specialize in distributing information, such as dictionaries, encyclopedias, travel guides, and other types of reference. Most of the publishing industry—especially within the educational sector—they already understand that some books are too expensive to produce for how fast they go out of date and for how easily the same information can be found online for free. Thus, some nonfiction publishers have completely stopped talking about books and now focus on content strategy, recognizing the need to deliver information through different channels, formats, and environments in adaptable forms.

Going even further than that, the CEO of one large educational publisher has said that his company's job is not to deliver information or content, but to develop services. By that, he means servicing universities, students, and professionals with online courses, assessments, workflow tools, communities, and of course, digital books.

Publishing futurists tend to draw a line in the sand between the future of novels or narrative, and the future of non-narrative books, such as what I just described. If you're working in a non-narrative form of publishing, you tend to be competing against multimedia offerings that didn't even exist in the 1990s. If you're working in narrative-driven publishing, such as fiction, then you tend to be more focused on how the digital age changes how those stories get discovered and consumed by readers, rather than how the stories need to be re-envisioned as multimedia. In other words, few people advocate that novels be written and developed as apps, although you will find experiments like that.

However, there are significant questions surrounding how readers may interact differently with digital books, and if the reading and writing process will become more social. Some of the most interesting work in this area has been pioneered by Bob Stein at the Institute for the Future of the Book. His argument is that reading has always been a social activity, and that our idea of reading as a solitary activity is fairly recent, something that arrived with widespread literacy. Furthermore, as we move from the printed page to the screen—to networked environments—the social aspect of reading and writing moves to the foreground. And once this shift happens, we see something very interesting: The lines begin to blur between reader and writer. Stein suggests that authors will take on the added role of moderators and leaders of communities in nonfiction areas, and as designers of complex worlds for readers to explore in fiction.

In nonfiction, there are numerous examples of this social and collaborative aspect, the most symbolic being Wikipedia, one of the grandest social writing and reading projects ever born. But it can be more difficult to understand what this might mean for fiction writers, but one area that might shed some light is transmedia.

You'll find considerable debate about the role of transmedia in book publishing—indeed, if it has any role to play at all. The idea of transmedia comes from the entertainment world. It focuses on the story world first and the methods of distribution second. The *Star Wars* franchise might be considered transmedia as something that spans film, TV, books, video games, merchandise, and more—but of course it didn't start out that way.

The most progressive people in media are looking at how stories can be established and grown without putting any one medium first, but instead growing or adapting the story in different ways across many channels.

If you look closely enough at book publishing, you will see signs of this. Small, nimble companies—often book packagers—are hiring writers to produce intellectual property that the publisher ultimately owns. The packager comes up with a concept that it thinks will catch fire, and outlines the story and characters in a collaborative manner, not too different from how TV and movie writers work. Then they find writers to produce the story with the appropriate voice and plot specifications they need. The writer gets paid, but they have no ownership or control over the story or intellectual property itself.

In another example, in 2012, a group of writers collaborated to produce a serialized story called *The Silent History*. The premise: What if children were born without the ability to acquire language? It was released over a period of six months through an iPhone app. Readers could also contribute to the story during that period and use their phones to unlock new chapters if they were in close geographic proximity to the specific setting of a particular chapter.

So we may slowly be moving into an era where we have an entirely new concept of what an author is and does. Rather than being the solitary creator who garrets himself away and produces a work of genius for the world, he may become more of a moderator or collaborator who synthesizes and expresses many people's ideas. Or the ownership of an idea will simply not be as important. We can already see this trend in Internet culture, with memes and remixing, as well as the formation of the creative commons as an alternative to traditional copyright.

Another area where we can find a strong social component and collaboration in reading and writing is in the fan fiction community. Fan fiction is when readers take well-known characters and story worlds, such as *Harry Potter* or *Star Wars*, and create new stories for their own enjoyment and to share within the community. E. L. James's bestselling novel *50 Shades of Grey* is a piece of fan fiction originally based on Stephanie Meyer's *Twilight*, and was posted as a work in progress on a public fan fiction website. It gathered fans and feedback over time before being formally published. Of course, one of the challenges of fan fiction is that writers can't readily make any money off it. It's copyright infringement after all, but Amazon recognized an opportunity in this challenge. In 2013, they launched Kindle Worlds to allow fan fiction writers to start publishing and earning money from their fan works through formalized licensing deals.

Even so, activity on Kindle Worlds is fairly minimal when compared with other sites where writers and readers congregate in the millions. One such site is Wattpad, which has a user base of more than 40 million. While fan fiction is one of the most predominant areas of activity on the site, Wattpad is more broadly a community of people who love to read and write stories. These stories are delivered primarily to mobile devices in serialized form, meaning the stories are in progress—readers have to wait for the next installment. If the fast growth of Wattpad and its youthful audience is any indicator, this type of interaction may shape the future of publishing.

One of the reasons that Wattpad is attractive to young writers is that it offers a real chance to directly reach and grow a readership, even if it means giving away the writing for free. Wattpad is able to ping a devoted readership whenever a new story or installment gets posted. And unlike traditional publishing or even self-publishing, where authors have limited insight into their readers without a means to have a conversation with them, Wattpad offers a platform for ongoing interaction. And Wattpad's larger vision is just that: To foster a stronger connection between the reader and the writer.

There's another motivation for writers to use Wattpad. It can be very daunting to write a book, but it's very easy to write one chapter. By building an audience and getting feedback right away, a writer may be encouraged to continue and build on their efforts rather than giving up when faced with a slump or self-doubt.

Once you have a huge fan base for your serialized Wattpad work, what do you do with it? Traditional publishing deals represent one path forward. Several authors have received six-figure deals from publishers for their serialized work, and agents regularly scout Wattpad for up-and-coming talent. But aside from a handful of partnerships, Wattpad itself hasn't made any moves to make money, so it remains to be seen what sustainable model might come from it.

While serials and fan fiction are sometimes dismissed by industry insiders as low-quality work that won't affect how traditional publishing operates, others have started to speculate that these markets might be in a position to do exactly that. One reason is that these sites deliver a social reading experience that's already leagues better than the traditional e-book experience. They deliver stories in smaller and more addictive chunks, and they integrate into pop culture far better than books do. And the authors are responsive to their readers.

If all this strikes you as not quite the future you had in mind—and definitely not a future you would want to participate in—there's yet another way you might find yourself unintentionally involved. Amazon and many others collect untold amounts of data through their reading platforms, and can calculate exactly how people read a particular book—how fast, how slow, and the exact paragraph where readers abandon a story.

There's already software that can recognize your mood, tell where your eye hits the screen, and tell whether or not you're paying attention. Conceivably, texts could eventually adapt to how they are being perceived while they're being read. Already, a book's first chapter has a critical role to play, since the first chapter of an e-book is often free, and when the first chapter ends, a reader needs to be compelled to buy the book. From an editorial perspective, we might begin to see writers and editors evaluate data to better understand where the readers lose interest, and how to avoid that in the future.

Of course, there's both burden and opportunity in that. More than a few see such developments as a threat. They say it doesn't help the art or the craft when authors build relationships with readers—and that it can ultimately be a distraction to be that responsive and engaged, or to be in conversation. The extent of this danger, however, totally depends on the values and goals of the writer. If the goal is sales and long-term readership growth, there might not be any harm at all. But if the activities impede the writer from pursuing what he considers his primary purpose, then we can see the call to engagement as detrimental.

In fact, this has been the conclusion of many literary writers, or people who see their purpose as producing art and meaning, something that goes beyond entertainment or satisfying the reader. Author Will Self said in an interview with *The Guardian*, "I don't really write for readers. I think that's a defining characteristic of being serious as a writer." What happens to such writers in the future of publishing if it's defined or driven by author-reader interaction?

I've often tried to tell writers of all genres that the Internet is the best thing to happen to them. Before the Internet, an author might be put upon by a publisher to do tours, talks, and other appearances that can be time-consuming and draining. Post Internet, the introverted author can decide exactly how, when, and where they want to interact with the public, and they can do it completely on their own terms. There's a great deal of control and planning that one never used to have over such activities, so the Internet, in short, is a great blessing for introverts.

But that doesn't really solve the problem of the author who has zero interest in putting on a show or being revealed. Serious authors tend to argue that distance is the writer's friend, and that mystery plays a significant role in our love of books. Therefore, by engaging more with readers, you're overexposing yourself and demystifying your work for everyone who follows you—and that makes you in fact lose potential readers.

So again, what's to come of the author who holds this philosophy? Does such a species survive in the future of publishing? Will publishing become more and more focused on reader interaction and favor a particular type of author, one who is comfortable serving his customer?

I believe our culture's concept of authorship is destined to change. As other thought leaders in publishing have pointed out, the concept of the author as original genius—it's a fairly recent one, which was invented not long after the printing press in tandem with copyright. The digital era may entail a new type of authorship, one that's built on resampling, remixing, and collaboration. Authors may indeed evolve to be leaders, moderators, and synthesizers of information, rather than the dictator in control of it.

One of the reasons I think this is true is because of one more dynamic we still need to discuss. This has been most notably pointed out by professor and author Clay Shirky. He's argued that publishing is the new literacy. What he means is that publishing is no longer a specialized process requiring professional training. Publishing has instead become a button on a screen that you click. That means anyone with a computer and an Internet connection possesses the tools to write and publish and potentially reach a global audience.

But being published doesn't guarantee attention like it once did. In fact, it's harder than it's ever been to gain attention for something you've written, even if you have a traditional publisher. This is important to understand, because by some accounts, we're now living in a time of universal authorship, where anyone and everyone writes for public consumption. While that might not mean writing a book for publication, it includes such things as commenting, blogging, posting updates on social media, and being active in online communities.

Put simply, we're swimming in free and cheap information and entertainment options. While the quality varies tremendously, this doesn't negate the fact that any single person has more good things to read, watch, or otherwise consume—often for free—than they could possibly need across several lifetimes. So the challenge becomes how to become more visible, valuable, or attention grabbing than the next person.

If your blog is read by 50,000 people, but your published book only reaches 10,000, which one was more worth your time? For many authors, that's not just a rhetorical question—it's a reality. This is why I think the author who is more engaged and responsive will be the author who has more options, more freedom, and more success in the future. There's enough choice and community out there that most of us only have time and money to devote to things we feel a part of, believe in, or simply can't get anywhere else.

Every decision you make as a writer has to be made with this bigger picture in mind, of how a particular book, article, blog post, or social media effort attracts a certain type of reader, and how you expect to funnel that reader to the next experience if they enjoy your work. Genre fiction authors have been experts at this, and they've built up incredible communities of fans who end up spreading the word on their behalf. Taking care of your readers means also taking care of your sales, and the digital era has brought us an abundance of models and means to engage and interact with readers and turn that into a sustainable living.

As I see it, the challenge isn't really about a lack of opportunities or models, but the average person's lack of time to pursue these things, or lack of stamina. Reader development strategies take time to pay off. It's rarely a quick win. If we are indeed living in an era where everyone can write and publish, it's the writers who know how to find and engage their readership or community, or who enter into collaborations with other authors and artists, who hold the advantage. Bob Stein has said that, "If the printing press empowered the individual, the digital world empowers collaboration."

Ultimately, when it comes to the future of publishing, you will get to decide. You'll choose how, when, and what to publish. Some publishers will fade and die. Some will consolidate. Some will become specialists in the book form and serve a devoted niche audience. Others may become multimedia operations, serving up stories across mediums. And some smart tech companies—those without a background in publishing and without a legacy system to support—they'll experiment and win big, and many will fail, too.

Authors will become known and be supported through many paths. Those with business savvy will be successful on their own, and others will have productive partnerships with publishers, editors, agents, and managers. Some authors will be known for making a living through their stories alone and others will capitalize on value-added or digital media endeavors. And yet another segment will continue writing without the expectation that their art should sustain a living. Some authors will go DIY first, others will go traditional first, and most will cross back and forth between the two, depending on the project, its needs, and its potential to spread beyond the written word.

A new generation of author is coming—a generation of those who enjoy the act of creating things across mediums and aren't tied to the book form. They'll use visuals, enjoy crafting a range of experiences, and maybe even be proficient with code.

You don't have to wait for someone to validate you before trying something new. You can reach your readers directly and experiment with how to deliver your story. There are so many new tools, services, and distribution methods, with low or no start-up costs, that your only limitation is your imagination.

So try to focus on the why of what you're doing. What is it that you stand for that's bigger than the specific book or story you want to publish? People gravitate toward individuals and communities that deeply resonate with them that lend meaning and identity, and align with their needs or values. You might hate thinking of yourself as a brand, but you can at least see yourself as having a unique voice with a unique perspective on the world. Use that to develop a strategy that encompasses many possible models for creating stories and sharing information. Focus on how you can connect directly with readers, and ultimately go beyond the traditional pitch-and-publish gatekeeper model.

Online Resources for Writers

Source	Description	URL
"279 Days to Overnight Success"	One writer's personal story of becoming a successful blogger	chrisguillebeau.com/files/2009/04/279days.pdf
AAR Online	Site of the Association of Authors' Representatives	aaronline.org
AgentQuery.com	Free database listing about 900 literary agents	agentyquery.com
Association of Writers and Writing Programs	Organization serving a community of nearly 500 writing programs; members receive special access to a mentorship program, job board, and opportunities for grants and awards	awpwriter.org
Authonomy	Online manuscript critique forum sponsored by HarperCollins	authonomy.com
Author Central	Provides data for tracking book sales in advance of the on-sale date	authorcentral.amazon.com
Authors Guild	National professional organization of book and magazine writers; provides information on standard book and magazine contracts	authorsguild.org
Book Blogger Directory	Lists book bloggers that you can pitch for review coverage	bookbloggerdirectory.wordpress.com

Source	Description	URL
Book Country	Online manuscript critique forum and self-publishing service provider	bookcountry.com
BookBub	E-mail marketing service that targets readers looking for inexpensive or free books	bookbub.com
Bowker Identifier Services	Official U.S. ISBN agency	myidentifiers.com
CreateSpace	Amazon's print-on-demand distributor for self-published authors	createspace.com
Duotrope	Paid database service; offers an updated listing of about 5,000 markets and an extensive list of nonpaying markets	duotrope.com
Editorial Freelancers Association	Professional association for freelance editors, writers, indexers, and other document specialists; provides information about rates and freelance agreements	the-efa.org
Goodreads	Social media site devoted to books and reading with 35 million members	goodreads.com
GrubStreet	Nonprofit organization in Boston that offers writing classes, manuscript consultants, and more	grubstreet.org
Guide to Literary Agents	Blog featuring posts about new agents, book marketing, and more	writersdigest.com/editor-blogs/guide-to-literary-agents

Source	Description	URL
The Independent Publishing Magazine	Reviews and discusses new self-publishing and digital services for writers	theindependent publishingmagazine.com
The IndieView	Lists independent online reviewers that you can pitch for coverage	theindieview.com
IngramSpark	Print-on-demand distributor for self-published authors	ingramspark.com
Kindle Direct Publishing	Retailer-specific e-book distribution and sales service	kdp.amazon.com
Kindle Scout	Amazon's crowdsourced publishing program	kindlescout.amazon.com
Kristin Nelson	Agent website that includes a blog offering "polite rants about queries, writers, and the publishing industry"	nelsonagency.com/kristin-nelson
Literary Rejections	Online support hub to help writers persevere through rejection; includes a database of submission policies for more than 300 agencies	literaryrejections.com
The Loft Literary Center	Nonprofit organization in Minneapolis that offers writing classes and hosts literary events	loft.org
Manuscript Wish List	Twitter list of what agents and editors are seeking	#MSWL or mswishlist.com

Source	Description	URL
Poets & Writers	Bimonthly magazine focused on the literary publishing community; maintains a database of opportunities for writers, especially those seeking grants, residencies, and prizes for their work	pw.org
Publishers Marketplace	Service for publishing industry professionals; offers a weekday newsletter, *Publishers Lunch*; job board; member database; and deals database	publishersmarketplace.com
QueryTracker.net	Database of more than 1,000 agents plus publisher listings	querytracker.net
Rachelle Gardner	Agent blog, offering advice for new authors, tips for finding an agent and getting published, and much more	rachellegardner.com
Rejection Wiki	Posts standard rejection letters from a range of publications	rejectionwiki.com/index.php?title=Literary_Journals_and_Rejections
Scott Berkun	Blog of a bestselling author and popular speaker on creativity, culture, business, and other subjects; check out his post "28 (Better) Things No One Tells You about Publishing"	scottberkun.com
Scribophile	Online manuscript critique forum	scribophile.com

Source	Description	URL
Script magazine	Source for writers of film and television scripts	scriptmag.com
Shaw Guides	Searchable database of upcoming writing conferences and workshops	shawguides.com
Shelf Awareness	Free daily e-newsletter for booksellers	http://www.shelf-awareness.com/
Smashwords	E-book publisher and distribution service	smashwords.com
Society for Editors and Proofreaders	Professional association for editors and proofreaders in the United Kingdom	sfep.org.uk
Submishmash	Lists potential creative opportunities available for writers and artists	submishmash.com
Submittable	Industry-wide standard online submission system	submittable.com
Wattpad	One of the most popular community sites for posting writing in serialized form	wattpad.com
The Writer	Monthly magazine that offers how-to information related to the craft and business of writing	writermag.com
Writer Beware	Hub for writers who have concerns about any publisher, service, or organization in the writing community	sfwa.org/other-resources/for-authors/writer-beware

Source	Description	URL
Writer's Digest	The most widely circulating how-to magazine for writers; also publishes instruction books and market guides, offers online education, and puts out an annual round-up of the 101 best websites for writers	writersdigest.com
Writer's Market	Longest continuously published market listings guide; website includes more than 9,000 market listings, articles on writing, and more	writersmarket.com
Writers Guild of America	Labor union for film and television scriptwriters and writers involved in new media (e.g., Internet work and mobile phone apps)	wga.org (Writers Guild, West) wgaeast.org (Writers Guild, East)

Bibliography

Writer's Digest Guides

Brewer, Robert, ed. *2016 Writer's Market*. Cincinnati: Writer's Digest, 2015.

———, ed. *2016 Poet's Market*. Cincinnati: Writer's Digest, 2015.

Randall, Rachel, ed. *2016 Novel and Short Story Writer's Market*. Cincinnati: Writer's Digest, 2015.

Sambuchino, Chuck, ed. *2016 Children's Writer's and Illustrator's Market*. Cincinnati: Writer's Digest, 2015.

———, ed. *2016 Guide to Literary Agents*. Cincinnati: Writer's Digest, 2015.

These informational directories on how and where to get your work published have been updated and released annually in one form or another since 1920. The oldest and most important one is *Writer's Market*, which covers all paying markets in both book publishing and magazine publishing. For fiction writers, *Novel and Short Story Writer's Market* is a more comprehensive, focused listing that includes smaller presses and literary journals that may pay very little or even nothing. *Children's Writer's and Illustrator's Market*, as its name implies, is specifically for writers seeking to publish anything in the juvenile market, from picture books to young adult novels. *Poet's Market* lists all places to publish individual poems, as well as full collections. The *Guide to Literary Agents* lists hundreds of literary agents, mostly those based in the United States and United Kingdom.

Other Practical Guides to Getting Published

Burt-Thomas, Wendy. *The Writer's Digest Guide to Query Letters*. Cincinnati: Writer's Digest, 2009. Aside from offering instruction in basic query writing, this guide includes query letter examples for each major genre and category.

Camenson, Blythe, and Marshall Cook. *Your Novel Proposal from Creation to Contract*. Cincinnati: Writer's Digest, 1999. This is one of the few guides on the market that will teach you how to write a novel synopsis. Although some of its information on the industry is now outdated (very few editors or agents ask for novel outlines or "proposals" these days), it still offers invaluable guidance on condensing complex stories into a few pages.

Eckstut, Arielle, and David Sterry. *The Essential Guide to Getting Your Book Published*. New York: Workman, 2010. The most comprehensive guide you'll find on how to get published, from start to finish—written by an agent and editor.

Herman, Jeff. *Jeff Herman's Guide to Book Publishers, Editors and Literary Agents*. 24th ed. Novato, CA: New World Library, 2014. This is the primary competitor to the Writer's Market series mentioned above, except it's not updated annually. It's edited by a longtime literary agent and offers more personality or color in the listings.

———. *Write the Perfect Book Proposal*. New York: John Wiley & Sons, 2001. A solid instructional guide for nonfiction authors writing a book proposal; written by a literary agent.

Kleinman, Jeff, and Ryan Lejarde. *The Science of Rejection Letters*. Amazon Digital Services, 2014. A short e-book by a literary agent that helps writers decipher the rejection letters they receive from agents and editors.

Larsen, Michael. *How to Write a Book Proposal*. 4th ed. Cincinnati: Writer's Digest, 2011. The industry-standard guide to book proposal writing by a literary agent. It first appeared in the 1980s and has been updated regularly ever since.

Lukeman, Noah. *How to Write a Great Query Letter*. Amazon Digital Services, 2014. One of the only guides to query letters you'll find by a literary agent.

Lyon, Elizabeth. *Nonfiction Book Proposals Anybody Can Write*. New York: Perigee, 2000. A friendly instruction book that makes the process of writing a book proposal more straightforward and manageable than the Larsen guide.

—————. *The Sell Your Novel Tool Kit*. New York: Perigee Books, 2002. One of the few instructional guides focused on how to sell fiction.

MacGregor, Chip. *Step by Step Pitches and Proposals*. Manzanita, OR: Benchmark Press, 2015. The only formal and focused instruction on pitching, by a literary agent.

Rabiner, Susan, and Alfred Fortunato. *Thinking like Your Editor: How to Write Great Serious Nonfiction and Get It Published*. New York: W.W. Norton & Co., 2003. A now-classic guide for any writer seeking to publish a nonfiction book, by a well-respected New York editor.

Sambuchino, Chuck. *Formatting and Submitting Your Manuscript*. 3rd ed. Cincinnati: Writer's Digest, 2009. An 8.5-by-11-inch format guide that offers visual examples of every type of manuscript page—by genre, category, and purpose.

—————. *Get a Literary Agent*. Cincinnati: Writer's Digest, 2015. A straightforward guide to literary agents, including how to query and pitch.

Writing Craft and Technique

Browne, Renni, and Dave King. *Self-Editing for Fiction Writers*. 2nd ed. New York: William Morrow, 2004. A bestselling guide on how to edit your novel manuscript.

Lukeman, Noah. *The First Five Pages*. New York: Simon & Schuster, 2000. One of the most insightful guides for beginning writers, showing with clear examples how agents and editors can tell within the first five pages if a manuscript is worth reading further.

Orr, Alice. *No More Rejections*. Cincinnati: Writer's Digest, 2004. Agent Alice Orr offers 50 insights into manuscripts that sell—primarily fiction focused.

Inspiration and Motivation

Lamott, Anne. *Bird by Bird*. New York: Random House, 1995. Probably the most well-known and beloved guide for writers, recommended by teachers everywhere. Lamott isn't everyone's cup of tea, but if you've heard the cliché about "shitty first drafts," this is where it comes from.

Pressfield, Steven. *The War of Art: Break through the Blocks and Win Your Inner Creative Battles*. New York: Black Irish Entertainment, 2012. A short but powerful read on the psychological battle of producing any kind of creative work. Applicable to all types of artists, including writers.

Working with Editors and Publishers

Gross, Gerald C. *Editors on Editing*. New York: Grove/Atlantic, 1993. This guide was originally released in 1962 and remains in print because of its timeless insights into the editing process.

Lerner, Betsy. *The Forest for the Trees: An Editor's Advice to Writers*. Revised and updated ed. New York: Riverhead Books, 2010. A New York editor's sage and timeless advice to writers who seek publication. (She's now an agent.)

Practical Advice on Self-Publishing

Kawasaki, Guy. *APE: Author, Publisher, Entrepreneur*. Nononina Press, 2013. An easy-to-digest guide to the self-publishing process for absolute beginners.

Levine, Mark. *The Fine Print of Self-Publishing*. 5th ed. Minneapolis: Bascom Hill Publishing Group, 2014. This has become the go-to book for self-publishing authors in the age of e-books and online retail.

Practical Guides on Author Platform and Book Marketing and Promotion

Gaughran, David. *Let's Get Visible*. Updated 2nd ed. Arriba Arriba Books, 2013. A successful indie author offers instruction on how to market and promote your self-published book, particularly online.

Grahl, Tim. *Your First 1,000 Copies*. Lynchburg, VA: Out:think, 2012. A short, helpful guide on how to sell your self-published book, by a professional marketer who has helped such bestselling authors as Daniel Pink, Pam Slim, and Hugh Howey.

Hyatt, Michael. *Platform: Get Noticed in a Noisy World*. Nashville: Thomas Nelson, 2012. A *New York Times*–bestselling book on how to build your author platform.

Jelen, Carole, and Michael McCallister. *Build Your Author Platform*. Dallas: BenBella Books, 2014. A detailed, step-by-step approach to building platform, particularly using digital media.

Katz, Christina. *Get Known before the Book Deal*. Cincinnati: Writer's Digest, 2008. How to build an author platform in multiple ways—not just online but through in-person events and other forms of professional development.

Penn, Joanna. *How to Market a Book*. 2nd ed. The Creative Penn Limited, 2014. A comprehensive guide to marketing self-published work, by someone with years of experience in the trenches.

Sambuchino, Chuck. *Create Your Writer Platform*. Cincinnati: Writer's Digest, 2012. Learn both the strategy and tactics of author platform building; includes a healthy section of author case studies.

Truant, Johnny, and Sean Platt. *Write. Publish. Repeat.* Realm & Sands, 2013. A broad strategical guide for new indie authors, written in a casual style by a successful self-publishing author team.

Critical Studies of the Book Publishing Industry

Bhaskar, Michael. *The Content Machine*. London: Anthem Press, 2013. As much a historical look at the book publishing industry as a meditation on how it needs to innovate to thrive in the future.

Epstein, Jason. *Book Business: Publishing Past, Present, and Future*. New York: W.W. Norton & Company, 2001. An industry insider discusses the crisis facing book publishing (in the context of the late 1990s); primarily a history of the industry during the second half of the 20th century.

McGuire, Hugh, and Brian O'Leary, eds. *Book: A Futurist's Manifesto*. Sebastopol, CA: O'Reilly Media, 2012. A series of thought-provoking essays by progressive players in the book publishing industry, primarily focusing on the digital innovation side.

Nash, Richard. "The Business of Literature." *Virginia Quarterly Review* 89, no. 2 (Spring 2013). A landmark essay by one of publishing's thought leaders on what the digital era augurs for the business of publishing.

Striphas, Ted. *The Late Age of Print*. New York: Columbia University Press, 2011. Helpful for understanding where book publishing has been and how it is changing (or might change) in response to the digital era.

Thompson, John B. *Merchants of Culture*. 2nd ed. New York: Plume, 2012. An engagingly written history of U.S. and U.K. trade publishing in the 21st century, by a Cambridge professor.

Other Useful References

Jassin, Lloyd, and Steven M. Schechter. *The Copyright Permission and Libel Handbook*. New York: John Wiley & Sons, 1998. One of the few guides on how to sort through legal issues in written work, particularly those pertaining to permissions.

Kirsch, Jonathan. *Kirsch's Guide to the Book Contract*. Los Angeles: Acrobat Books, 1998. The reference book that all agents have sitting on their desks.

Levine, Becky. *The Writing and Critique Book Survival Guide*. Cincinnati: Writer's Digest, 2010. Indispensable if you're trying to start a critique group or benefit from one.

May, Lori A. *The Low-Residency MFA Handbook*. New York: Continuum, 2011. For adult writers seeking to explore formal writing educational opportunities, a low-residency MFA is often the most viable option. This guide offers an overview of available programs and what issues to consider when applying to or selecting one.

Sheer, Laurie. *The Writer's Advantage*. Studio City, CA: Michael Wiese Productions, 2014. A forward-thinking writer's guide to storytelling across mediums and to understanding your genre.

Notes